W9-BVQ-641

Computational Handbook of

STATISTICS

Fourth Edition

Computational Handbook of
STATISTICS

Fourth Edition

James L. Bruning
Ohio University

B. L. Kintz
Western Washington University

 LONGMAN

An Imprint of Addison Wesley Longman, Inc.

New York • Menlo Park, California • Reading, Massachusetts • Harlow, England
Don Mills, Ontario • Sydney • Mexico City • Madrid • Amsterdam

Editor-in-Chief: Priscilla McGeehon
Developmental Editor: John Matthews
Project Coordination: Proof Positive/Farrowlyne Associates, Inc.
Design Administrator: Jess Schaal
Text and Cover Design: Kathy Burke
Production Administrator: Randee Wire
Compositor: Interactive Composition Corporation
Printer and Binder: R. R. Donnelley & Sons Company
Cover Printer: Lehigh Press Lithographers

Computational Handbook of Statistics, 4e

Library of Congress Cataloging-in-Publication Data

Bruning, James L.
    Computational handbook of statistics / James L. Bruning, B. L.
Kintz.
        p.   cm.
    Includes index.
    ISBN 0-673-99085-0
    1. Social sciences—Statistical methods.   2. Statistics.
I. Kintz, B. L.   II. Title
HA29.B835   1996
519.5—dc20   96-30391
                                                           CIP

    2   3   4   5   6   7   8   9   10—DOC—99   98   97

Preface

The emphasis of most statistics textbooks is on the theory and assumptions, the logic, and the derivations and formulas of the various statistical tests. Unfortunately, this approach promotes little understanding of how to apply statistical tests to actual data. Also, students often have little comprehension regarding which factors related to the type of data collected have an effect on the outcome of the tests used. This has become a particular problem as a result of the widespread availability of statistical packages that permit easy application of multiple analyses to any set of numbers.

The intent of the first three editions was to reverse this emphasis on theory, logic, and formulas, and to present statistical concepts and tests *as they are applied.* Our experience continues to indicate that this emphasis on applications and use of examples is extremely useful for researchers, students, and instructors. For researchers, we find that clearly described and worked examples can easily be generalized to a wide variety of situations. In this way, researchers can use the examples to help them design research projects, and when the data have been collected, decide the best analyses to apply to the data. For students, the step-by-step examples allow a quick and clear understanding of the meaning of the various formulas and terms presented in statistics textbooks. Also, by following a clearly worked example, students gain a much better understanding of the application of the various statistical tests and the corresponding formulas. Finally, for instructors, the worked examples can be used to demonstrate application of the various statistical formulas and tests to actual research problems. In this way, the *Handbook* allows for teaching by example and use of an easily understood problem-based approach to learning statistics. The book is also extremely useful to instructors of beginning laboratory courses in which students have completed only a basic statistics course. Use of the *Handbook* permits the design and analysis of more advanced experiments in which additional variables are manipulated or repeated measures taken.

As in the previous editions, the mathematical proofs and theoretical discussions that appear in most textbooks are excluded. Although the total amount of theoretical discussion presented in this book is minimal, assumptions and basic computational formulas for the various analyses are presented either at the beginning of each section or in the example. One significant change has been introduced in the fourth edition. For the standard deviation, the various t-tests, the Pearson product-moment correlation, and the Spearman's rank-order correlation, each of the computational steps is preceded by the appropriate term of the various computational formulas. This method provides a very easy and complete understanding of the actual computations called for by those formulas.

The major changes in this edition include a reorganization of the sections to correspond more closely to the typical sequence of topics taught in undergraduate statistics courses. There is also a new Part 2 on Confidence Intervals. As indicated above, each of the computational steps for the frequently used tests presented in Parts 1 and 3 is preceded by the appropriate term of the computational formula. In the other Parts of the fourth edition, examples have been updated and computational steps reduced or clarified.

An alternative approach is again taken for the sections on analysis of variance and multivariate analyses. In place of a presentation of assumptions and formulas, the Textbook Reference Chart allows the reader to cross-check the sections in the most widely used advanced statistics texts to find the theoretical discussions, logic, assumptions, and formulas of interest. There are three reasons for this approach. First, the design names and the terms used to describe the analyses vary widely from textbook to textbook. Second, there is no consistent system of mathematical notation and formula presentation in the various textbooks. The result is that translation from the notational system used by one author to that of another is often quite difficult. Third, presentaion of all of the necessary formulas and terms would have consumed more time and space than was deemed appropriate for a text of this type.

While most of the examples deal with the analysis of experimental findings in the behavioral and social sciences, this text is equally appropriate for courses and researchers in education, business, agriculture, and medical research, or any other area in which statistical analysis of data is required. In addition, because of its broad range of coverage, it is appropriate for courses at both the undergraduate and graduate levels. We also have found that research assistants with limited statistical backgrounds can use this text to quickly gain a good understanding of the design of projects on which they are working.

It would be impossible to thank everyone who has made either a direct or an indirect contribution to this edition of the book. There are, however, several persons whose influence warrants special recognition. Our publisher-author relationship has been all that could be desired, and we would like to extend special thanks to Chris Jennison, Executive Editor at HarperCollins, for his encouragement and assistance throughout the development of the fourth edition. We also wish to thank John Matthews, Developmental Editor, who provided us with timely advice and editorial assistance as the manuscript was being developed. We are deeply appreciative of the general encouragement, help, and assistance given by our wives, Marlene and Maria, during every phase of the manuscript development and revision.

We are grateful to the Literary Executor of the late Sir Ronald A. Fisher, F. R. S., and to Longman Group Ltd., London, for permission to reprint Tables III, V, and VI from their book *Statistical Tables for Biological, Agricultural and Medical Research* (6th edition, 1974).

JAMES L. BRUNING
Ohio University

B. L. KINTZ
Western Washington University

Contents

To the User

As explained in the Preface, this book approaches statistics from the applied, rather than the theoretical, point of view. We hope that the extensive use of examples and the step-by-step presentation of the computational procedures will not only provide models to be followed in computing analyses but also help the user to gain insights into how each segment or step fits into the final analysis. We also hope that by presenting nearly all the material in verbal rather than mathematical form, this book will help dispel the fears that many have of statistics. At the same time, we have included as aids to the user the basic assumptions and computational formulas for each analysis. These are either presented at the beginning of each section or incorporated into the computational example, except in the sections dealing with analysis of variance, multiple comparisons, and covariance. For these sections, textbook sources for the basic formulas and assumptions are presented in the Textbook Reference Chart following Part 4. This chart permits the user to identify the chapters in current advanced statistics textbooks where a complete discussion of the designs can be found. The following example demonstrates the methods of approach and presentation that are used throughout this book.

■ EXAMPLE

Assume that a physical education teacher has measured the heights of five students in one class and now wishes to compute the average, or mean, height of this group.

The mathematical formula for computation of the mean is

$$\overline{X} = \frac{\Sigma X}{N}$$

where $\overline{X}$ = mean of the scores
ΣX = sum of the scores
N = number of scores

Step 1.   Table the scores as follows. No particular order is necessary.

Subject	Height (inches)
S_1	60
S_2	53
S_3	57
S_4	52
S_5	58

Step 2.   Add all the scores to get the sum for the group.

$60 + 53 + 57 + 52 + 58 = \textbf{280}$

Step 3.   Computation of the mean: Divide the value of Step 2 by the number of scores (heights) that were added. (In the present example, there were 5 scores.)

$$\overline{X} = \frac{280}{5} = \textbf{56 inches}$$

While it is sometimes possible to use shortcuts and combine steps (as in the previous example), we recommend that, to avoid error and to more fully understand the meaning of each step, the user closely follow the steps we have outlined. During initial study or computation, the user should also label each step since this greatly facilitates the correction of errors and review of points that were not clear.   ■

PART 1

Organizing Data and Some Simple Computations

Research involves the making of systematic observations, organizing these observations in some meaningful fashion, and then, usually on the basis of statistical tests, drawing conclusions. Raw data—observations in their original form—are usually a mass of numbers or symbols that have little or no meaning. To allow even the most gross kinds of interpretations, the data must be organized in some fashion. Probably the simplest organization is the classification of data into categories. In this instance, a count is usually made of the observations that fall into one class as opposed to another. A good example is an observation of a crowd that is later classified according to the number of males versus females present. Statistical procedures to aid in the interpretation of data collected and organized in this fashion are *usually* (but not always) of the nonparametric type. These statistical tests are discussed in Part 7 of this book.

The form of data organization that is of interest in the first six parts of this book involves the use of measures that are recorded for each of several observations. These measures almost always imply some notion of varying magnitude or amount. This type of classification differs from the first in that it implies varying amounts of an observation rather than simply whether or not a particular observation was made. In the following sections, organization and computation of measures will be considered in relation to various simple statistical tests that experimenters use as aids in drawing conclusions regarding the outcome of their research.

Organizing Data (Sections 1.1, 1.2, and 1.3)

These first three sections discuss some of the basic procedures for making decisions regarding sample size, organizing the data, and putting it in an understandable form. While there are many other procedures for organizing data (such as frequency distributions, etc.), the ones presented in these chapters are those used most often.

Some Simple Computations (Sections 1.4, 1.5, 1.6, 1.7, and 1.8)

The first three of these sections are concerned primarily with demonstrating the basic uses of the t-test. These include the t for testing the difference between a sample and a population mean, the t for testing the difference between two sample means, and the t for related measures. The Sandler's A test also tests for related measures and is an alternative to the t-test. The final section deals with computations of sample size and power.

SECTION 1.1
Blocking and Tabling of Data

In most experiments involving the collection and analysis of data, the data are grouped, or blocked, to reduce variability and to make the scores more manageable for statistical analysis. The most commonly used method is to take the mean, median, or mode of several scores. The value obtained is then treated as a single score.

For example, if the number of correct responses on each of fifteen trials was the measure recorded, the raw data for Subject 1 might appear as follows:

Trial	1	2	3	4	5	6	7	8	9	10	11	12	13	14	15
Correct responses for S_1	1	4	2	6	1	3	5	9	7	9	4	9	14	10	14

Since there are fifteen trials, the most reasonable grouping would probably be to combine each consecutive set of three or five trials. If only one score were desired, the entire fifteen trials would be combined. The size of the group, or block, of data is entirely arbitrary.

The most common technique is to take the mean of each successive set of trials. In the above example, assume that the experimenter decides to block by taking the mean of each successive five scores. Thus, the fifteen scores of S_1 would be reduced to three scores, as follows:

Trial Block	1	2	3
Mean of 5 trials for S_1	2.8	6.6	10.2

If an overall mean were desired, the experimenter would simply add all the correct responses and divide by the number of trials given. For S_1 this would be 98/15, which equals 6.53.

Less frequently, the median or mode is used to block raw data. Use of these measures usually occurs only if the data within each set of scores are severely skewed. In the present example, the median would equal the middle score of each block of trials after the scores within each block had been rank ordered. Using the data presented above, the median of trials one through five would be 2, since there are two scores smaller than 2 (1, 1) and two larger (4, 6). The same type of computation would be made for trials six through ten and eleven through fifteen.

Trial Block	1	2	3
Median of 5 trials for S_1	2	7	10

The overall median in this example would be 6.

The mode is simply the score that occurs most often. When applied to blocks of five trials, the scores for S_1 become:

Trial Block	1	2	3
Mode of 5 trials for S_1	1	9	14

The overall mode would be 9, since that score occurs three times during the fifteen trials.

After the data have been blocked, they must be tabled so that statistical analyses can be undertaken. While the specific method of tabling depends upon the statistical analyses to be used, the most common technique involves simply identifying each subject and then entering the subject's score or scores in a row to the right. For example, using the mean scores in the above example:

Subject	Trial block		
	1	2	3
S_1	2.8	6.6	10.2
S_2	1.4	1.8	4.3
S_3	2.1	6.7	6.4

While it is apparent that different methods of blocking scores can result in different measures being recorded for each subject, the major point to note is that whenever raw data are blocked in some fashion, the statistical analyses may be based entirely on the blocked scores. In the above example, all analyses may be computed as though only three trials had been given or, if an overall score were used, as if only one score had been recorded. It is also important to note that for purposes of determining *degrees of freedom* (*df*), numbers of scores in a table, group means, etc., all computations and numerical counts are based on the blocked scores and not on the raw data.

SECTION 1.2
Range and Standard Deviation

By grouping and arranging scores, it is possible to get a fairly good understanding of the data that have been collected. In addition to grouping, however, it is usually desirable to obtain some idea of the dispersion of the scores. The simplest such measure is the *range*. This value is simply the difference between the largest and smallest scores in the distribution plus 1. For example, in the sample data presented below, the tallest child is 72 inches and the shortest is 43 inches; the range, then, is 29 plus 1, or 30 inches.

Although the range does give some information regarding the dispersion of the scores, its usefulness is limited. By far the most common and useful measure of dispersion is the *standard deviation* (s.d.). There are two ways to compute the standard deviation: directly, using difference scores; and indirectly, using the computational formula. As is shown in nearly all introductory textbooks, these two formulas produce the same numerical answer. Since the method that employs the computational formula is more generally applicable, it will be presented here.

■ EXAMPLE
This example is drawn from the field of developmental psychology. Assume that an experimenter is interested in obtaining information about the heights of twelve-year-olds who live in an area with a high level of natural fluorides in the water. To obtain this information, the experimenter collects a sample of data (the heights of twenty randomly selected twelve-year-olds living in this area) and proceeds to compute the standard deviation.

The mathematical formula for the standard deviation is

$$\text{s.d.} = \sqrt{\frac{\Sigma X^2 - \dfrac{(\Sigma X)^2}{N}}{N - 1}}$$

where ΣX^2 = the sum of the squared scores
$(\Sigma X)^2$ = the square of the sum of all of the scores
N = the total number of scores used in the computation

Step 1. Table the data as follows. No particular order is necessary.

Subject	Height (inches)
S_1	64
S_2	48
S_3	55
S_4	68
S_5	72
S_6	59
S_7	57
S_8	61
S_9	63
S_{10}	60
S_{11}	60
S_{12}	43
S_{13}	67
S_{14}	70
S_{15}	65
S_{16}	55
S_{17}	56
S_{18}	64
S_{19}	61
S_{20}	60

Step 2. Add all the scores.

$$64 + 48 + \cdots + 60 = \textbf{1208}$$

Step 3. Square all the scores, and add the squared values.

$$64^2 + 48^2 + \cdots + 60^2 = \textbf{73,894}$$

Step 4. Square the sum obtained in Step 2, and divide this value by the number of scores that were added to obtain the sum. The resultant value is called the *correction term*.

$$\frac{1208^2}{20} = \frac{1,459,264}{20} = \textbf{72,963}$$

Step 5. Subtract the value obtained in Step 4 from the sum in Step 3.

$$73,894 - 72,963 = \textbf{931}$$

Step 6. Divide the value obtained in Step 5 by $N - 1$*. (In this example, it would be $20 - 1 = 19$.) The resultant value is called the *variance*.

$$\frac{931}{19} = 49$$

Step 7. Take the square root of the value obtained in Step 6. This value is the standard deviation.

$$\sqrt{49} = 7 \text{ in.} \qquad \blacksquare$$

SECTION 1.3
Standard Error of the Mean

The standard error of the mean is extremely simple to compute once the steps outlined in Section 1.2 have been completed. All that must be done is to follow Steps 1 through 7 of Section 1.2 and divide the standard deviation obtained in Step 7 by the square root of the size of the sample.

In the example used in Section 1.2, the standard deviation obtained in Step 7 was 7 inches. Since there were twenty subjects in the sample ($N = 20$), simply divide 7 by the square root of 20 to obtain the standard error of the mean.

$$\frac{7}{\sqrt{20}} = \frac{7}{4.47} = 1.57$$

Note: The standard error of the mean usually is computed directly by use of the following formula. As can be seen, the result is identical with that obtained above using the steps of Sections 1.2 and 1.3.

$$\sqrt{\frac{\Sigma X^2 - \dfrac{(\Sigma X)^2}{N}}{N(N - 1)}}$$

Using the values from Section 1.2, we have:

$$\sqrt{\frac{73,894 - \dfrac{1,459,264}{20}}{20(20 - 1)}}$$

---

* This term is almost universally used since the division by $N - 1$ gives the unbiased *estimate* of the population variance rather than the *actual* variance of the sample. If the actual sample variance is desired, divide by N rather than $N - 1$. Step 7 is the same, regardless.

$$\sqrt{\frac{73{,}894 - 72{,}963}{380}}$$

$$\sqrt{\frac{931}{380}}$$

$$\sqrt{2.45} = \textbf{1.57}$$

SECTION 1.4

The *t*-Test for a Difference Between a Sample Mean and the Population Mean

One of the most commonly used tests of significance is the *t*-test. One use of this test assumes that the mean for some population or theoretical value, such as "poverty level of income," is known. Knowing the population or theoretical value, the experimenter can then determine whether the mean of the sample chosen is significantly different from the population mean.

■ EXAMPLE

This example uses the data presented in Section 1.2. Assume that after collecting measures of the heights of twenty randomly selected twelve-year-olds, the experimenter notices that while the standard deviation is large, the average height of the children in this sample is above the population average for twelve-year-olds. By use of the *t*-test, it can be determined whether this difference is significant.

The basic formula for testing the significance of a difference between a sample mean and population mean is

$$t = \frac{\bar{X} - \mu}{\text{standard error of the mean}} \quad \text{(Sections 1.2 and 1.3)}$$

or, in simplified form,

$$t = \frac{\bar{X} - \mu}{\sqrt{\dfrac{\Sigma X^2 - \dfrac{(\Sigma X)^2}{N}}{N(N-1)}}}$$

where $\bar{X}$ = the mean of the sample
μ = the mean of the population
ΣX^2 = the sum of the squared scores
$(\Sigma X)^2$ = the square of the sum of all of the scores
N = the number of scores recorded

Step 1.   Table the data as follows. No particular order is necessary.

Subject	Height (inches)
S_1	64
S_2	48
S_3	55
S_4	68
S_5	72
S_6	59
S_7	57
S_8	61
S_9	63
S_{10}	60
S_{11}	60
S_{12}	43
S_{13}	67
S_{14}	70
S_{15}	65
S_{16}	55
S_{17}	56
S_{18}	64
S_{19}	61
S_{20}	60

Step 2.   Add all the scores.

$$\Sigma X = 64 + 48 + \cdots + 60 = \textbf{1208}$$

Step 3.   Square all the scores, and add these squared values.

$$\Sigma X^2 = 62^2 + 48^2 + \cdots + 62^2 = \textbf{73,894}$$

Step 4.   Square the sum obtained in Step 2. Then divide this value by the number of scores that were added to get the sum. (In the present example, twenty scores were added.) The resultant value is called the correction term.

$$\frac{(\Sigma X)^2}{N} = \frac{1208^2}{20} = \frac{1,459,264}{20} = \textbf{72,963}$$

$$\Sigma X^2 - \frac{(\Sigma X)^2}{N} = 73,894 - 72,963 = \textbf{931}$$

Step 5.   Subtract the value obtained in Step 4 from the sum in Step 3.

Step 6.   Divide the value obtained in Step 5 by N times $N - 1$. In the present example, it would be $20 \times (20 - 1) = 380$.

$$\frac{931}{380} = \textbf{2.45}$$

Step 7.   Take the square root of the value obtained in Step 6.

$$\sqrt{2.45} = 1.57$$

Step 8.   Subtract the sample mean from the population mean (known from some other source such as growth tables).

$$\frac{\Sigma\ X}{N} = \frac{1208}{20} = 60.4 = sample\ mean$$

$$58.0 = population\ mean\ from\ growth\ tables$$

And, $60.4 - 58.0 = 2.4$

Note: For computational purposes, only the absolute difference between the means is important. The sign of the difference simply indicates whether the sample mean was larger or smaller than the population mean.

Step 9.   Divide the value obtained in Step 8 by the value obtained in Step 7. This yields the *t* value.

$$t = \frac{2.4}{1.57} = 1.53$$

Step 10.   To determine whether the *t* value is significant, the degrees of freedom must be obtained. For the test of significance of a sample mean and a population mean, the *df* are equal to $N - 1$. In this example, this would be $20 - 1 = 19$. The *t* for significance at the .05 level (two-tailed; see Appendix B) is 2.093. Since the *t* value in the present example is smaller than 2.093, it is concluded that there is no significant difference between this sample mean and the population mean.   ∎

SECTION 1.5
The *t*-Test for a Difference Between Two Independent Means

Probably the most common use of the *t*-test is to determine whether the performance difference between two groups of subjects is significant. In most experimental situations, the subjects are randomly assigned to the two groups; one of the groups is manipulated experimentally, and the effects of this manipulation are analyzed by comparing the performance of the two groups. However, there are many instances where the groups are already constituted (e.g., males versus females) and the experimenter wishes to determine whether they differ with respect to some other variable (e.g., height, weight, etc.).

∎ EXAMPLE
Assume that a principal wishes to determine whether there is a significant difference between the IQ scores of boys and girls in a particular grade. The

score on the Wechsler Intelligence Scale for Children (WISC) is recorded for each student.

The basic computational formula for the t-test of a difference between two independent means is

$$t = \frac{\bar{X}_1 - \bar{X}_2}{\sqrt{\left[\dfrac{\Sigma X_1^2 - \dfrac{(\Sigma X_1)^2}{N_1} + \Sigma X_2^2 - \dfrac{(\Sigma X_2)^2}{N_2}}{(N_1 + N_2) - 2}\right] \cdot \left[\dfrac{1}{N_1} + \dfrac{1}{N_2}\right]}}$$

where $\bar{X}_1$ = the mean of the first group of scores
$\bar{X}_2$ = the mean of the second group of scores
ΣX_1^2 = the sum of the squared score values of the first group
ΣX_2^2 = the sum of the squared score values of the second group
$(\Sigma X_1)^2$ = the square of the sum of the scores in the first group
$(\Sigma X_2)^2$ = the square of the sum of the scores in the second group
N_1 = the number of scores in the first group
N_2 = the number of scores in the second group

Step 1.   Table the data as follows. No particular order within groups is necessary.

Group 1 (boys)		Group 2 (girls)	
Subject	Score	Subject	Score
S_1	107	S_{13}	109
S_2	96	S_{14}	94
S_3	88	S_{15}	127
S_4	131	S_{16}	76
S_5	109	S_{17}	115
S_6	84	S_{18}	121
S_7	79	S_{19}	87
S_8	105	S_{20}	92
S_9	108	S_{21}	91
S_{10}	92	S_{22}	98
S_{11}	96	S_{23}	104
S_{12}	101	S_{24}	96
		S_{25}	110
		S_{26}	108

Step 2.   Add the scores in Group 1.

$\Sigma X_1 = 107 + 96 + \cdots + 101 = \mathbf{1196}$

Step 3.   Square every score in Group 1 and add these squared values.

$\Sigma X_1^2 = 107^2 + 96^2 + \cdots + 101^2 = \mathbf{121{,}318}$

Step 4. Square the value obtained in Step 2. Then divide the squared value by the number of scores on which the sum was based. (In this example, 12 scores were added.)

$$\frac{(\Sigma\ X_1)^2}{N_1} = \frac{1196^2}{12} = \frac{1,430,416}{12} = \mathbf{119,201}$$

Step 5. Subtract the value of Step 4 from the sum in Step 3.

$$\Sigma\ X_1^2 - \frac{(\Sigma\ X_1)^2}{N_1} = 121,318 - 119,201 = \mathbf{2117}$$

Step 6. Add the scores in Group 2.

$$\Sigma\ X_2 = 109 + 94 + \cdots + 108 = \mathbf{1428}$$

Step 7. Square every score in Group 2, and add these squared values.

$$\Sigma\ X_2^2 = 109^2 + 94^2 + \cdots + 108^2 = \mathbf{148,202}$$

Step 8. Square the value obtained in Step 6. Then divide the squared value by the number of scores on which the sum was based. (In the present example, 14 scores were added.)

$$\frac{(\Sigma\ X_2)^2}{N_2} = \frac{1428^2}{14} = \frac{2,039,184}{14} = \mathbf{145,656}$$

Step 9. Subtract the value of Step 8 from the sum in Step 7.

$$\Sigma\ X_2^2 - \frac{(\Sigma\ X_2)^2}{N_2} = 148,202 - 145,656 = \mathbf{2546}$$

Step 10. Add the values obtained in Step 5 and Step 9.

$$2117 + 2546 = \mathbf{4663}$$

Step 11. Divide the value obtained in Step 10 by $(N_1 + N_2) - 2$. (In the present example, $(12 + 14) - 2 = 24$.)

$$\frac{4663}{24} = \mathbf{194}$$

Step 12. Multiply the value obtained in Step 11 by $1/N_1 + 1/N_2$. (In the present example, this would equal $1/12 + 1/14$.)

$$194 \times \left(\frac{1}{12} + \frac{1}{14}\right) = 194 \times \frac{13}{84} = \mathbf{30.0}$$

Step 13.   Take the square root of the value obtained in Step 12.

$$\sqrt{30.0} = 5.48$$

Step 14.   Obtain the mean of Group 1 (sum in Step 2 divided by N_1) and the mean of Group 2 (sum in Step 6 divided by N_2).

$$\frac{\Sigma X_1}{N_1} = \frac{1196}{12} = 99.67 = mean\ of\ Group\ 1$$

$$\frac{\Sigma X_2}{N_2} = \frac{1428}{14} = 102.00 = mean\ of\ Group\ 2$$

Step 15.   Subtract the mean of Group 2 from the mean of Group 1.

$$99.67 - 102.00 = -2.33$$

(*Note:* For computational purposes, only the absolute difference between the means is important. The sign merely indicates the direction of the difference.)

Step 16.   Computation of t. Divide the value obtained in Step 15 (the numerator of the original equation) by the value obtained in Step 13 (the denominator of that equation).

$$t = \frac{2.33}{5.48} = .43$$

Step 17.   To determine whether the t value is significant, the degrees of freedom (*df*) must be computed. For a test of significance between two means, the *df* are equal to $(N_1 + N_2) - 2$. In the present example, $(12 + 14) - 2 = 24$. The t value that is significant at the .05 level for 24 *df* (two-tailed; see Appendix B) is equal to 2.064. Since the t value in the present example is less than 2.064, it is concluded that there is no significant difference between the IQ test scores of boys and girls in this particular class.   ■

SECTION 1.6
The *t*-Test for Related Measures

A somewhat rarer use of the *t*-test is to determine the significance of a difference between two correlated means. It is most commonly used when two scores are recorded for the same individuals. For instance, IQ test scores might be taken for each subject at the beginning (pre-test) and again at the end of a special training program (post-test) to determine if there has been an improvement in the scores.

The second use of this test occurs when pairs of subjects in two different groups are "matched" on the basis of some variable or set of variables—such as age, sex, race, years of education, etc.—to ensure that each of the pairs of subjects are the "same" before experimental manipulations are begun.

Points to Consider When Using the *t* for Related Measures

1. Both "groups" will have the same number of measures since they represent two measures on the same subjects or matched pairs of subjects.
2. If two measures are taken on the same subjects, the treatments-by-subjects analysis (see Section 4.5) is usually easier to compute and gives the same results since $t^2 = F$ for 1 and N df.

■ EXAMPLE

This example will demonstrate use of the *t* for related measures when "matched pairs" of subjects are used in the experiment. Exactly the same computational steps would be followed if repeated measures were taken on the same subjects (pre-test and post-test).

Assume an experimenter is interested in determining the effects of an early intervention program on the overall verbal skills of a group of underprivileged children. The first step is to match several pairs of students on the basis of some measure known to be related to overall verbal skills. Such a measure might be the Wechsler Intelligence Scale for Children.

The children are first matched and paired according to their performance on this test. One child from each pair is randomly assigned to the early intervention program; the remaining child in each pair is assigned to the other group, which receives no special training.

After six months, the overall verbal skills of every child is measured and the performance of the two groups compared to determine the effects of the program. In the present example, the pairs of matched subjects will be represented by S and S'; the test score of each S by X; and the test score of each S' by Y.

There are two formulas used for the *t* for related measures. The first involves computation of a correlation and is given by

$$t = \frac{\bar{X} - \bar{Y}}{\sqrt{\dfrac{S_X^2 + S_Y^2 - 2rS_XS_Y}{N}}}$$

where S_X^2 = variance of the X scores
$\quad\ \ S_Y^2$ = variance of the Y scores
$\quad\ \ r$ = correlation between X and Y
$\quad\ \ N$ = number of pairs of scores

The second formula, which gives *exactly* the same results, is much simpler and will be used to demonstrate the computational steps.

$$t = \frac{\bar{X} - \bar{Y}}{\sqrt{\dfrac{\Sigma D^2 - \dfrac{(\Sigma D)^2}{N}}{N(N - 1)}}}$$

where D = difference score between each X and Y pair
$\quad\ \ N$ = number of pairs of scores

Step 1.   Table the data as follows. No particular order is necessary, except that each pair (S and S') of scores must be in the same relative position.

Group 1 (no special treatment)		Group 2 (special treatment)	
Subject	Score	Subject	Score
S_1	89	S_1'	94
S_2	86	S_2'	94
S_3	96	S_3'	101
S_4	100	S_4'	105
S_5	94	S_5'	100
S_6	86	S_6'	84
S_7	81	S_7'	81
S_8	93	S_8'	96
S_9	87	S_9'	90
S_{10}	89	S_{10}'	88
S_{11}	110	S_{11}'	115
S_{12}	95	S_{12}'	100
S_{13}	107	S_{13}'	110
S_{14}	96	S_{14}'	102

Step 2.   Obtain the difference between each pair of scores.

$$89 - 94 = -5$$
$$86 - 94 = -8$$
$$96 - 101 = -5$$
$$100 - 105 = -5$$
$$94 - 100 = -6$$
$$86 - 84 = +2$$
$$81 - 81 = 0$$
$$93 - 96 = -3$$
$$87 - 90 = -3$$
$$89 - 88 = +1$$
$$110 - 115 = -5$$
$$95 - 100 = -5$$
$$107 - 110 = -3$$
$$96 - 102 = -6$$

Step 3.   Square all of the difference scores recorded in Step 2, and add these squared values.

$$\Sigma D^2 = (-5)^2 + (-8)^2 + \cdots + (-6)^2 = \textbf{293}$$

Step 4.   Obtain the *algebraic* sum of the difference scores obtained in Step 2. Square this value, and divide by the number of difference scores recorded.

$$\Sigma D = (-5) + (-8) + \cdots + (-6) = \textbf{-51}$$

and,

$$\frac{(\Sigma D)^2}{N} = \frac{-51^2}{14} = \frac{2601}{14} = \textbf{186}$$

Step 5.   Subtract the value of Step 4 from the sum in Step 3.

$$\Sigma D^2 - \frac{(\Sigma D)^2}{N} = 293 - 186 = \textbf{107}$$

Step 6.   Divide the result obtained in Step 5 by $N(N - 1)$. In the present example, this is $[14(14 - 1) = 182]$, since N refers to the number of difference scores. Then, take the square root of that quotient.

$$\sqrt{\frac{\Sigma D^2 - \dfrac{(\Sigma D)^2}{N}}{N(N - 1)}} = \sqrt{\frac{107}{182}} = \sqrt{.588} = \textbf{.767}$$

Step 7.   Obtain the mean score of each of the two groups—that is, add all of the scores in each group and divide each sum by the number of scores added to obtain it.

$$\Sigma X = 89 + 86 + \cdots + 96 = \textbf{1309} = \text{sum for Group 1}$$

$$\Sigma Y = 94 + 94 + \cdots + 102 = \textbf{1360} = \text{sum for Group 2}$$

$$\frac{\Sigma X}{N} = \frac{1309}{14} = \textbf{93.50} = \textit{mean for Group 1}$$

$$\frac{\Sigma Y}{N} = \frac{1360}{14} = \textbf{97.14} = \textit{mean for Group 2}$$

Step 8.   Subtract the mean for Group 2 from the mean for Group 1.

$$93.50 - 97.14 = \textbf{-3.64}$$

(*Note:* For computational purposes, only the absolute difference between the means is important. The sign indicates the direction of change and is important for interpretation of the results.)

Step 9.   Divide the value obtained in Step 8 by the value obtained in Step 6.

This yields the t value.

$$t = \frac{3.64}{.767} = \mathbf{4.74}$$

Step 10.   To determine whether the t value is significant, the degrees of freedom (df) first must be obtained. For the t for related measures, the $df = N - 1$ where N is the number of *difference* scores. In the present example, $N - 1 = 13$. From the t tables (see Appendix B), we find that the t value needed for significance at the .05 level with 13 df is 2.16. Since the obtained t is larger than 2.16, it is concluded that the special training program improved the overall verbal skills of the children.   ∎

SECTION 1.7
Sandler's *A* Test

An alternate and somewhat simpler technique for determining whether the difference between correlated samples is significant is Sandler's A test, which is derived directly from the t-test. Thus, the results of an analysis using the A test will be the same as those of the t-test for related measures described in Section 1.6.

The formula for A is

$$A = \frac{\text{Sum of the squared difference scores}}{\text{Sum of the difference scores squared}}, \quad \text{or} \quad \frac{\Sigma D^2}{(\Sigma D)^2}$$

To demonstrate the computation of the A statistic, the data presented in Section 1.6 will be used. Steps 1, 2, and 3 for the computation of A are the same as the computation of t for related measures.

Step 1.   Table the data as in Section 1.6.

Step 2.   Compute the difference scores as in 1.6.

Step 3.   Square and sum all of the difference scores. In the example from 1.6, this sum was equal to 293.

Step 4.   Obtain the algebraic sum of the difference scores computed in Step 2, and square that value. In the example used in Section 1.6, this sum computed in Step 2 was equal to -51.

$$-51^2 = \mathbf{2601}$$

(*Note:* You do *not* divide by the number of difference scores as in Step 4 of Section 1.6.)

Step 5. Divide the value obtained in Step 3 by the value obtained in Step 4.

$$A = \frac{293}{2601} = .113$$

Step 6. Turn to Appendix C and read into the table for 13 df (since there are 14 pairs of scores, $N - 1 = 13$). From this table we find that for an A value (two-tailed) to be significant at the .05 level, it must be equal to, *or smaller than*, .270. Since the obtained A is smaller (.113) than the tabled value, it is concluded that the difference is significant. ■

SECTION 1.8
Sample Size and Power

The power of a statistical test is defined as the probability of rejecting the null hypothesis when it is false. Stated in the terminology used by most researchers, power is the probability of finding a significant difference in an experiment when such a difference is present in the population. The power of a statistical test is dependent upon the following:

1. the level of significance chosen (the less stringent the alpha, the higher the power);
2. the variability of the measures recorded (the smaller the variance and standard deviation, the higher the power);
3. the size of the experimental (treatment) effect (the larger the treatment effect, the higher the power);
4. the size of the sample (the larger the sample size, the higher the power).

In theory, all of the above can be varied, but in fact, only the sample size can be changed with relative ease since the values usually chosen for α are .05 or .01. The variability of the measures almost always is at minimal levels through good research design, and the size of the treatment or experimental effect is determined by the actual size of the effect in the population.

Issues related to power must be considered before the experiment is undertaken. As indicated above, the major determinant of power that can be adjusted readily is the size of the sample. A great many experienced researchers use a rule-of-thumb sample size of approximately twenty. Significantly smaller samples ($N < 5-10$) often result in such low power values that differences are not detected, while very large samples ($N > 30-50$) produce power so great that very minute treatment effects of little practical importance may achieve statistical significance. If the reader is interested in a more complete discussion of power, almost any of the more advanced statistics textbooks are good sources. Citation of some of the commonly used advanced level texts precedes the reference table at the end of Part 4.

Before any calculations of the sample size needed to achieve a desired level of power can be undertaken, several decisions must be made. The first concerns the level of α chosen and its relationship to β, or, the probability of Type I and Type II errors. A guideline often followed is that the probability of a Type II error be set at four times that of a Type I error. Thus, if α is set at .05, then β would be set at .20. The desired level of power under this set of assumptions would then be equal to $1 - \beta$, or .80.

The remaining two decisions relate to the variability of the measures and the size of the treatment effects. Obviously, before the data are collected there is no way to know either the variability of the measures or the size of the treatment effects. Thus, estimates must be made.

The first value needed for calculation of the required size of sample is the *standardized effect size*. This value is a ratio of the estimated difference between the population means of the treatment groups and the estimated standard deviation of the population. For example, if the difference between the treatment means was 6 and the standard deviation was 8, the standardized effect size would be 6/8, or .75.

There are three generally accepted ways that the values needed to compute the standardized effect size can be obtained. First, pilot studies can be conducted to obtain likely values for estimation of the standard deviation and the mean differences. Second, prior research using similar conditions and response measures may provide information regarding the likely size of these parameters. Finally, Cohen[1] has suggested use of the following ratios to describe levels of standardized effect size. When the difference is expected to be small in relation to the standard deviation, a value of .20 is used (the difference between the means is expected to be approximately one-fifth the size of the standard deviation). When the ratio of the difference to the standard deviation is expected to be moderate, a value of .50 is used, and when the difference is expected to be large in relation to the standard deviation, a ratio value of .80 is suggested.

■ EXAMPLE 1

Assume that a two-group experiment is planned to determine the effect of loudness level of background music on the time required to memorize a set of mathematical formulas. Subjects will be assigned randomly to the two loudness conditions. Prior to conducting the research, the following decisions were made.

- The level of significance will be set at $\alpha = .05$.
- The power desired will be set at .80.
- A pilot study will be conducted to obtain estimates of the values needed to determine the size of sample necessary to achieve that level of power.

---

1. Cohen, J. *Statistical power analysis for the behavioral sciences,* Rev. ed. Academic Press, 1977. (See especially pages 20–27.)

The pilot data represent minutes required to memorize the formulas.

Group 1 (Soft Music)		Group 2 (Loud Music)	
S_1	3	S_7	4
S_2	4	S_8	3
S_3	6	S_9	1
S_4	4	S_{10}	2
S_5	3	S_{11}	5
S_6	5	S_{12}	3

Step 1. Turn to Section 1.5 and use the pilot data above to compute Steps 2 through 11. Then take the square root of the value obtained in Step 11. The result is the estimate of σ needed for computation of the standardized effect size. In the present example:

$$\sigma_{est} = \sqrt{14/10} = \mathbf{1.183}$$

Step 2. Compute the mean of the two groups. In the present example:

Mean of Group 1 = **4.167**

Mean of Group 2 = **3.000**

Step 3. Computation of the standardized effect size. This value is the difference between the means of the two groups divided by the standard deviation as computed in Step 1.

$$\text{Standardized effect size} = \frac{(\mu_{1(est)} - \mu_{2(est)})}{\sigma_{(est)}} = \frac{1.167}{1.183} = \mathbf{.99}$$

Step 4. Turn to Appendix P and find the table for Power = .80. Enter the table for $\alpha = .05$, $k = 2$, and 1.0σ. The value of N read from the table is **17**. Thus, to achieve a level of power of .80, the experimenter should assign 17 subjects to each group, or a total of 34 subjects in the experiment. (*Note:* Since the standardized effect size is slightly less than 1.0σ, N per group probably should be increased to 18.) ∎

■ EXAMPLE 2

Example 2 describes a four-group, completely randomized experiment as presented in Section 4.1. Assume the above experimenter now wishes to investigate the effects of four levels of background music on time required to memorize a more difficult set of mathematical formulas. Subjects will be assigned randomly to the four groups; α again will be set at .05, the desired level of power will be .80, and a pilot study will again be conducted to obtain estimates of the values needed to calculate the N per group required to achieve that level of power. The pilot data again represent minutes needed to memorize the formulas.

Group 1 (No Music)		Goup 2 (Soft Music)		Group 3 (Medium Music)		Group 4 (Loud Music)	
S_1	10	S_6	9	S_{11}	9	S_{16}	13
S_2	7	S_7	8	S_{12}	12	S_{17}	14
S_3	9	S_8	7	S_{13}	16	S_{18}	8
S_4	8	S_9	15	S_{14}	14	S_{19}	16
S_5	15	S_{10}	6	S_{15}	7	S_{20}	12

Step 1. Turn to Section 4.1 and compute Steps 2 through 11. The value needed to estimate σ is the ms_w. In the present example:

$$ms_w = SS_w/df = (\text{Step } 9)/16 = 177.2/16 = \textbf{11.075}$$

Then, take the square root of that value. This is the standard deviation needed for computation of the standardized effect size.

$$\sigma_{est} = \sqrt{11.075} = \textbf{3.328}$$

Step 2. Compute the mean of the two most extreme groups. In the present example, the mean performance of Group 2 was lowest and Group 4 highest.

Mean of Group 4 = **12.6**

Mean of Group 2 = **9.0**

Step 3. Compute the standardized effect size. This value is the difference between the means computed in Step 2 divided by the standard deviation computed in Step 1.

$$(\mu_{hi\,(est)} - \mu_{lo\,(est)})/\sigma_{(est)} = (12.6 - 9)/3.328 = \textbf{1.08}$$

Step 4. Turn to Appendix P and find the table for Power = .80. Enter the table for $\alpha = .05$, $k = 4$, and 1.0σ. The value of N read from the table is **23**. Thus, to achieve a power level of .80, the experimenter should assign 23 subjects per group, or a total of 92 subjects in the experiment. ∎

PART 2

Confidence Intervals

In the preceding section, the statistical tests were used to determine whether the differences between means were significant. The tests to be presented in Part 2 focus on a complementary topic, *interval estimation.*

In the behavioral sciences, interval estimation tends to be used less frequently than hypothesis testing procedures, even though interval estimates generally provide more information than the simple acceptance or rejection of the hypothesis. In most instances involving interval estimation, the researcher uses sample data to provide an estimate of the range of scores within which the population mean, or differences between means, are likely to fall.

In all computations of interval estimates, four types of statistical information must be decided or computed. The first is the level of confidence that the population mean (or mean difference) falls within the range or interval to be calculated. This value is decided by the researcher and is computed as $1 - \alpha$. In most instances the confidence coefficient will be $1 - .05$, or .95 (95%). The second and third types of information involve computation of the appropriate mean (or mean difference) and the appropriate standard error. These computations are based on the sample data collected. The final piece of information needed is the appropriate t or z value, which gives the distance from the mean known to contain .95 (95%) of the normal curve.

Where possible, the computations presented in Part 2 will use the data from Part 1 so that the reader can compare the types and amounts of information obtained from the two different approaches.

SECTION 2.1
Confidence Interval for the Mean

In Section 1.4, the researcher wished to determine whether the heights of a sample of twelve-year-olds who live in an area where the water is high in natural fluoride is significantly different from the population mean heights of twelve-year-olds. Section 2.1 focuses not on whether there is a significant difference between the mean heights of the twelve-year-olds who live in the high fluoride area and the population, but rather on the width of the interval that the researcher can be confident contains the mean height of the population of twelve-year-olds who live in that high fluoride area.

■ EXAMPLE

Recall that the data collected in Section 1.4 represented the heights of twenty randomly selected twelve-year-olds. To compute the confidence interval, the following steps must be undertaken.

Step 1. Select the confidence coefficient. This value is equal to $1 - \alpha$ and represents the level of certainty that the population mean falls within the range or interval to be computed. In almost all instances the coefficient selected will be equal to $1 - .05$, or .95.

Step 2. Obtain the mean of the sample. The value was computed in Step 8 of Section 1.4 and is equal to

Sample mean = **60.4**

Step 3. Obtain the standard error of the mean. To compute this value, follow Steps 1 through 7 of Section 1.4. From those computations, the value needed was found to equal

Standard error of the mean = **1.57**

Step 4. Obtain the tabled t value (two-tailed with $N - 1$ df) such that .95 of the distribution of scores will lie between these values. In the present example, twenty subjects were measured and the $t_{.05}$ value (Appendix B) for 19 df is equal to

$t_{.05} = \textbf{2.093}$

Step 5. The general formula for the computation of the confidence interval is

$\text{CI}_{.95} = \bar{X} \pm (t_{.05} \times \text{standard error of the mean})$

For the current example, the values are

$\text{CI}_{.95} = 60.4 \pm (2.093 \times 1.57)$

$= 60.4 \pm 3.29$

$= \textbf{57.11 to 63.69}$

Thus it is concluded, with a .95 (95%) level of confidence, that if all children who live in the high fluoride area were measured, the mean height of that population would fall between 57.11 and 63.69 inches. ■

Supplement

Three factors influence the width of the confidence interval. The first is the confidence coefficient chosen. If, in the above example, the experimenter wished to increase the level of confidence to .99 from the original .95, then the t value (two-tailed, 19 df) would be 2.861 instead of 2.093. Use of this t value in the calculation would result in the $CI_{.99} = 55.91$ to 64.89 as compared with the $CI_{.95} = 57.11$ to 63.69 calculated above. The result is an interval that provides a greater level of certainty that it contains the population mean (μ), but the cost is a wider interval.

The second and third factors affecting the width of the confidence interval are related to the size of the standard error of the mean. In all computations of confidence intervals, the smaller the standard error of the mean, the smaller the width of the interval. In some experimental situations, the size of the standard error of the mean can be reduced directly through better sampling or experimental procedures.

In most cases, however, the easiest and most practical way to reduce the size of the standard error of the mean is to employ the third factor. This involves increasing the sample size. For example, in the above problem, an increase in the sample size from 20 to 100 would have reduced the range or width of the confidence interval from 6.58 inches (57.11 to 63.69) to approximately 3.3 inches (58.75 to 62.05). The reader is encouraged to review Section 1.8, which discusses the factors that affect the power of a statistical test to detect differences. The same basic principles apply to the factors affecting the width of confidence intervals.

SECTION 2.2
Confidence Interval for a Difference Between Two Independent Means

The confidence interval procedures demonstrated in Section 2.1 for a single population mean can be generalized to the difference between two means. The data used to demonstrate these calculations will be taken from Section 1.5.

In Section 1.5, the principal was interested in determining whether there was a significant difference between the IQ scores of a sample of boys and girls in a particular school. The question to be considered in this section focuses not on whether the difference between the mean performance of the two groups is significant, but rather, on the width of the interval that the principal can be confident contains the mean difference between boys and girls if all children in the school were measured.

■ **EXAMPLE**

Recall that the data in Section 1.5 were taken from a random sample of twelve boys and fourteen girls. To compute the confidence interval for a difference between two independent means, the following steps must be undertaken.

Step 1.   Select the confidence coefficient. This value is equal to $1 - \alpha$ and represents the level of certainty that the mean difference in the population falls within the range or interval to be computed. In most instances the coefficient selected will be equal to $1 - .05$, or .95.

Step 2.   Obtain the mean difference between the two groups. This value was computed in Steps 14 and 15 of Section 1.5 and is equal to

Mean difference $= -2.33$

Step 3.   Obtain the standard error of the difference. To compute this value, follow Steps 1 through 13 of Section 1.5. From those computations, the value is equal to

Standard error of the difference $= 5.48$

Step 4.   Obtain the tabled t value (two-tailed for $N_1 + N_2 - 2$ degrees of freedom) such that .95 of the distribution will lie between these values. In the present example, $12 + 14 - 2 = 24$ df and the t value (Appendix B) is

$t_{.05}$ for 24 $df = 2.064$

Step 5.   The general formula for the computation of the confidence interval is

$$CI_{.95} = (\overline{X}_1 - \overline{X}_2) \pm (t_{.05} \times \text{standard error of the difference})$$

For the current example, the values are

$$CI_{.95} = (99.67 - 102.00) \pm (2.064 \times 5.48) = -2.33 \pm 11.31$$

$$= -13.64 \text{ to } +8.98$$

Thus, it is concluded with a .95 level of confidence that if the IQ test scores of all children in the school were obtained and compared, the mean difference between the IQ test performance of boys and girls would range from 13.64 points in favor of the girls to 8.98 points in favor of the boys.   ■

Supplement

The same three factors influence the size of the confidence interval for a difference between two independent means as affect the confidence interval for a single mean. The first factor is the confidence coefficient chosen. If the confidence coefficient had been increased to .99 from the original .95, then the t value (two-tailed, 24 df) would have been 2.797 instead of 2.064. Use of this t value in the computation would have resulted in a wider confidence interval that ranged from 17.66 points in favor of the girls to 13.00 points in favor of the boys.

The second factor also has the same effect as for a single mean. Any appropriate experimental or sampling procedure that reduces variability, and thus the size of the standard error of the difference, will reduce the width of the confidence interval. This will result in greater precision in estimating the mean difference between the two groups in the population.

The third factor, increasing the sample size, is probably the easiest way to gain greater precision and reduce the width of the confidence interval. In the above example, if the number of subjects in each group had been increased from $N_1 = 12$ and $N_2 = 14$ to $N_1 = 36$ and $N_2 = 42$, the width of the confidence interval would have decreased from 22.62 points (-13.64 to 8.98) to approximately 6.33 points (-5.49 to .83). Again, the reader is referred to Section 1.8 since the factors that affect the power of a statistical test to detect differences are much the same as those that affect the width of the confidence interval.

SECTION 2.3
Confidence Interval for a Difference Between Related Measures (Means)

The problem and data used to demonstrate this set of computations are taken from Section 1.6. In that section, the experimenter wished to determine whether a special education program resulted in a significant change in the verbal scores of a sample of underprivileged children. The basic question to be considered in Section 2.3 is not whether the change in verbal ability scores is significant, but rather the range of performance change that the experimenter can be confident will result from this special education program.

■ EXAMPLE
Recall that the data collected in Section 1.6 represented the scores of two groups of fourteen underprivileged children who were matched on their IQ test scores. To compute the confidence interval, the following steps must be undertaken. (*Note:* The same computational steps would be undertaken if the experimenter had used a single group of subjects and measured them twice, once prior to the special program [pre-test], and then after it was completed [post-test].)

Step 1. Determine the confidence coefficient. This value is equal to $1 - \alpha$ and represents the level of certainty that the mean change in the population falls within the range or interval to be computed. In almost all instances, this confidence coefficient will be equal to $1 - .05$, or .95.

Step 2. Obtain the mean difference (change) in performance resulting from the special program. This value was computed in Steps 8 and 9 of Section 1.6.

Mean difference (change) = **3.64**

Step 3. Obtain the standard error of the difference scores. To compute this value, follow Steps 1 through 7 of Section 1.6. From those computations, the value needed is found to be

Standard error of the difference scores = **.767**

Step 4.   Obtain the t value (two-tailed for $N - 1$ *pairs* of scores) such that .95 of the distribution lies between the scores. In the present example, fourteen difference scores were recorded and the $t_{.05}$ value (two-tailed; Appendix B) for 13 *df* is equal to

$$t_{.05} = \mathbf{2.160}$$

Step 5.   The general formula for the computation of the confidence interval is

$$\mathrm{CI}_{.95} = (\bar{X} - \bar{Y}) \pm (t_{.05} \times \text{Standard error of the difference scores})$$

For the current example, the values are

$$\mathrm{CI}_{.95} = (93.50 - 97.14) \pm (2.160 \times .767)$$

$$= 3.64 \pm 1.66$$

$$= \mathbf{1.98} \text{ to } \mathbf{5.30}$$

Thus, it is concluded with a .95 level of confidence that if all underprivileged children participating in this program were measured, the mean change (improvement) in scores on verbal skills would be between 1.98 and 5.30 points.   ∎

Supplement

The same three factors as discussed in the preceding two sections affect the width of the confidence interval. Increasing the confidence coefficient serves to increase the width of the interval, thus giving greater certainty that the population value is included. Precision, however, is reduced. Better matching or experimental procedures may have a direct effect on the size of the standard error of the difference scores and thus, the width of the confidence interval. Finally, increasing the number of subjects (or pairs of subjects as in the above example) will reduce the width of the confidence interval. An increase in the sample size from $N_{pairs} = 14$ to $N_{pairs} = 36$ would have reduced the width of the confidence interval from 3.32 (1.98 to 5.30) to .96 (3.16 to 4.12).

SECTION 2.4
Confidence Interval for a Proportion (Percent)

One of the most frequently computed confidence intervals is for a proportion or percent. In every election year, polls are taken and voter attitudes toward candidates and issues are presented in the news media. In reports of the results of these polls, the confidence interval usually is presented, but instead of using the term *confidence interval* media reports usually use the term *margin of error*.

∎ EXAMPLE
The local school board has decided to place a tax levy on the ballot in the upcoming election. One of the board members suggests that a poll be taken to get an idea of the likelihood of passage. A local polling firm offers to undertake

the task and randomly samples 550 residents who indicate that they plan to vote in the upcoming election. The key question in the survey asks each respondent whether he or she will vote in favor of the levy. The results indicate that 258 of the 550 total responded "yes," they will vote for the tax increase.

Step 1.   Determine the confidence coefficient. This value is equal to $1 - \alpha$ and represents the level of certainty that the proportion in the population who will vote "yes" falls within the interval to be computed. In almost all instances, the coefficient selected will be equal to $1 - .05$, or $.95$

Step 2.   Compute the proportion of the sample who indicated that they will vote "yes." This value is obtained by dividing the number who indicate they will vote "yes" ($n = 258$) by the total number sampled ($N = 550$). This value is p.

$p = 258/550 =$ **.469**

Step 3.   Compute the standard error of a proportion. This value is computed using the following formula:

$$\text{Standard error of a proportion} = \sqrt{\frac{pq}{N}}$$

where p = the proportion who indicate "yes." This value was computed
above and equals **.469.**
q = the proportion who do not indicate "yes." This value equals $1 - p$,
or **.531.**
N = the total number in the sample

In the present example we have

$$\text{Standard error of a proportion} = \sqrt{\frac{.469 \times .531}{550}} = \sqrt{\frac{.0249}{550}} = \textbf{.0213}$$

Step 4.   Obtain the appropriate z value. In the present example

$z_{.05} =$ **1.96**

Step 5.   The formula for computation of the confidence interval is

$\text{CI}_{.95} = p \pm (z \times \text{standard error of a proportion})$

For the current example, the values are

$\text{CI}_{.95} = .469 \pm (1.96 \times .0213)$

$= .469 \pm .042$

$=$ **.427** to **.511**

Thus, it is concluded with a .95 (95%) level of confidence that if the election were held at this time, between .427 and .511 (42.7% to 51.1%) of the voters would vote "yes" on the tax levy issue. (*Note:* Media reports of the above type of results usually take the following form: "The poll showed that 47% of the voters indicated that they will vote for the tax levy. The margin of error is ±4 percentage points." This method of reporting the results is easier for readers to understand and is correct because the actual sample value of .469 [47%] has a standard error of .0213 [2.13%] and it takes 1.96 standard errors in each direction [1.96 × .0213] to be 95% confident of voter behavior in the popula-tion.) ■

Supplement

The factors affecting the width of the confidence interval for a proportion are slightly different from those discussed in the previous sections. First, the selec-tion of the confidence coefficient has the same effect as presented earlier. A higher confidence coefficient (for example, .99 versus .95) results in a wider confidence interval. The second factor, sampling or experimental control, is somewhat different for a proportion. Because of the nature of the binomial distribution and the computation of the standard error of a proportion, better or poorer sampling and questioning techniques do not have a significant *statistical* effect on the standard error of a proportion. Of course, these factors can have a profound effect on the validity of the results obtained.

The most commonly used and easiest way to reduce the size of the standard error of the proportion, and thus the width of the confidence interval, is to increase the size of the sample. For example, if the N in the above example had been increased from 550 to 1100, the confidence interval or margin of error would have been reduced to slightly less than ±3 points as compared to the margin of slightly more than ±4 points calculated in the example above.

SECTION 2.5
Confidence Interval for the Difference Between Two Proportions (Percents)

The use of a confidence interval in relation to the difference between two proportions is used most frequently when attitude surveys and voter polls are taken. In almost all instances, the samples are large, and thus, the z statistic is appropriate.

■ EXAMPLE
A local politician wishes to determine the likely difference between men and women in terms of their voting attitudes toward her. To find out, the politician commissions a survey, and a total 560 men and 590 women are polled. Of the men polled, 270 indicate they will vote for the politician; among the women, 310 indicate they will vote for her.

Step 1.   Determine the confidence coefficient. This value is equal to $1 - \alpha$ and represents the level of certainty that the difference between men and women in the population falls within the interval to be computed. In almost all instances, the coefficient selected will be equal to $1 - .05$, or .95.

Step 2. Compute the proportion of males who indicate they will vote for the politician, and the proportion of females who indicate the same. These values are computed by dividing the number in each group who indicate they will vote "for" by the total number sampled in each group. The values computed are identified as p_1 and p_2.

$$p_1 = 270/560 = .482$$

$$p_2 = 310/590 = .525$$

Step 3. Compute the standard error of the difference between two proportions using the following formula:

$$\text{Standard error of the difference between two proportions} = \sqrt{\frac{p_1 q_1}{n_1} + \frac{p_2 q_2}{n_2}}$$

Where, in the present example:

p_1 = the proportion of men who indicate they will vote for the candidate. This value equals **.482.**

q_1 = the proportion of men who do not indicate they will vote for the candidate. This value is computed as $1 - p_1$ and is equal to **.518.**

p_2 = the proportion of women who indicate they will vote for the candidate. This value equals **.525.**

q_2 = the proportion of women who do not indicate they will vote for the candidate. This value is computed as $1 - p_2$ and is equal to **.475.**

n_1 = the number of men sampled. This value is **560.**

n_2 = the number of women sample. This value is **590.**

Thus, in the present example we have

Standard error of the difference between two proportions

$$= \sqrt{\frac{.482 \times .518}{560} + \frac{.525 \times .475}{590}}$$

$$= \sqrt{.000446 + .000423} = \sqrt{.000869} = .0295$$

Step 4. Obtain the appropriate z value. In the present example

$$z_{.05} = \mathbf{1.96}$$

Step 5. The formula for computation of the confidence interval is

$$\text{CI}_{.95} = (p_1 - p_2) \pm (z_{.05} \times \text{standard error of the difference between two proportions})$$

For the current example, the values are

$$= -.036 \pm (1.96 \times .0295)$$

$$= -.036 \pm .058$$

$$= \mathbf{-.094} \text{ to } \mathbf{+.022}$$

Thus, it is concluded with a .95 (95%) level of confidence that if the election were held at this time, the difference in the proportion of men and women who would support the candidate would range from a .094 (9.4%) higher level of support by women to a .022 (2.2%) higher level of support by men. (*Note:* Media reports of the above type of results usually take the following form: "The poll showed that compared to male voters, women favor the candidate by 52 to 48%. The margin of error for the poll is ±6 percentage points." This is easier for most readers to understand and reflects the rounded proportions of female and male voters who indicate they will vote for the candidate [.525 and .482], the standard error of the difference between the two proportions [.0295, or 2.95%], and the fact that it required 1.96 standard errors in each direction for us to be 95% confident of voter behavior in the population.)   ■

Supplement

The same three factors again can interact to affect the size of the confidence interval for a difference between two proportions. As in the case for a single proportion, increasing the size of the confidence coefficient will result in a wider interval. Similarly, better or poorer sampling, questioning, or measuring techniques do not have a significant *statistical* effect on the size of the standard error, but, of course, these factors will have an effect on the validity of the results. Finally, as in the previous sections, the easiest way to reduce the size of the standard error of a difference between two proportions, and thus the width of the confidence interval, is to increase the sample size. For example, if n_1 and n_2 in the above example had been doubled to 1120 and 1180, respectively, the width of the confidence interval (margin of error) would have been reduced from approximately ±6 points to approximately ±4 percentage points.

PART 3

Correlation and Related Topics

The sixteen sections in this part present six rather different kinds of analyses. These six types are listed below, followed by a more detailed description of the different kinds of problems that can be handled with each analysis. This material should enable you to quickly choose the section that most clearly suits your individual needs.

1. Pearson product-moment correlation (the common, or usual, correlation)
2. Rank-order correlation, point-biserial correlation, and the correlation ratio (*eta*)
3. Partial and multiple correlation, simple and multiple regression
4. Analyses of covariance
5. Tests for reliability of measurement
6. Significance tests for deciding whether two correlation coefficients are different in magnitude

Pearson Product-Moment Correlation (Section 3.1)

Use the correlation coefficient described in Section 3.1 if your numbers represent amounts of some measurable quantity—height, age, IQ, grade points, test scores, etc. This analysis assumes that the two variables for which you have measures are linearly related. If you have ranked data or are reasonably sure that the variables are related in some complex curved way, use one of the correlation coefficients below.

Rank-Order Correlation, Point-Biserial Correlation, and Eta (Sections 3.2, 3.3, 3.4, and 3.5)

If you have ranked data or wish to convert measures to ranks, use one of the rank-order correlations described in Sections 3.2 and 3.3. These analyses make no assumptions about the shape of the relationship between variables.

If you have measures along one variable, such as grade points, and have another variable that is dichotomized, such as sex, use the point-biserial correlation described in Section 3.4.

If you are fairly certain that the variables are related in some complex curved manner or if you have already computed an F ratio, you can use the correlation ratio (*eta*), described in Section 3.5, to express the relationship between the two variables.

Partial and Multiple Correlation, Simple and Multiple Regression (Sections 3.6, 3.7, 3.8, 3.9, and 3.10)

If you have three variables and wish to know how highly two of them are related when the mutual relationships with the third variable are taken out, use the partial correlation described in either Section 3.6 or Section 3.7.

If you have three variables and wish to know how highly two of them, taken together, are related to the third, use the multiple correlation described in Section 3.8.

Simple regression (Section 3.9) is used when a researcher wishes to use the scores on one variable to predict the scores on another variable.

Multiple regression (Section 3.10) is used if you wish to determine the weights which will give the highest possible correlation between the predicted and observed values of the criterion variable.

Covariance (Sections 3.11 and 3.12)

When you wish to make the kinds of tests of significance described in Sections 4.1 and 4.2 (the completely randomized design and the two-factor factorial design) but cannot select random groups that are essentially equal, you must make statistical corrections for such differences. For example, if one group is composed of grade school children and another of high school students, and you wish to measure the amount of verbal material learned in a certain interval of time, you would reasonably expect the groups to differ initially by a large amount because of their different levels of education. The analyses of covariance, described in Sections 3.11 and 3.12, provide a technique whereby you can equate the two groups before training begins.

A major condition that must be met if the analysis of covariance is to be unequivocally interpreted is that the group regressions are homogeneous. Whether this condition is met or not can be tested by referring to the supplements at the end of Sections 3.11 and 3.12.

Reliability of Measurement (Sections 3.13 and 3.14)

Whenever measures are gathered by some sort of testing, the validity of the measures depends upon the quality of the test being used. The tests for the reliability of measurement involve particular interpretations of a correlation coefficient. Sections 3.13 and 3.14 consider the topic of reliability of measurement.

Significance Tests of Differences Between Correlations (Sections 3.15 and 3.16)

Each correlation coefficient is regarded as being either (1) indicative of a real relationship or (2) due to chance variation. Each of Sections 3.1 through 3.8 presents a test to help you decide which of the two cases is more likely for a particular correlation value. However, it is often desirable to know whether two correlation coefficients differ by more than would be expected by chance. Sections 3.15 and 3.16 present tests to help evaluate differences between correlation values. If the two correlation coefficients are computed using completely different groups of people (that is, if the correlations are independent), use the test presented in Section 3.15. If the correlation values have been computed using the same people (that is, if the correlations are dependent), use the test presented in Section 3.16.

In this part, computational formulas will again be presented in those instances in which a complete analysis can be shown by a single formula or in which a standard set of terms and symbols is used in nearly all textbooks.

SECTION 3.1
Pearson Product-Moment Correlation

The Pearson product-moment correlation (r) is used to determine if there is a relationship between two sets of paired numbers. Generally, the paired numbers are either (1) two different measures on each of several objects or persons or (2) one measure on each of several pairs of objects or people where the pairing is based on some natural relationship, such as parent to child, or on some initial matching according to one specific variable, such as IQ score.

■ EXAMPLE

Assume that an experimenter wishes to determine whether there is a relationship between the grade point averages (GPAs) and the scores on a reading-comprehension test of fifteen college freshmen.

The basic computational formula for the Pearson product-moment correlation is

$$r = \frac{N \sum XY - (\sum X)(\sum Y)}{\sqrt{[N \sum X^2 - (\sum X)^2][N \sum Y^2 - (\sum Y)^2]}}$$

where N = number of pairs of scores
$\Sigma\ XY$ = sum of the products of the paired scores
$\Sigma\ X$ = sum of scores on one variable
$\Sigma\ Y$ = sum of scores on the other variable
$\Sigma\ X^2$ = sum of the squared scores on the X variable
$\Sigma\ Y^2$ = sum of the squared scores on the Y variable

Step 1.   The scores must be paired in some meaningful way in order to use the Pearson r. In the present example, the two different scores—reading comprehension and grade point average—are paired and recorded for each of the fifteen students.

Student	Reading score (X)	Freshman GPA (Y)
S_1	38	2.1
S_2	54	2.9
S_3	43	3.0
S_4	45	2.3
S_5	50	2.6
S_6	61	3.7
S_7	57	3.2
S_8	25	1.3
S_9	36	1.8
S_{10}	39	2.5
S_{11}	48	3.4
S_{12}	46	2.6
S_{13}	44	2.4
S_{14}	39	2.5
S_{15}	48	3.3

Step 2.   Multiply the two numbers in each pair, then add the products.

$\Sigma\ XY = (38 \times 2.1) + (54 \times 2.9) + \cdots + (48 \times 3.3) = \mathbf{1846.1}$

Step 3.   Multiply the number obtained in Step 2 by N, the number of *paired* scores (15 in this example).

$N\ \Sigma\ XY = 15 \times 1846.1 = \mathbf{27{,}691.5}$

Step 4.   Square each number in the first column, and add the squared values.

$\Sigma\ X^2 = 38^2 + 54^2 + \cdots + 48^2 = \mathbf{31{,}327}$

Step 5.   Multiply the sum of Step 4 by the number of paired scores ($N = 15$ in this example).

$N\ \Sigma\ X^2 = 15 \times 31{,}327 = \mathbf{469{,}905}$

Step 6. Add all the scores in the first column (in this example, the reading-comprehension scores).

$\Sigma X = 38 + 54 + \cdots + 48 = \mathbf{673}$

Step 7. Square the value obtained in Step 6.

$(\Sigma X)^2 = 673^2 = \mathbf{452{,}929}$

Step 8. Square each number in the second column, and add the squared values.

$\Sigma Y^2 = 2.1^2 + 2.9^2 + \cdots + 3.3^2 = \mathbf{110.2}$

Step 9. Multiply the result of Step 8 by the number of paired scores ($N = 15$ in this example).

$N \Sigma Y^2 = 15 \times 110.2 = \mathbf{1653}$

Step 10. Add all the scores in the second column (in this example, the freshman GPAs).

$\Sigma Y = 2.1 + 2.9 + \cdots + 3.3 = \mathbf{39.6}$

Step 11. Square the value obtained in Step 10.

$(\Sigma X)^2 = 39.6^2 = \mathbf{1568.16}$

Step 12. Multiply the final value of Step 6 by that of Step 10.

$(\Sigma X)(\Sigma Y) = 673 \times 39.6 = \mathbf{26{,}650.8}$

Step 13. The numerator of r is now computed by substracting the value obtained in Step 12 from that obtained in Step 3. Be careful to note whether the answer is positive or negative.

$N \Sigma XY - (\Sigma X)(\Sigma Y) = 27{,}691.5 - 26{,}650.8 = \mathbf{+1040.7}$

Step 14. The following four steps result in the computation of the denominator of r. First, subtract the value of Step 7 from that of Step 5.

$N \Sigma X^2 - (\Sigma X)^2 = 469{,}905 - 452{,}929 = \mathbf{16{,}976}$

Note: If the variance of these first-column scores is desired, divide the result of Step 14 by N^2, i.e., $16{,}976/15^2 = 16{,}976/225 = 75.45$. Or, if an estimate of the variance of the population from which these scores were drawn is desired, divide by $N(N - 1)$, i.e., $16{,}976/[15 (15 - 1)] = 16{,}976/210 = 80.84$.

Step 15. Subtract the result of Step 11 from that of Step 9.

$N \Sigma Y^2 - (\Sigma Y)^2 = 1653 - 1568.16 = \mathbf{84.84}$

Note: The variance of these second-column scores can be obtained by dividing this result by N^2, i.e., $84.84/15^2 = 84.84/225 = .38$. For the estimate of the population variance, divide by $N(N - 1)$, i.e., $84.84/210 = .40$.

Step 16.   Multiply the result of Step 14 by the result of Step 15.

$$[N \Sigma X^2 - (\Sigma X)^2][N \Sigma Y^2 - (\Sigma Y)^2] = 16,976 \times 84.84$$

$$= \mathbf{1,440,243.8}$$

Step 17.   Take the square root of the result of Step 16. This is the denominator of r.

$$\sqrt{1,440,243.8} = \mathbf{1200.1}$$

Step 18.   Divide the value of Step 13 by that of Step 17. This yields the value of the Pearson product-moment correlation. Be sure to note the sign which indicates whether the relationship is positive or negative.

$$r = \frac{+1040.7}{1200.1} = \mathbf{+.87}$$

Supplement

Testing the significance of r: Two different procedures are used to test the hypothesis that $r = 0$. If N (the number of pairs) is 30 or larger, a critical-ratio z-test can easily be done. If N is smaller than 30, a slightly more complicated t-test should be done.

Step 19.   If N is 30 or larger, compute $z = r\sqrt{N - 1}$. For example, suppose $r = -.56$ and $N = 37$. Then,

$$z = (-.56)\sqrt{37 - 1} = (-.56)\sqrt{36} = -.56 \times 6 = \mathbf{-3.36}$$

If z is greater than ± 1.96, then r is significant at the .05 level using a two-tailed test (see Appendix A).

Step 20.   If N is smaller than 30, compute $t = r\sqrt{(N - 2)/(1 - r^2)}$. Using the value of r from Step 18 and the value of N used to compute that r, we have $r = +.87$ and $N = 15$. Thus,

$$t = (+.87)\sqrt{\frac{15 - 2}{1 - .87^2}} = .87\sqrt{\frac{13}{1 - .76}}$$

$$= .87\sqrt{54.16} = .87 \times 7.36 = \mathbf{+6.40}$$

The degrees of freedom for this t are $N - 2$.

$$df = 15 - 2 = \mathbf{13}$$

With 13 degrees of freedom, a t value larger than ± 2.16 (see Appendix B) is significant at the .05 level when a two-tailed test is used.

Note: Several critical values of *r* are given in Appendix G for various degrees of freedom.   ■

SECTION 3.2

Spearman Rank-Order Correlation (*rho*)

Spearman's *rho* is used when an experimenter wishes to determine whether two sets of rank-ordered data are related.

■ **EXAMPLE**

The experimenter first asked that twenty children in a class be ranked according to what their teacher believed their intelligence to be. Then the children were tested and their actual Wechsler IQ scores obtained. The data were as follows.

Child	Teacher's ranking	IQ score
A	1	116
B	2	111
C	3	97
D	4	122
E	5	116
F	6	105
G	7	108
H	8	95
I	9	124
J	10	98
K	11	116
L	12	109
M	13	103
N	14	103
O	15	96
P	16	90
Q	17	134
R	18	87
S	19	96
T	20	91

The following formula for *rho* (ρ) describes the computational procedures:

$$rho = 1 - \frac{6 \, \Sigma \, D^2}{N(N^2 - 1)}$$

where D = difference score between each X and Y pair
       N = number of pairs of scores

Step 1.   Rank the IQ scores so that both variables are ranked.

Note: When two children have the same IQ score, the same rank is given to each. But notice that the rank given is the mean value of the two ranks for the two tied scores. For example, Child M and Child N both have IQ scores of 103. These scores should fall into ranks 11 and 12. But since both children have the same IQ score, both are ranked as 11.5 and the next score (Child J, with an IQ socre of 98) is ranked as 13.

Child	Teacher's ranking	IQ rank on the basis of test score
A	1	5
B	2	7
C	3	14
D	4	3
E	5	5
F	6	10
G	7	9
H	8	17
I	9	2
J	10	13
K	11	5
L	12	8
M	13	11.5
N	14	11.5
O	15	15.5
P	16	19
Q	17	1
R	18	20
S	19	15.5
T	20	18

Step 2.   Compute the difference between the two ranks for each child. The resulting value is called the *D value*. List these values in a column, making sure to note whether they are positive or negative.

Child	D Value	
A	**−4**	(1 − 5)
B	**−5**	(2 − 7)
C	**−11**	(3 − 14)
D	**+1**	(4 − 3)
E	**0**	(5 − 5)
F	**−4**	(6 − 10)
G	**−2**	(7 − 9)
H	**−9**	(8 − 17)

Child	D Value	
I	+7	(9 − 2)
J	−3	(10 − 13)
K	+6	(11 − 5)
L	+4	(12 − 8)
M	+1.5	(13 − 11.5)
N	+2.5	(14 − 11.5)
O	−0.5	(15 − 15.5)
P	−3	(16 − 19)
Q	+16	(17 − 1)
R	−2	(18 − 20)
S	+3.5	(19 − 15.5)
T	+2	(20 − 18)

Step 3.   Square all the D values from Step 2, and add all the squared values.

$$\Sigma D^2 = (-4^2) + (-5^2) + \cdots + 2^2 = \mathbf{668}$$

Step 4.   Multiply the result of Step 3 by the number 6. (*Note:* The number 6 is *always* used, regardless of the number of ranks, etc., involved.)

$$6 \Sigma D^2 = 6 \times 668 = \mathbf{4008}$$

Step 5.   Compute $N(N^2 - 1)$. (In our example, $N = 20$.)

$$N(N^2 - 1) = 20(400 - 1) = \mathbf{7980}$$

Step 6.   Divide the result of Step 4 by the result of Step 5.

$$\frac{6 \Sigma D^2}{N(N^2 - 1)} = \frac{4008}{7980} = \mathbf{.50}$$

Step 7.   Subtract the final value of Step 6 from the number 1. (*Note:* The number 1 is always used.) This yields the value of Spearman's *rho* (ρ). Be careful to record whether it is positive or negative.

$$\rho = 1 - \frac{6 \Sigma D^2}{N(N^2 - 1)} = 1 - .50 = \mathbf{+.50}$$

Supplement

Testing the significance of *rho*: Two different procedures are needed to test the hypothesis that *rho* = 0. If N (the number of ranks) is 30 or larger, a critical-ratio z-test can easily be done. If N is between 10 and 30, a slightly more complicated t-test should be done. No test is presented here for the significance of *rho* where N is less than 10 since it is rare that so few ranks would be considered.

Step 8.   When N is 30 or greater, compute $z = rho\sqrt{N - 1}$. For example, suppose $rho = -.21$ and $N = 50$. Then,

$$z = (-.21)\sqrt{50 - 1} = (-.21)\sqrt{49} = -.21 \times 7 = -1.47$$

If z is greater than ± 1.96, then rho is significant at the .05 level using a two-tailed test (see Appendix A).

Step 9.   When N is between 10 and 30, compute

$$t = rho\sqrt{\frac{N - 2}{1 - rho^2}}$$

Using the value of rho from Step 7 above and the value of N used to compute that rho, we have $rho = +.50$ and $N = 20$. Thus,

$$t = (+.50)\sqrt{\frac{20 - 2}{1 - rho^2}} = (+.50)\sqrt{\frac{18}{1 - .25}} = (+.50)\sqrt{\frac{18}{.75}}$$

$$= (+.50)\sqrt{24} = +.50 \times 4.9 = +2.45$$

The degrees of freedom for this t are $N - 2$. Thus,

$$df = 20 - 2 = 18$$

With 18 degrees of freedom, a t value larger than ± 2.10 (see Appendix B) is significant at the .05 level when a two-tailed test is used.   ■

SECTION 3.3
Kendall Rank-Order Correlation (*tau*)

Kendall's *tau* is sometimes used in place of Spearman's *rho*, presented in Section 3.2. If you have a pair of ranks for each of several individuals, the *tau* statistic can be computed to express the degree of relationship between the ranks. Its significance can be tested as follows.

■ EXAMPLE
Assume that an experimenter wishes to determine the degree of relationship between the ratings of two judges on ten contestants in a figure-skating contest. The measures recorded represent the ranks given to the contestants by each of the judges.

The usual formula for *tau* when there are no tied ranks is

$$tau = \frac{P = Q}{\frac{1}{2}N(N - 1)}$$

where P = total number of higher ranks
$\quad\quad Q$ = total number of lower ranks
$\quad\quad N$ = number of pairs of ranks

(*Note:* See the following for the explanation of "higher" and "lower.")

A more general computation, covering a case where some ranks are tied, is presented here. Steps 7 through 12 show how to correct for the tied ranks.

Step 1.   Table the data as follows. In computing *tau*, always arrange the first column of ranks so that they range from the lowest to the highest as you go down the column.

Contestant	Ranking by Judge A	Ranking by Judge B
A	1	3
B	2	5
C	3.5	1.5
D	3.5	4
E	5	1.5
F	6	6
G	8	8
H	8	7
I	8	10
J	10	9

Step 2.   The ranks in the first column run from lowest to highest. The ranks in the second column are "mixed up." We must determine the extent of the "mix-up" in Column 2. To do so, count the number of ranks in Column 2 that are higher than that for Contestant A—i.e., the number of ranks that are higher in numerical value than the number 3. In this example, only the two 1.5's are lower than 3; therefore there are seven numbers higher than 3.

No. of higher ranks = **7**

Then, count the number of ranks that are lower than 3.

No. of lower ranks = **2**

Step 3.   Next, count the number of ranks in Column 2 that are higher than the rank for Contestant B—i.e., the number of ranks higher than 5. In this example, 6, 8, 7, 10, and 9 are higher than 5. Thus,

No. of higher ranks = **5**

Then count the number of ranks lower than 5. Do *not* include ranks that have already been considered (Contestant A). With the ranking for A excluded,

No. of lower ranks = **3**

Step 4.   Now count the number of ranks that are higher than the rank for Contestant C—i.e., the number of ranks higher than 1.5. All ranks except the other 1.5 are higher, but ties are not counted, and we have already taken care of numbers 3 and 5 for Contestants A and B. Thus,

No. of higher ranks = **6**

Now count the number of ranks lower than 1.5.

No. of lower ranks = **0**

Step 5. Continue counting both the number of ranks higher and the number of ranks lower than the one under consideration for all the rest of the ranks in Column 2. Table the results as follows. (*Note:* The values for the bottom contestant are both zero since no ranks appear below them.)

Contestant	No. of higher ranks	No. of lower ranks
A	7	2
B	5	3
C	6	0
D	5	1
E	5	0
F	4	0
G	2	1
H	2	0
I	0	1
J	0	0

Step 6. Add the numbers in each of the columns in Step 5.

$7 + 5 + \cdots + 0 = \mathbf{36} = $ sum of Column 1 (higher ranks)

$2 + 3 + \cdots + 0 = \quad\mathbf{8} = $ sum of Column 2 (lower ranks)

Then, subtract the sum of Column 2 from the sum of Column 1. Be careful to record whether the result is positive or negative.

$36 - 8 = \mathbf{+28}$

Step 7. Go to the table in Step 1, and count the number of ranks that are tied in the first column (the ranks assigned by Judge A). Categorize each tie as being a set of two, three, four, etc., according to the number of contestants in that tie. Then, compute $x(x - 1)$ for each tie, where x is the number of contestants tied for that place—e.g., $2(2 - 1) = 2(1) = 2$; $5(5 - 1) = 5(4) = 20$; etc. Add these products, and divide by 2. (*Note:* The number 2 is always used.) In this example, Contestants C and D tied for the third and fourth positions (both were assigned the rank of 3.5), and Contestants G, H, and I tied for the seventh, eighth, and ninth places (all were assigned the rank of 8). In this example, there is one set of two and one set of three. Thus,

$$\frac{2(2-1) + 3(3-1)}{2} = \frac{2(1) + 3(2)}{2} = \frac{2+6}{2} = \frac{8}{2} = 4$$

Step 8.   Repeat all the computations of Step 7 using the ranks in the second column of Step 1 (the ranks assigned by Judge B). Notice that Contestants C and E are tied at a rank of 1.5. Thus, we have one set of two, so

$$\frac{2(2-1)}{2} = \frac{2(1)}{2} = \frac{2}{2} = 1$$

Step 9.   Compute $[N(N-1)]/2$, where N refers to the total number of ranks in each column (10 in this example).

$$\frac{N(N-1)}{2} = \frac{10(10-1)}{2} = \frac{10(9)}{2} = \frac{90}{2} = 45$$

Step 10.   Subtract the result of Step 7 from the result of Step 9.

$$45 - 4 = 41$$

Step 11.   Subtract the result of Step 8 from the result of Step 9.

$$45 - 1 = 44$$

Step 12.   Multiply the result of Step 10 by the result of Step 11.

$$41 \times 44 = 1804$$

Then, take the square root of the product.

$$\sqrt{1804} = 42.474$$

Step 13.   Divide the result of Step 6 by the result of Step 12. This yields the value of Kendall's *tau*.

$$tau = +\frac{28}{42.474} = +.66$$

Supplement

Testing the significance of *tau* (i.e., the hypothesis that *tau* = 0): When there are 10 or more ranks and when the number of tied ranks is not too great, the following significance test will yield approximate values.

Step 14.   Compute $[N(N-1)(2N+5)]/18$, where N is the total number of ranks in each column of Step 1 (10 in this example).

$$\frac{10(10-1)[2(10)+5]}{18} = \frac{10(9)(20+5)}{18} = \frac{90(25)}{18} = \frac{2250}{18} = 125$$

Step 15. Take the square root of the result of Step 14.

$$\sqrt{125} = \textbf{11.18}$$

Step 16. Divide the result of Step 6 by the answer of Step 15. This yields a z statistic.

$$z = +\frac{28}{11.18} = \textbf{+2.50}$$

If the result of Step 16 is larger than ± 1.96 (see Appendix A), then *tau* is significant at the .05 level using a two-tailed test. ∎

SECTION 3.4
Point-Biserial Correlation

The point-biserial correlation is used when a coefficient of relationship between one measure that is continuous and another that is dichotomous is desired.

■ EXAMPLE
Assume that an experimenter wishes to determine the relationship between scores on a certain college entrance examination and whether the student obtained a grade point average of C or better during the freshman year. Twelve students are picked at random, and their entrance examination scores and course grades are recorded.

The continuous variable in this example is the array of scores on the college entrance examination. The dichotomous variable is the grade point category, which is determined by whether the student got (1) C or better or (2) lower than C. The number 1 represents the grade of each person who obtained C or better. A cipher, 0, represents the grade of those who got lower than C.

The formula for the point-biserial correlation is

$$r_{pb} = \frac{\overline{Y}_1 - \overline{Y}_0}{s_y}\sqrt{\frac{N_1 N_0}{N(N-1)}}$$

where $\overline{Y}_1$ = the mean of the values of the continuous variable for persons in dichotomous category 1

$\overline{Y}_0$ = the mean of the values of the continuous variable for persons in dichotomous category 0

N_1 = the number of persons in dichotomous category 1

N_0 = the number of persons in dichotomous category 0

s_y = the estimated standard deviation of the population of continuous-variable values from which the sample was taken

N = the total number of persons in the sample ($N_1 + N_0$)

The formula for the estimated standard deviation of the population is

$$s_y = \sqrt{\frac{\Sigma Y^2}{N-1} - \frac{(\Sigma Y)^2}{N(N-1)}}$$

Step 1. Table the data as follows.

Student	College entrance examination score (Y)	GPA category
A	104	1
B	82	0
C	92	1
D	76	0
E	101	1
F	111	1
G	98	1
H	85	0
I	88	1
J	67	0
K	106	1
L	95	0

Step 2. Make a list of all those examination scores paired with the GPA category 1 and a list of all those scores paired with the GPA category 0.

Y_1 scores (paired with GPA 1)	Y_0 scores (paired with GPA 0)
104	82
92	76
101	85
111	67
98	95
88	
106	

Step 3. Compute the means of the two groups of scores.

$$\bar{Y}_1 = \frac{104 + 92 + \cdots + 106}{7} = \frac{700}{7} = \textbf{100}$$

$$\bar{Y}_0 = \frac{82 + 76 + \cdots + 95}{5} = \frac{405}{5} = \textbf{81}$$

Step 4. Perform the subtraction $\bar{Y}_1 - \bar{Y}_0$, noting and recording the sign of the result.

$$100 - 81 = \textbf{+19}$$

Step 5. Obtain $\sqrt{(N_1 N_0)/[N(N-1)]}$. (In our example, $N_1 = 7$, $N_0 = 5$, and $N = N_1 + N_0 = 12$.)

$$\sqrt{\frac{(7)(5)}{12(11)}} = \sqrt{\frac{35}{132}} = \sqrt{.265} = .515$$

Step 6. Square all the examination scores of Step 1, and add the squares. (*Note:* Steps 6 and 8 can be done at the same time if you are using a calculator.)

$$104^2 + 82^2 + \cdots + 95^2 = 103,625$$

Step 7. Multiply the value obtained in Step 6 by N (12 in our example).

$$103,625 \times 12 = 1,243,500$$

Step 8. Add all the examination scores.

$$104 + 82 + \cdots + 95 = 1105$$

Step 9. Square the value obtained in Step 8.

$$1105^2 = 1,221,025$$

Step 10. Subtract the result of Step 9 from the result of Step 7.

$$1,243,500 - 1,221,025 = 22,475$$

Step 11. Divide the result of Step 10 by $N(N-1)$.

$$\frac{22,475}{N(N-1)} = \frac{22,475}{12(11)} = \frac{22,475}{132} = 170.265$$

Step 12. Take the square root of the result of Step 11.

$$\sqrt{170.265} = 13.05$$

Step 13. Divide the result of Step 4 by the result of Step 12.

$$+\frac{19}{13.05} = +1.456$$

Step 14. Multiply the result of Step 13 by the result of Step 5. This yields the value of r_{pb}. (We see from Step 4 that the value will be positive when $\bar{Y}_1$ is larger than $\bar{Y}_0$.)

$$r_{pb} = +1.456 \times .515 = +.75$$

Supplement

Testing the significance of r_{pb}: The hypothesis that $r_{pb} = 0$ can be tested by the t-test

$$t = r_{pb} \sqrt{\frac{N - 2}{1 - r_{pb}^2}}$$

which has $N - 2$ degrees of freedom. In our example, $r_{pb} = +.75$ and $N = 12$. Thus,

$$t = (+.75) \sqrt{\frac{12 - 2}{1 - (+.75)^2}} = (+.75) \sqrt{\frac{10}{1 - .562}}$$

$$= (+.75) \sqrt{\frac{10}{.438}} = (+.75)\sqrt{22.831} = (+.75)(4.78) = \mathbf{+3.58}$$

With $N - 2 = 12 - 2 = 10$ degrees of freedom, a t value larger than ± 2.23 is significant at the .05 level using a two-tailed test (see Appendix B).   ■

SECTION 3.5
The Correlation Ratio (η)

As a measure of relationship between two variables, *eta* (η) can be useful when: (1) the relationship is sufficiently nonlinear to make you hesitant about using the Pearson r or (2) the experiment involves independent and dependent measures and you wish to know the degree of their relationship.

Step 1.   *Eta* is most clearly defined as

$$\eta = \sqrt{SS_{groups}/SS_{total}}$$

where $SS_{between\ groups}$ and SS_{total} are sums of squares computed in a typical analysis of variance. For illustration, we will use the $SS_{between\ groups}$ and the SS_{total} from the last step of Section 4.1.

$$SS_{between\ groups} = \mathbf{567} \quad \text{and} \quad SS_{total} = \mathbf{1132}$$

Step 2.   From these values we compute:

$$\eta = \sqrt{567/1132} = \sqrt{.50} = \mathbf{.71}$$

This value of η gives a rough indication of the correlation between the independent and dependent variables in the experiment discussed in Section 4.1.

The square of *eta* (η^2) can be compared with the square of the Pearson product-moment correlation (r^2), which gives an indication of the proportion of the variance that two variables hold in common. Thus, η^2 in the above example indicates that the independent and dependent variables share .50 of the total variance.

$$\eta^2 = .71^2 = .50$$

This sharing of variance is sometimes described as the proportion of the variance of the dependent variable that can be explained by knowing the values of the independent variable.

Step 3.   In order to compute η from the raw data, turn to Section 4.1 and follow all of the steps for the completely randomized design. To test the η for significance, complete the F-test for significance of the group means as given in Section 4.1. The results of that test are also the results of a significance test of η. For the example above, we see that η is judged to be significantly different from zero.

$$F = ms_{groups}/ms_{within} = 189/12.84 = \mathbf{14.71} \qquad df = 3/44$$

Regardless of which use of η (as presented at the beginning of this section) you wish to make, compute the sums of squares according to the steps presented in Section 4.1; then follow the directions in the present section.

Supplement

It is sometimes important to know the *eta* for research reported in a publication. The relationship between a particular independent variable and the dependent measure used as a criterion can be found if the F ratio and the degrees of freedom are reported. The procedure for computing *eta* from a given F value is as follows. We will use the data presented in Section 4.7 for the purposes of illustration.

Step 1.   Obtain the F of interest (here, the F for trials) and the appropriate degrees of freedom.

$$F = \mathbf{52.46} \qquad df = 2/60$$

Step 2.   Multiply the F value of Step 1 by the numerator df.

$$52.46 \times 2 = \mathbf{104.92}$$

Step 3.   Add the result of Step 2 to the denominator df from Step 1.

$$104.92 + 60 = \mathbf{164.92}$$

Step 4.   Divide the result of Step 2 by the result of Step 3. This yields the square of *eta*.

$$\frac{104.92}{164.92} = \mathbf{.64}$$

Step 5. Take the square root of the final value of Step 4.

$$eta = \sqrt{.64} = .80$$

This value of *eta* indicates the degree of relationship between the trials variable and the dependent variable, which is the number of correct responses per trial in the verbal-learning situation.   ∎

SECTION 3.6
Partial Correlation: Three Variables

Partial correlation is used when you have three sets of related measures and you wish to find the relationship between any two when the relationship effect of the third has been taken out of both variables.

■ EXAMPLE
Suppose you have measures of (*a*) incomes of a group of fathers, (*b*) incomes of their eldest sons, and (*c*) number of years of formal education of the sons. A correlation of +.60 between incomes of fathers and sons might be interpreted as being indicative that money-making characteristics run in families. However, an observer might argue that the most probable contributor to the similarity in incomes of fathers and sons is level of education. A partial correlation between incomes of fathers and sons with the effect of education "partialed" out would help solve the controversy.

The notation for partial correlation is $r_{ab.c}$, or "the partial correlation between variables *a* and *b* with the relational effects of *c* taken out." The formula for partial correlation is

$$r_{ab.c} = \frac{r_{ab} - r_{ac}r_{bc}}{\sqrt{1 - r_{ac}^2}\ \sqrt{1 - r_{bc}^2}}$$

Step 1. Compute the simple correlation between each of the three possible pairs of measures—r_{ab}, r_{ac}, and r_{bc}. To do this, follow the steps provided in Section 4.1 for each of the three correlation coefficients needed. Let us assume that the three correlations for this example turned out to be

$$r_{ab} = +.60 \qquad r_{ac} = +.70 \qquad r_{bc} = +.80$$

Step 2. Compute the partial correlation between *a* and *b*.

$$r_{ab.c} = \frac{.60 - (.70)(.80)}{\sqrt{1 - .70^2}\ \sqrt{1 - .80^2}} = \frac{.60 - .56}{\sqrt{1 - .49}\ \sqrt{1 - .64}}$$

$$= \frac{+.04}{\sqrt{.51}\ \sqrt{.36}} = \frac{+.04}{(.714)(.60)} = \frac{+.04}{.428} = +.09$$

Thus, the correlation $r_{ab} = +.60$ is reduced to $r_{ab.c} = +.09$ when the mutual relationships of the variables with *c* are partialed out. These data suggest that the hypothesis that money-making ability is hereditary is false, and that the reason fathers and sons tend to have similar incomes is that they tend to have similar levels of education.

Step 3. The other two partial correlations could be computed in a similar manner if desired.

$$r_{ac.b} = \frac{r_{ac} - r_{ab}r_{cb}}{\sqrt{1 - r_{ab}^2}\sqrt{1 - r_{cb}^2}} = \frac{.70 - (.60)(.80)}{\sqrt{1 - .60^2}\sqrt{1 - .80^2}} = \frac{+.22}{.48} = +.46$$

$$r_{bc.a} = \frac{r_{bc} - r_{ba}r_{ca}}{\sqrt{1 - r_{ba}^2}\sqrt{1 - r_{ca}^2}} = \frac{.80 - (.70)(.60)}{\sqrt{1 - .70^2}\sqrt{1 - .60^2}} = \frac{+.38}{.571} = +.67$$

SECTION 3.7
Partial Rank-Order Correlation (Using Kendall's *tau*)

The *tau* statistics of Section 3.3 may be extended to the case of partial correlation in either of two cases: (1) when there are no tied ranks or (2) when there are tied ranks but the rank-order correlations are expected to yield only rough indications of true values. No significance test for partial *tau* can be presented since the sampling distribution is unknown.

■ EXAMPLE
Suppose that a judge has rank-ordered fifteen individuals on the basis of IQ, personality, and poise. In this case, the experimenter wishes to determine the correlation between each possible pair of rankings when the effects of the third have been taken out. The data might appear as follows.

Subject	Ranking 1 (IQ)	Ranking 2 (Personality)	Ranking 3 (Poise)
S_1	1	3	1
S_2	2	5	4
⋮	⋮	⋮	⋮
S_{15}	15	13	12

Step 1. First, go to Section 3.3 and compute the *tau* value for each of the three possible pairs of rankings—1 with 2 (tau_{12}), 1 with 3 (tau_{13}), and 2 with 3 (tau_{23}). For this example, suppose

$$tau_{12} = +.50 \qquad tau_{13} = +.60 \qquad tau_{23} = +.80$$

Step 2.   Compute the partial correlation of 1 with 2, partialing out the relationships with 3.

$$tau_{12.3} = \frac{tau_{12} - tau_{13}\,tau_{23}}{\sqrt{1 - tau_{12}^2}\,\sqrt{1 - tau_{23}^2}} = \frac{.50 - (.60)(.80)}{\sqrt{1 - .60^2}\,\sqrt{-.80^2}}$$

$$= \frac{.50 - .48}{\sqrt{1 - .36}\,\sqrt{1 - .64}} = \frac{+.02}{\sqrt{.64}\,\sqrt{.36}} = \frac{+.02}{(.80)(.60)}$$

$$= \frac{+.02}{.48} = \mathbf{+.04}$$

Step 3.   In a similar manner, compute the partial correlation of 2 with 3, partialing out the relationships with 1.

$$tau_{23.1} = \frac{tau_{23} - tau_{21}\,tau_{31}}{\sqrt{1 - tau_{21}^2}\,\sqrt{1 - tau_{31}^2}} = \frac{.80 - (.50)(.60)}{\sqrt{1 - .50^2}\,\sqrt{1 - .60^2}}$$

$$= \frac{.80 - .30}{\sqrt{1 - .25}\,\sqrt{1 - .36}} = \frac{+.50}{\sqrt{.75}\,\sqrt{.64}} = \frac{+.50}{(.866)(.80)}$$

$$= \frac{+50}{.693} = \mathbf{+.72}$$

Step 4.   Finally, compute the partial correlation of 1 with 3, partialing out the relationships with 2.

$$tau_{13.2} = \frac{tau_{13} - tau_{12}\,tau_{23}}{\sqrt{1 - tau_{12}^2}\,\sqrt{1 - tau_{23}^2}} = \frac{.60 - (.50)(.80)}{\sqrt{1 - .50^2}\,\sqrt{1 - .80^2}}$$

$$= \frac{.60 - .40}{\sqrt{1 - .25}\,\sqrt{1 - .64}} = \frac{+.20}{\sqrt{.75}\,\sqrt{.36}} = \frac{+.20}{(.866)(.60)}$$

$$= \frac{+.20}{.520} = \mathbf{+.38}$$ ■

SECTION 3.8
Multiple Correlation: Three Variables

Multiple correlation is used when you wish to determine the relationship of one set of numbers (measures on a variable) with two other sets of numbers.

■ EXAMPLE
In a typical multiple-correlation situation, the first set of numbers represents measures on a criterion variable (in this example, freshman grade point average) and the other two sets of numbers are measures on predictors (here, high school

grades and college entrance examination scores). The multiple-correlation coefficient between the criterion variable and the two predictor variables will give an indication of the degree to which the predictors, taken together, actually predict.

Step 1. If you have measures on two predictor variables and one criterion variable, go to Section 3.1 and compute the three simple correlation coefficients according to the instructions there. Let's abbreviate the three variables as

1 = the criterion variable: freshman grade point average (GPA)
2 = the first predictor: high school grades
3 = the second predictor: entrance examination scores

The first correlation coefficient, r_{12}, is between GPA and high school grades; r_{13} is between GPA and examination scores; and r_{23} is between high school grades and examination scores. For the purposes of illustration, assume that the simple correlations in this case turned out to be

$$r_{12} = +.60 \qquad r_{13} = +.50 \qquad r_{23} = +.70$$

Step 2. The multiple correlation of 1 with 2 and 3 is given by

$$R_{1.23} = \sqrt{\frac{r_{12}^2 + r_{13}^2 - 2r_{12}r_{13}r_{23}}{1 - r_{23}^2}}$$

Step 3. Simply plug the values of the simple correlations in at the right spots, and carry out the operations.

$$R_{1.23} = \sqrt{\frac{.60^2 + .50^2 - 2(.60)(.50)(.70)}{1 - .70^2}}$$

$$= \sqrt{\frac{.36 + .25 - 1.20(.50)(.70)}{1 - .49}} = \sqrt{\frac{.61 - 1.20(.35)}{.51}}$$

$$= \sqrt{\frac{.19}{.51}} = \sqrt{.373} = .61$$

This is the value of the multiple correlation between the criterion variable and the two predictor variables. The correlation between high school grades and freshman GPA was .60, and the correlation between the entrance examination scores and freshman GPA was .50. By combining the high school grades with the entrance examination scores, the multiple correlation with freshman GPA was raised to .61. Thus, the combination of predictors produced a higher correlation with the criterion variable than either predictor taken separately.

Concerning the size of the correlation between the predictor variables and their joint correlation with the criterion: If the simple correlations between each of the predictors and the criterion remain unchanged, the value of R, the multiple correlation, will *increase* as the correlation between the predictors becomes smaller than .65, and the value of R will *decrease* as the correlation between predictors increases above .65. In other words, the more independent of each other the predictors are, the greater their value in jointly predicting the criterion, provided the simple correlations between each predictor and the criterion remain constant.

Computation of the multiple-correlation coefficient becomes much more complicated if there are more than two predictor variables. A procedure such as the Doolittle solution, as explained by McNemar,* can be used or, even better, a competent computer programmer can find a ready-made program that will do the job quickly and accurately.   ■

SECTION 3.9
Simple Regression: *X* Variable to Predict *Y*

Simple regression is used when an experimenter wishes to determine the weight for the X variable that will fit the straight line that minimizes the discrepancies between the observed and the predicted values of the criterion variable (i.e., the discrepancies between Y and Y').

■ **EXAMPLE**

A college football coach wishes to determine the best prediction equation for the grade-point averages of potential freshmen recruits. ACT (X) test scores for the current group of recruits as well as their grade-point averages ($Y_{observed}$) are available. Based on the available X (ACT) and Y (GPA) scores for this year's class, the prediction equation for next year's class can be calculated.

Step 1.   After the data have been collected, table them as follows. (*Note:* Since sums, sums of squares, and sums of cross products are required for computation of the regression equation, these can be calculated most easily by setting up the following table.)

Subjects	X (ACT)	Y (GPA)	XY (Cross products)
S_1	20	2.8	56.0
S_2	14	1.8	25.2
S_3	18	2.2	39.6
S_4	22	2.9	63.8
S_5	23	3.5	80.5

---

* Q. McNemar. *Psychological Statistics.* 4th ed. New York: John Wiley & Sons, Inc., 1969. Chapter 11, pp. 199–202.

Subjects	X (ACT)	Y (GPA)	XY (Cross products)
S_6	27	3.4	91.8
S_7	28	3.3	92.4
S_8	21	3.6	75.6
S_9	22	2.8	61.6
S_{10}	19	2.7	51.3
S_{11}	18	2.7	48.6
S_{12}	16	2.5	40.0
S_{13}	20	2.6	52.0
S_{14}	20	2.9	58.0
S_{15}	15	2.0	30.0
Sums:	**303**	**41.7**	**866.4**
Sums of Sqs.:	**6337**	**119.83**	

Step 2.   *Note:* The computational steps for prediction of grade-point average from ACT scores will be demonstrated in the present example. A similar set of computations, but with different results, would be undertaken if prediction of ACT scores from GPA were desired (X and Y would be reversed).

The formula for calculation of the regression line is

$$Y_{predicted} = b_{yx}X + a$$

where b_{yx} = the slope of the line that minimizes the discrepancies between the observed and predicted values of Y (observed and predicted GPAs)

a = the Y intercept, or the value of Y when $X = 0$

Step 3.   The computational formula for b_{yx} is

$$b_{yx} = \frac{N \Sigma XY - (\Sigma X)(\Sigma Y)}{N \Sigma X^2 - (\Sigma X)^2}$$

Using the data calculated in Step 1, the following results are obtained:

$$b_{yx} = \frac{15(866.4) - (303)(41.7)}{15(6337) - (303)^2}$$

$$= \frac{12,996.0 - 12,635.1}{95,055 - 91,809}$$

$$= \frac{360.9}{3246.0}$$

$$= .111$$

Step 4.   Computation of *a*: The *a* coefficient is found by use of the following formula:

$$a = \bar{Y} - b_{yx}\bar{X}$$

Using the values calculated in Step 2, we have

$$\bar{Y} = 41.7/15 = \textbf{2.78}$$
$$\bar{X} = 303/15 = \textbf{20.2}$$

Insertion of these values into the formula gives the following:

$$a = 2.78 - (.111)(20.2)$$
$$= 2.78 - 2.24$$
$$= \textbf{.54}$$

Step 5.   The needed values have been computed. Using the present example

$$Y_{predicted} = .111X + .54$$

Thus, if a recruit had an ACT score of 22, the recruit's predicted GPA would be 2.982, i.e.,

$$Y_{predicted} = (.111)(22) + .54$$
$$= 2.442 + .54$$
$$= \textbf{2.98}$$

Step 6.   It is rare that the predicted *Y* score will be identical with the obtained score. The estimate of the deviation is called the *standard error of estimate* and can be calculated using the raw score formula below.* The necessary sums, squares, and cross products were computed and recorded in Step 1.

$$s_{yx} = \sqrt{\frac{\left[\sum Y^2 - \frac{(\sum Y)^2}{N}\right] - \frac{\left[\sum XY - \frac{(\sum X)(\sum Y)}{N}\right]^2}{\left[\sum X^2 - \frac{(\sum X)^2}{N}\right]}}{N-2}}$$

---

*Equivalent formulas often reported in measurement textbooks include

$$s_{yx} = \sqrt{\frac{\sum y^2 - \frac{(\sum xy)^2}{\sum x^2}}{N-2}} \qquad \text{and} \qquad s_{yx} = s_y \sqrt{1 - r_{xy}^2} \cdot \sqrt{N - 1/N - 2}$$

Using the values calculated in Step 2, we have

$$S_{yx} = \sqrt{\frac{\left[119.83 - \frac{(41.7)^2}{15}\right] - \frac{\left[866.4 - \frac{(303)(41.7)}{15}\right]^2}{\left[6337 - \frac{(303)^2}{15}\right]}}{15 - 2}}$$

$$= \sqrt{\frac{[119.83 - 115.93] - \frac{[866.4 - 842.34]^2}{[6337 - 6120.6]}}{13}}$$

$$= \sqrt{\frac{1.22}{13}}$$

$$= \sqrt{.095}$$

$$= .308$$

The standard error of estimate may be interpreted in much the same way as a standard deviation. Both are measures of variation—the standard deviation around the mean, the standard error of estimate around the regression line values. In the present example, use of the standard error of estimate would lead to the expectancy that for a given value of X (ACT score), the grade-point averages of approximately 68 percent of the new recruits will fall between $\pm.308$ of their predicted value. Extending the range to two standard deviations, you can expect approximately 95 percent of the grade point averages to fall between $\pm.616$ of their predicted values.

Using the example calculated in Step 6, it would be predicted that 68 percent of new football recruits who score 22 on their ACT test will achieve a GPA between 2.67 and 3.29, and that 95 percent will achieve a grade point between 2.36 and 3.60. ■

SECTION 3.10
Multiple Regression: Two *X* Variables

Multiple regression is used when an experimenter wishes to determine the weights for each of the X variables that will give the highest possible correlation between the predicted and the observed values of the criterion variable (Y and Y').

■ EXAMPLE
An experimenter wishes to determine the best prediction equation for a group of disadvantaged college students. The ACT score (X_1) and the score on a reading-comprehension test (X_2) are available as well as the grade point average earned

by each student during his or her first year in college ($Y_{observed}$). Based on the X_1 and X_2 scores, the prediction equation for $Y_{predicted}$ can be obtained.

Step 1.   After the data have been collected, table them as follows:

Subjects	X_1	X_2	Y
S_1	12	18	2.2
S_2	7	13	1.4
S_3	9	9	1.8
S_4	11	18	1.6
S_5	13	17	2.5
S_6	10	12	1.9
S_7	14	12	2.0
S_8	12	16	2.4
S_9	8	17	2.6
S_{10}	6	11	1.8
S_{11}	13	18	1.7
S_{12}	15	15	2.0
S_{13}	11	10	1.7
S_{14}	14	14	2.0
S_{15}	15	18	2.3

Step 2.   Several sums, sums of squares, and sums of cross-products are required for the computation of the regression equation. These are done most easily by setting up the following table:

Subjects	X_1	X_2	Y	$X_1 Y$	$X_2 Y$	$X_1 X_2$
S_1	12	18	2.2	26.4	39.6	216
S_2	7	13	1.4	9.8	18.2	91
S_3	9	9	1.8	16.2	16.2	81
S_4	11	18	1.6	17.6	28.8	198
S_5	13	17	2.5	32.5	42.5	221
S_6	10	12	1.9	19.0	22.8	120
S_7	14	12	2.0	28.0	24.0	168
S_8	12	16	2.4	28.8	38.4	192
S_9	8	17	2.6	20.8	44.2	136
S_{10}	6	11	1.8	10.8	19.8	66
S_{11}	13	18	1.7	22.1	30.6	234
S_{12}	15	15	2.0	30.0	30.0	225
S_{13}	11	10	1.7	18.7	17.0	110
S_{14}	14	14	2.0	28.0	28.0	196
S_{15}	15	18	2.3	34.5	41.4	270
Sums:	**170**	**218**	**29.9**	**343.2**	**441.5**	**2524**
Sum X^2:	**2040**	**3310**	**61.29**			

Step 3.   Three Pearson product-moment correlations must be calculated. The basic computational formula for the Pearson product-moment correlation is

$$r = \frac{N \Sigma XY - (\Sigma X)(\Sigma Y)}{\sqrt{[N \Sigma X^2 - (\Sigma X)^2][N \Sigma Y^2 - (\Sigma Y)^2]}}$$

Values calculated in Step 2 can easily be inserted in appropriate positions in the above formula. Turn to Section 4.1 for a step-by-step set of instructions for calculating r.

$$r_{x_1 y} = \frac{15(343.2) - (170)(29.9)}{\sqrt{[15(2040) - (170)^2][15(61.29) - (29.9)^2]}} = \frac{65.0}{207.5} = .31$$

$$r_{x_2 y} = \frac{15(4415) - (218)(29.9)}{\sqrt{[15(3310) - (218)^2][15(61.29) - (29.9)^2]}} = \frac{104.3}{2321} = .45$$

$$r_{x_1 x_2} = \frac{15(2524) - (170)(218)}{\sqrt{[15(2040) - (170)^2][15(3310) - (218)^2]}} = \frac{800}{1901} = .42$$

Step 4.   The standard deviation of the three variables must also be calculated. The basic formula for the standard deviation is

$$s = \sqrt{\frac{\Sigma X^2 - \frac{(\Sigma X)^2}{N}}{N}}$$

Again, values calculated in Step 2 can be inserted into the above formula. A step by step summary of the computations can be found in Section 1.2.

$$s_{x_1} = \sqrt{\frac{2040 - \frac{(170)^2}{15}}{15}} = 2.75$$

$$s_{x_2} = \sqrt{\frac{3310 - \frac{(218)^2}{15}}{15}} = 3.07$$

$$s_y = \sqrt{\frac{61.29 - \frac{(29.9)^2}{15}}{15}} = .336$$

Step 5.   All preliminary calculations have been completed. The general formula for the regression equation is

$$Y_{\text{predicted}} = b_1 X_1 + b_2 X_2 + \cdots + b_x X_x + a$$

Since there are two variables in the present example, the formula would be

$$Y_{\text{predicted}} = b_1 X_1 + b_2 X_2 + a$$

Step 6. First, the regression coefficients, b_1 and b_2, must be obtained.

$$b_1 = \frac{s_y(r_{x_1y} - r_{x_2y}r_{x_1x_2})}{s_{x_2}(1 - r_{x_1x_2}^2)}$$

$$= \frac{.336[.31 - (.45)(.42)]}{2.75(1 - .42^2)} = \frac{.0407}{2.265} = .018$$

and,

$$b_2 = \frac{s_y(r_{x_2y} - r_{x_1y}r_{x_1x_2})}{s_{x_2}(1 - r_{x_1x_2}^2)}$$

$$= \frac{.336[.45 - (.31)(.42)]}{3.07(1 - .42^2)} = \frac{.1075}{2.528} = .0425$$

Step 7. Next, the constant, or adjustment, term, a, must be calculated. To calculate this term, the mean of X_1, X_2, and $Y_{observed}$ must be obtained. From the tabled data in Step 2 we find

$$\bar{X}_1 = \frac{170}{15} = 11.33$$

$$\bar{X}_2 = \frac{218}{15} = 14.53$$

$$\bar{Y} = \frac{29.9}{15} = 1.99$$

Then, substituting into the formula below, we have

$$a = \bar{Y} - b_1\bar{X}_1 - b_2\bar{X}_2$$

$$= 1.99 - (.018)(11.33) - (.0425)(14.53)$$

$$1.99 - 2.04 - .618$$

$$= 1.168$$

Step 8. All calculations needed to create the multiple-regression equation necessary to predict a Y score based on observed X scores have now been completed. Substituting into the formula presented in Step 3, we have

$$Y_{predicted} = b_1\bar{X}_1 + b_2\bar{X}_2 + a$$

$$= .018X_1 + .0425X_2 + 1.168$$

Continuing the initial example, if a student scored 15 on Test 1 (X_1) and 17 on Test 2 (X_2), the $Y_{predicted}$ would be

$$Y_{predicted} = (.018)(15) + (.0425)(17) + 1.168$$

$$= .270 + .7225 + 1.168$$

$$= 2.1605$$

Step 9.   If, in addition to the regression equation, a question is raised regarding the multiple correlation between $Y_{observed}$ and $Y_{predicted}$, the multiple correlation can be computed according to the following formula:

$$R^2_{yy'} = R^2_{y \cdot x_1 x_2} = \frac{r^2_{yx_1} + r^2_{x_2} - 2r_{yx_1}r_{yx_2}r_{x_1x_2}}{1 - r^2_{x_1x_2}}$$

$$= \frac{(.31)^2 + (.45)^2 - 2(.31)(.45)(.42)}{1 - .1764}$$

$$= \frac{.1814}{.8236}$$

$$= .22$$

and

$$R_{yy'} = \sqrt{.22} = .469$$

Step 10.   Test of significance of $R_{yy'}$. If both b_1 and b_2 are equal to zero, then $R_{yy'}$ will be equal to zero. A test of the null hypothesis that the population values β_1 and β_2 are equal to zero will be given by

$$F = \frac{R^2_{yy'}/k}{1 - R^2_{yy'}/(n - k - 1)}$$

$$= \frac{.22/2}{(1 - .22)/(15 - 2 - 1)}$$

$$= \frac{.11}{.065} = 1.69 \text{ with } df = k, n - k - 1 = \mathbf{2, 12}$$

Looking in the F tables under 2 and 12 df, we find that an F ratio of 3.88 is required for significance. Since the computed F was less than 3.88, we conclude that the R^2 is nonsignificant.   ■

SECTION 3.11

Simple Analysis of Covariance: One Treatment Variable

When experimental control of an important variable—such as age or IQ—is impossible or impractical, statistical control is possible by use of a covariance analysis. This section presents the procedures for such an analysis when there is only one treatment variable.

■ EXAMPLE

In order to make a decision concerning future equipment needs, an elementary school principal designed the following experiment to evaluate three different methods of teaching spelling. Eighteen first grade children were given a vocabulary test (the control measure) to determine their verbal ability before the program was begun. The X values below represent these test scores. The three different teaching methods were used for three months, and then a standard spelling test was given. The Y values represent these criterion spelling scores.

Step 1. Table the data as follows.

Teaching method 1			Teaching method 2			Teaching method 3		
Student	X	Y	Student	X	Y	Student	X	Y
A	32	62	G	21	72	M	38	95
B	46	66	H	24	85	N	45	88
C	27	64	I	18	61	O	52	104
D	35	48	J	32	87	P	48	86
E	31	51	K	35	69	Q	41	72
F	40	74	L	26	74	R	37	63

Step 2. Add the scores in each column.

	Method 1		Method 2		Method 3	
	X	Y	X	Y	X	Y
	32	62	21	72	38	95
	46	66	24	85	45	88
	⋮	⋮	⋮	⋮	⋮	⋮
Sums:	**211**	**365**	**156**	**448**	**261**	**508**

Step 3. Square all the numbers in the X columns (Step 1), and add the squared values.

$$32^2 + 46^2 + \cdots + 40^2 + 21^2 + 24^2 + \cdots$$
$$+ 26^2 + 38^2 + 45^2 + \cdots + 37^2 = \mathbf{23{,}448}$$

Step 4. Add the sums of the X columns (Step 2).

$$211 + 156 + 261 = \mathbf{628}$$

Step 5. Square the result of Step 4, and divide by the number of X values (18 in this example).

$$\frac{628^2}{18} = \frac{394{,}384}{18} = \mathbf{21{,}910.222}$$

Step 6. Subtract the result of Step 5 from the result of Step 3.

$$23{,}448 - 21{,}910.222 = \mathbf{1537.778}$$

Step 7. Square the three sums of the X columns (Step 2) and add the squares; then divide by the number of scores composing each sum (6 in this example).

$$\frac{211^2 + 156^2 + 261^2}{6} = \frac{136,978}{6} = \mathbf{22,829.667}$$

Step 8. Subtract the result of Step 5 from the result of Step 7.

$22,829.667 - 21,910.222 = \mathbf{919.445}$

Step 9. Subtract the value of Step 8 from the Step 6.

$1537.778 - 919.445 = \mathbf{618.333}$

Step 10. Square all the numbers in the Y columns (Step 1), and add the squares.

$$62^2 + 66^2 + \cdots + 74^2 + 72^2 + 85^2 + \cdots$$
$$+ 74^2 + 95^2 + 88^2 + \cdots + 63^2 = \mathbf{100,747}$$

Step 11. Add the sums of the Y columns (Step 2).

$365 + 448 + 508 = \mathbf{1321}$

Step 12. Square the result of Step 11, and divide by the number of Y values (18 in this example).

$$\frac{1321^2}{18} = \frac{1,745,041}{18} = \mathbf{96,946.722}$$

Step 13. Subtract the result of Step 12 from the result of Step 10.

$100,747 - 96,946.722 = \mathbf{3800.278}$

Step 14. Square the three sums of the Y columns (Step 2), and add the squares; then divide by the number of scores composing each sum (6 in this example).

$$\frac{365^2 + 448^2 + 508^2}{6} = \mathbf{98,665.500}$$

Step 15. Subtract the result of Step 12 from the result of Step 14.

$98,665.500 - 96,946.722 = \mathbf{1718.778}$

Step 16. Subtract the final value of Step 15 from that of Step 13.

$3800.278 - 1718.778 = \mathbf{2081.500}$

Step 17. Multiply each X score by its paired Y score (see Step 1), and add all the products.

$(32 \times 62) + (46 \times 66) + \cdots + (37 \times 63) = \mathbf{47,131}$

Step 18. Multiply the result of Step 4 by the result of Step 11, and divide by the number of XY pairs (18 in this example).

$$\frac{628 \times 1321}{18} = \frac{829,588}{18} = \mathbf{46,088.222}$$

Step 19. Subtract the final value of Step 18 from that of Step 17.

$47,131 - 46,088.222 = \mathbf{1042.778}$

Step 20. Multiply each X sum in Step 2 by its paired Y sum, and add the three products; then divide by the number of pairs under each method (6 in this example).

$$\frac{(211 \times 365) + (156 \times 448) + (261 \times 508)}{6} = \frac{279,491}{6} = \mathbf{46,581.833}$$

Step 21. Subtract the result of Step 18 from the result of Step 20.

$46,581.833 - 46,088.222 = \mathbf{493.611}$

Step 22. Subtract the value of Step 21 from that of Step 19.

$1042.778 - 493.611 = \mathbf{549.167}$

Step 23. Square the result of Step 19, and divide by the result of Step 6.

$$\frac{1042.778^2}{1537.778} = \frac{1,087,385.957}{1537.778} = \mathbf{707.115}$$

Step 24. Subtract the result of Step 23 from the result of Step 13.

$3800.278 - 707.115 = \mathbf{3093.163}$

Step 25. Square the result of Step 22, and divide by the result of Step 9.

$$\frac{549.167^2}{618.333} = \frac{301,584.394}{618.333} = \mathbf{487.738}$$

Step 26. Subtract the result of Step 25 from the result of Step 16.

$2081.500 - 487.738 = \mathbf{1593.762}$

Step 27. Divide the value of Step 26 by the number of degrees of freedom for the adjusted within-groups measures. The degrees of freedom will always be

$N - a - 1$, where N is the total number of XY pairs (18 in our example) and a is the number of different experimental groups (3 in our example, corresponding to the three methods of teaching).

$$\frac{1593.762}{N - a - 1} = \frac{1593.762}{18 - 3 - 1} = \frac{1593.762}{14} = \textbf{113.840}$$

Step 28.   Subtract the value of Step 26 from that of Step 24.

$$3093.163 - 1593.762 = \textbf{1499.401}$$

Step 29.   Divide the result of Step 28 by the number of degrees of freedom for the adjusted between-groups measures. This degree-of-freedom value will always be $a - 1$, where a is the number of different experimental groups (3 in our example).

$$\frac{1499.401}{a - 1} = \frac{1499.401}{3 - 1} = \frac{1499.401}{2} = \textbf{749.700}$$

Step 30.   Compute the F ratio by dividing the result of Step 29 by the result of Step 27.

$$F = \frac{749.700}{113.840} = \textbf{6.59}$$

This F has $df = (a - 1)/(N - a - 1)$. (This equals 2/14 in our example.) From Appendix E it is seen that with $df = 2/14$, an F ratio larger than 6.51 would be expected by chance alone less than one time in a hundred. Therefore, the F value is said to be significant at the .01 level. We conclude, then, that when the covariance analysis was used to equate statistically the groups according to vocabulary test score (this equating was necessary since the groups differed at the beginning of training), the methods of teaching provided significantly different results on the spelling test.

Supplement

In order to determine whether the individual group regressions are homogeneous with the overall regression, first compute the sum of squares (SS_x) and the sum of the cross products (SP) for each group of data.

Step 1.   Using the data from Step 1 of the original analysis, compute SS_x for each group. The basic formula for each computation is $\Sigma X^2 - (\Sigma X)^2/N_{(per\ gp.)}$.

$$\text{Group 1 } SS_x = 7655 - \frac{211^2}{6} = \textbf{234.8}$$

$$\text{Group 2 } SS_x = 4266 - \frac{156^2}{6} = \textbf{210.0}$$

$$\text{Group 3 } SS_x = 11{,}527 - \frac{261^2}{6} = \textbf{173.5}$$

Step 2. The SP values are computed in comparable fashion using the formula $\Sigma\,XY - \Sigma\,X\,\Sigma\,Y/N_{\text{(pairs of scores)}}$.

Group 1 SP $= 12{,}969 - \dfrac{211 \times 365}{6} =$ **133.2**

Group 2 SP $= 11{,}773 - \dfrac{156 \times 448}{6} =$ **125.0**

Group 3 SP $= 22{,}389 - \dfrac{261 \times 508}{6} =$ **291.0**

Step 3. Now compute SP^2/SS_x for each group.

Group 1 $= \dfrac{133.2^2}{234.8} =$ **75.56**

Group 2 $= \dfrac{125.0^2}{210.0} =$ **74.40**

Group 3 $= \dfrac{291.0^2}{173.5} =$ **488.10**

Step 4. Add the results of Step 3.

$75.56 + 74.4 + 488.1 =$ **638**

Step 5. Get the error sum of squares for Y from Section 3.11, Step 16, then subtract the result of Step 4.

$2081.5 - 638 =$ **1443.5**

Step 6. Divide the result of Step 5 by $df = N - 2a = 18 - 6 =$ **12**

$\dfrac{1443.5}{12} =$ **120.3**

Step 7. Get the adjusted error sum of squares for Y from Section 3.11, Step 26, then subtract the result of Step 5.

$1593.762 - 1443.5 =$ **150.26**

Step 8. Divide the result of Step 7 by $df = a - 1 = 3 - 1 =$ **2**

$\dfrac{150.26}{2} =$ **75.13**

Step 9. Compute the F ratio.

$\dfrac{75.13}{120.3} =$ **.62**

Since the F is very small we accept the hypothesis that the group regressions are homogeneous. ∎

SECTION 3.12
Factorial Analysis of Covariance: Two Treatment Variables

The following example presents the computational steps to be used when there are two treatment variables and it is necessary to have statistical control of some other variable to draw meaningful conclusions.

■ EXAMPLE

A certain university was engaged in teaching Peace Corps volunteers the foreign languages they would need during their tour of duty. The following experiment was carried out to determine the effectiveness of the different teaching methods used. All students were first given a language aptitude test, which provided the control measures (the X values presented in Step 1 below). It is obvious from these X values that the students' language aptitude scores differed widely. Since all the students were not able to participate in the experiment at the same time, they were placed in experimental groups on the basis of when they participated rather than on the basis of their aptitude scores. Because the average aptitude scores of the resulting experimental groups differed considerably, a covariance analysis was needed. Using statistical procedures, the covariance analysis equated the groups on aptitude scores, so that any differences found after the experiment could be interpreted as results of the experimental manipulations rather than of the original differences in aptitudes.

The experiment involved evaluating two methods of teaching the foreign languages and determining the value of language laboratory sessions. The two teaching methods were (1) formal classroom meetings with lectures and (2) no formal classroom meetings—only conversation periods held in a congenial atmosphere. In addition, half of the students being taught by each teaching method spent three hours a day in the language laboratory using the tape recording equipment. The other half of the students in each method group never entered the language lab.

Two years later, when the volunteers returned from overseas, they were asked to evaluate the degree to which their language training prepared them for their work. The ratings were on a 10-point scale ranging from 1 to 10. These ratings served as the criterion measures (the Y scores below).

Step 1. Table the data as follows.

Classroom group 1 (3 hrs./day in lab)			Conversation group 1 (3 hrs./day in lab)		
Subject	X	Y	Subject	X	Y
S_1	62	5	S_{11}	46	5
S_2	75	7	S_{12}	53	4
S_3	41	3	S_{13}	57	3
S_4	88	8	S_{14}	49	7
S_5	72	7	S_{15}	62	6

Classroom group 2 (No time in lab)			Conversation group 2 (No time in lab)		
Subject	X	Y	Subject	X	Y
S_6	84	2	S_{16}	58	9
S_7	91	3	S_{17}	72	10
S_8	68	1	S_{18}	61	8
S_9	77	1	S_{19}	65	8
S_{10}	85	3	S_{20}	59	10

Step 2. Add the scores in each column, and record the sums.

	Classroom 1/lab		Conversation 1/lab	
	X	Y	X	Y
	62	5	46	5
	75	7	53	4
	.	.	.	.
	.	.	.	.
Sums:	**338**	**30**	**267**	**25**

	Classroom 2/No lab		Conversation 2/No lab	
	X	Y	X	Y
	84	2	58	9
	91	3	72	10
	.	.	.	.
	.	.	.	.
Sums:	**405**	**10**	**315**	**45**

The Control Variable (Steps 3–15)

Step 3. Square all the numbers in the X columns (Step 1), and add the squares.

$$62^2 + \cdots + 72^2 + 84^2 + \cdots + 85^2 + 46^2 + \cdots + 62^2 + 58^2$$

$$+ \cdots + 59^2 = \mathbf{91{,}587}$$

Step 4. Add the sums for all four X columns (Step 2).

$$338 + 405 + 267 + 315 = \mathbf{1325}$$

Step 5.   Square the result of Step 4, and divide by the total number of X values (20 in this example).

$$\frac{1325^2}{20} = \frac{1,755,625}{20} = \mathbf{87,781.250}$$

Step 6.   Subtract the result of Step 5 from the result of Step 3.

$$91,587 - 87,781.25 = \mathbf{3805.750}$$

Step 7.   Add the sums of the X columns in the two classroom groups (Step 2), square that number, and divide it by the number of cases on which the sum is based (10 in our example).

$$\frac{(338 + 405)^2}{10} = \frac{743^2}{10} = \frac{552,049}{10} = \mathbf{55,204.900}$$

Step 8.   Add the sums of the X columns in the two conversation groups (Step 2), square that number, and divide it by the number of cases on which the sum is based (10 in our example).

$$\frac{(267 + 315)^2}{10} = \frac{582^2}{10} = \frac{338,724}{10} = \mathbf{33,872.400}$$

Step 9.   Add the result of Step 7 to the result of Step 8, and subtract the value of Step 5.

$$55,204.9 + 33,872.4 - 87,781.250 = \mathbf{1296.050}$$

Step 10.   Add the sums of the X columns in the two lab groups (Step 2), square that number, and divide it by the number of cases on which the sum is based (10 in our example).

$$\frac{(338 + 267)^2}{10} = \frac{605^2}{10} = \frac{366,025}{10} = \mathbf{36,602.500}$$

Step 11.   Add the sums of the X columns in the two no-lab groups (Step 2), square that number, and divide it by the number of cases on which the sum is based (10 in our example).

$$\frac{(405 + 315)^2}{10} = \frac{720^2}{10} = \frac{518,400}{10} = \mathbf{51,840}$$

Step 12.   Add the result of Step 10 to the result of Step 11; then subtract the value of Step 5.

$$36,602.500 + 51,840 - 87,781.250 = \mathbf{661.250}$$

Step 13.   Square each of the sums under the four X columns (Step 2), divide each square by the number of cases on which each sum is based (5 in our example), and then add the four quotients.

$$\frac{338^2}{5} + \frac{405^2}{5} + \frac{267^2}{5} + \frac{315^2}{5} = \frac{448,783}{5} = \mathbf{89,756.6}$$

Step 14.   Subtract the results of Steps 5, 9, and 12 from the value of Step 13.

$$89,756.6 - 87,781.250 - 1296.050 - 661.250 = \mathbf{18.05}$$

Step 15.   Subtract the result of Step 13 from that of Step 3.

$$91,587 - 89,756.6 = \mathbf{1830.4}$$

The Criterion Variable (Steps 16–28)

Step 16.   Square all the numbers in the Y columns (Step 1), and add the squares.

$$5^2 + \cdots + 7^2 + 2^2 + \cdots + 3^2 + 5^2 + \cdots + 6^2 + 9^2 + \cdots + 10^2 = \mathbf{764}$$

Step 17.   Add the sums for all the Y columns (Step 2).

$$30 + 10 + 25 + 45 = \mathbf{110}$$

Step 18.   Square the result of Step 17, and divide by the total number of Y values (20 in this example).

$$\frac{110^2}{20} = \frac{12,100}{20} = \mathbf{605}$$

Step 19.   Subtract the result of Step 18 from the result of Step 16.

$$764 - 605 = \mathbf{159}$$

Step 20.   Add the sums of the Y columns in the two classroom groups (Step 2), square that number, and divide it by the number of cases on which the sum is based (10 in our example).

$$\frac{(30 + 10)^2}{10} = \frac{40^2}{10} = \frac{1600}{10} = \mathbf{160}$$

Step 21.   Add the sums under the Y columns in the two conversation groups (Step 2), square that number, and divide it by the number of cases on which the sum is based (10 in our example).

$$\frac{(25 + 45)^2}{10} = \frac{70^2}{10} = \frac{4900}{10} = \mathbf{490}$$

Step 22.   Add the result of Step 20 to the result of Step 21, and subtract the result of Step 18.

$$160 + 490 - 605 = 45$$

Step 23.   Add the sums under the Y columns in the two lab groups (Step 2), square that number, and divide it by the number of cases on which the sum is based (10 in our example).

$$\frac{(30 + 25)^2}{10} = \frac{55^2}{10} = \frac{3025}{10} = 302.5$$

Step 24.   Add the sums under the Y columns in the two no-lab groups (Step 2), square that number, and divide it by the number of cases on which the sum is based (10 in our example).

$$\frac{(10 + 45)^2}{10} = \frac{55^2}{10} = \frac{3025}{10} = 302.5$$

Step 25.   Add the result of Step 23 to the result of Step 24, and subtract the result of Step 18.

$$302.5 + 302.5 - 605 = 0$$

Step 26.   Square each of the sums under the four Y columns (Step 2), divide each square by the number of cases on which each sum is based (5 in our example), and then add the quotients.

$$\frac{30^2}{5} + \frac{10^2}{5} + \frac{25^2}{5} + \frac{45^2}{5} = \frac{3650}{5} = 730$$

Step 27.   Subtract the results of Steps 18, 22, and 25 from the result of Step 26.

$$730 - 605 - 45 - 0 = 80$$

Step 28.   Subtract the value of Step 26 from that of Step 16.

$$764 - 730 = 34$$

Products of the Two Variables (Steps 29–53)

Step 29.   Multiply each of the X scores in Step 1 by its paired Y score, and add the products.

$$(62 \times 5) + \cdots + (72 \times 7) + (84 \times 2) + \cdots + (85 \times 3)$$
$$+ (46 \times 5) + \cdots + (62 \times 6) + (58 \times 9) + \cdots + (59 \times 10) = 7175$$

Step 30. Multiply the result of Step 4 by the value of Step 17; then divide by the number of XY pairs (20 in our example).

$$\frac{1325 \times 110}{20} = \frac{145,750}{20} = \textbf{7287.500}$$

Step 31. Subtract the result of Step 30 from the result of Step 29.

$$7175 - 7287.5 = \textbf{-112.5}$$

Step 32. From Step 2, obtain the X sum and the Y sum for the two classroom groups.

$$338 + 405 = \textbf{743} = X \text{ sum for classroom groups}$$

$$30 + 10 = \quad \textbf{40} = Y \text{ sum for classroom groups}$$

Multiply the X sum by the Y sum, and divide by the number of scores in each sum (10 in our example).

$$\frac{743 \times 40}{10} = \frac{29,720}{10} = \textbf{2972}$$

Step 33. From Step 2, obtain the X sum and the Y sum for the two conversation groups.

$$267 + 315 = \textbf{582} = X \text{ sum for conversation groups}$$

$$25 + 45 = \quad \textbf{70} = Y \text{ sum for conversation groups}$$

Multiply the X sum by the Y sum, and divide by the number of scores in each sum (10 in our example).

$$\frac{582 \times 70}{10} - \frac{40,740}{10} = \textbf{4074}$$

Step 34. Add the result of Step 32 to the result of Step 33, and subtract the value of Step 30.

$$2972 + 4074 - 7287.5 = \textbf{-241.5}$$

Step 35. From Step 2, obtain the X sum and the Y sum for the two lab groups.

$$338 + 267 = \textbf{605} = X \text{ sum for lab groups}$$

$$30 + 25 = \quad \textbf{55} = Y \text{ sum for lab groups}$$

Multiply the X sum by the Y sum, and divide by the number of scores in each sum (10 in our example).

$$\frac{605 \times 55}{10} = \frac{33,275}{10} = \textbf{3327.5}$$

Step 36.   From Step 2, obtain the X sum and the Y sum for the two no-lab groups.

$405 + 315 = \mathbf{720} = X$ sum for no-lab groups

$10 + 45 = \ \ \mathbf{55} = Y$ sum for no-lab groups

Multiply the X sum by the Y sum, and divide by the number of scores in each sum (10 in our example).

$$\frac{720 \times 55}{10} = \frac{39{,}600}{10} = \mathbf{3960}$$

Step 37.   Add the result of Step 35 to the result of Step 36, and subtract the result of Step 30.

$3327.5 + 3960 - 7287.5 = \mathbf{0}$

Step 38.   Multiply each X sum in Step 2 by its paired Y sum, divide each product by the number of scores on which each sum is based (5 in our example), and then add the quotients.

$$\frac{338 \times 30}{5} + \frac{405 \times 10}{5} + \frac{267 \times 25}{5} + \frac{315 \times 45}{5} = \frac{35{,}040}{5} = \mathbf{7008}$$

Step 39.   Subtract the results of Steps 30, 34, and 37 from the result of Step 38.

$7008 - 7287.5 - (-241.5) - 0 = \mathbf{-38}$

Step 40.   Subtract the value of Step 38 from the value of Step 29.

$7175 - 7008 = \mathbf{167}$

Step 41.   Square the result of Step 40, and divide by the value of Step 15.

$$\frac{167^2}{1830.4} = \frac{27{,}889}{1830.4} = \mathbf{15.237}$$

Then, subtract that quotient from the result of Step 28.

$34 - 15.237 = \mathbf{18.763}$

Step 42.   Add the result of Step 9 to the result of Step 15.

$1296.050 + 1830.4 = \mathbf{3126.45}$

Step 43.   Add the value of Step 22 to that of Step 28.

$45 + 34 = \mathbf{79}$

Step 44.   Add the result of Step 34 to the result of Step 40.

$(-241.5) + 167 = \mathbf{-74.5}$

Step 45. Square the result of Step 44, and divide by the result of Step 42.

$$\frac{(-74.5)^2}{3126.5} = \frac{5550.25}{3126.5} = \textbf{1.775}$$

Then, subtract that quotient and the result of Step 41 from the result of Step 43.

$79 - 1.775 - 18.763 = \textbf{58.462}$

Step 46. Add the final value of Step 12 to that of Step 15.

$661.250 + 1830.4 = \textbf{2491.65}$

Step 47. Add the result of Step 25 to that of Step 28.

$0 + 34 = \textbf{34}$

Step 48. Add the result of Step 37 to that of Step 40.

$0 + 167 = \textbf{167}$

Step 49. Square the result of Step 48, and divide by the result of Step 46.

$$\frac{167^2}{2491.65} = \frac{27,889}{2491.65} = \textbf{11.193}$$

Then subtract that quotient and the result of Step 41 from the result of Step 47.

$34 - 11.193 - 18.763 = \textbf{4.044}$

Step 50. Add the value of Step 14 to that of Step 15.

$18.05 + 1830.4 = \textbf{1848.450}$

Step 51. Add the value of Step 27 to that of Step 28.

$80 + 34 = \textbf{114}$

Step 52. Add the value of Step 39 to that of Step 40.

$(-38) + 167 = \textbf{129}$

Step 53. Square the result of Step 52, and divide by the result of Step 50.

$$\frac{129^2}{1848.45} = \frac{16,641}{1848.45} = \textbf{9.003}$$

Then, subtract that quotient and the result of Step 41 from the result of Step 51.

$114 - 9.003 - 18.763 = \textbf{86.234}$

Mean Squares and F Ratios (Steps 54–60)

Step 54.   Divide the result of Step 41, the adjusted-error sum of squares, by the degrees of freedom for adjusted error. The adjusted-error df are always $N - CL - 1$, where N is the total number of XY pairs (20 in this example), C is the number of experimental conditions on the first variable (2 in this example, for classroom versus conversation), and L is the number of experimental conditions on the other variable (2 in this example, for lab versus no lab). Thus, $N - CL - 1 = 20 - (2 \times 2) - 1 = 20 - 5 = 15$.

$$\frac{18.763}{N - CL - 1} = \frac{18.763}{15} = 1.251$$

This final value is the error mean square, which makes up the denominator for the three F-tests to follow.

Step 55.   Divide the result of Step 45, the adjusted sum of squares for teaching methods, by the appropriate degrees of freedom. The df are $C - 1$, where C is the number of experimental conditions in this variable (2 is this example, for classroom versus conversation).

$$\frac{58.462}{C - 1} = \frac{58.462}{1} = 58.462$$

Step 56.   Divide the value of Step 55 by that of Step 54. This will yield the F for teaching methods. The df are $(C - 1)/(N - CL - 1) = 1/15$.

$$F = \frac{58.462}{1.251} = 46.73$$

From Appendix E it is seen that with $df = 1/15$, an F ratio larger than 16.59 would be expected by chance alone less than one time in a thousand. Therefore, the F is said to be significant at the .001 level. This means that the different teaching methods were rated as being significantly different in their effectiveness.

Step 57.   Divide the result of Step 49, the adjusted sum of squares for language lab usage, by the appropriate degrees of freedom. The df are $L - 1$, where L is the number of experimental conditions in this variable (2 in this example, for lab versus no lab).

$$\frac{4.004}{L - 1} = \frac{4.044}{1} = 4.044$$

Step 58.   Divide the value of Step 57 by that of Step 54. This will yield the F for language lab usage. The df are $(L - 1)/(N - CL - 1) = (2 - 1)/(20 - 5) = 1/15$.

$$F = \frac{4.044}{1.251} = 3.23$$

Appendix E shows that the probability of getting a value larger than this F is between five and ten in one hundred. Therefore, we conclude that there is no difference in language effectiveness between those who spend three hours in the lab and those who spend no time in the lab.

Step 59.   Divide the result of Step 53, the adjusted sum of squares for the methods-by-lab interaction, by the appropriate degrees of freedom. The df are $(C - 1)(L - 1)$, or the product of the df from Step 55 and the df from Step 57.

$$\frac{86.234}{(C - 1)(L - 1)} = \frac{86.234}{1 \times 1} = \mathbf{86.234}$$

Step 60.   Divide the value of Step 59 by that of Step 54. This will yield the F for the methods-by-lab interaction.

$$F = \frac{86.234}{1.251} = \mathbf{68.93}$$

The df for this F are

$$\frac{(C - 1)(L - 1)}{N - CL - 1} = \frac{1}{15}$$

Appendix E shows that this F is significant at the .001 level. Since we have found that the teaching methods affect (interact with) the lab experience, we should seek out the source of the interaction. The statistical procedures to use for such an undertaking are presented in Section 5.10. If you find a significant interaction in your data, go to Section 5.10 and proceed.

Supplement

The test for homogeneity of regression when a factorial analysis of covariance is used is computed as follows:

Step 1.   Using the data from Step 1 of the original analysis, compute the sum of squares (SS_x) and the sum of the cross products (SP). The formula for SS_x is $\Sigma X^2 - (\Sigma X)^2/N_{(per\ gp.)}$ and for SP is $\Sigma XY - \Sigma X \Sigma Y/N_{(pairs)}$ for each group.

$$\text{Group 1 } SS_x = 24{,}078 - \frac{338^2}{5} = \mathbf{1229.2}$$

$$\text{Group 2 } SS_x = 14{,}419 - \frac{267^2}{5} = \mathbf{161.2}$$

$$\text{Group 3 } SS_x = 33{,}115 - \frac{405^2}{5} = \mathbf{310}$$

$$\text{Group 4 } SS_x = 19{,}975 - \frac{315^2}{5} = \mathbf{130}$$

$$\text{Group 1 SP} = 2166 - \frac{338 \times 30}{5} = \mathbf{138}$$

$$\text{Group 2 SP} = 1328 - \frac{267 \times 25}{5} = \mathbf{-7}$$

$$\text{Group 3 SP} = 841 - \frac{405 \times 10}{5} = \mathbf{31}$$

$$\text{Group 4 SP} = 2840 - \frac{315 \times 45}{5} = \mathbf{5}$$

Step 2. Compute SP^2/SS_x values for each group.

$$\text{Group 1} = \frac{138^2}{12,229.2} = \mathbf{15.5}$$

$$\text{Group 2} = \frac{(-7)^2}{161.2} = \mathbf{.3}$$

$$\text{Group 3} = \frac{31^2}{310} = \mathbf{3.1}$$

$$\text{Group 4} = \frac{5^2}{130} = \mathbf{.2}$$

Step 3. Add the results of Step 2.

$$15.5 + .3 + 3.1 + .2 = \mathbf{19.1}$$

Step 4. Get the error sum of squares for Y from Section 3.12, Step 28, and subtract the result of Step 3, above.

$$34 - 19.1 = \mathbf{14.9}$$

This SS represents the within-group regressions.

Step 5. Get the adjusted error sum of squares for Y from Section 3.12, Step 41, and subtract the result of Step 4, above.

$$18.763 - 14.9 = \mathbf{3.86}$$

This SS represents the between-group regression.

Step 6. Divide the result of Step 4 by its degrees of freedom.

$$df = n - 2a = 20 - 8 = \mathbf{12}$$

$$\frac{14.9}{12} = \mathbf{12.4}$$

Step 7.   Divide the result of Step 5 by its degrees of freedom.

$df = a - 1 = 4 - 1 = 3$

$$\frac{3.86}{3} = 1.29$$

Step 8.   Form the F ratio by dividing the result of Step 7 by the result of Step 6.

$$\frac{1.29}{1.24} = 1.04$$

Since this F is small, we accept the hypothesis that the regressions are homogeneous.   ■

SECTION 3.13
Reliability of Measurement: The Test as a Whole (Test-Retest, Parallel Forms, and Split Halves)

The three coefficients of reliability presented here all start with the computation of a Pearson product-moment correlation coefficient.

1. The *test-retest* reliability measure is computed when you have pairs of scores obtained from two different administrations of the same test to the same people. If you have such pairs of scores, label the scores obtained on the first administration as X and those obtained on the second administration as Y. Then, go to Section 3.1 and follow the instructions. The computed value will be the test-retest reliability coefficient (sometimes called the *coefficient of stability*).
2. The *parallel-forms* reliability measure is computed when you have pairs of test scores from two tests composed of "equated" items. If you have such pairs of scores, label them X and Y, go to Section 3.1, and follow the instructions. The computed value will be the parallel-forms reliability coefficient (sometimes called the *measure of equivalence and stability*).
3. The *split-halves* reliability measure is computed when you have given a test to several individuals and then formed pairs of scores by dividing the test items into two equal groups. (The usual method is to put even-numbered items in one group and odd-numbered items in the other group.) The pairs of scores are then used to compute the correlation. Carry out the following steps in order to compute the split-halves reliability coefficient.

Step 1.   Go to Section 3.1 and follow the instructions. When you have the correlation coefficient, return to this section and go on to the next step.

Step 2. In order to compute the correlation, you divide the test in half. This means the real or whole test is twice as long as either half used to compute the reliability coefficient. When a test is lengthened, the reliability increases. You must therefore "correct" the value obtained in Step 1 so that it effectively pertains to the whole test rather than to just half of it.

In order to correct the value of Step 1, first multiply the answer of Step 1 by the number 2. For example, suppose the correlation value from Step 1 is .83.

$$.83 \times 2 = \mathbf{1.66}$$

Step 3. Now add the number 1 to the result of Step 1.

$$1 + .83 = \mathbf{1.83}$$

Step 4. Divide the result of Step 2 by the result of Step 3.

$$\frac{1.66}{1.83} = \mathbf{.91}$$

This value is the split-halves reliability coefficient corrected so that it applies to the whole test. A high reliability value (.70 or higher) shows that the test is reliably (accurately) measuring the characteristic it was designed to measure.

SECTION 3.14
Reliability of Measurement: The Individual Items (Kuder-Richardson and Hoyt)

When your main concern is whether the items in a test are fairly homogeneous in terms of how the individuals responded to the items, the measure of reliability to be used is the Kuder-Richardson coefficient. The computational method presented here was actually developed by Hoyt. It uses the analysis of variance and is somewhat simpler than the original formulation. Hoyt's basic formula for reliability is

$$r_{tt} = \frac{V_e - V_r}{V_e}$$

where V_r = variance for remainder sum of squares
V_e = variance for examinees

■ EXAMPLE
Suppose that an experimenter wishes to test the reliability of a certain ten-item test administered to eight subjects. For the purposes of determining reliability, the experimenter records for each subject on each test item whether the question was answered correctly (indicated by the number 1) or incorrectly (indicated by the cipher, 0).

Step 1. Table the data as follows:

Subject	Test items									
	1	2	3	4	5	6	7	8	9	10
S_1	1	1	1	1	1	1	1	1	1	1
S_2	0	0	0	1	1	0	1	1	1	1
S_3	0	0	1	1	1	0	0	0	0	0
S_4	0	0	1	1	1	1	1	0	1	1
S_5	0	1	1	1	1	0	1	0	1	1
S_6	1	1	0	1	0	0	1	1	1	0
S_7	0	0	1	1	0	0	1	0	0	1
S_8	1	1	0	1	1	1	1	0	1	1

Step 2. Count the number of items that each subject answered correctly (in this example, 10 for the first subject, 6 for the second subject, etc.). List the totals for each subject.

Subject	No. of correct answers
S_1	10
S_2	6
S_3	3
S_4	7
S_5	7
S_6	6
S_7	4
S_8	8

Step 3. Add the number of correct answers (Step 2), and record the sum.

$$10 + 6 + \cdots + 8 = \mathbf{51}$$

Step 4. Square each number of correct answers in Step 2; then add the squares and divide that sum by the number of items in the test (10 in this example).

$$\frac{10^2 + 6^2 + \cdots + 8^2}{10} = \frac{359}{10} = \mathbf{35.9}$$

Step 5. Square the result of Step 3, and divide by the product of the number of people by the number of items ($8 \times 10 = 80$ in this example).

$$\frac{51^2}{80} = \frac{2601}{80} = \mathbf{32.512}$$

Step 6. Subtract the result of Step 5 from the result of Step 3.

$51 - 32.512 = \mathbf{18.488}$

Step 7. Subtract the result of Step 5 from the result of Step 4.

$35.9 - 32.512 = \mathbf{3.388}$

Step 8. Count the number of subjects who correctly answered each item. List the totals for each item.

Item	No. of persons correct
1	3
2	4
3	5
4	8
5	6
6	3
7	7
8	3
9	6
10	6

Step 9. Square each number of persons correct in Step 8; then add the squares and divide that sum by the number of people who took the test (8 in this example).

$$\frac{3^2 + 4^2 + \cdots + 6^2}{8} = \frac{259}{8} = \mathbf{36.125}$$

Step 10. Subtract the result of Step 5 from the result of Step 9.

$36.125 - 35.512 = \mathbf{3.613}$

Step 11. Subtract the result of Step 7 and the result of Step 10 from the result of Step 6.

$18.488 - 3.388 - 3.613 = \mathbf{11.487}$

Step 12. Divide the result of Step 7 by $N - 1$, where N is the number of subjects who took the test (8 in this example).

$$\frac{3.388}{N - 1} = \frac{3.388}{8 - 1} = \frac{3.388}{7} = \mathbf{.484}$$

Step 13. Divide the result of Step 11 by $(N - 1)(I - 1)$, where N is the number of subjects who took the test (8 in our example) and I is the number of items in the test (10 in our example).

$$\frac{11.487}{(N - 1)(I - 1)} = \frac{11.487}{7 \times 9} = \frac{11.487}{63} = .182$$

Step 14. Subtract the result of Step 13 from the result of Step 12.

.484 − .182 = **.302**

Step 15. Divide the result of Step 14 by the result of Step 12. This yields the value of the Kuder-Richardson (or Hoyt) reliability coefficient.

$$\frac{.302}{.484} = .62$$

A high reliability coefficient (.70 or higher) would mean that the test was accurately measuring some characteristic of the people taking it. Further, it would mean that the individual items on the test were producing similar patterns of responding in different people. Therefore, a high value would mean that the test items were homogeneous and reliable. ∎

SECTION 3.15
Test for Difference Between Independent Correlations

If you have two correlations computed from data that were gathered from two different groups of individuals, the correlation coefficients will be experimentally independent. In such a case, you may use the following procedure to test for significance of the difference between the correlations.

■ **EXAMPLE**

Suppose we have a correlation coefficient of +.68 that was computed between grades in an English class and IQ scores for thirty-eight people. Suppose further, that we have a correlation coefficient of +.36 between grades in a similar English class and IQ scores for a different group of seventy-three people. We wish to know whether these coefficients are different.

Step 1. First, change the two correlations into Fisher z scores. This can be done by means of any table of such transformations (see Appendix F):

Correlation of .68 = z of **.829**

Correlation of .36 = z of **.377**

Step 2. Subtract either z score of Step 1 from the other.

$$.829 - .377 = .452$$

Step 3. Subtract 3 from the number of people in the group for which the first correlation was computed (38 in this example). (*Note:* The number 3 is always used.)

$$38 - 3 = 35$$

Step 4. Divide the result of Step 3 into the number 1 (i.e., take the reciprocal of 35). Carry the answer to four decimal places.

$$\frac{1}{35} = .0286$$

Step 5. Subtract 3 from the number of people in the group for which the second correlation was computed (73 in this example).

$$73 - 3 = 70$$

Step 6. Divide the result of Step 5 into the number 1 (i.e., take the reciprocal of 70). Carry the answer to four decimal places.

$$\frac{1}{70} = .0143$$

Step 7. Add the result of Step 4 to the result of Step 6.

$$.0286 + .0143 = .0429$$

Then take the square root of the sum.

$$\sqrt{.0429} = .207$$

Step 8. Divide the result of Step 2 by the result of Step 7. This yields a z statistic.

$$z = \frac{.452}{.207} = 2.18$$

A z larger than 1.96 is significant at the .05 level using a two-tailed test (see Appendix A). A significant z tells us that the two correlation values are very likely different. ■

SECTION 3.16
Test for Difference Between Dependent (Related) Correlations

■ **EXAMPLE**
Assume you wish to determine whether a correlation of $+.70$ between grades in a statistics course and overall GPA for sixty-three students and a correlation

of $+.40$ between grades in an introductory psychology course and overall GPA for the same sixty-three students are significantly different. *Note:* Before you begin the test, you must compute the remaining correlation between statistics grades and introductory psychology grades for the sixty-three students (see Section 3.1). Suppose that computation yields a correlation of $+.30$.

Step 1. After you have computed all three correlations, compute the difference between the two correlations of interest (in this example, the first two): Recall, statistics with GPA $= +.70$; introductory psychology grades with GPA $= +.40$; and statistics grades with introductory psychology grades $= +.30$,

then, $.70 - .40 = $ **.30**

Step 2. Subtract 3 from the number of individuals measured ($N = 63$). (*Note:* The number 3 is always subtracted.)

$63 - 3 = $ **60**

Step 3. Add 1 to the third correlation computed in Step 1—i.e., the correlation in which you are not presently interested ($+.30$ in this example). (*Note:* The number 1 is always used.) Then, multiply the result of Step 2 by the computed sum and take the square root of that product.

$.30 + 1 = $ **1.30** and $60 \times 1.30 = $ **78** and $\sqrt{78} = $ **8.832**

Step 4. Multiply the result of Step 1 by the result of Step 3.

$.30 \times 8.832 = $ **2.65**

Step 5. Square each of the three correlation values from Step 1, then add the squares.

$.70^2 + .40^2 + .30^2 = .49 + .16 + .09 = $ **.74**

Step 6. Multiply the three correlation values from Step 1.

$.70 \times .40 \times .30 = $ **.084**

Step 7. Multiply the result of Step 6 by 2. (*Note:* The number 2 is always used.) Add 1 to the product. Then subtract the result of Step 5.

$(2 \times .084) + 1 = $ **1.168** and $1.168 - .74 = $ **.428**

Step 8. Multiply the result of Step 7 by 2. (*Note:* The number 2 is always used.) Take the square root of that product.

$.428 \times 2 = $ **.856** and $\sqrt{.856} = $ **.925**

Step 9. Divide the result of Step 4 by the result of Step 8. This yields a *t* statistic.

$t = 2.65/.925 = $ **2.86**

The appropriate degrees of freedom are given as the result of Step 2, i.e., 60 in this example. Since the computed *t* is larger than 2.00, with 60 *df* (see Appendix B), the correlation values of .70 and .40 are significantly different. ■

PART 4

Analysis of Variance

Most of the statistical tests presented in the previous sections are designed to determine the significance of relationships or differences between two groups. In actual practice, however, most experiments involve more than two groups. While it would be possible to test the difference between, say, four experimental groups by using t-tests of all possible combinations of two group means, the number of tests necessary to make these comparisons would be large. (The actual number of tests is equal to $N(N - 1)/2$. In the case of an experiment involving four experimental groups, six separate tests would be needed.)

In addition to posing computational problems, many multigroup experiments require that several variables be manipulated at the same time. For example, four groups of subjects might be presented with a learning task and their performance recorded over a series of several trials. The experimenter would very likely be interested not only in overall performance but also in whether the rate of learning of the several groups was the same. To determine this, statistical procedures are needed that are far more complex than the simple, two-group t statistic.

In subsequent Parts, several statistical analyses are introduced that permit evaluation of much more complicated experimental designs. To aid the user in determining which analysis is appropriate for a particular experimental design, a descriptive list of all the analyses of variance presented in Part 4 is presented below. In addition to indicating the type of problem for which each analysis is appropriate, the list also indicates some of the major strengths and weaknesses of each.

Following Part 4 is a textbook reference chart that provides a guide for seven of the most widely used statistics and design textbooks. This chart covers anova, multiple comparisons, covariance, power, trend analysis, and manova.

Completely Randomized Design (Section 4.1)

This design is basically an extension of the t-test to experiments involving three or more groups. This design would typically be used, for example, if an experimenter were interested in determining reactions to several different drugs. In this case, subjects would be randomly assigned to the several groups and a different drug administered to each group. After the performance of subjects in all groups had been measured, statistical analyses of the data would be undertaken to determine the differential effects of the drugs.

Factorial Design: Two Factors (Section 4.2)

This extension of the completely randomized design permits investigation of one set of variables in combination with some other set. For example, instead of being interested only in the effects of drugs, an experimenter might be interested in determining the effects of drugs in combination with varying amounts of sleep loss. In the simplest case, two drugs, A and B, would be paired with no sleep loss and with twenty-four-hour loss. This would result in the formation of four groups: Group 1—Drug A and no sleep loss; Group 2—Drug A and twenty-four-hour loss; Group 3—Drug B and no sleep loss; Group 4—Drug B and twenty-four-hour loss. Thus, it is possible to determine not only the effects of drugs and sleep loss but also whether the effects of Drugs A and B were enhanced or suppressed by sleep loss. Stated another way, it is possible to determine whether the variables interact.

The experimental procedure for the two-factor design is basically the same as for the completely randomized design. The subjects would be randomly assigned to the four (in this example) groups, sleep loss would be manipulated, and then the drugs would be administered. Again, after measuring performance, statistical analyses of the data would be undertaken.

Factorial Design: Three Factors (Section 4.3)

This is a commonly used extension of the two-factor design. The only difference is that a third factor, or dimension, is added. For example, an experimenter working with Drugs A and B and sleep versus sleep loss might also be interested in determining the effects of these factors in combination with a third factor, alcohol concentration in the blood. If only two concentrations are used, 0.0 and 0.2 percent, the experimental groups would be constituted as follows: Group 1—Drug A, no sleep loss, no alcohol; Group 2—Drug A, no sleep loss, alcohol; Group 3—Drug A, sleep loss, no alcohol; Group 4—Drug A, sleep loss, alcohol. Groups 5, 6, 7, and 8 would receive the above combinations of sleep loss and alcohol in combination with Drug B. The assignment of subjects, measurement of performance, and analysis of the results are basically the same as in the two-factor design.

Treatments-by-Levels Design (Section 4.4)

This represents a slight variation on the two-factor design discussed above. All the computations needed to analyze the treatments-by-levels design are the same as for the two-factor design; the only difference is in the intent of the design and interpretation of the results. In the treatments-by-levels, one of the factors usually represents some variable already known to affect performance. For example, if it were known that sleep loss generally heightens the effects of drugs, it would probably be wise for the experimenter to include different levels of sleep loss as a variable in the drug experiments. By so doing, variability due to the specific effects of different amounts of sleep loss could be statistically separated from the effects of the drugs.

Treatments-by-Subjects, or Repeated-Measures, Design (Section 4.5)

The treatments-by-subjects design is a variation of the completely randomized design. Instead of using several different groups of subjects with each group receiving a single drug, only one group of subjects would be used and each subject would receive all the drug treatments. If the treatments-by-subjects design were to be used for the drug experiment, the single group of subjects would probably receive one drug, perform the criterion task, and wait until the effects wore off. Then a second drug would be administered, the criterion task would be performed, and another waiting period would ensue. This same procedure would be repeated until every subject in the group had received every drug. Analysis of the findings would be based on the subjects' performance while under the influence of the several drugs. The major advantage of this design over the completely randomized design is that fewer subjects are required.* The major disadvantage is that there might be carryover effects from one treatment to the next. In the present example, it is possible that exposure to one drug would heighten or lessen sensitivity to other drugs administered later. Also, the subjects might become progressively more proficient at performing the criterion task and show an improvement in performance that would be due to learning and not to the effects of the drugs.

Treatments-by-Treatments-by-Subjects Design (Section 4.6)

This two-factor design bears the same relationship to the treatments-by-subjects design as the factorial bears to the completely randomized design. The treatments-by-treatments-by-subjects design is basically the same as the two-factor factorial design, with one notable exception. Instead of different subjects being assigned to the experimental groups, one group of subjects performs under all

---

* Very often the advantage of increased statistical power is also gained by using a repeated-measures design. The reason is that the random variability of a single subject from one measuring period to the next is usually much less than the variability introduced by measuring and comparing different subjects.

experimental conditions. Using the example from the two-factor factorial design, an experiment using the treatments-by-treatments-by-subjects design would probably be conducted as follows. First, all subjects would receive Drug A with no prior sleep loss, perform the criterion task, and then wait for the effects to wear off. After a suitable period, the same subjects would again receive Drug A, but this time the drug would follow a twenty-four-hour sleep loss. After performance measures had been recorded and a sufficient period allowed for the effects of the drug to wear off, the same procedures would be repeated with Drug B. The major advantage of this design over the factorial is that far fewer subjects are required. As in the treatments-by-subjects design, the major disadvantage is that there may be carryover effects from one treatment to the next.

Two-Factor Mixed Design: Repeated Measures on One Factor (Section 4.7)

This design is essentially a combination of the completely randomized and treatments-by-subjects designs. It involves the assignment of subjects to several experimental groups. However, instead of taking only one measure, as in the completely randomized design, the performance of the subjects would be measured repeatedly to determine the effects of the experimental variables over a prolonged period of time. This recording of repeated measures is, of course, identical with the procedure used in the treatments-by-subjects design.

To further clarify, let us continue with the example used to illustrate the completely randomized design. In the two-factor mixed design, subjects would again be assigned to the several experimental groups, and each group would be administered a different drug. Then, the subjects' performance on the criterion task would be measured several times.

Since measures are recorded over several successive test periods, this design permits (1) comparison of the overall performance of the experimental groups (as in the completely randomized design), (2) evaluation of performance changes from one measuring period to the next (as in the treatments-by-subjects design), and (3) evaluation of the drug effects in relation to the passage of time between measuring periods. This particular design is very widely used in the behavioral sciences.

Three-Factor Mixed Design: Repeated Measures on One Factor (Section 4.8)

This extension of the two-factor mixed design is essentially a combination of the factorial and repeated-measures designs. In the three-factor mixed design, the experimental groups are formed and subjects are assigned in exactly the same manner as in the factorial design. The basic difference (using the example of the factorial design) is that the effects of the drugs in combination with sleep loss would be measured several times rather than only once. Consequently, this design permits not only the evaluation of the overall experimental effects (as in the factorial design) but also the evaluation of general changes and interactions of the variables over the passage of time (as in the repeated-measures designs).

This particular design is probably the one used most often in behavioral science research. There are several slight variations of the format presented here, the most common of which involves presenting subjects with a task to be learned during a predetermined set of practice trials. In this situation, the repeated measures represent the learning rates of the subjects in the several experimental groups.

Three-Factor Mixed Design: Repeated Measures on Two Factors (Section 4.9)

This design is essentially a combination of the completely randomized and the treatments-by-treatments-by-subjects designs. As in the completely randomized design, subjects are randomly assigned to two or more experimental groups. For example, one group might be subjected to a twenty-four-hour sleep loss just prior to the experiment and the other group to no sleep loss. Each of these different groups would then be treated in the same fashion as in the treatments-by-treatments-by-subjects design. That is, two additional factors (say, Drug A versus Drug B and 0.0 versus 0.2 percent alcohol) would be combined and presented to each subject in both of the experimental groups. Consequently, all subjects in the sleep-loss and no-sleep-loss groups would receive Drug A with *no* alcohol, perform the criterion task, wait for the effects to dissipate, then receive Drug A *with* alcohol, etc., until all variable combinations had been experienced. The major advantage of the three-factor mixed design over the regular three-factor design discussed above is that far fewer subjects are required to conduct the experiment. Carryover effects represent the most serious drawback.

Latin Square Design: Simple (Section 4.10)

This design is a variation of the treatments-by-subjects, or repeated-measures, design. The basic difference in the Latin square design is that the presentation of the treatments is deliberately counterbalanced. Thus, instead of giving subjects the various drugs in the same order (Drug A, then B, then C, etc.) or randomly assigning the order of presentation of the drugs for each subject, a systematic order of presentation is set up so that order and carryover effects can be ascertained. Assume that three drugs are to be investigated. If the simple Latin square design were used, one third of the subjects would receive Drug A first, then B, then C; a second third would receive Drug C first, then A, then B; and the final third would receive Drug B first, then C, then A. As indicated above, this design permits the analysis not only of the effects of the drugs but also of the order in which they were given.

Latin Square Design: Complex (Section 4.11)

This design can be viewed as a variation of the two-factor mixed design or as an extension of the simple Latin square. As in the two-factor mixed design, subjects would be randomly assigned to different experimental groups (like sleep loss and no sleep loss). The drugs would then be administered to all subjects in both groups in the same manner as in the simple Latin square. Thus, one third of the subjects in the no-sleep-loss group would receive Drug A, then B, then C; a second third would receive Drug C, then A, then B; and a final third would receive Drug B, then C, then A. The same procedure would be used with the subjects in the sleep-loss group. Thus, this design permits not only the evaluation of the effects of the drugs and of sleep loss but also the effects of the order of drug administration in relation to the other two factors.

For most of Parts 4 and 5 of this book, only the verbal instructions for computing the analyses and the computed examples are presented. In place of symbols and formulas, the textbook sources of the several analyses are listed in the textbook reference chart that follows Part 4. The reasons for this are twofold. First, several of the more complex analyses require up to twenty separate computational formulas, plus additional ones for retabling the data. Second, and more important, there is no standard set of terms and symbols to indicate analysis-of-variance operations. These tend to be specific to each text, and translation from one text to another is difficult. To include all the symbols and terms currently in use or to develop a set of our own is beyond the scope of this book.

In Part 5, specific supplemental computations and the uses of multiple comparisons employed in conjunction with analyses of variance are discussed. Because of the relative specificity of these computations, the reader is encouraged to read the introductory comments at the beginning of Part 5 to determine whether a particular test is appropriate to use in a statistical analysis of specific experimental findings.

Dichotomous Data (Section 4.12)

This does not represent a special design but, rather, a situation in which the data recorded are usually "1" or "0." The actual computational steps are the same as those presented in earlier sections.

Rank-Order Data (Section 4.13)

In this situation, the data represent rank-ordered preferences. Once again, the computational steps are the same as those presented earlier.

SECTION 4.1
Completely Randomized Design

One of the more simple experimental designs that permits comparison of several groups is the *simple randomized,* or *completely randomized, design.*

Points to Consider When Using the Completely Randomized Design

1. For each subject in the experimental groups, there can be only *one* score. If many measures are taken for each subject, these measures must be combined in some fashion (added, etc.) so that there is only one score for each subject.
2. Although it is not necessary, it is usually best to have an equal number of subjects in each of the experimental groups. In most experiments, ten to fifteen subjects per group are used.
3. The number of experimental groups that may be compared is arbitrary. However, it is rare that more than four or five groups are compared in one experiment.

■ EXAMPLE

The example used to demonstrate the computational procedures is drawn from psychology. Assume that the experimenter is interested in determining the effect of shock on the time required to solve a set of difficult problems. Subjects are randomly assigned to four experimental conditions. Subjects in Group 1 receive no shock; Group 2, very-low-intensity shocks; Group 3, medium shocks; and Group 4, high-intensity shocks. The total time required to solve all the problems is the measure recorded for each subject.

Step 1.   After the experiment has been conducted and the data collected, table the data as follows:

Group 1 (No shock)		Group 2 (Low shock)		Group 3 (Medium shock)		Group 4 (High shock)	
Subject	Time (Min.)	Subject	Time (Min.)	Subject	Time (Min.)	Subject	Time (Min.)
S_1	10	S_{13}	3	S_{25}	19	S_{37}	23
S_2	7	S_{14}	8	S_{26}	12	S_{38}	14
S_3	9	S_{15}	7	S_{27}	16	S_{39}	16
S_4	8	S_{16}	5	S_{28}	14	S_{40}	18
S_5	15	S_{17}	6	S_{29}	7	S_{41}	12
S_6	3	S_{18}	10	S_{30}	8	S_{42}	13
S_7	8	S_{19}	12	S_{31}	13	S_{43}	16

Group 1 (No shock)		Group 2 (Low shock)		Group 3 (Medium shock)		Group 4 (High shock)	
Subject	Time (Min.)	Subject	Time (Min.)	Subject	Time (Min.)	Subject	Time (Min.)
S_8	9	S_{20}	4	S_{32}	10	S_{44}	17
S_9	11	S_{21}	7	S_{33}	19	S_{45}	19
S_{10}	9	S_{22}	6	S_{34}	9	S_{46}	14
S_{11}	5	S_{23}	5	S_{35}	15	S_{47}	16
S_{12}	17	S_{24}	15	S_{36}	14	S_{48}	17

Step 2.   Add the scores in each group to get the sum of *each group*.

	Group 1	Group 2	Group 3	Group 4
	10	3	19	23
	7	8	12	14
	.	.	.	.
	.	.	.	.
	.	.	.	.
Sums:	**111**	**88**	**156**	**195**

Step 3.   Square each number in the table, and add these squared values.

$$10^2 + 7^2 + \cdots + 17^2 + 3^2 + 8^2 + \cdots + 15^2 + 19^2 + 12^2$$
$$+ \cdots + 14^2 + 23^2 + 14^2 + \cdots + 17^2 = \mathbf{7434}$$

Step 4.   Add all the group sums (Step 2) together to obtain a grand total for the entire table.

$$111 + 88 + 156 + 195 = \mathbf{550}$$

Step 5.   Square the grand total (Step 4), and divide the squared value by the total number of measures recorded (see Step 1). (In the present example, the latter number is 48, since there are 4 groups of 12 subjects each.) The value obtained is the correction term.

$$\frac{550^2}{48} = \frac{302{,}500}{48} = \mathbf{6302}$$

Step 6.   Subtract the correction term (Step 5) from the sum of the squared values obtained in Step 3. The resultant value is the *sum of squares total*, or SS_t.

$$7434 - 6302 = \mathbf{1132}$$

Step 7.   Square the sum of each of the groups (Step 2), divide by the number of measures in each group, and then add these values.

$$\frac{111^2}{12} + \frac{88^2}{12} + \frac{156^2}{12} + \frac{195^2}{12} = \frac{82{,}426}{12} = \textbf{6869}$$

Step 8.   Subtract the correction term (Step 5) from the value obtained in Step 7. The resultant value is the *sum of squares between groups,* or SS_b.

$$6869 - 6302 = \textbf{567}$$

Step 9.   Subtract the sum of squares between groups (Step 8) from the sum of squares total (Step 6). This yields the *sum of squares within groups,* or SS_w.

$$1132 - 567 = \textbf{565}$$

Step 10.   All computations based directly on the data have now been completed. However, since the test of significance (*F*-test) is a ratio of the mean squares, these values must be computed. To compute the needed mean squares, the degrees of freedom (*df*) for each of the components (SS_t, SS_b, and SS_w) must be determined as follows:

df for SS_t = the total number of measures (see Step 1) minus 1

$$48 - 1 = \textbf{47}$$

df for SS_b = the number of experimental groups minus 1

$$4 - 1 = \textbf{3}$$

df for SS_w = the total df minus the between groups df.

$$47 - 3 = \textbf{44}$$

Step 11.   The mean squares are then computed as SS/df.

$$ms_t = \frac{SS_t}{df} \qquad \text{(This value is not needed for the analysis.)}$$

$$ms_b = \frac{SS_b}{df} = \frac{(\text{Step 8})}{3} = \frac{567}{3} = \textbf{189}$$

$$ms_w = \frac{SS_w}{df} = \frac{(\text{Step 9})}{44} = \frac{565}{44} = \textbf{12.84}$$

Step 12.   The test of significance (*F*) is equal to ms_b/ms_w.

$$F = \frac{189}{12.84} = \textbf{14.71}$$

Step 13.   Table the final analysis as follows.

Source	SS	df	ms	F	p
Total	1132	47	—	—	—
Between groups	567	3	189	14.71	<.001
Within groups	565	44	12.84	—	—

Since the *F* value (see Appendix E) of 14.71, with *df* of 3 and 44, would occur by chance less than once in one thousand times, it is concluded that level of shock intensity does affect the time required to solve these problems. ∎

SECTION 4.2
Factorial Design: Two Factors

Many times an experimenter wishes to determine the effects of two variables in combination with each other. For example, instead of investigating the effects of differing list difficulty on performance (memorizing the lists) in one experiment and then doing another experiment to determine the effects of varying room noise on performance, the experimenter may well wish to investigate these variables in combination with each other. The two-factor design permits such comparisons.

Points to Consider When Using the Two-Factor Factorial Design

1. For each subject in the experimental groups, there can be only *one* score. As in the simple randomized design, if many measures are taken for each subject, these must be combined (added, etc.) so that there is only one score for each subject.
2. It is usually best to have an equal number of subjects in each of the experimental groups. If equality cannot be obtained, the number of subjects in each of the groups should be proportional. In most experiments, ten to fifteen subjects per group are used.
3. The number of treatment groups within each factor to be compared is arbitrary. However, it is rare that more than four or five groups are included in either of the two factors.

∎ **EXAMPLE**

The example used to demonstrate the computational procedures is drawn from psychology. Assume that an experimenter is interested in determining the effects of high- versus low-intensity shock on the memorization of a difficult versus an easy list of nonsense syllables. Subjects are randomly assigned to four experimental conditions. Subjects in Group 1 receive periodic low-intensity shocks and must memorize an easy list; Group 2, high shock and an easy list; Group 3, low shock and a difficult list; and Group 4, high shock and a difficult list. The total number of errors made by each subject is recorded.

Step 1. After the experiment has been conducted, table the data as follows. (*Note:* If more than a 2 × 2 factorial—e.g., a 2 × 3, 3 × 3, etc.—is to be analyzed, simply table the additional treatment groups in their appropriate row or column. All other steps are the same.)

Group 1 (Low shock-easy list)		Group 2 (High shock-easy list)	
Subject	No. of errors	Subject	No. of errors
S_1	9	S_7	15
S_2	16	S_8	13
S_3	14	S_9	9
S_4	11	S_{10}	9
S_5	12	S_{11}	8
S_6	8	S_{12}	11

Group 3 (Low shock-difficult list)		Group 4 (High shock-difficult list)	
Subject	No. of errors	Subject	No. of errors
S_{13}	10	S_{19}	19
S_{14}	12	S_{20}	16
S_{15}	18	S_{21}	18
S_{16}	16	S_{22}	23
S_{17}	17	S_{23}	14
S_{18}	15	S_{24}	15

Step 2. Add the scores in each group.

	Group 1	Group 2	Group 3	Group 4
	9	15	10	19
	16	13	12	16
	⋮	⋮	⋮	⋮
Sums:	**70**	**65**	**88**	**105**

Step 3. Square each number in the entire table (Step 1), and add these squared values.

$$9^2 + 16^2 + \cdots + 15^2 + 13^2 + \cdots + 10^2 + 12^2$$
$$+ \cdots + 19^2 + 16^2 + \cdots + 15^2 = \mathbf{4832}$$

Step 4. Add the sums of all the groups (Step 2) to get the grand sum of the entire table.

$$70 + 65 + 88 + 105 = \mathbf{328}$$

Then, square this value, and divide by the total number of measures recorded in the table (see Step 1). This yields the correction term.

$$\frac{328^2}{24} = \frac{107{,}584}{24} = \mathbf{4483}$$

Step 5. Computation of the total sum of squares (SS_t): Simply subtract the correction term (Step 4) from the sum of the squared measures (Step 3).

$$4832 - 4483 = \mathbf{349} = SS_t$$

Step 6. Computation of the effects of the first factor (the overall effects of low shock versus high shock): First, add the sums of the two shock groups (see Step 2), disregarding the difficulty-of-list dimension.

$$70 + 88 = \mathbf{158} = \text{sum of the low-shock groups}$$
$$65 + 105 = \mathbf{170} = \text{sum of the high-shock groups}$$

Then, square the above sums, divide by the number of measures on which each of the sums was based, and add the quotients.

$$\frac{158^2}{12} + \frac{170^2}{12} = \frac{53{,}864}{12} = \mathbf{4489}$$

Then, subtract the correction term from the above value.

$$4489 - 4483 = \mathbf{6} = SS_{shock}$$

Step 7. Computation of the effects of the second factor (the overall effects of difficult versus easy list): First, add the sums of the two same-list-difficulty groups (see Step 2), disregarding the shock dimension.

$$70 + 65 = \mathbf{135} = \text{sum of easy-list groups}$$
$$88 + 105 = \mathbf{193} = \text{sum of difficult-list groups}$$

Then, square the above sums, divide by the number of measures on which each of the sums was based, and add the quotients.

$$\frac{135^2}{12} + \frac{193^2}{12} = \frac{55{,}474}{12} = \mathbf{4623}$$

Then, subtract the correction term from the above value.

$$4623 - 4483 = \mathbf{140} = SS_{list}$$

Step 8.   Computation of the interactive effects of shock and list difficulty: First, square the sums of each of the experimental groups (Step 2), divide by the number of measures on which each sum was based, then add the quotients.

$$\frac{70^2}{6} + \frac{65^2}{6} + \frac{88^2}{6} + \frac{105^2}{6} = \frac{27{,}894}{6} = \mathbf{4649}$$

Then, from this value, subtract the correction term (Step 4), SS_{shock} (Step 6), and SS_{list} (Step 7).

$$4649 - 4483 - 6 - 140 = \mathbf{20} = SS_{shock \times list}$$

Step 9.   Computation of the error-term sum of squares (SS_{error}): Simply subtract SS_{shock} (Step 6), SS_{list} (Step 7), and $SS_{shock \times list}$ (Step 8) from SS_{total} (Step 5).

$$349 - 6 - 140 - 20 = \mathbf{183} = SS_{error}$$

Step 10.   All computations based directly on the data have now been completed. However, since the F ratios are ratios of mean squares, the degrees of freedom (df) for each of the components must be computed.

df for SS_t = the total number of measures (see Step 1) minus 1.

$$24 - 1 = \mathbf{23}$$

df for SS_{shock} = the number of shock conditions minus 1.

$$2 - 1 = \mathbf{1}$$

df for SS_{list} = the number of list conditions minus 1.

$$2 - 1 = \mathbf{1}$$

df for $SS_{shock \times list}$ = the df for SS_{shock} times the df for SS_{list}.

$$1 \times 1 = \mathbf{1}$$

df for SS_{error} = the df for SS_t minus the df for SS_{shock}, SS_{list}, and $SS_{shock \times list}$.

$$23 - 1 - 1 - 1 = \mathbf{20}$$

Step 11.   The mean squares are then computed as SS/df.

ms_t (This value is not needed for the analysis.)

$$ms_{shock} = \frac{(\text{Step 6})}{1} = \frac{6}{1} = \mathbf{6}$$

$$ms_{list} = \frac{(\text{Step 7})}{1} = \frac{140}{1} = \mathbf{140}$$

$$ms_{shock\times list} = \frac{(Step\ 8)}{1} = \frac{20}{1} = 20$$

$$ms_{error} = \frac{(Step\ 9)}{20} = \frac{183}{20} = 9.15$$

Step 12.   The several F ratios are then computed as

$$\frac{ms_{shock}}{ms_{error}} \qquad \frac{ms_{list}}{ms_{error}} \qquad \frac{ms_{shock\times list}}{ms_{error}}$$

Step 13.   Table the final analysis as follows:

Source	SS	df	ms	F	p
Total	349	23	—	—	—
Shock	6	1	6	.66	n.s.
List	140	1	140	15.30	<.001
Shock × List	20	1	20	2.19	n.s.
Error	183	20	9.15	—	—

Therefore, we conclude (see Appendix E) that shock had no significant effect on performance and that the interaction of shock by list difficulty was also nonsignificant. However, the effect of list difficulty was significant and would be expected to occur by chance less than once in one thousand times.   ■

SECTION 4.3
Factorial Design: Three Factors

This design is a commonly used extension of the two-factor design discussed in Section 4.2. The one basic difference is that instead of determining the effects of two variables in combination with each other, this design permits evaluation of three variables.

Points to Consider When Using the Three-Factor Factorial Design

1. For each subject in the experimental groups, there can be only *one* score. As in the two-factor design, if many measures are taken for each subject, these must be combined (added, etc.) so that there is only one score for each subject.
2. It is usually best to have an equal number of subjects in each experimental group. In most experiments, ten to fifteen subjects per group are used.

3. The number of treatment groups within each factor to be compared is arbitrary. However, it is rare that more than four or five groups are included in any of the factors.

■ EXAMPLE

The example used to demonstrate the computational procedures is drawn from the field of psychology and is essentially an extension of the one used in Section 4.2. Assume that the experimenter, in addition to determining the effects of high- and low-intensity shock on the memorization of easy and difficult lists, is also concerned with determining the effects of rate of list presentation on learning in the above conditions. Obviously, the experimenter could conduct one two-factor experiment at a fast rate and another at a slow rate. As an alternative, rate of presentation could be included as an additional dimension and the entire experiment conducted as one three-factor design.

In the present example, then, the variables are high versus low shock, difficult versus easy list, and fast versus slow rate of presentation. Subjects are randomly assigned to one of eight experimental conditions. Subjects in Group 1 receive periodic low-intensity shock and must memorize an easy list presented at a slow rate; Group 2—low-intensity shock, easy list, fast rate; Group 3—low-intensity shock, difficult list, slow rate; Group 4—low-intensity shock, difficult list, fast rate. Groups 5, 6, 7, and 8 receive the same treatment as Groups 1, 2, 3, and 4, except that high-intensity shocks are administered: Group 5—high-intensity shock, easy list, slow rate; Group 6—high-intensity shock, easy list, fast rate; Group 7—high-intensity shock, difficult list, slow rate; Group 8—high-intensity shock, difficult list, fast rate.

The total number of errors made by each subject is the measure recorded.

Step 1. After the experiment has been completed, table the data as follows. (*Note:* If other than a $2 \times 2 \times 2$ factorial—e.g., $2 \times 2 \times 3$, $3 \times 2 \times 3$, etc.—is to be analyzed, simply table the additional treatment groups in their appropriate row or column. All other steps are the same.)

Group 1 (Low, easy, slow)		Group 2 (Low, easy, fast)		Group 3 (Low, difficult, slow)		Group 4 (Low, difficult, fast)	
Subject	No. of errors	Subject	No. of errors	Subject	No. of errors	Subject	No. of errors
S_1	15	S_7	23	S_{13}	11	S_{19}	25
S_2	8	S_8	16	S_{14}	16	S_{20}	27
S_3	9	S_9	17	S_{15}	8	S_{21}	29
S_4	7	S_{10}	17	S_{16}	14	S_{22}	34
S_5	8	S_{11}	14	S_{17}	20	S_{23}	38
S_6	4	S_{12}	11	S_{18}	16	S_{24}	26

Group 5 (High, easy, slow)		Group 6 (High, easy, fast)		Group 7 (High, difficult, slow)		Group 8 (High, difficult, fast)	
Subject	No. of errors	Subject	No. of errors	Subject	No. of errors	Subject	No. of errors
S_{25}	14	S_{31}	24	S_{37}	11	S_{43}	39
S_{26}	6	S_{32}	16	S_{38}	17	S_{44}	32
S_{27}	3	S_{33}	10	S_{39}	12	S_{45}	38
S_{28}	5	S_{34}	18	S_{40}	14	S_{46}	39
S_{29}	6	S_{35}	13	S_{41}	21	S_{47}	33
S_{30}	7	S_{36}	17	S_{42}	18	S_{48}	31

Step 2.   Add the scores in each group.

	Group 1	Group 2	Group 3	Group 4
	15	23	11	25
	8	16	16	27
	⋮	⋮	⋮	⋮
Sums:	**51**	**98**	**85**	**179**

	Group 5	Group 6	Group 7	Group 8
	14	24	11	39
	6	16	17	32
	⋮	⋮	⋮	⋮
Sums:	**41**	**98**	**93**	**212**

Step 3.   Square each number in the entire table (Step 1), and add these squared values.

$$15^2 + 8^2 + \cdots + 31^2 = \mathbf{20{,}083}$$

Step 4.   Add all the group sums (Step 2) to get the grand sum of the entire table.

$$51 + 98 + 85 + 179 + 41 + 98 + 93 + 212 = \mathbf{857}$$

Then, square the above value and divide by the number of scores added (recorded in Step 1) to obtain the grand sum. (In the present example, 48 scores were added.) This yields the correction term.

$$\frac{857^2}{48} = \frac{734{,}449}{48} = \mathbf{15{,}301}$$

Step 5. Computation of the total sum of squares (SS_t): Simply subtract the correction term (Step 4) from the sum of the squared measures (Step 3).

$$20{,}083 - 15{,}301 = \mathbf{4782} = SS_t$$

Step 6. Computation of the effects of the first factor (the overall effects of high versus low shock): First, add the scores of the two same-intensity-shock groups (see Step 2), disregarding the difficulty-of-list and rate-of-presentation dimensions.

$$51 + 98 + 85 + 179 = \mathbf{413} = \text{sum of the low-shock groups}$$

$$41 + 98 + 93 + 212 = \mathbf{444} = \text{sum of the high-shock groups}$$

Then, square the above sums, divide by the number of measures on which each of the sums was based, and add the quotients.

$$\frac{413^2}{24} + \frac{444^2}{24} = \frac{367{,}705}{24} = \mathbf{15{,}321}$$

Then, subtract the correction term (Step 4) from the above value.

$$15{,}321 - 15{,}301 = \mathbf{20} = SS_{\text{shock}}$$

Step 7. Computation of the effects of the second factor (the overall effects of difficult versus easy list): First, sum the scores of the two same-list-difficulty groups (Step 2), disregarding the shock-intensity and rate-of-presentation dimensions.

$$51 + 98 + 41 + 98 = \mathbf{288} = \text{sum of the easy-list groups}$$

$$85 + 179 + 93 + 212 = \mathbf{569} = \text{sum of the difficult-list groups}$$

Then, square the above sums, divide by the number of measures on which each was based, and add the quotients.

$$\frac{288^2}{24} + \frac{569^2}{24} = \frac{406{,}705}{24} = \mathbf{16{,}946}$$

Then, subtract the correction term (Step 4) from the above value.

$$16{,}946 - 15{,}301 = \mathbf{1645} = SS_{\text{list}}$$

Step 8. Computation of the effects of the third factor (the overall effects of fast versus slow rate of presentation): First, sum the scores of the two same-rate-of-presentation groups (Step 2), disregarding the shock-intensity and list-difficulty dimensions.

$$51 + 85 + 41 + 93 = \mathbf{270} = \text{sum of the slow-rate groups}$$

$$98 + 179 + 98 + 212 = \mathbf{587} = \text{sum of the fast-rate groups}$$

Then, square the above sums, divide by the number of measures on which each was based, and add the quotients.

$$\frac{270^2}{24} + \frac{587^2}{24} + \frac{417,469}{24} = \mathbf{17,394}$$

Then, subtract the correction term from the above value.

$$17,394 - 15,301 = \mathbf{2093} = SS_{rate}$$

Step 9. Computation of the interactive effects of the first and second factors (shock × list): First, sum the scores of the groups which have the same pairings of shock intensity and list difficulty, disregarding the rate-of-presentation dimension.

$51 + 98 = \mathbf{149}$ = sum of the low-shock, easy-list groups

$85 + 179 = \mathbf{264}$ = sum of the low-shock, difficult-list groups

$41 + 98 = \mathbf{139}$ = sum of the high-shock, easy-list groups

$93 + 212 = \mathbf{305}$ = sum of the high-shock, difficult-list groups

Then, square the above sums, divide by the number of scores on which each sum was based, and add the quotients.

$$\frac{149^2}{12} + \frac{264^2}{12} + \frac{139^2}{12} + \frac{305^2}{12} = \frac{204,243}{12} = \mathbf{17,020}$$

Then, from this value, subtract the correction term (Step 4), the SS_{shock} (Step 6), and the SS_{list} (Step 7).

$$17,020 - 15,301 - 20 - 1645 = \mathbf{54} = SS_{shock \times list}$$

Step 10. Computation of the interactive effects of the first and third factors (shock × rate of presentation): First, sum the scores of the groups that have the same pairings of shock intensity and rate of presentation. Disregard the difficulty-of-list dimension.

$51 + 85 = \mathbf{136}$ = sum of the low-shock, slow-rate groups

$98 + 179 = \mathbf{277}$ = sum of the low-shock, fast-rate groups

$41 + 93 = \mathbf{134}$ = sum of the high-shock, slow-rate groups

$98 + 212 = \mathbf{310}$ = sum of the high-shock, fast-rate groups

Then, square the above sums, divide by the number of scores on which each is based, and add the quotients.

$$\frac{136^2}{12} + \frac{277^2}{12} + \frac{134^2}{12} + \frac{310^2}{12} = \frac{209,281}{12} = \mathbf{17,440}$$

Then, from the above value, subtract the correction term (Step 4), the SS_{shock} (Step 6), and the SS_{rate} (Step 8).

$$17,440 - 15,301 - 20 - 2093 = \mathbf{26} = SS_{shock \times rate}$$

Step 11.   Computation of the interactive effects of the second and third factors (difficulty $\times$ rate of presentation): First, sum the scores of the groups that have the same pairings of difficulty of material and rate of presentation. Disregard the shock dimension.

$$51 + 41 = \mathbf{92} = \text{sum of the easy-list, slow-rate groups}$$

$$98 + 98 = \mathbf{196} = \text{sum of the easy-list, fast-rate groups}$$

$$85 + 93 = \mathbf{178} = \text{sum of the difficult-list, slow-rate groups}$$

$$179 + 212 = \mathbf{391} = \text{sum of the difficult-list, fast-rate groups}$$

Then, square the above sums, divide by the number of scores on which each is based, and add the quotients.

$$\frac{92^2}{12} + \frac{196^2}{12} + \frac{178^2}{12} + \frac{391^2}{12} = \frac{231,445}{12} = \mathbf{19,287}$$

Then, from the above value, subtract the correction term (Step 4), the SS_{list} (Step 7), and the SS_{rate} (Step 8).

$$19,287 - 15,301 - 1645 - 2093 = \mathbf{248} = SS_{list \times rate}$$

Step 12.   Computation of the interactive effects of the first, second, and third factors (shock $\times$ list difficulty $\times$ rate of presentation): First, square the sums of each of the experimental groups (Step 2), divide by the number of measures on which each sum was based, and then add the quotients.

$$\frac{51^2}{6} + \frac{98^2}{6} + \frac{85^2}{6} + \frac{179^2}{6} + \frac{41^2}{6} + \frac{98^2}{6} + \frac{93^2}{6} + \frac{212^2}{6}$$

$$= \frac{116,349}{6} = \mathbf{19,391}$$

Then, from this value, subtract the correction term (Step 4), the SS_{shock} (Step 6), the SS_{list} (Step 7), the SS_{rate} (Step 8), the $SS_{shock \times list}$ (Step 9), $SS_{shock \times rate}$ (Step 10), and the $SS_{list \times rate}$ (Step 11).

$$19,391 - 15,301 - 20 - 1645 - 2093 - 54 - 26 - 248$$

$$= \mathbf{4} = SS_{shock \times list \times rate}$$

Step 13.   Computation of the error-term sum of squares (SS_{error}): Simply subtract SS_{shock} (Step 6), SS_{list} (Step 7), SS_{rate} (Step 8), $SS_{shock \times list}$ (Step 9),

$SS_{shock \times rate}$ (Step 10), $SS_{list \times rate}$ (Step 11), and $SS_{shock \times list \times rate}$ (Step 12) from the SS_{total} (Step 5).

$$4782 - 20 - 1645 - 2093 - 54 - 26 - 248 - 4 = \mathbf{692} = SS_{error}$$

Step 14. All of the computations based directly on the data have been completed. However, since the F ratios are ratios of mean squares, the degrees of freedom (df) for each of the components must be computed.

df for SS_t = the total number of measures (see Step 1) minus 1.

$$48 - 1 = \mathbf{47}$$

df for SS_{shock} = the number of shock conditions minus 1.

$$2 - 1 = \mathbf{1}$$

df for SS_{list} = the number of list difficulties minus 1.

$$2 - 1 = \mathbf{1}$$

df for SS_{rate} = the number of rates of presentation minus 1.

$$2 - 1 = \mathbf{1}$$

df for $SS_{shock \times list}$ = the df for shock times the df for list.

$$1 \times 1 = \mathbf{1}$$

df for $SS_{shock \times rate}$ = the df for shock times the df for rate.

$$1 \times 1 = \mathbf{1}$$

df for $SS_{list \times rate}$ = the df for list items the df for rate.

$$1 \times 1 = \mathbf{1}$$

df for $SS_{shock \times list \times rate}$ = the df for shock times the df for list times the df for rate.

$$1 \times 1 \times 1 = \mathbf{1}$$

df for SS_{error} = the df for SS_t minus the df for SS_{shock}, SS_{list}, SS_{rate}, $SS_{shock \times list}$, $SS_{list \times rate}$, $SS_{shock \times rate}$, and $SS_{shock \times list \times rate}$.

Step 15. The mean squares are then computed as SS/df.

ms_t (This value is not needed for the analysis.)

$$ms_{shock} = \frac{(\text{Step 6})}{1} = \frac{20}{1} = \mathbf{20}$$

$$ms_{list} = \frac{(\text{Step 7})}{1} = \frac{1645}{1} = \mathbf{1645}$$

$$ms_{rate} = \frac{(Step\ 8)}{1} = \frac{2093}{1} = \mathbf{2093}$$

$$ms_{shock \times list} = \frac{(Step\ 9)}{1} = \frac{54}{1} = \mathbf{54}$$

$$ms_{shock \times rate} = \frac{(Step\ 10)}{1} = \frac{26}{1} = \mathbf{26}$$

$$ms_{list \times rate} = \frac{(Step\ 11)}{1} = \frac{248}{1} = \mathbf{248}$$

$$ms_{shock \times list \times rate} = \frac{(Step\ 12)}{1} = \frac{4}{1} = \mathbf{4}$$

$$ms_{error} = \frac{(Step\ 13)}{40} = \frac{692}{40} = \mathbf{17.30}$$

Step 16. The several F ratios are then computed as

$$\frac{ms_{shock}}{ms_{error}} \qquad \frac{ms_{shock \times list}}{ms_{error}}$$

$$\frac{ms_{list}}{ms_{error}} \qquad \frac{ms_{shock \times rate}}{ms_{error}}$$

$$\frac{ms_{rate}}{ms_{error}} \qquad \frac{ms_{list \times rate}}{ms_{error}}$$

$$\frac{ms_{shock \times list \times rate}}{ms_{error}}$$

Step 17. Table the final analysis as follows:

Source	SS	df	ms	F	p
Total	4782	47	—	—	—
Shock	20	1	20	1.16	n.s.
List	1645	1	1645	95.09	<.001
Rate	2093	1	2093	120.98	<.001
Shock × list	54	1	54	3.12	n.s.
Shock × rate	26	1	26	1.50	n.s.
List × rate	248	1	248	14.34	<.001
Shock × list × rate	4	1	4	23	n.s.
Error	692	40	17.30	—	—

Therefore, it is concluded (see Appendix E) that list difficulty and presentation rate affect error-making in a word-memorizing situation, and that the effects of list difficulty and presentation rate are interactive.   ■

SECTION 4.4
Treatments-by-Levels Design

Occasionally a researcher is faced with a group of subjects who either come from distinctly different populations or are tested at different times and places. In this case, it might be reasonable to expect the subjects in the various samples to differ in some systematic fashion. To control for this source of bias and confusion, a variation of the factorial design, the treatments-by-levels design, is appropriate.

Points to Consider When Using the Treatments-by-Levels Design

1. For each subject in the experimental groups, there can be only *one* score. As in the factorial designs, if many measures are taken for each subject, these must be combined so that there is only one score for each subject.
2. It is best to have an equal number of subjects in each experimental group and within each level or replication. In most experiments, ten to fifteen subjects per group are used.
3. The number of treatment groups is arbitrary. The same is true of the number of levels or replications employed. However, it is rare that more than four or five groups or levels are employed.

■ **EXAMPLE**

One of the most common uses of the treatments-by-levels design occurs in the field of education, when children are drawn from various schools that differ markedly in quality and location. For this example, assume that an experimenter wishes to investigate the effectiveness of three different methods of teaching arithmetic. Because there is reason to believe that the success of the teaching methods depends on the overall quality of the school and the type of students enrolled, one school is selected from an upper-class neighborhood, another from a middle-class area, and a third from a slum area. In each school, one class is taught by the usual teacher-only method, a second class by a teacher plus teaching machines, and the third by television plus teaching machines. An achievement test is given to each student at the beginning of the term and again at the end. The score recorded for each student is the amount of improvement (in test points) shown.

Step 1. After the experiment has been completed, table the data as follows.

LEVEL 1 (UPPER-CLASS SCHOOL)					
Group 1 (Teacher only)		Group 2 (Teacher + machines)		Group 3 (Television + machines)	
Subject	Points	Subject	Points	Subjects	Points
S_1	74	S_7	94	S_{13}	87
S_2	79	S_8	96	S_{14}	76
S_3	94	S_9	92	S_{15}	94
S_4	90	S_{10}	84	S_{16}	92
S_5	88	S_{11}	85	S_{17}	98
S_6	87	S_{12}	89	S_{18}	71

LEVEL 2 (MIDDLE-CLASS SCHOOL)					
Group 4		Group 5		Group 6	
S_{19}	70	S_{25}	76	S_{31}	70
S_{20}	78	S_{26}	91	S_{32}	86
S_{21}	96	S_{27}	94	S_{33}	91
S_{22}	86	S_{28}	86	S_{34}	74
S_{23}	80	S_{29}	87	S_{35}	88
S_{24}	92	S_{30}	91	S_{36}	77

LEVEL 3 (LOWER-CLASS SCHOOL)					
Group 7		Group 8		Group 9	
S_{37}	92	S_{43}	91	S_{49}	70
S_{38}	86	S_{44}	84	S_{50}	86
S_{39}	84	S_{45}	80	S_{51}	81
S_{40}	71	S_{46}	73	S_{52}	71
S_{41}	74	S_{47}	69	S_{53}	65
S_{42}	78	S_{48}	71	S_{54}	63

Step 2. Add the scores in each group.

LEVEL 1		
Group 1	Group 2	Group 3
74	94	87
79	96	76
⋮	⋮	⋮
Sums: **512**	**540**	**518**

LEVEL 2		
Group 4	Group 5	Group 6
70	76	70
78	91	86
$\vdots$	$\vdots$	$\vdots$

Sums: **502**   **525**   **486**

LEVEL 3		
Group 7	Group 8	Group 9
92	91	70
86	84	86
$\vdots$	$\vdots$	$\vdots$

Sums: **485**   **468**   **436**

Step 3. Square each number in the entire table (Step 1), and add these squared values.

$$74^2 + 79^2 + \cdots + 63^2 = \mathbf{374{,}776}$$

Step 4. Add the sums of each group (Step 2) to get the grand sum of the entire table.

$$512 + 540 + 518 + 502 + 525 + 486 + 485 + 468 + 436 = \mathbf{4472}$$

Then, square this value, and divide by the total number of measures recorded in the table (see Step 1). This yields the correction term.

$$\frac{4472^2}{54} = \frac{19{,}998{,}784}{54} = \mathbf{370{,}347}$$

Step 5. Computation of the total sum of squares (SS_t): Simply subtract the correction term (Step 4) from the sum of the squared measures (Step 3).

$$374{,}776 - 370{,}347 = \mathbf{4429} = SS_t$$

Step 6. Computation of the effects of levels (the overall performance of students in the upper-, middle-, and lower-class schools): First, add the sums of the three levels, disregarding the other dimension, method of teaching (see Step 2).

$$512 + 540 + 518 = \mathbf{1570} = \text{sum for the upper-class school}$$

$$502 + 525 + 486 = \mathbf{1513} = \text{sum for the middle-class school}$$

$$485 + 468 + 436 = \mathbf{1389} = \text{sum for the lower-class school}$$

Then, square the above sums, divide by the number of measures on which each of the sums was based, and add the quotients.

$$\frac{1570^2}{18} + \frac{1513^2}{18} + \frac{1389^2}{18} = \frac{6,683,390}{18} = \mathbf{371,299}$$

Then, subtract the correction term from the above value.

$$371,299 - 370,347 = \mathbf{952} = SS_{levels}$$

Step 7.   Computation of the treatment effects (the overall effects of, teacher only, teacher plus machines, and television plus machines): First, add the sums of the three treatment conditions, disregarding the levels dimension (see Step 2).

$$512 + 502 + 485 = \mathbf{1499} = \text{sum for teacher-only groups}$$

$$540 + 525 + 468 = \mathbf{1533} = \text{sum for teacher-plus-machines groups}$$

$$518 + 486 + 436 = \mathbf{1440} = \text{sum for television-plus-machines groups}$$

Then, square the above sums, divide by the number of measures on which each was based, and add the quotients.

$$\frac{1499^2}{18} + \frac{1533^2}{18} + \frac{1440^2}{18} = \frac{6,670,690}{18} = \mathbf{370,594}$$

Then, subtract the correction term from the above value.

$$370,594 - 370,347 = \mathbf{247} = SS_{treatments}$$

Step 8.   Computation of the interactive effects of treatments and levels: First, square the sums of each of the experimental groups (Step 2), divide by the number of measures on which each of the sums was based, then add the quotients.

$$\frac{512^2}{6} + \frac{540^2}{6} + \frac{518^2}{6} + \frac{502^2}{6} + \frac{525^2}{6} + \frac{486^2}{6} + \frac{485^2}{6} + \frac{468^2}{6} + \frac{436^2}{6}$$

$$= \frac{2,230,238}{6} = \mathbf{371,706}$$

Then, subtract the correction term (Step 4), the SS_{levels} (Step 6), and the $SS_{treatments}$ (Step 7) from the above value.

$$371,706 - 370,347 - 952 - 247 = \mathbf{160} = SS_{treatments \times levels}$$

Step 9.   Computation of the error-term sum of squares (SS_{error}): Simply subtract SS_{levels} (Step 6), $SS_{treatments}$ (Step 7), and $SS_{treatments \times levels}$ (Step 8) from SS_t (Step 5).

$$4429 - 952 - 247 - 160 = \mathbf{3070} = SS_{error}$$

Step 10. All computations based directly on the data have now been completed. Since the F ratios are ratios of mean squares, the degrees of freedom (df) must be computed for each of the components.

df for SS_t	= the total number of measures (see Step 1) minus 1.
	$54 - 1 = \mathbf{53}$
df for SS_{levels}	= the number of levels used in the experiment minus 1.
	$3 - 1 = \mathbf{2}$
df for $SS_{treatments}$	= the number of treatment conditions minus 1.
	$3 - 1 = \mathbf{2}$
df for $SS_{treatments\times levels}$	= df for treatments times the df for levels.
	$2 \times 2 = \mathbf{4}$
df for SS_{error}	= the df for SS_t minus the dfs for SS_{levels}, $SS_{treatments}$, and $SS_{treatments\times levels}$.
	$53 - 2 - 2 - 4 = \mathbf{45}$

Step 11. The mean squares are then computed as SS/df.

ms_t	(This value is not needed for the analysis.)
ms_{levels}	$= \dfrac{(Step\ 6)}{2} = \dfrac{952}{2} = \mathbf{476}$
$ms_{treatments}$	$= \dfrac{(Step\ 7)}{2} = \dfrac{247}{2} = \mathbf{123.5}$
$ms_{treatments\times levels}$	$= \dfrac{(Step\ 8)}{4} = \dfrac{160}{4} = \mathbf{40}$
ms_{error}	$= \dfrac{(Step\ 9)}{45} = \dfrac{3070}{45} = \mathbf{68.22}$

Step 12. The several F ratios are then computed as

$$\frac{ms_{levels}}{ms_{error}} \qquad \frac{ms_{treatments}}{ms_{error}} \qquad \frac{ms_{treatments\times levels}}{ms_{error}}$$

Step 13.   Table the final analysis as follows:

Source	SS	df	ms	F	p
Total	4429	53	—	—	—
Levels	952	2	476	6.98	<.005
Treatments	247	2	123.5	1.81	n.s.
Treatments × levels	160	4	40	.58	n.s.
Error	3070	45	68.22	—	—

Therefore, it is concluded (see Appendix E) that while the expected differences in the overall arithmetic achievements of the students in the three schools were present, there were no differences due to the three methods of instruction and the methods of instruction did not interact with the schools of the students.   ■

SECTION 4.5
Treatments-by-Subjects, or Repeated-Measures, Design

Whenever two or more different treatments are given to the same subjects, a very powerful statistical design can be used. This design, which permits analysis of repeated measures on the same individuals, is known by various names and is treated in considerable detail in most textbooks.

Points to Consider When Using the Treatments-by-Subjects Design

1. Each subject is tested under, and a score is entered for, each treatment condition.
2. The number of subjects employed and the number of treatments given each subject is arbitrary. However, most experiments use ten to fifteen subjects, and it is rare that more than four or five treatments are compared.

■ EXAMPLE
In addition to analyzing the effects of successive experimental manipulations, this design is often used to indicate and evaluate the stability of measures over a prolonged period. This use will be illustrated in the following example. Assume that an experimenter wishes to know whether the mean scores on an intelligence test remain stable from year to year or whether they differ to a degree larger than could be expected by chance alone. To answer this question, the experimenter

chooses twenty subjects, all twelve years old, and obtains an IQ score for each. Then, each year after that, for three years, another IQ test is given to the same twenty students. The IQ scores on each of these four tests are the data recorded.

Step 1. At the end of four years, when the data have been collected, they are tabled as follows:

Subject	IQ—Age 12	IQ—Age 13	IQ—Age 14	IQ—Age 15
S_1	98	102	113	108
S_2	104	100	105	111
S_3	126	131	128	136
S_4	74	79	84	81
S_5	86	85	90	88
S_6	92	92	88	95
S_7	98	96	101	103
S_8	110	115	107	118
S_9	118	122	129	120
S_{10}	97	96	104	100
S_{11}	83	85	80	88
S_{12}	124	128	135	138
S_{13}	133	132	130	138
S_{14}	101	112	115	114
S_{15}	112	108	116	114
S_{16}	96	91	95	98
S_{17}	89	96	90	97
S_{18}	95	101	99	104
S_{19}	87	95	94	97
S_{20}	93	99	92	102

Step 2. Add the scores in each treatment (age level in the present example) to get the sum for each treatment.

Subject	Age 12	Age 13	Age 14	Age 15
S_1	98	102	113	108
S_2	104	100	105	111
⋮	⋮	⋮	⋮	⋮
Sums:	**2016**	**2065**	**2095**	**2150**

Step 3. Square each number in the table (Step 1), and add these squared values together.

$$98^2 + 104^2 + \cdots + 102^2 = \mathbf{886{,}376}$$

Step 4.   Add the sums for each treatment (Step 2) to obtain a grand total for the entire table.

$$2016 + 2065 + 2095 + 2150 = \textbf{8326}$$

Step 5.   Square the grand total (Step 4), and divide by the total number of measures recorded (see Step 1). This yields the correction term.

$$\frac{8326^2}{80} = \textbf{866,528}$$

Step 6.   Computation of the total sum of squares (SS_t): Subtract the correction term (Step 5) from the sum of the squared values obtained in Step 3.

$$886,376 - 866,528 = \textbf{19,848} = SS_t$$

Step 7.   Add the four scores recorded for each subject, and write the twenty sums in a column.

Subject	Age 12		Age 13		Age 14		Age 15	Sums
S_1	98	+	102	+	113	+	108	**421**
S_2	104	+	100	+	105	+	111	**420**
$\vdots$	$\vdots$		$\vdots$		$\vdots$		$\vdots$	$\vdots$
S_{20}	93	+	99	+	92	+	102	**386**

Step 8.   Square all the sums obtained in Step 7, and add the squares.

$$412^2 + 420^2 + \cdots + 386^2 = \textbf{3,540,914}$$

Step 9.   Divide the value obtained in Step 8 by the number of scores that were added to get each of the sums in Step 7. (In the present example, 4 numbers were added to get each of the sums.)

$$\frac{3,540,914}{4} = \textbf{885,228}$$

Step 10.   Computation of the sum of squares for subjects (SS_{subjects}): Subtract the correction term (Step 5) from the value obtained in Step 9.

$$885,228 - 866,528 = \textbf{18,700} = SS_{\text{subjects}}$$

Step 11.   Square each of the values obtained in Step 2, and add the squares.

$$2016^2 + 2065^2 + 2095^2 + 2150^2 = \textbf{17,340,006}$$

Then, divide by the number of scores on which each sum in Step 2 was based. (In the present example, this would be 20.)

$$\frac{17,340,006}{20} = \mathbf{867,000}$$

Step 12. Computation of the sum of squares for treatments ($SS_{treatments}$): Subtract the correction term (Step 5) from the value of Step 11.

$$867,000 - 866,528 = \mathbf{472} = SS_{treatments}$$

Step 13. Computation of the error-term sum of squares (SS_{error}): Subtract the $SS_{subjects}$ (Step 10) and the $SS_{treatments}$ (Step 12) from the SS_t (Step 6).

$$19,848 - 18,700 - 472 = \mathbf{676} = SS_{error}$$

Step 14. All computations based directly on the data have been completed. However, since the test of significance (F ratio) is a ratio of the mean squares, these values must be computed. To do this, the degrees of freedom (df) must be determined for each of the components, as follows:

df for SS_t = the total number of measures (see Step 1) minus 1.

$$80 - 1 = \mathbf{79}$$

df for $SS_{subjects}$ = the total number of subjects used in the experiment minus 1.

$$20 - 1 = \mathbf{19}$$

df for $SS_{treatments}$ = the total number of treatments given each subject minus 1.

$$4 - 1 = \mathbf{3}$$

df for SS_{error} = the total df minus the df for subjects and the df for treatments.

$$79 - 19 - 3 = \mathbf{57}$$

Step 15. The mean squares are then computed as SS/df.

ms_t (This value is not needed for analysis.)

$ms_{subjects}$ (This also is not needed.)

$$ms_{treatments} = \frac{(\text{Step 12})}{3} = \frac{472}{3} = \mathbf{157.33}$$

$$ms_{error} = \frac{(\text{Step 13})}{57} = \frac{676}{57} = \mathbf{11.86}$$

Step 16. Table the analysis as follows. The test of significance (F) is equal to $ms_{treatment}/ms_{error}$.

Source	SS	df	ms	F	p
Total	19,848	79	—	—	—
Subjects	18,700	19	—	—	—
Treatments	472	3	157.33	13.27	< .001
Error	676	57	11.86	—	—

Since the F value of 13.27, with df of 3 and 57, would occur by chance less than once in one thousand times (see Appendix E), it is concluded that the IQ scores were not stable over the four-year period.   ■

SECTION 4.6

Treatments-by-Treatments-by-Subjects, or Repeated-Measures: Two Factors, Design

The treatments-by-treatments-by-subjects design is a very efficient analysis that can be used when all treatments in a two-factor experiment are administered to each subject.

Points to Consider When Using the Treatments-by-Treatments-by-Subjects Design

1. Each subject is tested and scored for each treatment condition within both of the factors.
2. The number of subjects employed and the number of treatments given within each factor are arbitrary. However, most experiments use ten to fifteen subjects, and it is rare that the effects of more than four or five treatments within either or both factors are compared.

■ **EXAMPLE**

Consider a memorization experiment where the experimenter wants to study the relationship between short-term and long-term retention on the one hand and easy and difficult items on the other. The experimenter has each subject learn both easy and difficult items, measuring the retention of these items over short and long periods of time. In this experiment, the experimenter is not interested in analyzing performance over several trials. Therefore, the experimenter will consider only the total number of correct responses. (*Note:* If he were also to consider trials, this would add another dimension and make this a treatments-by-treatments-by-treatments-by-subjects design.) The scores recorded for each subject are the subject's total number of correct responses on the easy and difficult items when the subject is tested after a short and after a long period of time.

Step 1. Table the data as follows. Remember, each subject performs under each treatment condition within both factors.

Subject	Short-term retention		Long-term retention	
	Easy items	Difficult items	Easy items	Difficult items
S_1	83	100	75	40
S_2	100	83	71	41
S_3	100	100	50	43
S_4	89	92	74	47
S_5	100	90	83	62
S_6	100	100	100	70
S_7	92	92	72	44
S_8	100	89	83	62
S_9	50	54	33	38
S_{10}	100	100	72	50

Step 2. Add the scores in each treatment for both factors.

Subject	STR–easy	STR–difficult	LTR–easy	LTR–difficult
S_1	83	100	75	40
S_2	100	83	71	41
⋮	⋮	⋮	⋮	⋮
Sums:	**914**	**900**	**713**	**497**

Step 3. Square each number in the table (Step 1), and add the squares.

$$83^2 + 100^2 + \cdots + 50^2 = \mathbf{248{,}212}$$

Step 4. Add the sums for each treatment for both factors (Step 2) to obtain a grand total for the entire table.

$$914 + 900 + 713 + 497 = \mathbf{3024}$$

Step 5. Square the grand total of Step 4, and divide by the total number of measures recorded in Step 1 (40 in this example). This yields the correction term.

$$\frac{3024^2}{40} = \frac{9{,}144{,}576}{40} = \mathbf{228{,}614.4}$$

Step 6.   Subtract the correction term (Step 5) from the sum of the squares obtained in Step 3.

$$248,212 - 228,614.4 = \textbf{19,597.6} = SS_t$$

Step 7.   Add all the scores recorded for each subject in Step 1, and put these sums in a column.

	Short-term retention			Long-term retention		
Subject	Easy items		Difficult items	Easy items	Difficult items	Sums
S_1	83	+	100	+	75	+	40	**298**
S_2	100	+	83	+	71	+	41	**295**
⋮	⋮		⋮		⋮		⋮	⋮
S_{10}	100	+	100	+	72	+	50	**322**

Step 8.   Square all the sums obtained in Step 7, and add the squares.

$$298^2 + 295^2 + \cdots + 322^2 = \textbf{937,872}$$

Step 9.   Divide the value obtained in Step 8 by the number of scores that were added to get each of the sums in Step 7 (4 scores were added in this example).

$$\frac{937,872}{4} = \textbf{234,468}$$

Step 10.   Subtract the correction term of Step 5 from the value of Step 9.

$$234,468 - 228,614.4 = \textbf{5853.6} = SS_{\text{subjects}}$$

Step 11.   Computation of the sum of squares for the first factor (the differential effects of STR versus LTR—$SS_{\text{retention}}$): First, add the sums of the STR and the LTR treatments (Step 2), disregarding the difficulty-of-items dimension.

$$914 + 900 = \textbf{1814} = \text{sum of the STR treatment}$$

$$713 + 497 = \textbf{1210} = \text{sum of the LTR treatment}$$

Then, square the above sums, divide by the number of measures on which each sum was based (20 in this example), and add the quotients.

$$\frac{1814^2}{20} + \frac{1210^2}{20} = \frac{4,754,696}{20} = \textbf{237,734.8}$$

Then, subtract the correction term (Step 5) from the above value.

$$237,734.8 - 228,614.4 = \textbf{9120.4} = SS_{\text{retention}}$$

Step 12.   Computation of the effects of the second factor (the effects of easy versus difficult items—$SS_{\text{difficulty}}$): First, sum the scores on the easy items and the difficult items (Step 2), disregarding the retention dimension.

$914 + 713 = \textbf{1627} =$ sum of the easy items

$900 + 497 = \textbf{1397} =$ sum of the difficult items

Then, square the above sums, divide by the number of measures on which each sum was based (20 in this example), and add the quotients.

$$\frac{1627^2}{20} + \frac{1397^2}{20} + \frac{4,598,738}{20} = \textbf{229,936.9}$$

Then, subtract the correction term (Step 5) from the above value.

$229,936.9 - 228,614.4 = \textbf{1322.5} = SS_{\text{difficulty}}$

Step 13. Computation of the interactive effects of the first and second factors ($SS_{\text{retention}\times\text{difficulty}}$): First, square the sums of each of the experimental treatments (Step 2), divide by the number of measures on which each sum was based (10 in this example), and add the quotients.

$$\frac{914^2}{10} + \frac{900^2}{10} + \frac{713^2}{10} + \frac{497^2}{10} = \frac{2,400,774}{10} = \textbf{240,077.4}$$

Then, subtract the correction term (Step 5), the sum of squares for retention (Step 11), and the sum of squares for difficulty (Step 12) from the above value.

$240,077.4 - 228,614.4 - 9120.4 - 1322.5 = \textbf{1020.1} = SS_{\text{retention}\times\text{difficulty}}$

Step 14. Computation of the error term for retention ($SS_{\text{error for retention}}$): This requires that the data be retabled as follows. For each subject, add the number of correct responses made to the tests of STR and those of LTR (disregarding the difficulty-of-items dimension).

Subject	STR	LTR
S_1	183 (83 + 100)	115 (75 + 40)
S_2	183 (100 + 83)	112 (71 + 41)
S_3	200	93
S_4	181	121
S_5	190	145
S_6	200	170
S_7	184	116
S_8	189	145
S_9	104	71
S_{10}	200	122

Then, square all the sums in the above table, and add the squares.

$183^2 + 183^2 + \cdots + 122^2 = \textbf{489,622}$

Then, divide the above value by the number of scores added to get each of the sums entered in the table in Step 14 (2 in this example).

$$\frac{489,622}{2} = \textbf{244,811}$$

Then, from this value, subtract the correction term (Step 5), the sum of squares for subjects (Step 10), and the sum of squares for retention (Step 11).

$$244{,}811 - 228{,}614.4 - 5853.6 - 9120.4 = \textbf{1222.6} = SS_{\text{error for retention}}$$

Step 15. Computation of the error term for item difficulty ($SS_{\text{error for difficulty}}$): Again, the data must first be retabled. For each subject, add the number of correct responses made on the easy and the difficult items (disregarding the retention conditions).

Subject	Easy	Difficult
S_1	158 (83 + 75)	140 (100 + 40)
S_2	171 (100 + 71)	124 (83 + 41)
S_3	150	143
S_4	163	139
S_5	183	152
S_6	200	170
S_7	164	136
S_8	183	151
S_9	83	92
S_{10}	172	150

Then, square all the sums in the above table, and add the squares.

$$158^2 + 171^2 + \cdots + 150^2 = \textbf{472{,}632}$$

Then divide this value by the number of scores added to get each of the sums in the above table (2 in this example).

$$\frac{472{,}632}{2} = \textbf{236{,}316}$$

Then, from this value, subtract the correction term (Step 5), the sum of squares for subjects (Step 10), and the sum of squares for difficulty (Step 12).

$$236{,}316 - 228{,}614.4 - 5853.6 - 1322.5 = \textbf{525.5} = SS_{\text{error for difficulty}}$$

Step 16. Computation of the error term for retention-by-difficulty interaction ($SS_{\text{error for retention}\times\text{difficulty}}$): From the total sum of squares (Step 6), subtract the sum of squares for subjects (Step 10), sum of squares for retention (Step 11), sum of squares for difficulty (Step 12), sum of squares for difficulty by retention (Step 13), error of retention (Step 14), and error for difficulty (Step 15).

$$19{,}597.6 - 5853.6 - 9120.4 - 1322.5 - 1020.1 - 1222.6 - 525.5$$

$$= \textbf{532.9} = SS_{\text{error for retention}\times\text{difficulty}}$$

Step 17. All computations based directly on the data have been completed. However, since the test of significance (F ratio) is a ratio of mean squares, the degrees of freedom must be determined for each of the components.

df for SS_t = the total number of measures recorded in Step 1 minus 1.

$$40 - 1 = \textbf{39}$$

df for $SS_{subjects}$ = the number of subjects used in experiment minus 1.

$$10 - 1 = \textbf{9}$$

df for $SS_{retention}$ = the number of retention conditions minus 1.

$$2 - 1 = \textbf{1}$$

df for $SS_{error\ for\ retention}$ = the df for $SS_{subjects}$ times the df for $SS_{retention}$.

$$9 \times 1 = \textbf{9}$$

df for $SS_{difficulty}$ = the number of difficulty conditions minus 1.

$$2 - 1 = \textbf{1}$$

df $SS_{error\ for\ difficulty}$ = the df for $SS_{subjects}$ times the df for $SS_{difficulty}$.

$$9 \times 1 = \textbf{9}$$

df $SS_{retention \atop \times difficulty}$ = the df for $SS_{retention}$ times the df for $SS_{difficulty}$.

$$1 \times 1 = \textbf{1}$$

df for $SS_{error\ for\ retention \atop \times difficulty}$ = the df for $SS_{subjects}$ times the df for $SS_{retention}$ times the df for $SS_{difficulty}$.

$$9 \times 1 \times 1 = \textbf{9}$$

Step 18. The desired mean squares are then computed as SS/df.

$$ms_{retention} = \frac{(Step\ 11)}{1} = \frac{9120.4}{1} = \textbf{9120.4}$$

$$ms_{difficulty} = \frac{(Step\ 12)}{1} = \frac{1322.5}{1} = \textbf{1322.5}$$

$$ms_{difficulty \times retention} = \frac{(Step\ 13)}{1} = \frac{1020.1}{1} = \textbf{1020.1}$$

$$ms_{retention\ error} = \frac{(Step\ 14)}{9} = \frac{1222.6}{9} = \textbf{135.844}$$

$$ms_{\text{difficulty error}} = \frac{(\text{Step } 15)}{9} = \frac{525.5}{9} = \textbf{58.389}$$

$$ms_{\text{difficulty}\times\text{retention error}} = \frac{(\text{Step } 16)}{9} = \frac{532.9}{9} = \textbf{59.211}$$

Step 19.   Table the analysis as follows. The tests of significance (F ratios) are computed as

$$\frac{ms_{\text{retention}}}{ms_{\text{error for retention}}} \qquad \frac{ms_{\text{difficulty}}}{ms_{\text{error for difficulty}}}$$

$$\frac{ms_{\text{difficulty}\times\text{retention}}}{ms_{\text{error for difficulty}\times\text{retention}}}$$

Source	SS	df	ms	F	p
Total	19,597.6	39	—	—	—
Subjects	5853.6	9	—	—	—
Retention	9120.4	1	9120.4	67.14	<.001
Difficulty	1322.5	1	1322.5	22.65	<.005
Difficulty × retention	1020.1	1	1020.1	17.23	<.005
Error retention	1222.6	9	135.84	—	—
Error difficulty	525.5	9	58.39	—	—
Error retention × difficulty	532.9	9	59.21	—	—

Therefore, it is concluded (see Appendix E) that:

1. the length of the retention interval had a significant effect on the amount retained;
2. the difficulty of the learned material significantly affected the amount retained;
3. the effects of difficulty of material and retention interval interacted to a significant degree.   ∎

SECTION 4.7
Two-Factor Mixed Design: Repeated Measures on One Factor

This two-factor mixed design is basically a combination of the completely randomized design and the treatments-by-subjects design. Not only does this design permit comparison of the differences in the overall performance of the subjects in the several experimental groups, but it also permits evaluation of the changes in performance shown by the subjects during the experimental session.

Points to Consider When Using the Two-Factor Mixed Design

1. If trials for observations are blocked, each block is treated as one score.
2. Although it is not necessary, it is usually best to have an equal number of subjects in each experimental group.
3. The number of experimental groups compared, the number of subjects per group, and the number of trials or observations (scores) recorded for each subject are arbitrary. However, it is rare that more than four or five experimental groups are compared in one experiment or that more than five or six scores are entered and analyzed for each subject. In most experiments, ten to fifteen subjects are assigned to each experimental group.

■ **EXAMPLE**

Assume that an experimenter wishes to determine the effects of meaningfulness of material on rate of learning. The subjects are randomly assigned to three groups, one of which must learn a low-meaningful list of nonsense syllables, the second a medium-meaningful list, and the third a high-meaningful list. All subjects are given fifteen trials, and the number of correct responses per trial is recorded. To simplify the analysis, the experimenter blocks the number of correct responses into three blocks of five trials each. Thus, the scores used in the analysis represent the number of correct responses for each successive block of five trials.

Step 1. After the experiment has been conducted, table the data as follows.

| | Group 1 (low-meaningful material) | | |
Subject	Trial block 1	Trial block 2	Trial block 3
S_1	3	3	4
S_2	3	4	4
S_3	1	3	4
S_4	1	2	3
S_5	2	3	5
S_6	4	5	6
S_7	4	5	6
S_8	1	4	5
S_9	1	4	5
S_{10}	2	3	3
S_{11}	2	2	4

	Group 2 (medium-meaningful material)		
Subject	Trial block 1	Trial block 2	Trial block 3
S_{12}	2	3	6
S_{13}	1	4	5
S_{14}	3	6	7
S_{15}	2	4	6
S_{16}	1	2	3
S_{17}	4	5	5
S_{18}	1	3	4
S_{19}	1	2	4
S_{20}	2	3	4
S_{21}	3	5	6
S_{22}	4	6	7

	Group 3 (high-meaningful material)		
S_{23}	2	4	8
S_{24}	3	6	3
S_{25}	4	7	7
S_{26}	1	7	4
S_{27}	3	7	12
S_{28}	1	4	2
S_{29}	1	5	3
S_{30}	2	5	6
S_{31}	3	6	6
S_{32}	1	5	12
S_{33}	4	9	7

Step 2. Add the scores in each group for each trial block (hereafter, referred to simply as "trials").

	Group 1		
Subject	Trial 1	Trial 2	Trial 3
S_1	3	3	4
S_2	3	4	4
$\vdots$	$\vdots$	$\vdots$	$\vdots$
Sums:	**24**	**38**	**49**

	Group 2		
S_{12}	2	3	6
S_{13}	1	4	5
$\vdots$	$\vdots$	$\vdots$	$\vdots$
Sums:	**24**	**43**	**57**

Group 3			
Subject	Trial 1	Trial 2	Trial 3
S_{23}	2	4	8
S_{24}	3	6	3
$\vdots$	$\vdots$	$\vdots$	$\vdots$
Sums:	**25**	**65**	**70**

Step 3. Obtain the sum for each group by adding the sums of the individual trials (Step 2).

$$24 + 38 + 49 = \mathbf{111} = \text{sum of Group 1}$$

$$24 + 43 + 57 = \mathbf{124} = \text{sum of Group 2}$$

$$25 + 65 + 70 = \mathbf{160} = \text{sum of Group 2}$$

Step 4. Add the scores for *each* subject in each group.

Group 1						
Subject	Trial 1		Trial 2		Trial 3	Sums
S_1	3	+	3	+	4	**10**
S_2	3	+	4	+	4	**11**
$\vdots$	$\vdots$		$\vdots$		$\vdots$	$\vdots$
S_{11}	2	+	2	+	4	**8**
Group 2						
S_{12}	2	+	3	+	6	**11**
S_{13}	1	+	4	+	5	**10**
$\vdots$	$\vdots$		$\vdots$		$\vdots$	$\vdots$
S_{22}	4	+	6	+	7	**17**
Group 3						
S_{23}	2	+	4	+	8	**14**
S_{24}	3	+	6	+	3	**12**
$\vdots$	$\vdots$		$\vdots$		$\vdots$	$\vdots$
S_{33}	4	+	9	+	7	**20**

Step 5.   Square each score in the entire table (Step 1), and add these squared values for a grand sum of the squared values.

$$3^2 + 3^2 + \cdots + 7^2 = \textbf{2043}$$

Step 6.   Add the group totals (Step 3) for the grand sum of the entire table.

$$111 + 124 + 160 = \textbf{395}$$

Step 7.   Square the grand sum (Step 6), and divide it by the total number of measures in the entire table—i.e., the number of subjects times the number of measures per subject (see Step 1). (In the present example, this would be $33 \times 3 = 99$.) The resultant value is the correction term.

$$\frac{395^2}{99} = \frac{156,025}{99} = \textbf{1576}$$

Step 8.   Computation of the total sum of squares (SS_t): Simply subtract the correction term (Step 7) from the sum of the squared scores (Step 5).

$$2043 - 1576 = \textbf{467} = SS_t$$

Between-Subjects Effects (Steps 9–11)

Step 9.   Computation of the between-subjects sum of squares (SS_b): First, square the sum of each subject's scores (Step 4), and add these squared values.

$$10^2 + 11^2 + \cdots + 20^2 = \textbf{5271}$$

Then, divide this value by the number of trials given each subject.

$$\frac{5271}{3} = \textbf{1757}$$

Then, subtract the correction term from the above value.

$$1757 - 1576 = \textbf{181} = SS_b$$

Step 10.   Computation of the effects of the experimental conditions on overall performance (SS_c): (In the present example, these are the meaningfulness effects.) First, square the sum for each experimental group (Step 3), and divide these values by the number of measures in each experimental group. (In the present example, this would be 11 subjects $\times$ 3 trials per subject, or 33.) Then, add these quotients.

$$\frac{111^2}{33} + \frac{124^2}{33} + \frac{160^2}{33} = \frac{53,297}{33} = \textbf{1615}$$

Then, subtract the correction term from the above value.

$$1615 - 1576 = \textbf{39} = SS_c$$

Step 11. Computation of the between-subjects error term (error$_b$): Simply subtract the SS$_c$ (Step 10) from the SS$_b$ (Step 9).

$$181 - 39 = \mathbf{142} = \text{error}_b$$

Within-Subjects Effects (Steps 12–15)

Step 12. Computation of the within-subjects sum of squares (SS$_w$): Simply subtract the SS$_b$ (Step 9) from the SS$_t$ (Step 8).

$$467 - 181 = \mathbf{286} = \text{SS}_w$$

Step 13. Computation of the sum of squares for trials (SS$_{tr}$): First, add the sums of Trial 1 (Step 2) for all experimental groups.

$$24 + 24 + 25 = \mathbf{73} = \text{sum for Trial 1}$$

Do the same for Trial 2 and Trial 3.

$$38 + 43 + 65 = \mathbf{146} = \text{sum for Trial 2}$$

$$49 + 57 + 70 = \mathbf{176} = \text{sum for Trial 3}$$

Then, square each of these sums, and divide the products by the number of measures on which each sum was based.

$$\frac{73^2}{33} + \frac{146^2}{33} + \frac{176^2}{33} = \frac{57{,}621}{33} = \mathbf{1746}$$

Then, subtract the correction term from the above value.

$$1746 - 1576 = \mathbf{170} = \text{SS}_{tr}$$

Step 14. Computation of the sum of squares for the trials-by-conditions interaction (SS$_{tr \times c}$): First, square the sums of each trial in each of the experimental groups (Step 2), divide by the number of measures on which each sum was based, and add these quotients.

$$\frac{24^2}{11} + \frac{38^2}{11} + \frac{49^2}{11} + \frac{24^2}{11} + \frac{43^2}{11} + \frac{57^2}{11} + \frac{25^2}{11} + \frac{65^2}{11} + \frac{70^2}{11} = \frac{19{,}845}{11}$$

$$= \mathbf{1804}$$

Then, from this value, subtract the correction term (Step 7), SS$_c$ (Step 10), and SS$_{tr}$ (Step 13).

$$1804 - 1576 - 39 - 170 = \mathbf{19} = \text{SS}_{tr \times c}$$

Step 15. Computation of the within-subjects error term (error$_w$): Simply subtract SS$_{tr}$ (Step 13) and SS$_{tr \times c}$ (Step 14) from the SS$_w$ (Step 12).

$$286 - 170 - 19 = \mathbf{97} = \text{error}_w$$

Step 16.   All computations based directly on the data have been completed:

SS_t = 467 (Step 8)
SS_b = 181 (Step 9)
SS_c = 39 (Step 10)
SS_{error_b} = 142 (Step 11)
SS_w = 286 (Step 12)
SS_{tr} = 170 (Step 13)
$SS_{tr \times c}$ = 19 (Step 14)
SS_{error_w} = 97 (Step 15)

However, since the tests of significance (*F*-tests) are ratios of *mean* squares, we must compute these values. To do this, the degrees of freedom (*df*) for each of the components must be determined, as follows:

df for SS_t = the total number of measures recorded minus 1.

$$99 - 1 = \mathbf{98}$$

df for SS_b = the total number of subjects minus 1.

$$33 - 1 = \mathbf{32}$$

df for SS_c = the total number of experimental groups minus 1.

$$3 - 1 = \mathbf{2}$$

df for SS_{error_b} = the *df* for SS_b minus the *df* for SS_c.

$$32 - 2 = \mathbf{30}$$

df for SS_w = the *df* for SS_t minus the *df* for SS_b.

$$98 - 32 = \mathbf{66}$$

df for SS_{tr} = the number of trials given each subject minus 1.

$$3 - 1 = \mathbf{2}$$

df for $SS_{tr \times c}$ = the *df* for SS_{tr} times the *df* for SS_c.

$$2 \times 2 = \mathbf{4}$$

df for SS_{error_w} = the *df* for SS_w minus the *df* for SS_{tr} minus the *df* for $SS_{tr \times c}$.

$$66 - 2 - 4 = \mathbf{60}$$

Step 17.   The mean squares are then computed as SS/df.

ms_t (This value is not needed.)
ms_b (This value is not needed.)
ms_c $= \dfrac{\text{(Step 10)}}{2} = \dfrac{39}{2} = \mathbf{19.5}$

$$ms_{error_b} = \frac{(Step\ 11)}{30} = \frac{142}{30} = \textbf{4.73}$$

$ms_w \qquad$ (This value is not needed.)

$$ms_{tr} = \frac{(Step\ 13)}{2} = \frac{170}{2} = \textbf{85}$$

$$ms_{tr \times c} = \frac{(Step\ 14)}{4} = \frac{19}{4} = \textbf{4.75}$$

$$ms_{error_w} = \frac{(Step\ 15)}{60} = \frac{97}{60} = \textbf{1.62}$$

Step 18. Table the final analysis as follows. The tests of significance (*F*-tests) are equal to

$$\frac{ms_c}{ms_{error_b}} \qquad \frac{ms_{tr}}{ms_{error_w}} \qquad \frac{ms_{tr \times c}}{ms_{error_w}}$$

Source	SS	df	ms	F	p
Total	467	98	—	—	—
Between subjects	181	32	—	—	—
Conditions	39	2	19.50	4.12	<.05
Error_b	142	30	4.73	—	—
Within subjects	286	66	—	—	—
Trials	170	2	85.00	52.46	<.001
Trials × conditions	19	4	4.75	2.93	<.05
Error_w	97	60	1.62	—	—

Hence, it is concluded (see Appendix E) that:

1. Meaningfulness of material significantly affected the overall amount learned.
2. Subjects learned as a function of practice (trials).
3. The groups of subjects learned at different rates. ∎

SECTION 4.8

Three-Factor Mixed Design: Repeated Measures on One Factor

The three-factor mixed design is basically a combination of the factorial design and the treatments-by-subjects design. Not only does this design permit examination of the effects of two factors in combination with each other, but it also permits examination of performance variations shown by the subjects during the experimental session.

Points to Consider When Using the Three-Factor Mixed Design

1. As in the other designs, if trials are blocked, each block is treated as one score.
2. It is usually best to have an equal number of subjects in each of the experimental groups. If equality cannot be obtained, the number of subjects in each group should be proportional. In most experiments, ten to fifteen subjects are assigned per group.
3. The number of experimental groups within each factor is arbitrary. However, it is rare that more than four or five groups are included in either of the two factors. Similarly, it is rare that more than five or six scores are entered and analyzed for each of the subjects.

■ EXAMPLE

Assume that an experimenter wishes to determine the effects of high and low performance expectancy in combination with failure and success feedback on the learning of verbal material. Subjects are randomly assigned to one of four groups. The subjects in Group 1 (high expectancy/failure) are initially told that they are likely to perform the task very well. During the learning period, however, they are periodically told that they are actually performing quite poorly and must try harder. Group 2 subjects (high expectancy/success) are also initially told that they are likely to perform well. During the learning period, they are told that they are indeed doing well and should continue their excellent performance. Group 3 subjects (low expectancy/failure) are initially told that their performance is likely to be very low. During the practice period, they are told that they are doing poorly, as expected, but if possible, they should try harder. Group 4 subjects (low expectancy/success) are also told that their performance is likely to be very low. During the practice period, however, they are told that they are actually doing very well and should continue their excellent performance.

The subjects in all four groups are given a total of twenty trials to learn a list of low-meaningful nonsense syllables. The number of syllables recited correctly on each trial is recorded. For analysis purposes, the experimenter blocks the scores on each of the twenty trials into four blocks of five trials each.

The number of correct responses within each of these blocks of five trials is recorded.

Step 1.   After the experiment has been conducted, table the data as follows.

Subject	Group 1 (high expectancy/failure)			
	Trial block 1	Trial block 2	Trial block 3	Trial block 4
S_1	4	6	7	9
S_2	6	7	9	11
S_3	5	8	10	13
S_4	3	4	6	9

Group 1 (high expectancy/failure)			
Subject	Trial block 1	Trial block 2	Trial block 3	Trial block 4
S_5	4	6	9	10
S_6	5	5	6	8
S_7	7	8	9	12

Group 2 (high expectancy/success)			
S_8	5	8	9	12
S_9	3	5	10	14
S_{10}	7	10	12	13
S_{11}	5	8	11	15
S_{12}	4	9	13	15
S_{13}	3	5	9	12
S_{14}	6	7	8	11

Group 3 (low expectancy/failure)			
S_{15}	3	4	4	5
S_{16}	5	6	8	9
S_{17}	5	6	6	8
S_{18}	5	6	7	8
S_{19}	3	4	4	5
S_{20}	7	7	8	7
S_{21}	6	8	8	8

Group 4 (low expectancy/success)			
S_{22}	4	8	10	14
S_{23}	5	10	14	18
S_{24}	3	7	12	18
S_{25}	5	8	11	17
S_{26}	6	11	15	19
S_{27}	6	8	10	15
S_{28}	5	11	17	20

Step 2.   Add the scores in each group for each trial block (hereafter referred to as "trial").

Group 1			
Subject	Trial 1	Trial 2	Trial 3	Trial 4
S_1	4	6	7	9
S_2	6	7	9	11
⋮	⋮	⋮	⋮	⋮
Sums:	**34**	**44**	**56**	**72**

		Group 2		
Subject	Trial 1	Trial 2	Trial 3	Trial 4
S_8	5	8	9	12
S_9	3	5	10	14
:	:	:	:	:
Sums:	**33**	**52**	**72**	**92**

		Group 3		
S_{15}	3	4	4	5
S_{16}	5	6	8	9
:	:	:	:	:
Sums:	**34**	**41**	**45**	**50**

		Group 4		
S_{22}	4	8	10	14
S_{23}	5	10	14	18
:	:	:	:	:
Sums:	**34**	**63**	**89**	**121**

Step 3.   Obtain the sum for each group by adding the sums of the individual trials.

$$34 + 44 + 56 + 72 = \mathbf{206} = \text{sum for Group 1}$$
$$33 + 52 + 72 + 92 = \mathbf{249} = \text{sum for Group 2}$$
$$34 + 41 + 45 + 50 = \mathbf{170} = \text{sum for Group 3}$$
$$34 + 63 + 89 + 121 = \mathbf{307} = \text{sum for Group 4}$$

Step 4.   Add the scores for *each* subject in each group.

				Group 1				
Subject	Trial 1		Trial 2		Trial 3		Trial 4	Sums
S_1	4	+	6	+	7	+	9	**26**
S_2	6	+	7	+	9	+	11	**33**
:	:		:		:		:	:
S_7	7	+	8	+	9	+	12	**36**

Subject	Trial 1		Trial 2		Trial 3		Trial 4	Sums
				Group 2				
S_8	5	+	8	+	9	+	12	34
S_9	3	+	5	+	10	+	14	32
⋮	⋮		⋮		⋮		⋮	⋮
S_{14}	6	+	7	+	8	+	11	32
				Group 3				
S_{15}	3	+	4	+	4	+	5	16
S_{16}	5	+	6	+	8	+	9	28
⋮	⋮		⋮		⋮		⋮	⋮
S_{21}	6	+	8	+	8	+	8	30
				Group 4				
S_{22}	4	+	8	+	10	+	14	36
S_{23}	5	+	10	+	14	+	18	47
⋮	⋮		⋮		⋮		⋮	⋮
S_{28}	5	+	11	+	17	+	20	53

Step 5.   Square each score in the entire table (Step 1), and add these squared values for the grand sum of the squared numbers.

$$4^2 + 6^2 + \cdots + 20^2 = \mathbf{9412}$$

Step 6.   Add the group totals (Step 3) to get the grand sum of the entire table.

$$206 + 249 + 170 + 307 = \mathbf{932}$$

Step 7.   Square the grand sum, and divide it by the total number of measures in the entire table—i.e., the number of subjects times the number of measures per subject (see Step 1). The value obtained is the correction term.

$$\frac{932^2}{112} = \mathbf{7755}$$

Step 8.   Computation of the total sum of squares (SS_t): Simply subtract the correction term (Step 7) from the sum of squares (Step 5).

$$9412 - 7755 = \mathbf{1657} = SS_t$$

Between-Subjects Effects (Steps 9–13)

Step 9. Computation of the between-subjects sum of squares (SS_b): First, square the sum of each subject's scores (Step 4), and add these squared values.

$$26^2 + 33^2 + \cdots + 53^2 = \textbf{33,324}$$

Then, divide by the number of trials given to each subject.

$$\frac{33,324}{4} = \textbf{8331}$$

Then, subtract the correction term (Step 7) from the above value.

$$8331 - 7755 = \textbf{576} = SS_b$$

Step 10. Computation of the effects of the first experimental condition on overall performance (the overall effects of high versus low expectancy—$SS_{expectancy}$): First, sum the scores of the two expectancy groups (Step 3), disregarding the success or failure feedback.

$$\begin{aligned}
206 &= \text{sum for Group 1 (high expectancy/failure)}\\
+\ 249 &= \text{sum for Group 2 (high expectancy/success)}\\
\hline
\textbf{455} &= \text{sum for all high expectancy subjects}
\end{aligned}$$

$$\begin{aligned}
170 &= \text{sum for Group 3 (low expectancy/failure)}\\
+\ 307 &= \text{sum for Group 4 (low expectancy/success)}\\
\hline
\textbf{477} &= \text{sum for all low expectancy subjects}
\end{aligned}$$

Then, square the sums of the two experimental conditions obtained above, and divide each product by the number of measures added to get each of the sums. (In the present example, the divisor is 56 in both cases: 7 subjects per group $\times$ 2 groups $\times$ 4 trials per subject.) Then, add the quotients.

$$\frac{455^2}{56} + \frac{477^2}{56} = \textbf{7759}$$

Then, subtract the correct term (Step 7) from the above value.

$$7759 - 7755 = \textbf{4} = SS_{expectancy}$$

Step 11. Computation of the effects of the second experimental condition on overall performance (the effects of failure versus success feedback—$SS_{feedback}$): First, sum the scores of the two failure and success groups (Step 3), disregarding the high or low expectancy.

$$\begin{aligned}
206 &= \text{sum for Group 1 (high expectancy/failure)}\\
+\ 170 &= \text{sum for Group 3 (low expectancy/failure)}\\
\hline
\textbf{376} &= \text{sum for all subjects who "failed"}
\end{aligned}$$

$$\begin{aligned}
249 &= \text{sum for Group 2 (high expectancy/success)}\\
+\ 307 &= \text{sum for Group 4 (low expectancy/success)}\\
\hline
\textbf{556} &= \text{sum for all subjects who "succeeded"}
\end{aligned}$$

Then, square the sums of these two experimental conditions, and divide by the number of measures added to get each sum. (Here, each sum was obtained by adding 56 scores.) Then, add the quotients.

$$\frac{376^2}{56} + \frac{556^2}{56} = \textbf{8045}$$

Then, subtract the correction term (Step 7) from the above value.

$$8045 - 7755 = \textbf{290} = SS_{feedback}$$

Step 12.   Computation of the interactive effects of the two experimental conditions: (In this example, we are attempting to determine whether the effects of failure or success feedback are influenced by the expectancy of the subject— $SS_{expectancy \times feedback}$.) First, square the sum of each of the experimental groups (Step 3); then, divide these products by the number of measures added to get each. (Here, 28 scores were added.) Then add the quotients.

$$\frac{206^2}{28} + \frac{249^2}{28} + \frac{170^2}{28} + \frac{307^2}{28} = \textbf{8128}$$

Then, from this value, subtract the correction term (Step 7), the $SS_{expectancy}$ (Step 10), and the $SS_{feedback}$ (Step 11).

$$8128 - 7755 - 4 - 290 = \textbf{79} = SS_{expectancy \times feedback}$$

Step 13.   Computation of the between-subjects error term (error$_b$): Simply subtract the $SS_{expectancy}$ (Step 10), $SS_{feedback}$ (Step 11), and $SS_{expectancy \times feedback}$ (Step 12) from the SS_b (Step 9).

$$576 - 4 - 290 - 79 = \textbf{203} = error_b$$

Within-Subjects Effects (Steps 14–19)

Step 14.   Computation of the within-subjects sum of squares (SS_w): Simply subtract the SS_b (Step 9) from the SS_t (Step 8).

$$1657 - 576 = \textbf{1081} = SS_w$$

Step 15.   Computation of the sum of squares for trials (SS_{trials}): First, add the sums of each trial for *all* experimental groups (Step 2).

$$34 + 33 + 34 + 34 = \textbf{135} = \text{sum of Trial 1}$$
$$44 + 52 + 41 + 63 = \textbf{200} = \text{sum of Trial 2}$$
$$56 + 72 + 45 + 89 = \textbf{262} = \text{sum of Trial 3}$$
$$72 + 92 + 50 + 121 = \textbf{335} = \text{sum of Trial 4}$$

Then, square each of these sums, divide each square by the number of measures on which that sum was based, and add the quotients.

$$\frac{135^2}{28} + \frac{200^2}{28} + \frac{262^2}{28} + \frac{335^2}{28} = \textbf{8539}$$

Then, subtract the correction term (Step 7) from the above value.

$$8539 - 7755 = \mathbf{784} = SS_{trials}$$

Step 16. Computation of the sum of squares for the trials-by-first-condition interaction (here, the trials-by-expectancy interaction—$SS_{trials \times expectancy}$): First, sum the scores of the two expectancy groups on each trial (Step 2), disregarding the failure or success feedback.

	Trial 1	Trial 2	Trial 3	Trial 4
Group 1 (high expectancy/failure)	34	44	56	72
Group 2 (high expectancy/success)	33	52	72	92
Sums of all high-expectancy $S_s =$	**67**	**86**	**128**	**164**
Group 3 (low expectancy/failure)	34	41	45	50
Group 4 (low expectancy/success)	34	63	89	121
Sum of all low-expectancy $S_s =$	**68**	**104**	**134**	**171**

Then, square the sums of each trial, divide by the number of measures on which each of the sums was based, and add the quotients together.

$$\frac{67^2}{14} + \frac{96^2}{14} + \frac{128^2}{14} + \frac{164^2}{14} + \frac{68^2}{14} + \frac{104^2}{14} + \frac{134^2}{14} + \frac{171^2}{14} = \mathbf{8544}$$

Then, from this value, subtract the correction term (Step 7), $SS_{expectancy}$ (Step 10), and SS_{trials} (Step 15).

$$8544 - 7755 - 4 - 784 = \mathbf{1} = SS_{trials \times expectancy}$$

Step 17. Computation of the sum of squares for the trials-by-second-condition interaction (here, the trials-by-feedback interaction—$SS_{trials \times feedback}$): First, sum the scores of the two failure or success groups on each trial (Step 2), disregarding high and low expectancy.

	Trial 1	Trial 2	Trial 3	Trial 4
Group 1 (high expectancy/failure)	34	44	56	72
Group 3 (low expectancy/failure)	34	41	45	50
Sums for all "failure" $S_s =$	**68**	**85**	**101**	**122**
Group 2 (high expectancy/success)	33	52	72	92
Group 4 (low expectancy/success)	34	63	89	121
Sums for all "success" $S_s =$	**67**	**115**	**161**	**213**

Then, square the sums of each trial, divide by the number of measures on which each of the sums was based, and add the quotients together.

$$\frac{68^2}{14} + \frac{85^2}{14} + \frac{101^2}{14} + \frac{122^2}{14} + \frac{67^2}{14} + \frac{115^2}{14} + \frac{161^2}{14} + \frac{213^2}{14} = \mathbf{8996}$$

Then, from this value, subtract the correction term (Step 7), $SS_{feedback}$ (Step 11), and SS_{trials} (Step 15).

$$8996 - 7755 - 290 - 784 = \mathbf{167} = SS_{trials \times feedback}$$

Step 18. Computation of the sum of squares for the trials-by-first-condition-by-second-condition interaction (here, the interaction of trials by expectancy by feedback—$SS_{trials \times expectancy \times feedback}$): First, square the sums of each trial in each of the experimental groups (Step 2). Divide each squared value by the number of measures on which each sum was based, then add the quotients together.

$$\frac{34^2}{7} + \cdots + \frac{72^2}{7} + \frac{33^2}{7} + \cdots + \frac{92^2}{7} + \frac{34^2}{7}$$

$$+ \cdots + \frac{50^2}{7} + \frac{34^2}{7} + \cdots + \frac{121^2}{7} = \frac{63,902}{7} = \mathbf{9129}$$

Then, from this value, subtract the correction term (Step 7), $SS_{expectancy}$ (Step 10), $SS_{feedback}$ (Step 11), $SS_{expectancy \times feedback}$ (Step 12), SS_{trials} (Step 15), $SS_{trials \times expectancy}$ (Step 16), and $SS_{trials \times feedback}$ (Step 17).

$$9129 - 7755 - 4 - 290 - 79 - 784 - 1 - 167$$

$$= \mathbf{49} = SS_{trials \times expectancy \times feedback}$$

Step 19. Computation of the within-subjects error term ($error_w$): Subtract SS_{trials} (Step 15), $SS_{trials \times expectancy}$ (Step 16), $SS_{trials \times feedback}$ (Step 17), and $SS_{trials \times expectancy \times feedback}$ (Step 18) from SS_w (Step 14).

$$1081 - 784 - 1 - 167 - 49 = \mathbf{80} = error_w$$

Step 20. All computations have now been completed.

SS_t	= 1657 (Step 8)
SS_b	= 576 (Step 9)
$SS_{expectancy}$	= 4 (Step 10)
$SS_{feedback}$	= 290 (Step 11)
$SS_{expectancy \times feedback}$	= 79 (Step 12)
SS_{error_b}	= 203 (Step 13)
SS_w	= 1081 (Step 14)
SS_{trials}	= 784 (Step 15)
$SS_{trials \times expectancy}$	= 1 (Step 16)
$SS_{trials \times feedback}$	= 167 (Step 17)
$SS_{trials \times expectancy \times feedback}$	= 49 (Step 18)
SS_{error_w}	= 80 (Step 19)

However, since the tests of significance (F-tests) are ratios of *mean* squares, we must compute these values. To do so, the degrees of freedom (df) for each of the components must be determined, as follows.

df for SS_t = the total number of measures recorded minus 1.

$$112 - 1 = \mathbf{111}$$

df for SS_b = the total number of subjects minus 1.

$$28 - 1 = \mathbf{27}$$

df for $SS_{expectancy}$ = the number of expectancy groups minus 1.

$$2 - 1 = \mathbf{1}$$

df for $SS_{feedback}$ = the number of feedback groups minus 1.

$$2 - 1 = \mathbf{1}$$

df for $SS_{expectancy \times feedback}$ = the df for expectancy times the df for feedback.

$$1 \times 1 = \mathbf{1}$$

df for SS_{error_b} = the df for SS_b minus the df for expectancy feedback and expectancy by feedback.

$$27 - 1 - 1 - 1 = \mathbf{24}$$

df for SS_w = the df for the SS_t minus the df for SS_b.

$$111 - 27 = \mathbf{84}$$

df for SS_{trials} = the number of trials given each subject minus 1.

$$4 - 1 = \mathbf{3}$$

df for $SS_{trials \times expectancy}$ = the df for SS_{trials} times the df for $SS_{expectancy}$.

$$3 \times 1 = \mathbf{3}$$

df for $SS_{trials \times feedback}$ = the df for SS_{trials} times the df for $SS_{feedback}$.

df for $SS_{trials \times expectancy \times feedback}$ = the df for SS_{trials} times the df for $SS_{feedback}$ times the df for $SS_{expectancy}$.

$$3 \times 1 \times 1 = \mathbf{3}$$

df for SS_{error_w} = the df for SS_w minus the df for SS_{trials}, $SS_{trials \times expectancy}$, $SS_{trials \times feedback}$, and $SS_{trials \times expectancy \times feedback}$.

$$84 - 3 - 3 - 3 - 3 = \mathbf{72}$$

Step 21. The mean squares are then computed as SS/df.

ms_t (This value is not needed.)

ms_b (This value is not needed.)

$$ms_{expectancy} = \frac{(\text{Step 10})}{1} = \frac{4}{1} = 4$$

$$ms_{feedback} = \frac{(\text{Step 11})}{1} = \frac{290}{1} = 290$$

$$ms_{expectancy \times feedback} = \frac{(\text{Step 12})}{1} = \frac{79}{1} = 79$$

$$ms_{error_b} = \frac{(\text{Step 13})}{24} = \frac{203}{24} = 8.46$$

ms_w (This value is not needed.)

$$ms_{trials} = \frac{(\text{Step 15})}{3} = \frac{784}{8} = 231.33$$

$$ms_{trials \times expectancy} = \frac{(\text{Step 16})}{3} = \frac{1}{3} = .33$$

$$ms_{trials \times feedback} = \frac{(\text{Step 17})}{3} = \frac{167}{3} = 55.67$$

$$ms_{trials \times expectancy \times feedback} = \frac{(\text{Step 18})}{3} = \frac{49}{3} = 16.33$$

$$ms_{error_w} = \frac{(\text{Step 19})}{72} = \frac{80}{72} = 1.11$$

Step 22. Table the final analysis as follows. The tests of significance (F ratios) are equal to the mean squares of the experimental conditions divided by their appropriate error terms.

Source	SS	df	ms	F	p
Total	1657	111	—	—	—
Between subjects	576	27	—	—	—
Expectancy (high/low)	4	1	4	<1	—
Feedback (success/failure)	290	1	290	34.27	<.001
Expectancy × feedback	79	1	79	9.34	<.001
Error$_b$	203	24	8.46	—	
Within subjects	1081	84	—	—	—
Trials	784	3	261.43	235.43	<.001
Trials × expectancy	1	3	.33	<1	—
Trials × feedback	167	3	55.67	50.15	<.001
Trials × expectancy × feedback	49	3	16.33	14.71	<.001
Error$_w$	80	72	1.11	—	—

Hence, it is concluded (see Appendix E) that:

1. the type of feedback given the subjects (failure or success) affects the overall performance level;
2. the effect of the feedback, is dependent upon (interacts with) the expectancy of the subjects;
3. all subjects did learn as a function of practice (trials);
4. the rate of learning is dependent upon the type of feedback;
5. the rate of learning is dependent upon both the expectancy level of the subjects and the feedback they receive.   ■

SECTION 4.9
Three-Factor Mixed Design: Repeated Measures on Two Factors

This design is basically a combination of the treatments-by-treatments-by-subjects design and the completely randomized design. Instead of only one group of subjects receiving all the treatment conditions (as in the treatments-by-treatments-by-subjects design), two or more experimental groups are compared (as in the completely randomized design). Thus, this design permits the comparison of several groups' performances and the evaluation of the variations in performance shown by the subjects under all treatment conditions within both factors presented.

Points to Consider When Using the Three-Factor Mixed Design

1. Each subject in a particular experimental group is tested under each treatment condition within both of the factors.
2. The number of subjects used in each experimental group is arbitrary. Again, while it is not necessary, it is best to have an equal number of subjects in each group. In most experiments, ten to fifteen subjects are assigned to each group.
3. The number of treatments given within each of the factors is arbitrary. However, it is rare that more than four or five treatments within either or both of the factors are compared.

■ EXAMPLE
Consider a situation where two groups of subjects practice a coordination task using a pursuit rotor apparatus. All subjects in *both* groups practice for four 60-second trials with the rotor moving clockwise. Then all subjects practice for four 60-second trials with the rotor moving counterclockwise. (*Note:* If the

experimenter decided to counterbalance and have half the subjects practice under the counterclockwise condition first, this would be a Latin square design.)

The two experimental groups are formed as follows. One group practices under a schedule whereby the four 60-second practice trials (under clockwise and counterclockwise conditions) are followed by 60 seconds of rest between each practice trial. The other group practices for 60 seconds with only 10 seconds of rest between each trial. Thus, the present experiment permits evaluation of (1) the effects of the amount of rest between practice trials, (2) the effects of the direction of rotation, and (3) changes across practice trials. The response measured for all subjects under all treatments is time on target during each 60-second trial.

Step 1. After the data have been collected, they are tabled as follows:

	GROUP 1 (60-SECOND PRACTICE/60-SECOND REST)							
	Clockwise				Counterclockwise			
Subject	Trial 1	Trial 2	Trial 3	Trial 4	Trial 1	Trial 2	Trial 3	Trial 4
S_1	21	26	35	43	2	9	20	24
S_2	18	28	41	46	5	10	14	15
S_3	25	24	45	48	10	15	21	21
S_4	19	20	38	37	1	3	8	7
S_5	14	18	25	33	4	7	12	20
S_6	17	16	28	29	8	10	18	25
S_7	12	18	29	35	6	13	24	28
S_8	15	17	27	30	1	7	17	26
S_9	20	28	26	29	2	4	16	14
S_{10}	18	20	31	38	9	23	36	39
	GROUP 2 (60-SECOND PRACTICE/10-SECOND REST)							
S_{11}	15	17	26	30	11	14	17	20
S_{12}	6	9	17	24	15	14	19	22
S_{13}	22	23	28	26	10	18	16	13
S_{14}	18	26	29	32	16	18	15	21
S_{15}	11	16	15	18	2	1	6	9
S_{16}	14	22	22	32	7	11	10	14
S_{17}	19	21	24	29	9	12	11	17
S_{18}	16	17	17	22	13	17	21	20
S_{19}	12	16	25	23	4	9	14	19
S_{20}	10	12	16	17	8	10	15	15

Step 2.   Add the scores for each treatment in both experimental groups.

	GROUP 1							
	Clockwise				Counterclockwise			
Subject	Trial 1	Trial 2	Trial 3	Trial 4	Trial 1	Trial 2	Trial 3	Trial 4
S_1	21	26	35	43	2	9	20	24
S_2	18	28	41	46	5	10	14	15
.	.	.	.	.	.	.	.	.
.	.	.	.	.	.	.	.	.
Sums:	**179**	**215**	**325**	**368**	**48**	**101**	**186**	**219**

	GROUP 2							
S_1	15	17	26	30	11	14	17	20
S_2	6	9	17	24	15	14	19	22
.	.	.	.	.	.	.	.	.
.	.	.	.	.	.	.	.	.
Sums:	**143**	**179**	**219**	**253**	**95**	**124**	**144**	**170**

Step 3.   Square each number in the entire table (Step 1), then add the squares.

$21^2 + 18^2 + \cdots + 15^2 = \textbf{69,810}$

Step 4.   Add all the sums obtained in Step 2 to get the grand sum for the entire table.

$179 + \cdots + 48 + \cdots + 143 + \cdots + 95 + \cdots + 170 = \textbf{2968}$

Step 5.   Square the grand sum obtained in Step 4, and divide it by the total number of measures recorded—i.e., the total number of subjects times the number of measures recorded for each subject (in this example, $20 \times 8 = 160$). This yields the correction term.

$$\frac{2968^2}{160} = \frac{8,809,024}{160} = \textbf{55,056.4}$$

Step 6.   Computation of the total sum of squares (SS_t): Simply subtract the correction term (Step 5) from the sum of the squared values in Step 3.

$69,810 - 55,056.4 = \textbf{14,753.6} = SS_t$

Between-Subjects Effects (Steps 7–9)

Step 7.   Computation of the effects of the experimental conditions on overall performance (in the present example, the effects of 60- and 10-second rest periods—SS_{groups}): First, add all the trial sums obtained in Step 2 for Group 1 and for Group 2.

$$179 + 215 + 325 + 368 + 48 + 101 + 186 + 219 = \mathbf{1641}$$

$$= \text{sum for Group 1}$$

$$143 + 179 + 219 + 253 + 95 + 124 + 144 + 170 = \mathbf{1327}$$

$$= \text{sum for Group 2}$$

Then, square each of these totals, divide each square by the number of scores added to get the total (80 in this example), and add the quotients.

$$\frac{1641^2}{80} + \frac{1327^2}{80} = \frac{4,453,810}{80} = \mathbf{55,672.6}$$

Then, subtract the correction term (Step 5) from the above value.

$$55,672.6 - 55,056.4 = \mathbf{616.2} = SS_{groups}$$

Step 8.   Computation of the between-subjects sum of squares (SS_b): First, add the scores for each subject in each group.

Subject	Trial 1		Trial 2		Trial 3		Trial 4		Trial 1		Trial 2		Trial 3		Trial 4	Sums
							Group 1									
S_1	21	+	26	+	35	+	43	+	2	⏐	9	+	20	+	24	**180**
S_2	18	+	28	+	41	+	46	+	5	+	10	+	14	+	15	**177**
⋮	⋮		⋮		⋮		⋮		⋮		⋮		⋮		⋮	⋮
S_{10}	18	+	20	+	31	+	38	+	9	+	23	+	36	+	39	**214**
							Group 2									
S_{11}	15	+	17	+	26	+	30	+	11	+	14	+	17	+	20	**150**
S_{12}	6	+	9	+	17	+	24	+	15	+	14	+	19	+	22	**126**
⋮	⋮		⋮		⋮		⋮		⋮		⋮		⋮		⋮	⋮
S_{20}	10	+	12	+	16	+	17	+	8	+	10	+	15	+	15	**103**

Then, square the sum of each subject's scores, and add these squares.

$$180^2 + 177^2 + \cdots + 103^2 = \mathbf{460,482}$$

Then, divide the above value by the number of scores added to get the sum for each subject. (In the present example, 8 scores were added to get each of the above sums.)

$$\frac{460,482}{8} = \mathbf{57,560.25}$$

Then, subtract the correction term (Step 5) from the above value.

$$57,560.25 - 55,056.4 = \textbf{2503.8} = SS_b$$

Step 9. Computation of the between-subjects error term (SS_{error_b}): Simply subtract the sum of squares for groups (Step 7) from the sum of squares for between subjects (Step 8).

$$2503.8 - 616.2 = \textbf{1887.6} = SS_{error_b}$$

Within-Subjects Effects (Steps 10–20)

Step 10. Computation of the within-subjects sum of squares (SS_w): Simply subtract the between-subjects sum of squares (Step 8) from the total sum of squares (Step 6).

$$14,753.6 - 2503.8 = \textbf{12,249.8} = SS_w$$

Step 11. Computation of the sum of squares of the first within-subjects factor (here, the clockwise versus counterclockwise rotation—$SS_{rotation}$): First, add the sums for the clockwise and the counterclockwise conditions (Step 2), disregarding the trials and the rest-period dimensions.

$$170 + 215 + 325 + 368 + 143 + 179 + 219 + 253$$

$$= \textbf{1881} = \text{sum for clockwise}$$

$$48 + 101 + 186 + 219 + 95 + 124 + 144 + 170$$

$$= \textbf{1087} = \text{sum for counterclockwise}$$

Then, square each of these sums, and divide each square by the number of scores added to get each sum. (In this example 80 scores were added to obtain each sum.) Then, add the quotients.

$$\frac{1881^2}{80} + \frac{1087^2}{80} = \frac{4,719,730}{80} = \textbf{58,996.6}$$

Then, subtract the correction term (Step 5) from the above value.

$$58,996.6 - 55,056.4 = \textbf{3940.2} = SS_{rotation}$$

Step 12. Computation of the sum of squares for the second within-subjects factor (here, the effects of trials—SS_{trials}): First, sum the scores for each of the four trials (Step 2), disregarding the rotational-direction and rest-period dimensions:

$$170 + 143 + 48 + 95 = \textbf{465} = \text{sum for Trial 1}$$
$$215 + 179 + 101 + 124 = \textbf{619} = \text{sum for Trial 2}$$
$$325 + 219 + 186 + 144 = \textbf{874} = \text{sum for Trial 3}$$
$$368 + 253 + 219 + 170 = \textbf{1010} = \text{sum for Trial 4}$$

Then, square these sums, and divide each square by the number of scores added to get each of the above sums. (In this example, each of the above sums represents a total of 40 scores, since 10 subjects' scores were added to get each of the sums in Step 2.) Then, add the quotients.

$$\frac{465^2}{40} + \frac{619^2}{40} + \frac{874^2}{40} + \frac{1010^2}{40} + \frac{2,383,362}{40} = \mathbf{59,584.0}$$

Then, subtract the correction term (Step 5) from the above value.

$$59,584.0 - 55,056.4 = \mathbf{4527.6} = SS_{trials}$$

Step 13. Computation of the interaction between experimental groups (rest interval) and the first factor (rotational direction)—$SS_{groups \times rotation}$: First, add the sums for each treatment for each of the two groups (Step 2). In this example, disregard the trials dimension and obtain the sums for the clockwise treatment in Group 1 and the counterclockwise treatment in Group 1. Do the same for Group 2.

$$179 + 215 + 325 + 368 = \mathbf{1087} = \text{sum for Group 1, clockwise}$$
$$143 + 179 + 219 + 253 = \mathbf{794} = \text{sum for Group 2, clockwise}$$
$$48 + 101 + 186 + 219 = \mathbf{554} = \text{sum for Group 1, counterclockwise}$$
$$95 + 124 + 144 + 170 = \mathbf{533} = \text{sum for Group 2, counterclockwise}$$

Then, square these sums, and divide by the number of scores added to obtain each sum. (In the present example, each of the above sums represents a total of 40 scores.) Then add the quotients.

$$\frac{1087^2}{40} + \frac{794^2}{40} + \frac{554^2}{40} + \frac{533^2}{40} + \frac{2,403,010}{40} = \mathbf{60,075.2}$$

Then, subtract the correction term (Step 5), the sum of squares for groups (Step 7), and the sum of squares for rotational direction (Step 11), from the above value.

$$60,075.2 - 55,056.4 - 616.2 - 3940.2 = \mathbf{462.4} = SS_{groups \times rotation}$$

Step 14. Computation of the interaction between experimental groups (rest interval) and the second factor (trials)—$SS_{groups \times trials}$: First, add the sums for each trial for each of the two groups (Step 2). In the present example, disregard the rotational-direction dimension and obtain the sums for Trials 1, 2, 3, and 4 in Group 1. Do the same for Group 2.

$$179 + 48 = \mathbf{227} = \text{sum for Group 1, Trial 1}$$
$$215 + 101 = \mathbf{316} = \text{sum for Group 1, Trial 2}$$
$$325 + 186 = \mathbf{511} = \text{sum for Group 1, Trial 3}$$
$$368 + 219 = \mathbf{587} = \text{sum for Group 1, Trial 4}$$
$$143 + 95 = \mathbf{238} = \text{sum for Group 2, Trial 1}$$
$$179 + 124 = \mathbf{303} = \text{sum for Group 2, Trial 2}$$
$$219 + 144 = \mathbf{363} = \text{sum for Group 2, Trial 3}$$
$$253 + 170 = \mathbf{423} = \text{sum for Group 2, Trial 4}$$

Then, square each of these sums, and divide by the number of scores added to obtain each sum. (In the present example, each sum represents a total of 20 scores: 10 subjects and 2 scores per subject.) Then, add the quotients.

$$\frac{227^2}{20} + \frac{316^2}{20} + \cdots + \frac{423^2}{20} = \frac{1,216,226}{20} = \textbf{60,811.3}$$

Then, subtract the correction (Step 5), the sum of squares for groups (Step 7), and the sum of squares for trials (Step 12) from the above value.

$$60,811.3 - 55,056.4 - 616.2 - 4527.6 = \textbf{611.1} = SS_{groups \times trials}$$

Step 15.   Computation of the interaction between the first factor (rotational direction) and the second factor (trials)—$SS_{rotation \times trials}$: First, add the sums for each trial for both rotational-direction conditions (Step 2). In the present example, disregard the groups' effects and obtain the sum for Trials 1, 2, 3, and 4 under the clockwise condition. Then do the same for the counterclockwise condition.

$$179 + 143 = \textbf{322} = \text{sum for Trial 1, clockwise}$$
$$215 + 179 = \textbf{394} = \text{sum for Trial 2, clockwise}$$
$$325 + 219 = \textbf{544} = \text{sum for Trial 3, clockwise}$$
$$368 + 253 = \textbf{621} = \text{sum for Trial 4, clockwise}$$
$$48 + 95 = \textbf{143} = \text{sum for Trial 1, counterclockwise}$$
$$101 + 124 = \textbf{225} = \text{sum for Trial 2, counterclockwise}$$
$$186 + 144 = \textbf{330} = \text{sum for Trial 3, counterclockwise}$$
$$219 + 170 = \textbf{389} = \text{sum for Trial 4, counterclockwise}$$

Then, square each of these sums, and divide by the number of scores added to obtain each sum. (In the present example, each sum represents a total of 20 scores: 10 subjects and 2 scores per subject.) Then, add the quotients.

$$\frac{322^2}{20} + \frac{394^2}{20} + \cdots + \frac{389^2}{20} = \frac{1,217,792}{20} = \textbf{63,589.6}$$

Then, subtract the correction term (Step 5), the sum of squares for rotation (Step 11), and the sum of squares for trials (Step 12) from the above value.

$$63,589.6 - 55,056.4 - 3940.2 - 4527.6 = \textbf{65.4} = SS_{rotation \times trials}$$

Step 16.   Computation of the interaction among groups, rotation, and trials ($SS_{groups \times rotation \times trials}$): First, square each sum obtained by Step 2, and divide each square by the number of scores added to obtain each sum. (In the present example, each sum represents a total of 10 scores.) Then add the quotients.

$$\frac{179^2}{10} + \frac{215^2}{10} + \cdots + \frac{170^2}{10} = \frac{652,874}{10} = \textbf{65,287.4}$$

Then, from this value, subtract the correction term (Step 5), the sum of squares for groups (Step 7), the sum of squares for rotation (Step 11), the sum of squares for trials (Step 12), the sum of squares for groups by rotation (Step 13), the sum of squares for groups by trials (Step 14), and the sum of squares for rotation by trials (Step 15).

$$65,287.4 - 55,056.4 - 616.2 - 3940.2 - 4527.6 - 462.4 - 611.1$$

$$- 65.4 = \mathbf{8.1} = SS_{groups \times rotation \times trials}$$

Step 17. Computation of the total error for within subjects (SS_{error_w}): (*Note:* This error term is not used in any of the F-tests, but it is needed for later computations.) Subtract the final values of Steps 11, 12, 13, 14, 15, and 16 from the final value of Step 10.

$$12,249.8 - 3940.2 - 4527.6 - 462.4 - 611.1 - 65.4 - 8.1 = \mathbf{2635.0}$$

$$= SS_{error_w}$$

Step 18. Computation of the error term for the rotation and for the rotation-by-groups interaction (SS_{error}): This requires that the data be retabled as follows. Sum the scores of each subject for the four trials within each rotational-direction condition.

	Group 1	
Subject	Clockwise	Counterclockwise
S_1	125 (21 + 26 + 35 + 43)	55 (2 + 9 + 20 + 24)
S_2	133 (18 + 28 + 41 + 46)	44 (5 + 10 + 14 + 15)
$\vdots$	$\vdots$	$\vdots$
S_{10}	107	107

	Group 2	
S_{11}	88	62
S_{12}	56	70
$\vdots$	$\vdots$	$\vdots$
S_{20}	55	48

Then, square each of these sums, and divide the squares by the number of scores added to obtain each sum. (In this example, each sum is based on 4 scores.) Then, add the quotients.

$$\frac{125^2}{4} + \frac{133^2}{4} + \cdots + \frac{48^2}{4} = \frac{254,140}{4} = \mathbf{63,535}$$

Then, from this value, subtract the correction term (Step 5), the sum of squares for between subjects (Step 8), the sum of squares for rotation (Step 11), and the sum of squares for rotation by groups (Step 13).

$$63,535 - 55,056.4 - 2503.8 - 3940.2 - 462.4 = \mathbf{1572.2} = SS_{error_1}$$

Step 19. Computation of the error term for trials and for the groups-by-trials interaction (SS_{error_2}): This requires that the data be retabled once again. Sum the scores of each subject on the four trials, disregarding the rotation-direction dimension.

Subject	Trial 1	Trial 2	Trial 3	Trial 4
		Group 1		
S_1	23(21 + 2)	35(26 + 9)	55(35 + 20)	67(43 + 24)
S_2	23(18 + 5)	38(28 + 10)	55(41 + 14)	61(46 + 15)
⋮	⋮	⋮	⋮	⋮
S_{10}	27	43	67	77
		Group 2		
S_{11}	26	31	43	50
S_{12}	21	23	36	46
⋮	⋮	⋮	⋮	⋮
S_{20}	18	22	31	32

Then, square all the sums in this table, and divide each square by the number of scores added to obtain each sum. (In the present example, 2 scores were added.) Then, add the quotients.

$$\frac{23^2}{2} + \frac{23^2}{2} + \cdots + \frac{32^2}{2} = \frac{126,418}{2} = \textbf{63,209}$$

Then, from this value, subtract the correction term (Step 5), the sum of squares for between subjects (Step 8), the sum of squares for trials (Step 12), and the sum of squares for groups-by-trials (Step 14).

$$63,209 - 55,056.4 - 2503.8 - 4527.6 - 611.1 = \textbf{510.1} = SS_{error_2}$$

Step 20. Computation of the error term for the trials-by-rotation interaction and for the trials-by-rotation-by-groups interaction (SS_{error_3}): Simply subtract the final values of Steps 18 and 19 from the final value of Step 17.

$$2635.0 - 1572.2 - 510.1 = \textbf{552.7} = SS_{error_3}$$

Step 21. All the computations based directly on the data have been completed. However, to compute the F ratios, the degrees of freedom (df) are required. These are computed as follows:

df for SS_t = the total number of scores entered in Step 1 minus 1.

$$160 - 1 = \textbf{159}$$

df for SS_b	= the total number of subjects used in the experiment minus 1.
	$20 - 1 = \mathbf{19}$
df for SS_{groups}	= the number of groups minus 1.
	$2 - 1 = \mathbf{1}$
df for SS_{error_b}	= the between-subjects df minus the groups df.
	$19 - 1 = \mathbf{18}$
df for SS_w	= the total df minus the between-subjects df.
	$159 - 19 = \mathbf{140}$
df for $SS_{rotation}$	= the number of different (rotation) conditions minus 1.
	$2 - 1 = \mathbf{1}$
df for SS_{trials}	= the number of trials given within each condition minus 1.
	$4 - 1 = \mathbf{3}$
df for $SS_{groups \times rotation}$	= the df for groups times the df for rotation.
	$1 \times 1 = \mathbf{1}$
df for $SS_{groups \times trials}$	= the df for groups times the df for trials.
	$1 \times 3 = \mathbf{3}$
df for $SS_{rotation \times trials}$	= the df for rotation times the df for trials.
	$1 \times 3 = \mathbf{3}$
df for $SS_{groups \times rotation \times trials}$	= the df for groups times the df for rotation times the df for trials.
	$1 \times 1 \times 3 = \mathbf{3}$
df for SS_{error_w}	= the df for within subjects minus the df for rotation, trials, groups-by-rotation, groups-by-trials, rotation-by-trials, and groups-by-rotation-by-trials.
	$140 - 1 - 3 - 1 - 3 - 3 - 3 = \mathbf{126}$
df for SS_{error_1} (rotation and rotation-by-groups)	= the df for rotation, times the total number of subjects, minus the number of groups.
	$1 \times (20 - 2) = \mathbf{18}$

df for SS_{error_2} (trials and groups-by-trials)	= the df for trials, times the total number of subjects, minus the number of groups.

$$3 \times (20 - 2) = 54$$

df for SS_{error_3} (rotation-by-trials and groups-by-rotation-by-trials)	= the df for rotation, times the df for trials, times the total number of subjects, minus the number of groups.

$$1 \times 3 \times (20 - 2) = 54$$

Step 22.   The mean squares are then computed as SS/df.

$$ms_{groups} = \frac{(Step\ 7)}{1} = \frac{616.2}{1} = 616.2$$

$$ms_{error_b} = \frac{(Step\ 9)}{18} = \frac{1887.6}{18} = 104.9$$

$$ms_{rotation} = \frac{(Step\ 11)}{1} = \frac{3940.2}{1} = 3940.2$$

$$ms_{trials} = \frac{(Step\ 12)}{3} = \frac{4527.6}{3} = 1509.2$$

$$ms_{groups \times rotation} = \frac{(Step\ 13)}{1} = \frac{462.4}{1} = 462.4$$

$$ms_{groups \times trials} = \frac{(Step\ 14)}{3} = \frac{611.1}{3} = 203.7$$

$$ms_{rotation \times trials} = \frac{(Step\ 15)}{3} = \frac{65.4}{3} = 21.8$$

$$ms_{groups \times rotation \times trials} = \frac{(Step\ 16)}{3} = \frac{8.1}{3} = 2.7$$

$$ms_{error_1} = \frac{(Step\ 18)}{18} = \frac{1572.2}{18} = 87.3$$

$$ms_{error_2} = \frac{(Step\ 19)}{54} = \frac{510.1}{54} = 9.4$$

$$ms_{error_3} = \frac{(Step\ 20)}{54} = \frac{552.7}{54} = 10.2$$

Step 23.   The appropriate F ratios are as follows.

$$\text{Experimental groups: } \frac{ms_{groups}}{ms_{error_b}}$$

$$\text{Rotation direction: } \frac{ms_{rotation}}{ms_{error_1}}$$

$$\text{Trials: } \frac{ms_{trials}}{ms_{error_2}}$$

$$\text{Groups-by-rotation: } \frac{ms_{G \times R}}{ms_{error_1}}$$

$$\text{Groups-by-trials: } \frac{ms_{G \times T}}{ms_{error_2}}$$

$$\text{Rotation-by-trials: } \frac{ms_{R \times T}}{ms_{error_3}}$$

$$\text{Groups-by-rotation-by-trials: } \frac{ms_{G \times R \times T}}{ms_{error_3}}$$

Step 24.   Table the results as follows:

Source	SS	df	ms	F	p
Total	14,753.6	159	—	—	—
Between subjects	2,503.8	19	—	—	—
Groups	616.2	1	616.2	5.88	<.05
Error$_b$	1,887.6	18	104.9	—	—
Within subjects	12,249.8	140	—	—	—
Rotation	3,940.2	1	3940.2	45.11	<.001
Trials	4,527.6	3	1509.2	159.77	<.001
G × R	462.4	1	462.4	5.29	<.05
G × T	611.1	3	203.7	21.56	<.001
R × T	65.4	3	21.8	2.13	n.s.
G × R × T	8.1	3	2.7	<1	n.s.
Error$_1$	1,572.2	18	87.3	—	—
Error$_2$	510.1	54	9.4	—	—
Error$_3$	552.7	54	10.2	—	—

Therefore, it is concluded (see Appendix E) that:

1. the overall performance of the groups was different;
2. the effects of directional change (rotation) were significant;
3. the subjects' performance changed across trials;
4. there was a significant groups-by-direction (rotation) interaction;
5. there was a significant trials-by-groups interaction.   ■

SECTION 4.10
Latin Square Design: Simple

This Latin square design is basically equivalent to the treatments-by-subjects design of Section 4.5, except that the effects of the order of treatment presentation can also be analyzed.

Points to Consider When Using the Simple Latin Square Design

1. All subjects in all the experimental subgroups receive the same treatments. The only difference between the subgroups is in the order of presentation of these treatments, which is systematically counterbalanced. For example, if three drugs are being tested, every subject receives each of the drugs, but one third of the subjects are given Drug 1 first; the second third, Drug 2 first, and the final third, Drug 3 first.
2. There should be an equal number of subjects in each of the experimental subgroups. In most experiments, five or fifteen subjects are assigned to each subgroup.
3. It is rare that more than four or five treatments are administered to each of the subjects. (*Note:* The number of treatments is always equal to the number of experimental subgroups in a Latin square design.)

■ EXAMPLE

Assume that an experimenter wishes to determine the effects of three different shock intensities on the galvanic skin responses of a group of subjects. Since it seems reasonable to expect that the order in which the shocks are presented might affect the results, the experimenter decides to counterbalance the effects of the shock by using a Latin square design. To do this, one third of the subjects receive low-intensity shock, followed by medium, and then high. The second third of the subjects receive medium-intensity shock first, followed by high, and then low. The remaining third receive high, low, and then medium. The measure recorded is the number of responses above a certain criterion during the fifteen trials given under each shock condition.

In this experiment, the presentation of the shock intensities will be as follows. (The subgroups will hereafter be referred to simply as "groups.")

	Shock intensity		
Order of Presentation	Low	Medium	High
First	Group 1	Group 2	Group 3
Second	Group 3	Group 1	Group 2
Third	Group 2	Group 3	Group 1

Or, rearranging the group and order-of-presentation dimensions, the above becomes:

Group	Shock intensity		
	Low	Medium	High
Group 1	First	Second	Third
Group 2	Third	First	Second
Group 3	Second	Third	First

(*Note:* This rearrangement permits computations to be made more easily but does not affect the actual computational procedures.)

Step 1. After the experiment has been conducted, table the data as follows:

Subject	Group 1 (Order: low, medium, high)		
	Low shock (First)	Medium shock (Second)	High shock (Third)
S_1	4	6	7
S_2	6	8	9
S_3	5	8	10
S_4	3	5	6
S_5	4	5	9
S_6	5	6	6
S_7	7	19	10

	Group 2 (Order: medium, high, low)		
	(Third)	(First)	(Second)
S_8	8	6	2
S_9	9	4	6
S_{10}	11	8	9
S_{11}	6	6	6
S_{12}	14	8	17
S_{13}	9	5	6
S_{14}	8	5	8

	Group 3 (Order: high, low, medium)		
Subject	Low shock (Second)	Medium shock (Third)	High shock (First)
S_{15}	8	9	9
S_{16}	8	9	12
S_{17}	10	9	10
S_{18}	9	11	11
S_{19}	7	8	9
S_{20}	10	8	13
S_{21}	7	4	8

Step 2. Add the scores in each group for each shock intensity.

	Group 1		
Subject	Low (First)	Medium (Second)	High (Third)
S_1	4	6	7
S_2	6	8	9
.	.	.	.
Sums:	**34**	**57**	**57**

	Group 2		
	(Third)	(First)	(Second)
S_8	8	6	2
S_9	9	4	6
.	.	.	.
Sums:	**65**	**42**	**54**

	Group 3		
	(Second)	(Third)	(First)
S_{15}	8	9	9
S_{16}	8	9	12
.	.	.	.
Sums:	**59**	**58**	**72**

Step 3.   Obtain the sum for each group by adding the sums of the shock intensities.

$34 + 57 + 57 =$ **148** $=$ sum for Group 1
$65 + 42 + 54 =$ **161** $=$ sum for Group 2
$59 + 58 + 72 =$ **189** $=$ sum for Group 3

Step 4.   Add the scores for *each* subject in each group.

Subject	Low		Medium		High	Sums
			Group 1			
$\cdot\, S_1$	4	+	6	+	7	**17**
S_2	6	+	8	+	9	**23**
$\vdots$	$\vdots$		$\vdots$		$\vdots$	$\vdots$
S_7	7	+	19	+	10	**36**
			Group 2			
S_8	8	+	6	+	2	**16**
S_9	9	+	4	+	6	**19**
$\vdots$	$\vdots$		$\vdots$		$\vdots$	$\vdots$
S_{14}	8	+	5	+	8	**21**
			Group 3			
S_{15}	8	+	9	+	9	**26**
S_{16}	8	+	9	+	12	**29**
$\vdots$	$\vdots$		$\vdots$		$\vdots$	$\vdots$
S_{21}	7	+	4	+	8	**19**

Step 5.   Square each score in the entire table (Step 1), and add these squared values to get a grand sum of the squares. (Note that in the following example we are considering the scores as they go across—not down—the table.)

$$4^2 + 6^2 + 7^2 + 6^2 + 8^2 + 9^2 + \cdots + 7^2 + 4^2 + 8^2 = \textbf{4500}$$

Step 6.   Add the group sums (Step 3) to get the grand sum of the entire table.

$$148 + 161 + 189 = \textbf{498}$$

Step 7.   Square the grand sum and divide it by the total number of measures in the entire table—i.e., the number of subjects times the number of measures per subject ($21 \times 3 = 63$ in this example). This yields the correction term.

$$\frac{498^2}{63} = \frac{248,004}{63} = \textbf{3936.571}$$

Step 8.   Computation of the total sum of squares (SS_t): Simply subtract the correction term (Step 7) from the sum of the squares (Step 5).

$$4500 - 3936.571 = \mathbf{563.429} = SS_t$$

Between-Subjects Effects (Steps 9–11)

Step 9.   Computation of the between-subjects sum of the squares (SS_b): First, square the sum of each subject's scores (Step 4), and add these squared values.

$$17^2 + 23^2 + \cdots + 19^2 = \mathbf{12{,}756}$$

Then, divide this value by the number of different shock intensities given each subject (i.e., the number of different orders).

$$\frac{12{,}756}{3} = \mathbf{4252}$$

Then, subtract the correction term (Step 7) from the above value.

$$4252 - 3936.571 = \mathbf{315.429} = SS_b$$

Step 10.   Computation of the effects of groups—SS_G (i.e., the effects of order of presentation of the shock intensities on the overall group performance): First, square the sum of each of the experimental groups (Step 3), divide each squared value by the number of measures on which the sum was based, and then add these values.

$$\frac{148^2}{21} + \frac{161^2}{21} + \frac{189^2}{21} = \frac{83{,}546}{21} = \mathbf{3978.381}$$

Then, subtract the correction term (Step 7) from the above value.

$$3978.381 - 3936.571 = \mathbf{41.810} = SS_G$$

Step 11.   Computation of the between-subjects error term (SS_{error_b}): Simply subtract the SS_G (Step 10) from the SS_b (Step 9).

$$315.429 - 41.810 = \mathbf{273.619} = SS_{error_b}$$

Within-Subjects Effects (Steps 12–16)

Step 12.   Computation of the within-subjects sum of squares (SS_w): Simply subtract the SS_b (Step 9) from the SS_t (Step 8).

$$563.429 - 315.429 = \mathbf{248.0} = SS_w$$

Step 13.   Computation of the treatment effects (in this example, the effects of low-, medium-, and high-intensity shock—SS_s): First, add the sums of all subjects when they received low shock (Step 2). Do the same for medium and high shock.

$$34 + 65 + 59 = \textbf{158} = \text{sum for low shock}$$
$$57 + 42 + 58 = \textbf{157} = \text{sum for medium shock}$$
$$57 + 54 + 72 = \textbf{183} = \text{sum for high shock}$$

Then, square each of these sums, divide by the number of measures on which each sum was based, and add the quotients.

$$\frac{158^2}{21} + \frac{157^2}{21} + \frac{183^2}{21} = \frac{83,102}{21} = \textbf{3957.238}$$

Then, subtract the correction term (Step 7) from the above value.

$$3957.238 - 3936.571 = \textbf{20.667} = SS_s$$

Step 14. Computation of the order effects—SS_O (i.e., the general effects of firstness, secondness, and thirdness, irrespective of the particular shock intensity): First, add the sums of the shock intensities presented first, second, and third (Step 2).

$$34 + 42 + 72 = \textbf{148} = \text{sum of shocks presented first}$$
$$57 + 54 + 59 = \textbf{170} = \text{sum of shocks presented second}$$
$$57 + 65 + 58 = \textbf{180} = \text{sum of shocks presented third}$$

Then, square the sums, divide by the number of measures on which each sum was based, then add the quotients.

$$\frac{148^2}{21} + \frac{170^2}{21} + \frac{180^2}{21} = \frac{83,204}{21} = \textbf{3962.095}$$

Then, subtract the correction term (Step 7) from the above value.

$$3962.095 - 3936.571 = \textbf{25.524} = SS_O$$

Step 15. Computation of the effects of a particular shock intensity being presented first, second, and third—SS_{SO_w} (SS for shock $\times$ order within subjects): First, square the sums of each shock intensity in each of the nine experimental groups (Step 2), divide by the number of measures on which the sums were based (7 in this example), then add the quotients.

$$\frac{34^2}{7} + \frac{57^2}{7} + \frac{57^2}{7} + \frac{65^2}{7} + \frac{42^2}{7} + \frac{54^2}{7} + \frac{59^2}{7} + \frac{58^2}{7} + \frac{72^2}{7}$$

$$= \frac{28,588}{7} = \textbf{4084.0}$$

Then, from this value, subtract the correction term (Step 7).

$$4084 - 3936.571 = \textbf{147.429}$$

Then, from this value, subtract SS_G (Step 10), SS_S (Step 13), and SS_O (Step 14).

$$147.429 - 41.810 - 20.667 - 25.524 = \mathbf{59.428} = SS_{SO_w}$$

Step 16.   Computation of the within-subject error term (SS_{error_w}): Simply subtract SS_S (Step 13), SS_O (Step 14), and SS_{SO_w} (Step 15) from SS_w (Step 12).

$$248 - 20.667 - 25.524 - 59.428 = \mathbf{142.381} = SS_{error_w}$$

Step 17.   All computations based on the data have been completed:

$$
\begin{aligned}
SS_t &= 563.429 \text{ (Step 8)} \\
SS_b &= 315.429 \text{ (Step 9)} \\
SS_G &= 41.810 \text{ (Step 10)} \\
SS_{error_b} &= 273.619 \text{ (Step 11)} \\
SS_w &= 248.000 \text{ (Step 12)} \\
SS_S &= 20.667 \text{ (Step 13)} \\
SS_O &= 25.524 \text{ (Step 14)} \\
SS_{SO_w} &= 59.428 \text{ (Step 15)} \\
SS_{error_w} &= 142.381 \text{ (Step 16)}
\end{aligned}
$$

Since the F ratios are the ratios of mean squares (SS/df), the df must be determined as follows:

df for SS_t = total number of measures recorded minus 1.

$$63 - 1 = \mathbf{62}$$

df for SS_b = total number of subjects minus 1.

$$21 - 1 = \mathbf{20}$$

df for SS_G = number of experimental subject groups minus 1.

$$3 - 1 = \mathbf{2}$$

df for SS_{error_b} = df for SS_b minus the df for SS_G.

$$20 - 2 = \mathbf{18}$$

df for SS_w = df for SS_t minus the df for SS_b.

$$62 - 20 = \mathbf{42}$$

df for SS_S = number of treatment conditions minus 1.

$$3 - 1 = \mathbf{2}$$

df for SS_O = number of different orders of presentation minus 1.

$$3 - 1 = \mathbf{2}$$

df for SS_{SO_w} = number of treatment groups minus 2, times the number of orders minus 1.

$$(3 - 2) \times (3 - 1) = \mathbf{2}$$

df for SS_{error_w} = df for SS_w minus the df for SS_s, SS_o, and SS_{so_w}.

$$42 - 2 - 2 - 2 = 36$$

Step 18. Compute the mean squares needed for the analysis (SS/df).

ms_t (This value is not needed.)

ms_b (This value is not needed.)

$$ms_G = \frac{(Step\ 10)}{2} = \frac{41.810}{2} = 20.905$$

$$ms_{error_b} = \frac{(Step\ 11)}{18} = \frac{273.619}{18} = 15.201$$

ms_w (This value is not needed.)

$$ms_S = \frac{(Step\ 13)}{2} = \frac{20.667}{2} = 10.333$$

$$ms_O = \frac{(Step\ 14)}{2} = \frac{25.524}{2} = 12.762$$

$$ms_{SO_w} = \frac{(Step\ 15)}{2} = \frac{59.428}{2} = 29.714$$

$$ms_{error_w} = \frac{(Step\ 16)}{36} = \frac{142.381}{36} = 3.955$$

Step 19. Compute the F ratios, and table the data as follows.

Source	SS	df	ms	F	p
Total	563.429	62	—	—	—
Between subjects	315.429	20	—	—	—
Groups (SO$_b$)	41.810	2	20.905	1.38	n.s.
Error$_b$	273.619	18	15.201	—	—
Within subjects	248.00	42	—	—	—
Shock (S)	20.667	2	10.333	2.61	n.s.
Order (O)	25.524	2	12.762	3.23	n.s.
Shock × order$_w$ (SO$_w$)	59.428	2	29.714	7.51	<.005*
Error$_w$	142.381	36	3.955	—	—

---

*The p value listed is taken from an F table for the appropriate degrees of freedom. However, according to Lindquist (1953, p. 280), in the instances where the source of variation is mixed (SO$_b$ and SO$_w$), each component should be tested at the $X/2\%$ level. In that case, it would be concluded that the SO$_w$ interaction is significant at the .025 rather than the .005 level.

Therefore, it is concluded (see Appendix E) that the within-subjects shock and order effects were interactive. All other effects were nonsignificant. ■

SECTION 4.11
Latin Square Design: Complex

The complex Latin square design is essentially an extension of the simple Latin square. The basic difference is that one extra between-subjects dimension is added. The major advantage of this Latin square design is that it allows the use of far fewer groups of subjects to cover the treatment combinations of interest.

Points to Consider When Using the Complex Latin Square Design

1. Two or more main experimental subject groups are employed and are either *treated* differently or are *selected* on the basis of some criterion so that they differ (for example, high-, medium-, and low-anxiety subjects).
2. Within each of the main experimental subject groups, a number of subgroups are formed, corresponding to the size of the Latin square (i.e., if the square is 3 × 3, then each main group is divided into three subgroups).
3. An equal number of subjects should be assigned to each of the subgroups. In most experiments, five to fifteen subjects are assigned to each subgroup.
4. It is rare that more than four or five treatments are administered to each of the subjects. (*Note:* The number of treatments administered to each subject is always equal to the number of subgroups in a Latin square design.)

■ EXAMPLE

Assume that an experimenter wishes to determine the effects of three different difficulties of verbal material on the learning ability of high- versus low-anxiety subjects. However, she hypothesizes that if the three different difficulties of material were given to each subject, the order in which they were presented would affect the rate of learning. Therefore, instead of presenting the lists in the same order (for example, difficult, medium, then easy) to all the subjects in both experimental groups (high- versus low-anxiety), she decides to counterbalance the difficulty effects by using a Latin square design. Consequently, within *both* the high- and low-anxiety conditions, the order of presentation of the lists is systematically varied so that an equal proportion of the subjects receive the difficult, medium, and easy lists first, second, and third in counterbalanced order. The measure recorded by the experimenter is the number of trials needed to reach the criterion of one perfect recitation of each of the lists.

For the high- and low-anxiety subjects, the presentation of the lists is as follows: (the subgroups will hereafter be referred to simply as "groups")

| Order of presentation | Low-anxiety subjects Type of list | | |
	Hard	Medium	Easy
First	Group 1	Group 2	Group 3
Second	Group 3	Group 1	Group 2
Third	Group 2	Group 3	Group 1
	High-anxiety subjects		
First	Group 4	Group 5	Group 6
Second	Group 6	Group 4	Group 5
Third	Group 5	Group 6	Group 4

Or, rearranging the group and order-of-presentation dimensions for both the high- and low-anxiety subjects, the above becomes:

| Group | Low-anxiety subjects Type of list | | |
	Hard	Medium	Easy
1	First	Second	Third
2	Third	First	Second
3	Second	Third	First
	High-anxiety subjects		
4	First	Second	Third
5	Third	First	Second
6	Second	Third	First

Note: This rearrangement permits computations to be made more easily, but it in no way affects the actual computational procedures.

Step 1.   After the experiment has been completed, table the data as follows:

LOW-ANXIETY SUBJECTS		
Group 1 (Order: hard, medium, easy)		
Subject	Hard list (First)	Medium list (Second)	Easy list (Third)

Subject	Hard list (First)	Medium list (Second)	Easy list (Third)
S_1	20	16	9
S_2	14	15	7
S_3	18	10	11
S_4	16	12	10
S_5	18	9	12
S_6	19	14	10

Group 2 (Order: medium, easy, hard)		
	(Third)	(First)	(Second)
S_7	17	17	9
S_8	16	18	9
S_9	12	15	8
S_{10}	11	15	10
S_{11}	13	13	12
S_{12}	15	16	12

Group 3 (Order: easy, hard, medium)		
	(Second)	(Third)	(First)
S_{13}	19	9	11
S_{14}	14	8	13
S_{15}	13	6	14
S_{16}	14	12	10
S_{17}	16	10	15
S_{18}	18	16	13

HIGH-ANXIETY SUBJECTS		
Group 4 (Order: hard, medium, easy)		
Subject	Hard list (First)	Medium list (Second)	Easy list (Third)
S_{19}	26	16	7
S_{20}	23	16	6
S_{21}	21	11	8
S_{22}	19	11	6
S_{23}	24	10	8
S_{24}	27	12	10

| Group 5 (Order: medium, easy, hard) | | |
Subject	Hard list (First)	Medium list (Second)	Easy list (Third)
S_{25}	14	17	8
S_{26}	15	18	6
S_{27}	11	16	6
S_{28}	13	16	9
S_{29}	15	13	11
S_{30}	13	11	10

| Group 6 (Order: easy, hard, medium) | | |
	(Second)	(Third)	(First)
S_{31}	19	10	10
S_{32}	15	9	11
S_{33}	14	7	6
S_{34}	13	12	10
S_{35}	15	10	9
S_{36}	17	11	8

Step 2. Add the scores in each group for each level of list difficulty.

| LOW-ANXIETY SUBJECTS | | |
| Group 1 | | |
Subject	Hard (First)	Medium (Second)	Easy (Third)
S_1	20	16	9
S_2	14	15	7
⋮	⋮	⋮	⋮
Sums:	**105**	**76**	**59**

| Group 2 | | |
	(Third)	(First)	(Second)
S_7	17	17	9
S_8	16	18	9
⋮	⋮	⋮	⋮
Sums:	**84**	**94**	**60**

LOW-ANXIETY SUBJECTS		
Group 3		
Subject	Hard (Second)	Medium (Third)	Easy (First)
---	---	---	---
S_{13}	19	9	11
S_{14}	14	8	13
⋮	⋮	⋮	⋮
Sums:	**94**	**61**	**76**

HIGH-ANXIETY SUBJECTS		
Group 4		
Subject	Hard (First)	Medium (Second)	Easy (Third)
---	---	---	---
S_{19}	26	16	7
S_{20}	23	16	6
⋮	⋮	⋮	⋮
Sums:	**140**	**76**	**45**

Group 5		
	(Third)	(First)	(Second)
---	---	---	---
S_{25}	14	17	8
S_{26}	15	18	6
⋮	⋮	⋮	⋮
Sums:	**81**	**91**	**50**

Group 6		
	(Second)	(Third)	(First)
---	---	---	---
S_{31}	19	10	10
S_{32}	15	9	11
⋮	⋮	⋮	⋮
Sums:	**93**	**59**	**54**

Step 3.   Obtain the sum for each group by adding the sums for each level of list difficulty.

$105 + 76 + 59 = \mathbf{240} =$ sum for Group 1
$84 + 94 + 60 = \mathbf{238} =$ sum for Group 2
$94 + 61 + 76 = \mathbf{231} =$ sum for Group 3
$140 + 76 + 45 = \mathbf{261} =$ sum for Group 4
$81 + 91 + 50 = \mathbf{222} =$ sum for Group 5
$93 + 59 + 54 = \mathbf{206} =$ sum for Group 6

Step 4.   Add the scores for *each* subject in each group.

LOW-ANXIETY SUBJECTS				
Group 1				
Subject	Hard	Medium	Easy	Sums
S_1	20 +	16 +	9	**45**
S_2	14 +	15 +	7	**36**
:	:	:	:	:
S_6	19 +	14 +	10	**43**
Group 2				
S_7	17 +	17 +	9	**43**
S_8	16 +	18 +	9	**43**
:	:	:	:	:
S_{12}	15 +	16 +	12	**43**
Group 3				
S_{13}	19 +	9 +	11	**39**
S_{14}	14 +	8 +	13	**35**
:	:	:	:	:
S_{18}	18 +	16 +	13	**47**

HIGH-ANXIETY SUBJECTS				
Group 4				
Subject	Hard	Medium	Easy	Sums
S_{19}	26 +	16 +	7	**49**
S_{20}	23 +	16 +	6	**45**
:	:	:	:	:
S_{24}	27 +	12 +	10	**49**

		Group 5		
Subject	Hard	Medium	Easy	Sums
S_{25}	14 +	17 +	8	39
S_{26}	15 +	18 +	6	39
.	.	.	.	.
.	.	.	.	.
.	.	.	.	.
S_{30}	13 +	11 +	10	34

		Group 6		
S_{31}	19 +	10 +	10	39
S_{32}	15 +	9 +	11	35
.	.	.	.	.
.	.	.	.	.
.	.	.	.	.
S_{36}	17 +	11 +	8	36

Step 5. Square each score in the entire table (Step 1), and add these squared values to get a grand sum of the squared numbers.

$$20^2 + 16^2 + 9^2 + 14^2 + 15^2 + 7^2 + \cdots + 17^2 + 11^2 + 8^2 = \textbf{20,106}$$

Step 6. Add the group totals (Step 3) to get the grand sum for the entire table.

$$240 + 238 + 231 + 261 + 222 + 206 = \textbf{1398}$$

Step 7. Square the grand sum of Step 6, and divide it by the total number of measures recorded in Step 1—i.e., the number of subjects times the number of measures per subject ($36 \times 3 = 108$, in this example). This yields the correction term.

$$\frac{1398^2}{108} = \frac{1,954,404}{108} = \textbf{18,096.333}$$

Step 8. Computation of the total sum of squares (SS_t): Simply subtract the correction term (Step 7) from the sum of squares obtained in Step 5.

$$20,106 - 18,096.333 = \textbf{2009.667} = SS_t$$

Between-Subjects Effects (Steps 9–13)

Step 9. Computation of the between-subjects sum of squares (SS_b): First, square the sum of each subject's scores (Step 4), and add these squared values.

$$45^2 + 36^2 + \cdots + 36^2 = \textbf{55,080}$$

Then, divide this value by the number of scores added to obtain each of the sums obtained in Step 4. (In the present example, each sum represents 3 scores.)

$$\frac{55,080}{3} = \textbf{18,360}$$

Then, subtract the correction term from the above value.

$$18,360 - 18,096.333 = \textbf{263.667} = SS_b$$

Step 10. Computation of the "pure" between-groups effects (SS_A): (The other "between" components in this design are partially between- and partially within-subjects sources of variance. In the present example, the overall effects of high versus low anxiety are not confounded.) First, add the group sums (Step 3) for the subjects in the low-anxiety conditions (Groups 1, 2, and 3) and for subjects in the high-anxiety conditions (Groups 4, 5, and 6).

$$240 + 238 + 231 = \textbf{709} = \text{sum for low-anxiety } Ss$$
$$261 + 222 + 206 = \textbf{689} = \text{sum for high-anxiety } Ss$$

Then, square each of these sums, divide by the total number of scores that make up each sum, and add the quotients.

$$\frac{709^2}{54} + \frac{689^2}{54} = \frac{977,402}{54} = \textbf{18,100.037}$$

Then, subtract the correction term (Step 7) from the above value.

$$18,100.037 - 18,096.333 = \textbf{3.704} = SS_A$$

Step 11. Computation of the between-subjects list-by-order interaction (SS_{LO_b}): First add the sums for the groups that received the same order of presentation of the lists (Step 3), disregarding the effects of high versus low anxiety.

$$
\begin{array}{rl}
240 = & \text{sum for Group 1} \\
+\ 261 = & \text{sum for Group 4} \\
\hline
\textbf{501} = & \text{sum for all } Ss \text{ who received the lists} \\
& \text{in the order: hard, medium, easy}
\end{array}
$$

$$
\begin{array}{rl}
238 = & \text{sum for Group 2} \\
+\ 222 = & \text{sum for Group 5} \\
\hline
\textbf{460} = & \text{sum for all } Ss \text{ who received the lists} \\
& \text{in the order: easy, hard, medium}
\end{array}
$$

$$
\begin{array}{rl}
231 = & \text{sum for Group 3} \\
+\ 206 = & \text{sum for Group 5} \\
\hline
\textbf{437} = & \text{sum for all } Ss \text{ who received the lists} \\
& \text{in the order: medium, easy, hard}
\end{array}
$$

Then, square the above sums, divide each squared value by the number of measures on which the sum was based, then add the quotients.

$$\frac{501^2}{36} + \frac{460^2}{36} + \frac{437^2}{36} = \frac{653,570}{36} = \mathbf{18,154.722}$$

Then, subtract the correction term (Step 7) from the above value.

$$18,154.722 - 18,096.333 = \mathbf{58.389} = SS_{LO_b}$$

Step 12. Computation of the between-subjects list-by-order-by-anxiety interaction (SS_{LOA_b}): First, square the sum of each of the experimental groups (Step 3), divide each squared value by the number of measures on which the sum is based, and add the quotients.

$$\frac{240^2}{18} + \frac{238^2}{18} + \frac{231^2}{18} + \frac{261^2}{18} + \frac{222^2}{18} + \frac{206^2}{18} = \frac{327,446}{18} = \mathbf{18,191.444}$$

Then, from the above value, subtract the correction term (Step 7), the SS_A (Step 10), and the SS_{LO_b} (Step 11).

$$18,191.444 - 18,096.333 - 3.704 - 58.389 = \mathbf{33.018} = SS_{LOA_b}$$

Step 13. Computation of the between-subjects error term (SS_{error_b}): Simply subtract the SS_A (Step 10), SS_{LO_b} (Step 11), and SS_{LOA_b} (Step 12) from the SS_b (Step 9).

$$263.667 - 3.704 - 58.389 - 33.018 = \mathbf{168.556} = SS_{error_b}$$

Within-Subjects Effects (Steps 14–21)

Step 14. Computation of the within-subjects sum of squares (SS_w): Simply subtract the SS_b (Step 9) from the SS_t (Step 8)

$$2009.667 - 263.667 = \mathbf{1746.0} = SS_w$$

Step 15. Computation of the list effects (SS_L): (In this example, these are the effects of a hard versus medium versus easy list, disregarding the order and anxiety effects.) First, add the scores of all the subjects on the hard list (Step 2). Do the same for the medium and easy lists.

$$105 + 84 + 94 + 140 + 81 + 93 = \mathbf{597} = \text{sum for hard list}$$
$$76 + 94 + 61 + 76 + 91 + 59 = \mathbf{457} = \text{sum for medium list}$$
$$59 + 60 + 76 + 45 + 50 + 54 = \mathbf{344} = \text{sum for easy list}$$

Then, square each of these sums, divide by the number of measures on which each sum was based, and add the quotients.

$$\frac{597^2}{36} + \frac{457^2}{36} + \frac{344^2}{36} = \frac{683,594}{36} = \mathbf{18,988.722}$$

Then, subtract the correction term (Step 7) from the above value.

$$18,988.722 - 18,096.333 = \textbf{892.389} = SS_L$$

Step 16. Computation of the order effects (SS_O): (In this example, these are the general effects of firstness versus secondness or thirdness of list presentation, irrespective of anxiety level or the particular list presented.) First, add the sums of the lists presented first, second, and third (Step 2).

$$105 + 94 + 76 + 140 + 91 + 54 = \textbf{560} = \text{sum of lists presented first}$$
$$76 + 60 + 94 + 76 + 50 + 93 = \textbf{449} = \text{sum of lists presented second}$$
$$59 + 84 + 61 + 45 + 81 + 59 = \textbf{389} = \text{sum of lists presented third}$$

Then, square these sums, divide by the number of measures on which each sum was based, and add the quotients.

$$\frac{560^2}{36} + \frac{449^2}{36} + \frac{389^2}{36} = \frac{666,522}{36} = \textbf{18,514.5}$$

Then, subtract the correction term (Step 7) from the above value.

$$18,514.5 - 18,096.333 = \textbf{418.167} = SS_O$$

Step 17. Computation of the effects of each type of list being presented first versus second versus third, disregarding the effects of anxiety (SS_{LO_w}): First, add the sums of the high- and low-anxiety groups for each of the treatment and order combinations (Step 2).

$$105 + 140 = \textbf{245} = \text{sum of difficult list first}$$
$$76 + 76 = \textbf{152} = \text{sum of medium list second}$$
$$59 + 45 = \textbf{104} = \text{sum of easy list third}$$
$$94 + 91 = \textbf{185} = \text{sum of medium list first}$$
$$60 + 50 = \textbf{110} = \text{sum of easy list second}$$
$$84 + 81 = \textbf{165} = \text{sum of difficult list third}$$
$$76 + 54 = \textbf{130} = \text{sum of easy list first}$$
$$94 + 93 = \textbf{187} = \text{sum of difficult list second}$$
$$61 + 59 = \textbf{120} = \text{sum of medium list third}$$

Then, square each of the above sums, divide each square by the number of measures on which each sum is based, then add the quotients.

$$\frac{245^2}{12} + \frac{152^2}{12} + \cdots + \frac{120^2}{12} = \frac{233,764}{12} = \textbf{19,480.333}$$

Then, from this value, subtract the correction term (Step 7), the sum of squares for LO_b (Step 11), the sum of squares for lists (Step 15), and the sum of squares for order (Step 16).

$$19,480.333 - 18,096.333 - 58.389 - 892.389 - 418.167$$

$$= \textbf{15.055} = SS_{LO_w}$$

Step 18. Computation of the treatments-by-"pure"-between-groups interaction (in this example, the list-by-anxiety interaction—SS_{LA}): First, add the sums of the difficult, medium, and easy lists within each of the anxiety conditions (Step 2), disregarding the effects of order of presentation of these lists.

$$105 + 84 + 94 = \textbf{283} = \text{sum of difficult lists, low-anxiety } Ss$$
$$76 + 94 + 61 = \textbf{231} = \text{sum of medium lists, low-anxiety } Ss$$
$$59 + 60 + 76 = \textbf{195} = \text{sum of easy lists, low-anxiety } Ss$$
$$140 + 81 + 93 = \textbf{314} = \text{sum of difficult lists, high-anxiety } Ss$$
$$76 + 91 + 59 = \textbf{226} = \text{sum of medium lists, high-anxiety } Ss$$
$$45 + 50 + 54 = \textbf{149} = \text{sum of easy lists, high-anxiety } Ss$$

Then, square the above sums, divide by the number of measures on which each sum is based, and add these quotients.

$$\frac{283^{24}}{18} + \frac{231^2}{18} + \frac{195^2}{18} + \frac{314^2}{18} + \frac{226^2}{18} + \frac{149^2}{18} = \frac{343,348}{18} = \textbf{19,074.889}$$

Then, from this value, subtract the correction term (Step 7), the sum of squares for anxiety (Step 10), and the sum of squares for lists (Step 15).

$$19,074.889 - 18,096.333 - 3.704 - 892.389 - 82.463 = SS_{LA}$$

Step 19. Computation of the order-by-"pure"-between-groups interaction (here, the order-by-anxiety interaction—SS_{OA}): First, add the sums of the lists presented first versus second versus third within each of the anxiety conditions (Step 2) disregarding the effects of list difficulty.

$$105 + 94 + 76 = \textbf{275} = \text{sum of first lists, low-anxiety } Ss$$
$$76 + 60 + 94 = \textbf{230} = \text{sum of second lists, low-anxiety } Ss$$
$$59 + 84 + 61 = \textbf{204} = \text{sum of third lists, low-anxiety } Ss$$
$$140 + 91 + 54 = \textbf{285} = \text{sum of first lists, high-anxiety } Ss$$
$$76 + 50 + 93 = \textbf{219} = \text{sum of second lists, high-anxiety } Ss$$
$$45 + 81 + 59 = \textbf{185} = \text{sum of third lists, high-anxiety } Ss$$

Then, square the above sums, divide by the number of measures on which each sum was based, and add these quotients.

$$\frac{275^2}{18} + \frac{230^2}{18} + \frac{204^2}{18} + \frac{285^2}{18} + \frac{219^2}{18} + \frac{185^2}{18} = \frac{333,552}{18} = \textbf{18,530.667}$$

Then, from this value, subtract the correction term (Step 7), the sum of squares for anxiety (Step 10), and the sum of squares for order (Step 16).

$$18,530.667 - 18,096.333 - 3.704 - 418.167 = \textbf{12,463} = SS_{OA}$$

Step 20. Computation of the within-subjects lists-by-order-by-anxiety interaction (SS_{LOA_w}): First, square the sums of each list within each experimental group (Step 2), divide by the number of measures on which each sum was based, and add the quotients.

$$\frac{105^2}{6} + \frac{76^2}{6} + \frac{59^2}{6} + \frac{84^2}{6} + \frac{94^2}{6} + \frac{60^2}{6} + \cdots + \frac{93^2}{6} + \frac{59^2}{6} + \frac{54^2}{6}$$

$$= \frac{117,896}{6} = \mathbf{19,649.333}$$

From the above value, subtract the correction term (Step 7), the sum of squares for anxiety (Step 10), the sum of squares LO_b (Step 11), the sum of squares LOA_b (Step 12), the sum of squares for lists (Step 15), the sum of squares for order (Step 16), the sum of squares LO_w (Step 17), the sum of squares LA (Step 18), and the sum of squares OA (Step 19).

$$19,649.333 - 18,096.333 - 3.704 - 58.389 - 33.018 - 892.389$$

$$- 418.167 - 15.055 - 82.463 - 12.463 = \mathbf{37.352} = SS_{LOA_w}$$

Step 21. Computation of the within-subjects error term (SS_{error_w}): From the within-subjects sum of squares (Step 14), subtract the sums of squares for lists (Step 15), order (Step 16), lists × order within (Step 17), lists × anxiety (Step 18), order × anxiety (Step 19), and list × order × anxiety (Step 20).

$$1746.000 - 892.389 - 418.167 - 15.055 - 82.463 - 12.463 - 37.352$$

$$= \mathbf{288.111} = SS_{error_w}$$

Step 22. All computations based on the data have been completed:

$$
\begin{aligned}
SS_t &= 2009.667 \ (\text{Step 8}) \\
SS_b &= 263.667 \ (\text{Step 9}) \\
SS_A &= 3.704 \ (\text{Step 10}) \\
SS_{LO_b} &= 58.389 \ (\text{Step 11}) \\
SS_{LOA_b} &= 33.018 \ (\text{Step 12}) \\
SS_{error_b} &= 168.556 \ (\text{Step 13}) \\
SS_w &= 1746.000 \ (\text{Step 14}) \\
SS_L &= 892.389 \ (\text{Step 15}) \\
SS_O &= 418.167 \ (\text{Step 16}) \\
SS_{LO_w} &= 15.055 \ (\text{Step 17}) \\
SS_{LA} &= 82.463 \ (\text{Step 18}) \\
SS_{OA} &= 12.463 \ (\text{Step 19}) \\
SS_{LOA_w} &= 37.352 \ (\text{Step 20}) \\
SS_{error_w} &= 288.111 \ (\text{Step 21})
\end{aligned}
$$

Since the F ratios are ratios of mean squares (SS/df), the df must be determined as follows:

df for SS_t = total number of measures recorded minus 1.

$$108 - 1 = \mathbf{107}$$

df for SS_b = total number of subjects minus 1.

$$36 - 1 = \mathbf{35}$$

df for SS_A = number of "pure" between-subjects groups minus 1.

$$2 - 1 = \mathbf{1}$$

df for SS_{LO_b} = number of treatments (lists) minus 1.

$$3 - 1 = \mathbf{2}$$

df for SS_{LOA_b} = number of treatments minus 1, times the number of "pure" between-subjects groups minus 1.

$$(3 - 1) \times (2 - 1) = \mathbf{2}$$

df for SS_{error_b} = df for SS_b minus the df for SS_A, SS_{LO_b}, and SS_{LOA_b}.

$$35 - 1 - 2 - 2 = \mathbf{30}$$

df for SS_W = df for SS_t minus the df for SS_b.

$$107 - 35 = \mathbf{72}$$

df for SS_L = number of treatment groups minus 1.

$$3 - 1 = \mathbf{2}$$

df for SO_O = number of orders of presentation minus 1.

$$3 - 1 = \mathbf{2}$$

df for SS_{LO_w} = number of treatments minus 1, times the number of orders minus 2.

$$(3 - 1) \times (3 - 2) = \mathbf{2}$$

df for SS_{LA} = number of treatments minus 1, times the number of "pure" between factors minus 1.

$$(3 - 1) \times (2 - 1) = \mathbf{2}$$

df for SS_{OA} = number of orders minus 1, times the number of "pure" between factors minus 1.

$$(3 - 1) \times (2 - 1) = \mathbf{2}$$

df for SS_{LOA_w} = number of treatments minus 1, times the number of "pure" between factors minus 1.

$$(3 - 1) \times (2 - 1) = \mathbf{2}$$

df for SS_{OA} = number of orders minus 1, times the number of "pure" between factors minus 1.

$$(3 - 1) \times (2 - 1) = \mathbf{2}$$

df for SS_{LOA_w} = number of treatments minus 1, times the number of orders minus 2, times the number of "pure" between factors minus 1.

$$(3 - 1) \times (3 - 2) \times (2 - 1) = 2$$

df for SS_{error_w} = df for SS_w minus the df for SS_L, SS_O, SS_{LO_w}, SS_{LA}, SS_{OA}, and SS_{LOA_w}.

$$72 - 2 - 2 - 2 - 2 - 2 - 2 = 60$$

Step 23. Computation of the mean squares needed for the analysis ($ms = SS/df$):

ms_t (This value is not needed.)

ms_b (This value is not needed.)

$$ms_A = \frac{\text{(Step 10)}}{1} = \frac{3.704}{1} = 3.704$$

$$ms_{LO_b} = \frac{\text{(Step 11)}}{2} = \frac{58.389}{2} = 29.194$$

$$ms_{LOA_b} = \frac{\text{(Step 12)}}{2} = \frac{33.018}{2} = 16.509$$

$$ms_{error_b} = \frac{\text{(Step 13)}}{30} = \frac{168.556}{30} = 5.619$$

ms_w (This value is not needed.)

$$ms_L = \frac{\text{(Step 15)}}{2} = \frac{892.389}{2} = 446.194$$

$$ms_O = \frac{\text{(Step 16)}}{2} = \frac{418.167}{2} = 209.083$$

$$ms_{LO_w} = \frac{\text{(Step 17)}}{2} = \frac{15.055}{2} = 7.527$$

$$ms_{LA} = \frac{\text{(Step 18)}}{2} = \frac{82.463}{2} = 41.231$$

$$ms_{OA} = \frac{\text{(Step 19)}}{2} = \frac{12.463}{2} = 6.231$$

$$ms_{LOA_w} = \frac{\text{(Step 20)}}{2} = \frac{37.352}{2} = 18.676$$

$$ms_{error_w} = \frac{\text{(Step 21)}}{60} = \frac{288.111}{60} = 4.802$$

Step 24.   Compute the F ratios, and table the data as follows:

Source	SS	df	ms	F	p
Total	2009.667	107	—	—	—
Between subjects	263.667	35	—	—	—
Anxiety	3.704	1	3.704	.66	n.s.
List × order$_b$	58.389	2	29.194	5.20	<.025*
List × order$_b$ × anxiety$_b$	33.018	2	16.509	2.94	n.s
Error$_b$	168.556	30	5.619	—	—
Within subjects	1746.000	72	—	—	—
List	892.389	2	446.194	92.92	<.001
Order	418.167	2	209.083	43.54	<.001
List × order$_w$	15.055	2	7.527	1.57	n.s.
List × anxiety	82.463	2	41.231	8.59	<.001
Order × anxiety	12.463	2	6.231	1.30	n.s.
List × order$_w$ × anxiety$_w$	37.352	2	18.676	3.89	<.05
Error$_w$	288.111	60	4.802	—	—

Therefore, it is concluded (see Appendix E) that:

1. the effects of list difficulty and order of presentation interacted;
2. the overall effects of list difficulty were significant;
3. the overall effects of order of presentation were significant;
4. the effects of anxiety and list difficulty interacted. ■

SECTION 4.12
Analysis of Variance for Dichotomous Data

This section and the one that follows are not designs of experiments but, rather, represent special situations in which the data recorded the dichotomous or rank-ordered. The actual computational steps are the same as those presented in earlier sections. The only real difference is in the data collection and recording.

Points to Consider When Analyzing Dichotomous Data

1. The design used and the analyses undertaken depend on the type of problem and the experimental treatments, or groups, employed.
2. The data recorded for each subject will be a "1" or a "0."

---

* The p values listed are those taken from F tables for the appropriate degrees of freedom. However, according to Lindquist (1953, p. 280), in those instances where the sources of variation are mixed (LO_b and LO_w, and LOA_b and LOA_w), each component should be tested at the $X/2\%$ level. In that case, it would be concluded that only the LO_b of the mixed sources is significant (at the .05 rather than the .025 level).

■ **EXAMPLE**

The design used to demonstrate the analysis of dichotomous data will be the Repeated Measures Design presented in Section 4.5.

For this example, assume that three different automobiles are being evaluated by automotive experts. Several different questions are asked, but the question of particular interest is the final one, "If you had the necessary funds, would you purchase this car?" *Yes* responses are given a value of "1"; *No* responses are recorded as "0."

Step 1.   Table the data as follows:

Expert judges	Car #1	Car #2	Car #3
S_1	1	1	0
S_2	1	1	0
S_3	0	0	1
S_4	1	1	0
S_5	0	0	1
S_6	0	0	1
S_7	1	1	0
S_8	0	1	0
S_9	1	1	0
S_{10}	1	0	0

Turn to Section 4.5, and follow the instructions in Steps 2 through 16.   ■

SECTION 4.13
Analysis of Variance for Rank-Order Data

This section also deals with the type of data recorded rather than focusing on experimental design. For the example in this section, the data represent rank-ordering of preferences. As with analysis of dichotomous data, the computational steps are the same as those presented in earlier designs.

Points to Consider When Analyzing Rank-Order Data

1. The experimental design used and the analysis undertaken depend on the type of problem under investigation and the experimental treatments, or groups, employed.
2. The data recorded for each subject will be a rank or a series of ranks.

■ **EXAMPLE**

The example used to demonstrate analysis of rank-order data will be the Repeated Measures Design of Section 4.5.

Assume that an experimenter wishes to determine whether there is a difference in taste preference for three brands of cola drinks. Appropriate experimental controls (randomized presentation, double blind, etc.) are used, and the data recorded are the rankings of the three drinks in order of preference. (*Note:* If the presentation of the cola drinks for tasting were systematically counterbalanced, the appropriate analysis would be the Latin Square presented in Section 4.10.)

Step 1.   Table the data as follows:

Subject	Cola #1	Cola #2	Cola #3
S_1	3	2	1
S_2	2	3	1
S_3	1	2	3
S_4	2	3	1
S_5	3	2	1
S_6	2	1	3
S_7	2	3	1
S_8	3	1	2
S_9	3	2	1
S_{10}	2	3	1
S_{11}	1	2	3
S_{12}	3	2	1

Turn to Section 4.5, and follow Steps 2 through 16. (*Note:* An analysis of rank-order data will always result in a sum of squares for subjects [Step 10] equal to zero.)

Textbook Reference Chart for Anova, Multiple Comparisons, Covariance, Power, Trend Analysis Using Orthogonal Polynomials, and Manova

The following chart is provided as a guide for using *Computational Handbook of Statistics* in conjunction with seven of the most widely used statistics and design texts. The names and section numbers in the *Handbook* are presented across the top row, with the corresponding pages and names used by the various other textbooks listed directly below them. Texts referred to in the chart include the following:

Bruning, J. L., and Kintz, B. L. *Computational handbook of statistics,* 4th ed. Addison Wesley Longman, Inc., 1997.

Hays, W. L. *Statistics,* 5th ed. Harcourt Brace, 1994.

Keppel, G. *Design and analysis: A researcher's handbook,* 3rd ed. Prentice-Hall, 1991.

Kirk, R. *Experimental design: Procedures for the behavioral sciences,* 3rd ed. Brooks/Cole, 1995.

Lindeman, R. H., Merenda, P. F., and Gold, R. Z. *Introduction to bivariate and multivariate analysis.* Scott, Foresman, 1980.

Myers, J. L., and Well, A. *Research design and statistical analysis.* Harper-Collins, 1991.

Tatsuoka, M. M., and Lohners, P. *Multivariate analysis.* Macmillan, 1988.

Winer, B. J., Brown, D. R., and Michels, K. M. *Statistical principles in experimental design,* 3rd ed. McGraw-Hill, 1991.

ANOVA, MULTIPLE COMPARISONS, COVARIANCE, POWER, TREND
ANALYSIS, AND MANOVA: Cross References

Bruning & Kintz Section	Completely randomized design 4.1	Factorial design: two factors 4.2
Hays Pages	Model I: Fixed Effects 385–405	Two-Factor Design 472–504
Keppel Pages	Completely Randomized Design 18–19, 28–40	Factorial Designs 187–278
Kirk Pages	Completely Randomized Design, or CR-k 164–202	Completely Randomized Factorial, or CRF-pq 364–431
Myers & Well Pages	Between-Subjects One-Factor Design 87–112	Between-Subjects Two-Factor Design 126–134
Winer, Brown, & Michels Pages	Single Factor Experiments 74–219	Factorial Experiments 284–313

Bruning & Kintz Section	Factorial design: three factors 4.3	Treatment by levels 4.4
Hays Pages	Three Factor Design 505–518	Randomized Blocks 557–567
Keppel Pages	Higher Order Factorial 421–459	Nested Designs 562–576
Kirk Pages	Completely Randomized Factorial, or CRF-pqr 437–443	Randomized Block Factorial, or RBF-p 34–37, 251–308
Myers Pages	Between-Subjects Three Factor Design 139–153	Treatment by Blocks 157–158
Winer, Brown, & Michels Pages	Factorial Experiments 313–321	Randomized Complete Blocks Design 210–216

Bruning & Kintz Section	Treatments-by-subjects, or repeated measures 4.5	Treatments-by-treatments-by-subjects 4.6
Hays Pages	Repeated Measures 567–570	Repeated Measures 570–571
Keppel Pages	Single-Factor Within Subjects 344–364	Two-Factor Within Subjects 461–478
Kirk Pages	Randomized Block, or RB-p 251–308	Randomized Block Factorial, or RB-pq 454–472
Myers Pages	Repeated Measures 234–244	Two-Factor Repeated Measures 259–271
Winer, Brown, & Michels Pages	Single Factor-Repeated Measures 220–281	Multi-Factor-Repeated Measures 497–509

Bruning & Kintz Section	Two-factor mixed: repeated measures on one 4.7	Three-factor mixed: repeated on one 4.8
Hays	Not Discussed	Not Discussed
Keppel Pages	Mixed Two-Factor Within Subjects 367–415	Mixed Three-Factor, One Within Factor 494–495
Kirk Pages	Split-Plot Factorial, or SPF-p.q 512–540	Split-Plot Factorial, or SPF-pr.q 540–553
Myers Pages	One Between and One Within Subjects 290–306	Two Between and One Within Subjects 307–311
Winer, Brown, & Michels Pages	Two Factor with Repeated Measures on One 509–513	Three Factor with Repeated Measures on One 547–579

Bruning & Kintz Section	Three factor with repeated measures on two 4.9	Latin square 4.10
Hays	Not discussed	Not discussed
Keppel	Mixed Factorial Two Within-S Factors	Latin Square
Pages	495–496	336–339
Kirk	Split-Plot Factorial, or SPF-p.qr	Latin Square
Pages	553–562	319–356
Myers	One Between and Two Within Subjects	Latin Square
Pages	311–317	344–374
Winer, Brown, & Michels	Three Factor with Repeated Measures	Latin Square
Pages	531–547	679–733

Bruning & Kintz Section	Multiple comparisons 5.4–5.9	Covariance 3.11–3.12
Hays	Multiple Comparisons	Covariance
Pages	454–463	810–838
Keppel	Multiple Comparisons	Covariance
Pages	170–177	301–326
Kirk	Multiple Comparisons	Covariance
Pages	113–159	273–277, 525–526, 760
Myers	Simple Effects	Covariance
Pages	134–136, 304–305	435–460
Winer, Brown, & Michels	Comparisons Among Treatment Means	Covariance
Pages	140–197	739–836

Bruning & Kintz Section	Sample size and power 1.8	Trend analysis using orthogonal polynomials 5.11
Hays Pages	Power 284–295	Orthogonal Polynomials 778–789
Keppel Pages	Power 76–89	Orthogonal Polynomials 151–153
Kirk Pages	Power 58–65	Orthogonal Polynomials 191, 761–764
Myers Pages	Power 54–56, 147–149	Orthogonal Polynomials 210–215
Winer, *et al.* Pages	Power 120–140	Orthogonal Polynomials 199–206

	MANOVA Cross Reference		
Bruning & Kintz Section	Manova sample-pop. 6.1	Manova matched pairs 6.2	Manova two groups 6.3
Lindeman, *et al.* Pages	180		181
Myers Pages			247–250
Tatsuoka Pages	82–85		85–88

Bruning & Kintz Section	Manova change scores 6.4	Manova more than two groups 6.5	Manova two factors 6.6
Lindeman, *et al.* Pages		220–229	229–244
Myers Pages		247–250	247–250
Tatsuoka Pages		88–96	267–279

PART 5

Supplemental Computations for Analysis of Variance

The next eleven sections present supplemental computations that are often needed to make a more complete and accurate analysis of data than is possible with the tests in Part 4. The eleven tests specifically treated in these sections are grouped below into three general types; a more detailed description of each test follows. This introductory material should help you decide which test (or tests) will satisfy your particular demands.

1. Tests for equality of variances
2. Tests for "simple effects"—usually used when an interaction is found to be significant
3. Trend tests—used to determine whether linear, quadratic, and higher complex relationships are present in the data

Tests for Equality of Variances (Sections 5.1, 5.2, and 5.3)

Most statistical tests have a clearly stated requirement that population variances be equal. Sections 5.1, 5.2, and 5.3 present simple tests to determine whether this is true. Any one of these tests may also be used to determine whether two experimental treatments produce an effect in terms of different variances.

Section 5.1 presents a test for equality of two independent variances. Section 5.2 is concerned with a test for equality of two related variances. (Related variances are variances computed from two measures of the same people or measures of matched people.) Section 5.3 presents a test for equality of several independent variances.

Tests for Simple Effects (Sections 5.4–5.10)

When the more complex analyses, such as those presented in Part 4 are completed, a researcher often wishes to determine which specific means differ from each other. Sections 5.4–5.9 present several ways of dealing with such "simple effects."

There is, however, considerable controversy regarding which of several tests is most appropriate. The only point where there seems to be agreement is that in order to use *t*-tests for multiple comparisons, you must state the specific hypotheses regarding which means were expected to differ *before* the experiment is carried out. If you wait until the experiment has been completed, look at the data, and then do *t*-tests on only a few of the most widely differing values, you are guilty of a severe violation of probability theory—the tabled probability values hold only when you have planned from the beginning of the data-gathering phase to compare specific means.

On the other hand, if you choose specific differences to compare after the data have been collected, you must use a test that will correct the probability for your choosing to state your comparisons after the fact. See the Textbook Reference Chart for a discussion of the complex issues regarding which of the several available tests gives the accurate probability estimate for the comparisons.

The computational procedures of all of the tests are highly similar. The *t*-test (Section 5.4), Tukey (Section 5.7), and the Scheffé (Section 5.8) tests all use a single critical difference for making all comparisons, but the last two tests use tables that correct for the total number of means being compared. The Duncan's (Section 5.5) and Newman-Keul's (Section 5.6) tests, on the other hand, employ the so-called layer approach where the critical difference is determined by the range of the two specific means being compared. The Dunnett test (Section 5.9) is a specialized test for comparing experimental group means only with the control group rather than making all possible comparisons.

The same example will be used in Sections 5.4–5.9 to demonstrate the computation of the various tests. A table following Section 5.9 will summarize the results and the differences in conclusions that would be drawn from the various tests.

When the very complex analyses of Sections 4.6–4.11 are used, there are several complete factorial or completely randomized analyses that may be computed *before* the more simple comparisons of two means are made. Section 5.10 presents a series of questions that might be asked and subsequently answered in such complex research situations.

Tests for Trend (Section 5.11)

Occasionally, a researcher is confronted with a problem that requires describing the shape of the data points, or the type of equation that best fits these points. In this case, the analyses presented in Section 5.11 would best serve this need.

SECTION 5.1

Test for Difference Between Variances of Two Independent Samples (Test for Homogeneity of Independent Variances)

There are two cases in which it is desirable to do a significance test of the difference between two independent variances: (1) when an experimental hypothesis is concerned with the variability of the samples, and (2) when there is doubt concerning the requirement of equality of variances in a mean-difference test. In either case, the following procedure may be followed in testing the hypothesis of equal variances.

Step 1.   Presumably, you already have the two variances (or the two variance estimates, i.e., mean squares). If you do not, go to Section 1.2 and follow the instructions in the first six steps. The value arrived at in Step 6 will be the variance for one of the samples. When you have both variances, go on to Step 2 of this section.

Step 2.   Obtain the F ratio by placing the larger variance of Step 1 over the smaller. For example, suppose the two variances are

variance$_1$ = 126.81

variance$_2$ = 35.27

Then,

$$F = \frac{126.81}{35.27} = \textbf{3.60}$$

Step 3.   Before the F value can be evaluated for significance, the degrees of freedom associated with each variance must be determined. In all cases, the degrees of freedom for a variance (actually population-variance estimate) will be one less than the number of cases on which the variance is based. For example, suppose variance$_1$ of Step 2 had been computed from a sample of 41 cases. Then,

df for variance$_1$ = 41 − 1 = **40**

In the same way, suppose variance$_2$ had been computed from a sample of 31 cases. Then,

df for variance$_2$ = 31 − 1 = **30**

Step 4.   The F value of Step 2 (3.60 in this example) has the two degrees of freedom 40 and 30 associated with it. From tabled F values (see Appendix E), we find that when $df = 40/30$,* F values larger than 2.47 are significant at the .01 level. Since the ratio of the variances in the present example equals 3.60, it is concluded that the variances are not homogeneous (equal).

However, there is one slight complication due to the fact that we selected *only* the larger variance as the numerator of the F ratio. For this reason, a correction is needed. In all cases, this correction is accomplished by simply multiplying the probability value by 2. Thus, an F value of 2.47, with degrees of freedom equal to 24/30, is considered significant at the .02 level rather than at the .01 level. ∎

SECTION 5.2
Test for Difference Between Variances of Two Related Samples (Test for Homogeneity of Related Variances)

There are two cases in which it is desirable to do a significance test of the difference between two related (correlated) variances: (1) when an experimental hypothesis is concerned with the variability of the samples, and (2) when there is doubt concerning the requirement of equality of variances in a mean-difference test. In either case, the following procedure may be followed in testing the hypothesis of equal variances.

Step 1.   Presumably, you already have the two variances (or the two variance estimates, i.e., mean squares). If you do not, go to Section 1.2 and follow the instructions in the first six steps. The value arrived at in Step 6 will be the variance for one of the samples. When you have both variances, go on to Step 2 of this section.

Step 2.   Since these samples are related (correlated), the degree of the relationship must be determined. Compute the correlation between the pairs of scores. This is done by following the directions from Step 1 through Step 18 in Section 3.1. For the present example, suppose the computed correlation is +.64.

Step 3.   Subtract the smaller variance of Step 1 from the larger variance. For example, suppose

$\text{variance}_1 = 65.27$

$\text{variance}_2 = 243.61$

Then,

$243.61 - 65.27 = \mathbf{178.34}$

---

*Since the df of 40/30 are not listed, go to the next closest df values. In this instance, they would be 24/30.

Step 4. Multiply the two variances together.

$243.61 \times 65.27 = \mathbf{15{,}900.425}$

Step 5. There were two groups of scores from which the two variances of Step 1 were computed. Subtract 2 from the number of cases in one group. For example, suppose each group is composed of 36 scores.

$36 - 2 = \mathbf{34}$

Step 6. Take the square root of the final value of Step 5.

$\sqrt{34} = \mathbf{5.831}$

Step 7. Multiply the final value of Step 6 by the final value of Step 3.

$5.831 \times 178.34 = \mathbf{1039.9}$

Step 8. Subtract the result of Step 2 from the number 1. (*Note:* The number 1 is always used.)

$1 - .64 = \mathbf{.36}$

Step 9. Multiply the final value of Step 4 by the number 4. (*Note:* The number 4 is always used.)

$4 \times 15{,}900.425 = \mathbf{63{,}601.7}$

Step 10. Multiply the value obtained in Step 9 by the result of Step 8.

$63{,}601.7 \times .36 = \mathbf{22{,}896.612}$

Then, take the square root of the product.

$\sqrt{22{,}896.612} = \mathbf{151.316}$

Step 11. Divide the final value of Step 7 by the final value of Step 10. This yields the *t* statistic.

$$t = \frac{1039.9}{151.316} = \mathbf{6.87}$$

Step 12. The degrees of freedom for the *t* is the result of Step 5 (34 in this example). At *t* with 34 degrees of freedom that is larger than 2.042 (see Appendix B) is significant at the .05 level using a two-tailed test. If the computed *t* value is large enough to be significant, this means that the variances are very likely different. ■

SECTION 5.3

Test for Differences Among Several Independent Variances (F-Maximum Test for Homogeneity of Variances)*

There are two cases in which it is desirable to do a significance test of the differences among several independent variances: (1) when an experimental hypothesis is concerned with the variability of the samples, and (2) when there is doubt concerning the requirement of equality of variances in a mean-difference test. In either case, the following procedure may be followed in testing the hypothesis of equal variances. There is one restriction on the use of this F_{max} test: the sizes of all the samples *must be the same.*

Step 1.   Presumably, you already have the several variances (or the variance estimates, i.e., mean squares). If you do not, go to Section 1.2 and follow the instructions in the first six steps. The value arrived at in Step 6 will be the variance for one of the samples. When you have all the variances, go on to Step 2 of this section.

Step 2.   Obtain the F_{max} ratio by placing the largest variance of Step 1 over the smallest. For example, suppose we had computed five variances in Step 1:

$variance_1 = 18.99$
$variance_2 = 27.62$
$variance_3 = 92.63$
$variance_4 = 77.38$
$variance_5 = 26.40$

Then,

$$F_{max} = \frac{92.63}{18.99} = \textbf{4.88}$$

Step 3.   The number of degrees of freedom is always one less than the number of cases in each sample. Suppose that the size of each sample is 18. Then,

$$df = 18 - 1 = \textbf{17}$$

Step 4.   The significance of the F_{max} ratio computed in Step 2 is obtained from a table of F_{max} values (see Appendix I). We must know both the number of degrees of freedom (17 in this example) and the number of variances being

---

*A Master's thesis completed at Ohio University in 1967 by Mr. Henry Winkler, titled "An empirical sampling study testing the robustness of several tests of homogeneity of variance and Type I errors in the simple randomized analysis of variance," dealt with the power of the F_{max} as well as Bartlett's, Cochran's, and Levine's two tests for homogeneity of variances. His results indicate that the F_{max} test and Bartlett's test are the most robust and are to be preferred over the others. Because of its simplicity, the F_{max} is probably the best choice.

considered (5 in this example). From the table of F_{max} values, we see that when $df = 17$ and the number of variances $= 5$, a value larger than 4.37 is significant at the .05 level. Since the value computed in Step 2 above (4.88) is larger than 4.37, we conclude that these variances are not homogeneous (i.e., they are different). ∎

SECTION 5.4
The *t*-Test for Differences Among Several Means

The *t*-test is used to determine which specific means differ significantly from each other *if* these differences have been hypothesized *prior to the collection of the experimental data.*

■ **EXAMPLE**
The set of data used to demonstrate the computational procedures is that used for the simple randomized design presented in Section 4.1. The summary table presented in the final analysis was:

Source	SS	df	ms	F	p
Total	1132	47	—	—	—
Between groups	567	3	189.00	14.71	<.001
Within groups	565	44	12.84	—	—

The basic computational formula for computing the critical difference is

$$\text{C. diff.} = t \sqrt{\frac{2 \text{ ms}_{\text{within gp. error}}}{n(\text{per gp.})}}$$

where *t* is obtained from the *t* tables presented in Appendix B. The significance of the overall *F* indicates only that out of the means of the four groups, at least two differ. The problem is to determine *which* pairs of means are significantly different.

Step 1. Obtain the mean score for each group. (In this example, there are 12 scores in each group.)

Sum of Group 1 = 111 $\dfrac{111}{2}$ = **9.25** = mean of Group 1

Sum of Group 2 = 88 $\dfrac{88}{12}$ = **7.33** = mean of Group 2

Sum of Group 3 = 156 $\dfrac{156}{12}$ = **13.00** = mean of Group 3

Sum of Group 4 = 195 $\dfrac{195}{12}$ = **16.25** = mean of Group 4

Step 2.   Derive the standard error of the difference among means by

$$\sqrt{\frac{2 \text{ ms}_{within}}{n(\text{per gp.})}}$$

For this example,

$$\sqrt{\frac{2 \times 12.84}{12}} = \sqrt{2.14} = \mathbf{1.463}$$

If there are unequal numbers of cases in some groups, you must account for those unequal ns. If the ns are not too disparate (as a rough rule of thumb, if there are not more than twice as many in the largest group as in the smallest group), you may use $\bar{n}$, the harmonic mean of the numbers, where

$$\bar{n} = \frac{\text{number of groups}}{\dfrac{1}{n_1} + \dfrac{1}{n_2} + \dfrac{1}{n_3} + \cdots + \dfrac{1}{n_i}}$$

For example, suppose that $n_1 = 16$, $n_2 = 12$, $n_3 = 8$, and $n_4 = 12$. Then,

$$\bar{n} = \frac{4}{\frac{1}{16} + \frac{1}{12} + \frac{1}{8} + \frac{1}{12}} = \frac{4}{.353} = \mathbf{11.33}$$

So the standard error of the differences between means would be

$$\sqrt{\frac{2(12.84)}{11.33}} = \sqrt{2.266} = \mathbf{1.51}$$

If the ns are widely different, the standard error must be computed separately for each comparison as

$$\sqrt{\text{ms}_{within}\left(\frac{1}{n_1} + \frac{1}{n_2}\right)}$$

For example, if $n_1 = 18$, $n_2 = 6$, and $\text{ms}_{within} = 12.84$, we would have

$$\sqrt{12.84(\tfrac{1}{18} + \tfrac{1}{6})} = \sqrt{\frac{12.84}{18} + \frac{12.84}{6}} = \sqrt{.713 + 2.14}$$

$$= \sqrt{2.853} = \mathbf{1.69}$$

A new standard error must then be computed for each new t-test.

Step 3.   The needed t value is obtained from Appendix B ($p = .05$). The table is entered at the row headed by the df for the mean square within groups. In the present example, the df for ms_{within} is 44. Since 44 is not listed, go to the next closest df, which is 40. Reading into the table, for 40 df, at the .05 level,

$$t = 2.02$$

Step 4.   Now multiply the t value of Step 3 by the value obtained in Step 2. This gives the critical difference against which the several mean differences will be compared.

$$2.02 \times 1.463 = \mathbf{2.955} = \text{C. diff.}$$

Step 5. Testing the differences between the various means: In all instances, if the difference between any two means (see Step 1) is larger than the critical difference (in this case, 2.955), then the means are assumed to be significantly different.

Group 1 vs. Group 4 (C. diff. = 2.955):
    16.25 − 9.25 **= 7.00** (significant)

Group 1 vs. Group 3 (C. diff. = 2.955):
    13.00 − 9.25 **= 3.75** (significant)

Group 1 vs. Group 2 (C. diff. = 2.955):
    9.25 − 7.33 **= 1.92** (nonsignificant)

Group 2 vs. Group 4 (C. diff. = 2.955):
    16.25 − 7.33 **= 8.92** (significant)

Group 2 vs. Group 3 (C. diff. = 2.955):
    13.00 − 7.33 **= 5.67** (significant)

Group 3 vs. Group 4 (C. diff. = 2.955):
    16.25 − 13.00 **= 3.25** (significant) ∎

SECTION 5.5
Duncan's Multiple-Range Test

The Duncan's multiple-range test involves the so-called layer or stair-step approach to the making of multiple comparisons. Instead of making all comparisons in relation to a single critical difference (as in the t-test), the size of the critical difference is adjusted depending upon whether the two means being compared are adjacent, or whether one or more other means fall between those being compared.

■ EXAMPLE

The data used to demonstrate the computational procedures are those used for the simple randomized design presented in Section 4.1. Recall that the summary table was as follows:

Source	SS	df	ms	F	p
Total	1132	47	—	—	—
Between groups	567	3	189.00	14.71	<.001
Within groups	565	44	12.84	—	—

The basic computational formula for the Duncan's multiple-range test is

$$\text{C. diffs.} = k_r \sqrt{\frac{\text{ms}_{\text{within gp. error}}}{n(\text{per gp.})}}$$

where the several k values are obtained from tables presented in Appendix J.

Step 1. Obtain the mean score for each group. (In this example, there are 12 scores per group.)*

Sum of Group 1 = 111 $\dfrac{111}{12} = \textbf{9.25}$ = mean of Group 1

Sum of Group 2 = 88 $\dfrac{88}{12} = \textbf{7.33}$ = mean of Group 2

Sum of Group 3 = 156 $\dfrac{156}{12} = \textbf{13.00}$ = mean of Group 3

Sum of Group 4 = 195 $\dfrac{195}{12} = \textbf{16.25}$ = mean of Group 4

Step 2. Derive the standard error of the means by

$$\sqrt{\frac{\text{ms}_{\text{within}}}{n(\text{per gp.})}}$$

For this example,

$$\sqrt{\frac{12.84}{12}} = \sqrt{1.07} = \textbf{1.03}$$

If there are unequal numbers of cases in some groups, you must account for those unequal ns. If the ns are not too disparate (as a rough rule of thumb, if there are not more than twice as many in the largest group as in the smallest group), you may use $\bar{n}$, the harmonic mean of the numbers, where

$$\bar{n} = \frac{\text{number of groups}}{\dfrac{1}{n_1} + \dfrac{1}{n_2} + \dfrac{1}{n_3} + \cdots + \dfrac{1}{n_i}}$$

For example, suppose that $n_1 = 16$, $n_2 = 12$, $n_3 = 8$, and $n_4 = 12$. Then,

$$\bar{n} = \frac{4}{\frac{1}{16} + \frac{1}{12} + \frac{1}{8} + \frac{1}{12}} = \frac{4}{.353} = \textbf{11.33}$$

So the standard error of the means would be

$$\sqrt{\frac{12.84}{11.33}} = \sqrt{1.13} = \textbf{1.06}$$

---

* For unequal ns, see C. Y. Kramer, "Extension of multiple range tests to group means with unequal numbers of replications," *Biometrics*, 1956, **12**, 307–310.

Step 3. Go to Appendix J ($p = .05$) to obtain the "significant studentized ranges." The table is entered at the row headed by the df for the mean square within groups. In the present example, the df for ms_{within} is 44. Since 44 df is not listed, use the next closest df, which is 40. Reading to the right in this row, for the different ranges of means (r) to be compared, the values are

$r = 2$: $k = 2.86$
$r = 3$: $k = 3.01$
$r = 4$: $k = 3.10$

Step 4. Multiply each significant range by the value obtained in Step 2. The values obtained are the minimum critical differences for the given ranges of comparisons.

$r = 2$:   C. diff.$_2$ = 2.86 × 1.03 = **2.95**
$r = 3$:   C. diff.$_3$ = 3.01 × 1.03 = **3.10**
$r = 4$:   C. diff.$_4$ = 3.10 × 1.03 = **3.19**

Step 5. Testing the differences between the various means: The means must first be *ranked* from *smallest* to *largest* so the appropriate critical difference for each comparison will be used. In this example, the means are ranked as: Gp. 2 = 7.33, Gp. 1 = 9.25, Gp. 3 = 13.00, Gp. 4 = 16.25. In each instance, if the difference between the means (see Step 1) is larger than the minimum for that range (Step 4), it is considered to be significant.

Group 2 vs. Group 4 (C. diff.$_4$ = 3.19)

16.25 − 7.33 = **8.92** (significant)

Group 2 vs. Group 3 (C. diff.$_2$ = 3.10)

13.00 − 7.33 = **5.67** (significant)

Group 2 vs. Group 1 (C. diff.$_2$ = 2.95)

9.25 − 7.33 = **1.92** (nonsignificant)

Group 1 vs. Group 4 (C. diff.$_3$ = 3.10)

16.25 − 9.25 = **7.00** (significant)

Group 1 vs. Group 3 (C. diff.$_2$ = 2.95)

13.00 − 9.25 = **3.75** (significant)

Group 3 vs. Group 4 (C. diff.$_2$ = 2.95)

16.25 − 13.00 = **3.25** (significant)

Therefore, it is concluded that Groups 2 and 4, 2, and 3, 1 and 4, 1 and 3, and 3 and 4 differ significantly in terms of their overall performance. ∎

SECTION 5.6
The Newman-Keuls' Multiple-Range Test

A somewhat more stringent layer approach for making multiple comparisons is the Newman-Keuls' multiple-range test. The computational steps for the Newman-Keuls' are the same as for the Duncan's, except the tabled values that determine the critical ranges are different. Many statisticians argue that the mathematical bases for the Newman-Keuls' tables are more defensible than those for the Duncan's.

■ **EXAMPLE**
Again, the data from the simple randomized design of Section 4.1 are used.

Source	SS	df	ms	F	p
Total	1132	47	—	—	—
Between groups	567	3	189.00	14.71	<.001
Within groups	565	44	12.84	—	—

The basic computational formula for the Newman-Keuls' is

$$\text{C. diffs.} = q_r \sqrt{\frac{\text{ms}_{\text{within gp. error}}}{n(\text{per gp.})}}$$

where the several q values are obtained from tables presented in Appendix K.

Step 1.   Obtain the mean score for each group. (In this example, there are 12 scores per group.)*

Sum of Group 1 = 111 $\frac{111}{12}$ = **9.25** = mean of Group 1

Sum of Group 2 = 88 $\frac{88}{12}$ = **7.33** = mean of Group 2

Sum of Group 3 = 156 $\frac{156}{12}$ = **13.00** = mean of Group 3

Sum of Group 4 = 195 $\frac{195}{12}$ = **16.25** = mean of Group 4

Step 2.   Derive the standard error of the means by

$$\sqrt{\frac{\text{ms}_{\text{within}}}{n(\text{per gp.})}}$$

---

*For unequal ns, see C. Y. Kramer, "Extension of multiple range tests to group means with unequal numbers of replications," *Biometrics*, 1956, **12**, 307–10.

For this example,

$$\sqrt{\frac{12.84}{12}} = \sqrt{1.07} = \mathbf{1.03}$$

If there are unequal numbers of cases in some groups, you must account for those unequal ns. If the ns are not too disparate (as a rough rule of thumb, if there are not more than twice as many in the largest group as in the smallest group), you may use $\bar{n}$, the harmonic mean of the numbers, where

$$\bar{n} = \frac{\text{number of groups}}{\dfrac{1}{n_1} + \dfrac{1}{n_2} + \dfrac{1}{n_3} + \cdots + \dfrac{1}{n_i}}$$

For example, suppose that $n_1 = 16$, $n_2 = 12$, $n_3 = 8$, and $n_4 = 12$. Then,

$$\bar{n} = \frac{4}{\frac{1}{16} + \frac{1}{12} + \frac{1}{8} + \frac{1}{12}} = \frac{4}{.353} = \mathbf{11.33}$$

So the standard error of the means would be

$$\sqrt{\frac{12.84}{11.33}} = \sqrt{1.13} = \mathbf{1.06}$$

Step 3. Go to Appendix K ($p = .05$) to obtain the "significant studentized ranges." The table is entered at the row headed by the df for the error mean square within groups. In the present example, the df for ms_{within} is 44. Since 44 df is not listed, use the next closest df, which is 40. Reading to the right in this row, for the different ranges of means (r) to be compared, the values are

$r = 2$: $q = 2.86$
$r = 3$: $q = 3.44$
$r = 4$: $q - 3.79$

Step 4. Multiply each significant range by the value obtained in Step 2. The values obtained are the minimum critical differences for the given ranges of comparisons.

$r = 2$:   C. diff.$_2$ = 2.86 × 1.03 = **2.95**
$r = 3$:   C. diff.$_3$ = 3.44 × 1.03 = **3.54**
$r = 4$:   C. diff.$_4$ = 3.79 × 1.03 = **3.90**

Step 5. Testing the differences between the various means: The means must first be ranked from smallest to largest in order that the range (r value) for each difference can be determined. In this example, the means are ranked as: Gp. $2 = 7.33$, Gp. $1 = 9.25$, Gp. $3 = 13.00$, Gp. $4 = 16.25$. In each instance, if the difference between the means (see Step 1) is larger than the minimum for that range (Step 4), it is considered to be significant.

Group 2 vs. Group 4 (C. diff.$_4$ = 3.90)

$\qquad$ 16.25 − 7.33 = **8.92** (significant)

Group 2 vs. Group 3 (C. diff.$_3$ = 3.54)

$\qquad$ 13.00 − 7.33 = **5.67** (significant)

Group 2 vs. Group 1 (C. diff.$_2$ = 2.95)

$\qquad$ 9.25 − 7.33 = **1.92** (nonsignificant)

Group 1 vs. Group 4 (C. diff.$_3$ = 3.54)

$\qquad$ 16.25 − 9.25 = **7.00** (significant)

Group 1 vs. Group 3 (C. diff.$_2$ = 2.95)

$\qquad$ 13.00 − 9.25 = **3.75** (significant)

Group 3 vs. Group 4 (C. diff.$_2$ = 2.95)

$\qquad$ 16.25 − 13.00 = **3.25** (significant)

Therefore, it is concluded that Groups 2 and 4, 2 and 3, 1 and 4, 1 and 3, and 3 and 4 differ significantly in terms of their overall performance. ∎

SECTION 5.7
The Tukey Test

Tukey's test is similar to the t-test in that a single critical difference is computed for making all the comparisons between the means; but it is also similar to the Duncan's and Newman-Keuls' tests in that the size of this critical difference is dependent upon the number of comparisons being made. The computational procedures for Tukey's test are basically the same as those for the Newman-Keuls' multiple-range test.

■ **EXAMPLE**

The set of data used to demonstrate the computational procedures is again that used for the simple randomized design presented in Section 4.1. Data from the final analysis of that example are:

Source	SS	df	ms	F	p
Total	1132	47	—	—	—
Between groups	567	3	189.00	14.71	<.001
Within groups	565	44	12.84	—	—

The basic computational formula for Tukey's test is

$$\text{C. diff.} = q_r \sqrt{\frac{\text{ms}_{\text{within gp. error}}}{n(\text{per gp.})}}$$

where the needed q value is obtained from tables presented in Appendix K.

Step 1.   Obtain the mean score for each group. (In this example, there are 12 scores per group.)*

Sum of Group 1 = 111 $\dfrac{111}{12}$ = **9.25**   = mean of Group 1

Sum of Group 2 = 88 $\dfrac{88}{12}$ = **7.33**   = mean of Group 2

Sum of Group 3 = 156 $\dfrac{156}{12}$ = **13.00** = mean of Group 3

Sum of Group 4 = 195 $\dfrac{195}{12}$ = **16.25** = mean of Group 4

Step 2.   Derive the standard error of the means by

$$\sqrt{\frac{\text{ms}_{\text{within}}}{n(\text{per gp.})}}$$

For this example,

$$\sqrt{\frac{12.84}{12}} = \sqrt{1.07} = \textbf{1.03}$$

If there are unequal numbers of cases in some groups, you must account for those unequal ns. If the ns are not too disparate (as a rough rule of thumb, if there are not more than twice as many in the largest group as in the smallest group), you may use $\bar{n}$, the harmonic mean of the numbers, where

$$\bar{n} = \cfrac{\text{number of groups}}{\dfrac{1}{n_1} + \dfrac{1}{n_2} + \dfrac{1}{n_3} + \cdots + \dfrac{1}{n_i}}$$

For example, suppose that $n_1 = 16$, $n_2 = 12$, $n_3 = 8$, and $n_4 = 12$. Then,

$$\bar{n} = \cfrac{4}{\frac{1}{16} + \frac{1}{12} + \frac{1}{8} + \frac{1}{12}} = \frac{4}{.353} = \textbf{11.33}$$

---

* For unequal ns, see C. Y. Kramer, "Extension of multiple range tests to group means with unequal numbers of replications," *Biometrics,* 1956, **12**, 307–10.

So the standard error of the means would be

$$\sqrt{\frac{12.84}{11.33}} = \sqrt{1.13} = \mathbf{1.06}$$

Step 3. The needed q value is obtained from Appendix K ($p = .05$). The table is entered at the column headed by the number of means to be compared and the row headed by the df for the mean square within groups. In the present example, the df for ms_{within} is 44. Since 44 is not listed, go to the next closest df, which is 40. At the .05 level for four means ($r = 4$) and 40 df, we find:

$$r = 4: \quad q = 3.79$$

Step 4. Now multiply the q value of Step 3 by the value obtained in Step 2. This gives the critical difference against which the several mean differences will be compared.

$$3.79 \times 1.03 = \mathbf{3.90} = \text{C. diff.}$$

Step 5. Testing the differences between the various means: In all instances, if the difference between any two means (see Step 1) is larger than the critical difference (in this case 3.90), then the means are assumed to be significantly different.

Group 1 vs. Group 4 (C. diff. = 3.90)

$$16.25 - 9.25 = \mathbf{7.00} \text{ (significant)}$$

Group 1 vs. Group 3 (C. diff. = 3.90)

$$13.00 - 9.25 = \mathbf{3.75} \text{ (nonsignificant)}$$

Group 1 vs. Group 2 (C. diff. = 3.90)

$$9.25 - 7.33 = \mathbf{1.92} \text{ (nonsignificant)}$$

Group 2 vs. Group 4 (C. diff. = 3.90)

$$16.25 - 7.33 = \mathbf{8.92} \text{ (significant)}$$

Group 2 vs. Group 3 (C. diff. = 3.90)

$$13.00 - 7.33 = \mathbf{5.67} \text{ (significant)}$$

Group 3 vs. Group 4 (C. diff. = 3.90)

$$16.25 - 13.00 = \mathbf{3.25} \text{ (nonsignificant)}$$ ■

Step 2.   Derive the standard error of the difference among means by

$$\sqrt{\frac{2 \text{ ms}_{\text{within}}}{n(\text{per gp.})}}$$

For this example,

$$\sqrt{\frac{2 \times 12.84}{12}} = \sqrt{2.14} = \textbf{1.46}$$

If there are unequal numbers of cases in some groups, you must account for those unequal ns. If the ns are not too disparate (as a rough rule of thumb, if there are not more than twice as many of the largest group as in the smallest group), you may use $\bar{n}$, the harmonic mean of the numbers, where

$$\bar{n} = \frac{\text{number of groups}}{\dfrac{1}{n_1} + \dfrac{1}{n_2} + \dfrac{1}{n_3} + \cdots + \dfrac{1}{n_i}}$$

For example, suppose that $n_1 = 16$, $n_2 = 12$, $n_3 = 8$, and $n_4 = 12$. Then,

$$\bar{n} = \frac{4}{\frac{1}{16} + \frac{1}{12} + \frac{1}{8} + \frac{1}{12}} = \frac{4}{.353} = \textbf{11.33}$$

So the standard error of the differences between means would be

$$\sqrt{\frac{2(12.84)}{11.33}} = \sqrt{2.266} = \textbf{1.51}$$

If the ns are widely different, the standard error must be computed separately for each comparison as

$$\sqrt{\text{ms}_{\text{within}}\left(\frac{1}{n_1} + \frac{1}{n_2}\right)}$$

For example, if $n = 16$, $n = 6$, and $\text{ms}_{\text{within}} = 12.84$, we would have

$$\sqrt{12.84(\tfrac{1}{18} + \tfrac{1}{6})} = \sqrt{\frac{12.84}{18} + \frac{12.84}{6}} = \sqrt{.713 + 2.14}$$

$$= \sqrt{2.853} = \textbf{1.69}$$

Step 3.   The needed F value is obtained from Appendix E ($p = .05$) for df equal to the number of groups minus 1, and the df for mean square$_{\text{within}}$. In this example, the appropriate df would be 3 and 44. However, since 44 is not listed, go to the next smallest tabled df, which would be 40.

$$F(3, 40) = 2.84$$

Step 4. Multiply this value by the number of groups minus 1, i.e.,

$$4 - 1 = 3 \times 2.84 = \mathbf{8.52}$$

Step 5. Take the square root of the above value and multiply by the value obtained in Step 2. The final result is the critical difference needed for comparison of the several means.

$$\sqrt{8.52} = 2.92$$

Then,

$$2.92 \times 1.46 = \mathbf{4.26} = \text{C. diff.}$$

Step 6. Testing the differences between the various means: In all instances, if the difference between any two means (see Step 1) is larger than the critical difference (in this case, 4.09), then the means are assumed to be significantly different.

Group 1 vs. Group 4 (C. diff. = 4.26)

$$16.25 - 9.25 = \mathbf{7.00} \text{ (significant)}$$

Group 1 vs. Group 3 (C. diff. = 4.26)

$$13.00 - 9.25 = \mathbf{3.75} \text{ (nonsignificant)}$$

Group 1 vs. Group 2 (C. diff. = 4.26)

$$7.33 - 9.25 = \mathbf{1.92} \text{ (nonsignificant)}$$

Group 2 vs. Group 4 (C. diff. = 4.26)

$$16.25 - 7.33 = \mathbf{8.92} \text{ (significant)}$$

Group 2 vs. Group 3 (C. diff. = 4.26)

$$13.00 - 7.33 = \mathbf{5.67} \text{ (significant)}$$

Group 3 vs. Group 4 (C. diff. = 4.26)

$$16.25 - 13.00 = \mathbf{3.25} \text{ (nonsignificant)}$$ ∎

SECTION 5.9
Dunnett's Test

The Dunnett is a specialized multiple-comparison test that is used in those instances when the only comparisons desired are between the control group and the various experimental groups (all possible comparisons involving all experimental groups are not made). The computational procedures of the Dunnett test are basically the same as those for the t-test and Scheffé's. As in those tests, a single critical difference is calculated against which all mean comparisons are made.

■ EXAMPLE

The data used to demonstrate the computational procedures are those used for the simple randomized design of Section 4.1. For this example, however, it will be assumed that Group 1 was the control group and Groups 2, 3, and 4 were experimental groups.

Source	SS	df	ms	F	p
Total	1132	47	—	—	—
Between groups	567	3	189.00	14.71	<.001
Within groups	565	44	12.84	—	—

The computational formula for Dunnett's test is

$$\text{C. diff.} = d_r \sqrt{\frac{2 \text{ ms}_{\text{within gp. error}}}{n(\text{per gp.})}}$$

where the needed d value is obtained from the tables presented in Appendix L.

Step 1. Obtain the mean score for each group. (In this example, there are 12 scores in each group.)

Sum of Group 1 = 111 $\dfrac{111}{12}$ = **9.25** = mean of Group 1

Sum of Group 2 = 88 $\dfrac{88}{12}$ = **7.33** = mean of Group 2

Sum of Group 3 = 156 $\dfrac{156}{12}$ = **13.00** = mean of Group 3

Sum of Group 4 = 195 $\dfrac{195}{12}$ = **16.25** = mean of Group 4

Step 2. Derive the standard error of the difference among means by

$$\sqrt{\frac{2 \text{ ms}_{\text{within}}}{n(\text{per gp.})}}$$

For this example,

$$\sqrt{\frac{2 \times 12.84}{12}} = \sqrt{2.14} = \textbf{1.46}$$

If there are unequal numbers of cases in some groups, you must account for those unequal ns. If the ns are not too disparate (as a rough rule of thumb, if there are not more than twice as many in the largest group as in the smallest group), you may use $\bar{n}$, the harmonic mean of the numbers, where

$$\bar{n} = \frac{\text{number of groups}}{\dfrac{1}{n_1} + \dfrac{1}{n_2} + \dfrac{1}{n_3} + \cdots + \dfrac{1}{n_i}}$$

For example, suppose that $n_1 = 16$, $n_2 = 12$, $n_3 = 8$, and $n_4 = 12$. Then,

$$\bar{n} = \frac{4}{\frac{1}{16} + \frac{1}{12} + \frac{1}{8} + \frac{1}{12}} = \frac{4}{.353} = \textbf{11.33}$$

So the standard error of the differences between means would be

$$\sqrt{\frac{2(12.84)}{11.33}} = \sqrt{2.266} = \textbf{1.51}$$

If the ns are widely different, the standard error must be computed separately for each comparison as

$$\sqrt{\text{ms}_{\text{within}}\left(\frac{1}{n_1} + \frac{1}{n_2}\right)}$$

For example, if $n_1 = 18$, $n_2 = 6$, and $\text{ms}_{\text{within}} = 12.84$, we would have

$$\sqrt{12.84(\tfrac{1}{18} + \tfrac{1}{6})} = \sqrt{\frac{12.84}{18} + \frac{12.84}{6}} = \sqrt{.713 + 2.14}$$
$$= \sqrt{2.853} = \textbf{1.69}$$

Step 3. The needed d value is obtained from Appendix L ($p = .05$). The table is entered at the column headed by the number of means to be compared and the row headed by the df for the error mean square within groups. In the present example, the df for $\text{ms}_{\text{within}}$ is 44, but since that value is not listed, read the table at the next smallest value, which is 40. Thus for 4 groups and 40 df, the d value is:

$r = 4$: $\qquad d = 2.44$

Step 4. Multiply the value obtained in Step 2 by the value of Step 3 to obtain the critical difference.

$1.46 \times 2.44 = \textbf{3.56} = \text{C. diff.}$

Step 5.   Testing the differences between the control and experimental groups: In all instances, if the difference between the means is larger than the critical difference obtained in Step 4 (3.56 in this example), the means are assumed to be significantly different.

Group 1 vs. Group 2 (C. diff. = 3.56)

$9.25 - 7.33 = \textbf{1.92}$ (nonsignificant)

Group 1 vs. Group 3 (C. diff. = 3.56)

$13.00 - 9.25 = \textbf{3.75}$ (significant)

Group 1 vs. Group 4 (C. diff. = 3.56)

$16.25 - 9.25 = \textbf{7.00}$ (significant)

See page 203 for a summary of the differences in the several test results.

■

SECTION 5.10
F-Tests for Simple Effects

The *F*-test for simple effects is most commonly used when one of the factorial or mixed designs yields a significant interaction.

■ **EXAMPLE**

To demonstrate some of the more commonly used tests of simple effects, a complete analysis of the two-factor mixed design of Section 4.7 will be presented. Although the presentation in this section represents a considerably more detailed analysis than is usually carried out, the several operations are presented for the sake of completeness.

First, recall the final analysis of the mixed design of Section 4.7.

Source	SS	df	ms	F	p
Total	467	98	—	—	—
Between subjects	181	32	—	—	—
Conditions	39	2	19.50	4.12	<.05
Error$_b$	142	30	4.73	—	—
Within subjects	286	66	—	—	—
Trials	170	2	85.00	52.46	<.001
Trials × Conditions	19	4	4.75	2.93	<.05
Error$_w$	97	60	1.62	—	—

SUMMARY TABLE

	t-test	Duncan's	Newman-Keuls'	Tukey's	Scheffé's	Dunnett's
	C. diff. = 2.94	C. diff. = $2.94_{(r=2)}$ $3.10_{(r=3)}$ $3.19_{(r=4)}$	C. diff. = $2.94_{(r=2)}$ $3.54_{(r=3)}$ $3.90_{(r=4)}$	C. diff. = 3.90	C. diff. = 4.26	C. diff. = 3.56
Gp 2 vs. 4 7.33 vs. 16.25	Significant	Significant	Significant	Significant	Significant	—
Gp 2 vs. 3 7.33 vs. 13.00	Significant	Significant	Significant	Significant	Significant	—
Gp 2 vs. 1 7.33 vs. 9.25	Nonsignificant	Nonsignificant	Nonsignificant	Nonsignificant	Nonsignificant	Nonsignificant
Gp 1 vs. 4 9.25 vs. 16.25	Significant	Significant	Significant	Nonsignificant	Nonsignificant	Significant
Gp 1 vs. 3 9.25 vs. 13.00	Significant	Significant	Significant	Significant	Significant	Significant
Gp 3 vs. 4 13.00 vs. 16.25	Significant	Significant	Significant	Nonsignificant	Nonsignificant	—

Figure 1

The conclusions drawn from this analysis were:

1. Meaningfulness of material significantly affected overall amount learned.
2. The overall tendency of the subjects was to change (learn) as a function of practice (trials).
3. The subjects in the various groups learned at different rates.

The specific questions to be answered by the analyses of simple effects relate to the differences noted above and can be stated as follows.

First Questions.   The first two questions relate to the significant main effects of "Conditions" and "Trials." In the case of "Conditions," the significant F ratio merely means that of the three groups, at least two differ significantly. The problem is to determine which specific pairs differ. Similarly, the significant overall F for "Trials" means that on at least two trials, a change in performance took place. Thus, further tests are needed to determine on which specific trials a significant change occurred. In both instances, the Newman-Keuls' range test will be applied to analyze the difference.* The graphical representation of the group means (Question 1a) being compared is presented in Figure 1. (*Note:* In most instances where there is a significant interaction, as is the case in this example, analyses of the main effects would not be undertaken and the researcher would proceed directly to the third question, listed below.)

Question 1a.   Which of the three groups (conditions) differ significantly from each other in terms of overall performance?

Step 1.   Obtain the overall mean for each of the three groups. The sums obtained in Step 3 of the original analysis (Section 4.7) must be divided by the number of subjects in each of the experimental groups times the number of

_____

* Obviously, Scheffé's, etc., tests could also be used.

scores recorded for each subject (in this case, 33, since 33 measures were recorded in each group).

Sum of Group 1 = 111 $\dfrac{111}{33}$ = **3.36** = mean of Group 1

Sum of Group 2 = 124 $\dfrac{124}{33}$ = **3.76** = mean of Group 2

Sum of Group 3 = 160 $\dfrac{160}{33}$ = **4.85** = mean of Group 3

Step 2. Derive the standard error by

$$\sqrt{\frac{ms_{errors}}{n(\text{measures per group})}} = \sqrt{\frac{4.73}{33}} = \sqrt{.1433} = \textbf{.38}$$

Step 3. The significant studentized ranges are obtained from Appendix K of Newman-Keuls' multiple-range values ($p = .05$). The table is entered at the row headed by the *df* for ms_{error_b}, which is 30. Reading to the right in this row, for the different ranges of means (*r*) to be compared, the values are

$r = 2$: $q = 2.89$

$r = 3$: $q = 3.49$

Step 4. Multiply each significant range by the value obtained in Step 2. This gives the minimum critical differences against which the actual differences in the means will be compared.

$r = 2$:   C. diff. = $2.89 \times .38$ = **1.10**

$r = 3$:   C. diff. = $3.49 \times .38$ = **1.32**

Step 5. Testing the difference between the various means: First, rank the means from smallest to largest. In each instance, if the difference between the means (see Step 1) is larger than the minimum for that range (Step 4), it is considered to be significant.

Group 3 vs. Group 1 ($R_3 = 1.32$)

$4.85 - 3.36$ = **1.49** (significant)

Group 3 vs. Group 2 ($R_2 = 1.10$)

$4.85 - 3.76$ = **1.09** (nonsignificant)

Group 2 vs. Group 1 ($R_2 = 1.10$)

$3.76 - 3.36$ = **.40** (nonsignificant)

Therefore, it is concluded that only Groups 1 and 3 differ significantly in terms of their overall performance.

Question 1b.   On which of the three trials is there a significant change in the average performance of the three groups?

Step 1.   Obtain the overall mean for each of the three trials. The sums obtained in Step 13 of the original analysis (Section 4.7) must be divided by the number of subjects in each group times the number of groups (in this case, 33 since there were 11 subjects in each of the three groups).

Sum of Trial 1 = 73 $\dfrac{73}{33} = \mathbf{2.21} =$ overall mean of Trial 1

Sum of Trial 2 = 146 $\dfrac{146}{33} = \mathbf{4.42} =$ overall mean of Trial 2

Sum of Trial 3 = 176 $\dfrac{176}{33} = \mathbf{5.33} =$ overall mean of Trial 3

Step 2.   Derive the standard error by

$$\sqrt{\dfrac{ms_{error_w}}{n(\text{total number of measures per trial})}} = \sqrt{\dfrac{1.62}{33}} = \sqrt{.049} = \mathbf{.22}$$

Step 3.   The significant studentized ranges are obtained from Appendix K. The table is entered at the row headed by the df for ms_{error_w}, which is 60.

$r = 2$: $q = 2.83$

$r = 3$: $q = 3.40$

Step 4.   Multiply each significant range by the value obtained in Step 2.

$r = 2$:   C. diff. $= 2.83 \times .22 = \mathbf{.62}$

$r = 3$:   C. diff. $= 3.40 \times .22 = \mathbf{.75}$

Step 5.   Testing the difference between the various means: First, rank the means from smallest to largest. In each instance, if the difference (Step 1) is larger than the minimum for that range (Step 4), it is considered to be significant.

Trial 3 vs. Trial 1 $(R_3 = .75)$

$5.33 - 2.21 = \mathbf{3.12}$ (significant)

Trial 2 vs. Trial 1 $(R_2 = .62)$

$4.42 - 2.21 = \mathbf{2.21}$ (significant)

Trial 3 vs. Trial 2 $(R_2 = .62)$

$5.33 - 4.42 = \mathbf{.91}$ (significant)

Therefore, it is concluded that the overall means of the three trials differ significantly from each other.

Question 2. Although the overall tendency of the groups was to change (learn) as a function of trials (practice), did each of the groups actually improve? (*Note:* In actuality, most researchers would not be interested in this question until the third question had been answered. However, since this is merely an example, the various significant effects will be treated in order.) The graphical representation of the effect being analyzed is presented in Figure 2.

Step 1. From Step 2 of the original analysis (Section 4.7), obtain the sums of the trials for Group 1.

Sum for Trial 1 = **24**
Sum for Trial 2 = **38**
Sum for Trial 3 = **49**

Step 2. Square each of these values, divide by the number of scores on which each sum was based (in this case, 11), and add the quotients.

$$\frac{24^2}{11} + \frac{38^2}{11} + \frac{49^2}{11} = \frac{4421}{11} = \mathbf{401.91}$$

Step 3. Obtain the grand sum for Group 1.

$$24 + 38 + 49 = \mathbf{111}$$

Then, square this sum and divide by the total number of scores recorded in Group 1.

$$\frac{111^2}{33} = \frac{12{,}321}{33} = \mathbf{373.36}$$

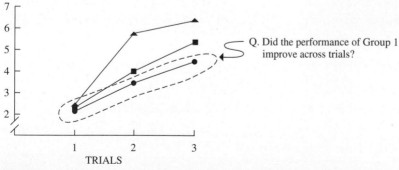

Q. Did the performance of Group 1 improve across trials?

TRIALS

Figure 2

Step 4.   Subtract the value of Step 3 from that of Step 2. This yields the Group 1 sum of squares for trials.

$$401.91 - 373.36 = \textbf{28.55} = SS_{trials} \text{ for Group 1}$$

Step 5.   The df for this component are equal to the number of trials minus 1.

$$3 - 1 = 2$$

Step 6.   Computation of the mean square for the simple trials effects: Merely divide the SS_{trials} for Group 1 (Step 4) by the df (Step 5).

$$\frac{28.55}{2} = \textbf{14.27} = ms_{trials} \text{ for Group 1}$$

Step 7.   The test of significance (F-test) of the trials effect for Group 1 is $ms_{trials(Gp1)}/ms_{error_w(total)}$.

$$F = \frac{14.27}{1.62} = \textbf{8.81}$$

From Appendix E, it is found that this value, with df 2 and 60, is significant ($p < .001$). Therefore, it is concluded that performance of the subjects in Group 1 changed as a function of practice. The same procedures should be repeated for Groups 2 and 3. In each instance, the F ratio equals $ms_{trials(Gp.2 \text{ or } 3)}/ms_{error_w(total)}$.

Alternate Analysis to Answer Question 2.   The analysis presented above merely indicates that there was an overall tendency for the performance of subjects in Group 1 to change over trials. By use of the Newman-Keuls' analysis presented below, it will be possible to determine which specific trials within Group 1 (or any other group to which the analysis might be applied) differ significantly from each other.

Step 1.   From Step 2 of the original analysis, obtain the mean score for each trial in Group 1.

Sum for Trial 1 = 24 $\dfrac{24}{11} = \textbf{2.18} =$ mean for Group 1/Trial 1

Sum for Trial 2 = 38 $\dfrac{38}{11} = \textbf{3.45} =$ mean for Group 1/Trial 2

Sum for Trial 3 = 49 $\dfrac{49}{11} = \textbf{4.45} =$ mean for Group 1/Trial 3

Step 2.   Derive the standard error as

$$\sqrt{\frac{ms_{error_w}}{n(\text{number of measures per trial})}} = \sqrt{\frac{1.62}{11}} = \sqrt{.147} = \textbf{.38}$$

Step 3.   The significant studentized ranges are obtained from Appendix K. The table is entered at the row headed by the *df* for ms_{error_w}.

$r = 2$: $q = 2.83$

$r = 3$: $q = 3.40$

Step 4.   Multiply each significant range by the value obtained in Step 2.

$r = 2$:   C. diff. $= 2.83 \times .38 =$ **1.08**

$r = 3$:   C. diff. $= 3.40 \times .38 =$ **1.29**

Step 5.   Testing the difference between the various means: First, rank the means from the smallest to largest. In each instance, if the difference (Step 1) is larger than the minimum for that range (Step 4), it is considered to be significant.

Trial 3 vs. Trial 1 ($R_3 = 1.29$)

$4.45 - 2.18 =$ **2.27** (significant)

Trial 2 vs. Trial 1 ($R_2 = 1.08$)

$3.45 - 2.18 =$ **1.27** (significant)

Trial 3 vs. Trial 2 ($R_2 = 1.08$)

$4.45 - 3.45 =$ **1.00** (nonsignificant)

Therefore, it is concluded that trials 1 and 2, and 1 and 3 in Group 1 differ significantly from each other.

Question 3:   The trials-by-conditions interaction indicates that at least two of the groups of subjects learned at different rates. Which groups were they? Comparisons must be made between Groups 1 and 2, Groups 1 and 3, and Groups 2 and 3. In the present example, the first comparison will be made between Groups 1 and 2. The graphical representation of the comparison is presented in Figure 3.

Q. Did Groups 1 & 2 learn at different rates?

Figure 3

Step 1. From Step 2 of the original analysis (Section 4.7), obtain the sums of each of the trials for Group 1 and Group 2.

	Trial 1	Trial 2	Trial 3
Sums for Group 1 =	24	38	49
Sums for Group 2 =	24	43	57

Step 2. Obtain the overall sum for each of the groups.

$24 + 38 + 49 = \mathbf{111} =$ sum for Group 1

$24 + 43 + 57 = \mathbf{124} =$ sum for Group 2

Then, square these sums, divide by the number of scores on which each sum was based, and add the quotients.

$$\frac{111^2}{33} + \frac{124^2}{33} = \frac{27,697}{33} = \mathbf{839.30}$$

Step 3. Obtain the grand sum for both groups.

$111 + 124 = \mathbf{235}$

Then, square this value, and divide it by the total number of scores recorded in Groups 1 and 2. This yields the correction term for the Group 1 versus Group 2 comparison.

$$\frac{235^2}{66} = \frac{55,225}{66} = \mathbf{836.74}$$

Step 4. Computation of the Group 1 versus Group 2 effects: Merely subtract the correction term (Step 3) from the value obtained in Step 2.

$839.30 - 836.74 = \mathbf{2.56} = \mathrm{SS}_{\mathrm{groups}}$ for Groups 1 and 2

Step 5. Computation of the effects of trials for Groups 1 and 2: First, obtain the sum of Trials 1, 2, and 3 for both experimental groups (see Step 1).

$24 + 24 = \mathbf{48} =$ sum for Trial 1

$38 + 43 = \mathbf{81} =$ sum for Trial 2

$49 + 57 = \mathbf{106} =$ sum for Trial 3

Then, square each of these sums, divide by the number of scores on which each was based, and add the quotients.

$$\frac{48^2}{22} + \frac{81^2}{22} + \frac{106^2}{22} = \frac{20,101}{22} = \mathbf{913.68}$$

Then, subtract the correction term (Step 3) from the above value.

913.68 − 836.74 **= 76.94** $=$ SS$_{trials}$ for Groups 1 and 2

Step 6. Computation of interaction of trials by conditions (groups) for Groups 1 and 2: First, square each of the sums for each trial for Groups 1 and 3 (Step 1). Divide each value by the number of scores on which each sum was based, then add the quotients.

$$\frac{24^2}{11} + \frac{38^2}{11} + \frac{49^2}{11} + \frac{24^2}{11} + \frac{43^2}{11} + \frac{57^2}{11} = \frac{10,095}{11} = \textbf{917.73}$$

Then, subtract the correction term (Step 3), the SS$_{groups}$ (Step 4), and SS$_{trials}$ (Step 5) from the above value.

917.73 − 836.74 − 2.56 − 76.94

$$= \textbf{1.48} = SS_{trials \times groups} \text{ for Groups 1 and 2}$$

Step 7. The *df* for this component is equal to the number of trials minus 1, times the number of groups minus 1.

(3 − 1)(2 − 1) **= 2**

Step 8. Computation of the ms for the trials-by-groups interaction for Groups 1 and 2: Merely divide the SS$_{trials \times groups}$ (Step 6) by the *df* (Step 7).

$$\frac{1.48}{2} = \textbf{.74} = ms_{trials \times groups} \text{ for Groups 1 and 2}$$

Step 9. The test of significance (*F*-test) is computed as

$$F = \frac{ms_{trials \times groups (Gps.1 and 2)}}{ms_{error_w (total)}}$$

Thus,

$$F = \frac{.74}{1.62} = \textbf{.46}$$

From Appendix E, it is found that this *F* value, with *df* = 2 and 60, is nonsignificant. Therefore, it is concluded that the subjects in Groups 1 and 2 did not learn at different rates. The remaining tests of simple interactions are carried out in exactly the same way except that Groups 1 and 3 are compared, and then Groups 2 and 3. In all instances, the test of significance is $F = ms_{trials \times groups}/ms_{error_w}$.

Alternate Approaches to Question 3.   Since both the overall conditions effect and the trials-by-conditions interaction were significant in the present example, it may be of interest to determine exactly where (on which trials) the groups

Q. Are there differences among the initial performance levels of the three groups?

Figure 4

differed significantly. One of the most common techniques is to compare the performance of the several groups on each trial. Although many analyses are used (Newman-Keuls', Tukey's, etc.), the F-test is employed most often and is a series of completely randomized designs for each trial. The F-test of group differences for Trial 1* is presented below. The graphical representation of this analysis is shown in Figure 4.

Step 1. From Step 1 of the original analysis (Section 4.7), obtain the scores for each subject in all three groups on Trial 1. Table these scores as follows:

	TRIAL 1				
Group 1		Group 2		Group 3	
Subject	Score	Subject	Score	Subject	Score
S_1	3	S_{12}	2	S_{23}	2
S_2	3	S_{13}	1	S_{24}	3
S_3	1	S_{14}	3	S_{25}	4
S_4	1	S_{15}	2	S_{26}	1
S_5	2	S_{16}	1	S_{27}	3
S_6	4	S_{17}	4	S_{28}	1
S_7	4	S_{18}	1	S_{29}	1
S_8	1	S_{19}	1	S_{30}	2
S_9	1	S_{20}	2	S_{31}	3
S_{10}	2	S_{21}	3	S_{32}	1
S_{11}	2	S_{22}	4	S_{33}	4

---

* There are occasions when this analysis might be applied even if the trials-by-conditions interaction were not significant. Although the problem is not present in this example, sometimes there is a question as to whether the groups might have differed significantly on the first trial (sampling error). If this were the case, any differences noted in the overall analysis would reflect this error rather than any real differences due to treatment effects.

Step 2.   Turn to the completely randomized design as presented in Section 4.1, and continue with Step 2 of that analysis. The final F value (Step 12) will indicate whether there are significant differences among the group means on this particular trial. Repeat the same procedure for the remaining trials.

Note: If, when the above analyses have been completed, significant conditions (group) effects are found, one of the multiple comparisons tests may be used to determine which specific pairs of groups differ.

The second alternative to answering Question 3 proceeds in nearly the same fashion as the method presented above, except that the comparisons between the groups are made against a single, pooled error term. It should be noted that this approach is recommended by many authors but is considered dubious by others. This pooled error term is computed as follows*:

Step 1.   Secure the needed mean square$_{\text{within cell}}$ which will serve as the error term for all comparisons. The sums of squares and df values are obtained from the summary table of the original analysis.

$$\text{ms}_{\text{within cells}} = \frac{\text{SS}_{\text{error}_b} + \text{SS}_{\text{error}_w}}{df_{\text{error}_b} + df_{\text{error}_w}}$$

$$= \frac{142 + 97}{30 + 60}$$

$$= \frac{239}{90}$$

$$= \mathbf{2.66} \text{ with } df = 90$$

Step 2.   Proceed to compute the mean square$_{\text{conditions}}$ for each trial. First, secure the sums for Groups 1, 2, and 3 on the first trial, and obtain the overall sum for that trial.

Sum for Group 1 on Trial 1 = **24**

Sum for Group 2 on Trial 1 = **24**

Sum for Group 3 on Trial 1 = **25**
Overall Sum for Trial 1 = **73**

Step 3.   Square each sum for Trial 1, and divide that value by the number of scores on which the sum was based. Add those values.

$$\frac{24^2}{11} + \frac{24^2}{11} + \frac{25^2}{11} = \frac{1777}{11} = \mathbf{161.54}$$

---

* See Winer (1991) *pp.* 530–31 for a discussion of an alternate method to calculate the df for ms$_{\text{within cells}}$.

Step 4. Square the overall sum for Trial 1, and divide that value by the number of scores added to obtain that sum.

$$\frac{73^2}{33} = \frac{5329}{33} = \mathbf{161.48}$$

Step 5. Computation of $SS_{conditions}$ for Trial 1: Subtract the value of Step 4 from that of Step 3.

$$161.54 - 161.48 = \mathbf{.06}$$

Step 6. Computation of the mean square$_{conditions\ for\ Trial\ 1}$: The df are equal to the number of groups minus 1, and the mean square is computed as $SS_{conditions}/df_{conditions}$.

$$ms_{conditions} = \frac{.06}{2} = \mathbf{.03}$$

Step 7. The F ratio to test for differences among the groups of Trial 1 is as follows:

$$F = \frac{ms_{conditions\ at\ Trial\ 1}}{ms_{within\ cells}} = \frac{.03}{2.66} = \mathbf{.01}$$

For $df = 2$ and 90, and F ratio of approximately 3.15 is needed to achieve significance. Obviously, the computed F ratio of .01 falls far short of the value required.

Step 8. Repeat steps 2, 3, 4, 5, and 6 for the remaining trials. In all cases, the error term for the F ratio will be the value computed in Step 1 ($ms_{within\ cells}$). ∎

SECTION 5.11
Use of Orthogonal Components in Tests for Trend

In general, after an F ratio has been found to be significant, the only additional tests are those for simple effects (Sections 5.4–5.10). Occasionally, however, it is of interest to determine the shape of the curves that best fit the data points of the various experimental groups. If the treatments form an increasing or decreasing continuum, such as trials or variations in shock intensity or anxiety level, the treatment effects can be further subdivided into trend components by use of orthogonal polynomials.

Three examples will be presented: The first is based on the data of Section 4.1 (the completely randomized design), the second on data presented in Section 4.7 (the two-factor mixed design), and the third on data from Section 4.8 (the three-factor mixed design). These examples represent the most frequent instances where this type of trend analysis is used, but they by no means exhaust the possibilities of application since the analysis can be used with any design. It is important to note that this type of trend analysis merely gives information regarding the shape of the performance curves. The nature of the data and the purpose of the experiment determine entirely whether these analyses are worthwhile.

■ EXAMPLE 1

This example is based on the data and results of the completely randomized analysis presented in Section 4.1. First, recall the final analysis of that section:

Source	SS	df	ms	F	p
Total	1132	47	—	—	—
Between groups	567	3	189.00	14.71	<.001
Within groups	565	44	12.84	—	—

Question. What degree polynomial best approximates the form of the curve that connects the data points (group means) of the four groups?

Step 1. Turn to Appendix N and obtain the appropriate coefficients for the re-analysis. Since there are four groups, the coefficients for $k = 4$ are

Linear:	-3	-1	$+1$	$+3$
Quadratic:	$+1$	-1	-1	$+1$
Cubic:	-1	$+3$	-3	$+1$

Step 2. The linear component will be analyzed first. To do this, multiply the *sum* of each group (Step 2 of the original analysis) by its appropriate linear coefficient.

Sum of Group 1 = 111 $111 \times (-3) = \mathbf{-333}$

Sum of Group 2 = 88 $88 \times (-1) = \mathbf{-88}$

Sum of Group 3 = 156 $156 \times (+1) = \mathbf{+156}$

Sum of Group 4 = 195 $195 \times (+3) = \mathbf{+585}$

Step 3. Get the algebraic sum of the values obtained in Step 2.

$$(-333) + (-88) + 156 + 585 = \mathbf{+320}$$

Then, square that sum.

$$320^2 = \mathbf{102,400}$$

Step 4. Square each of the linear coefficients (Step 1), and sum these squared values.

$$(-3)^2 + (-1)^2 + 1^2 + 3^2 = \mathbf{20}$$

Then, multiply the sum by the number of subjects in each group (12 in the present example).

$$20 \times 12 = \mathbf{240}$$

Step 5. Divide the value of Step 3 by that of Step 4.

$$\frac{102{,}400}{240} = \mathbf{426.67} = SS_{linear}$$

Step 6. The test for linear trend is an F ratio that is equal to the value of Step 5 divided by the mean square within groups of the original analysis. (In the present example, $ms_{within} = 12.84$.) Compute this F, and record the value for future use.

$$F_{linear} = \frac{426.67}{12.84} = \mathbf{33.22}$$

The degrees of freedom (df) for this F ratio are always equal to 1 and the df for ms_{within} of the original analysis (1, 44 in the present example).

After the linear computations are completed, the same basic steps must be repeated to analyze the quadratic component.

Step 1. From Step 1 of the linear analysis (or Appendix N), obtain the coefficients for the quadratic component. In the present example, where $k = 4$, these are:

Quadratic: +1   −1   −1   +1

Step 2. This time multiply the sum of each group by its appropriate quadratic coefficient.

Sum of Group 1 = 111 $111 \times (+1) = \mathbf{+111}$

Sum of Group 2 = 88 $88 \times (-1) = \mathbf{-88}$

Sum of Group 3 = 156 $156 \times (-1) = \mathbf{-156}$

Sum of Group 4 = 195 $195 \times (+1) = \mathbf{+195}$

Step 3. Get the algebraic sum of the values obtained in Step 2.

$$111 + (-88) + (-156) + 195 = \mathbf{+62}$$

Then, square this sum.

$$+62^2 = \mathbf{3844}$$

Step 4. Square the quadratic coefficients, and sum these squared values.

$$1^2 + (-1)^2 + (-1)^2 + 1^2 = \mathbf{4}$$

Then, multiply this sum by the number of subjects in each group. (In the present example, 12)

$$4 \times 12 = \mathbf{48}$$

Step 5. Divide the value of Step 3 by that of Step 4.

$$\frac{3844}{48} = \mathbf{80.08} = SS_{quadratic}$$

Step 6. The test for quadratic trend is an F ratio that is equal to the value of Step 5 divided by the mean square within groups of the original analysis. Compute this F, and record the value for future use.

$$F_{quadratic} = \frac{80.08}{12.84} = \mathbf{6.23}$$

The df for this F ratio are always equal to 1 and the df for ms_{within} of the original analysis (44 in this example).

Once again the computations must be repeated; this time, analyze the cubic component.

Step 1. From Step 1 of the linear analysis (or Appendix N), obtain the cubic coefficients. In the present example, where $k = 4$, these are

Cubic: -1 $+3$ -3 $+1$

Step 2. Multiply the sum of each group by the appropriate cubic coefficient.

Sum of Group 1 = 111 $111 \times (-1) = \mathbf{-111}$

Sum of Group 2 = 88 $88 \times (+3) = \mathbf{+264}$

Sum of Group 3 = 156 $156 \times (-3) = \mathbf{-468}$

Sum of Group 4 = 195 $195 \times (+1) = \mathbf{+195}$

Step 3. Get the algebraic sum of the values obtained in Step 2.

$$(-111) + 264 + (-468) + 195 = \mathbf{-120}$$

Then, square this sum.

$$-120^2 = \mathbf{14,400}$$

Step 4. Square each of the cubic coefficients, and sum these squared values.

$$(-1)^2 + 3^2 + (-3)^2 + 1^2 = \mathbf{20}$$

Then, multiply that sum by the number of subjects in each group (12 in this example).

$$20 \times 12 = \mathbf{240}$$

Step 5. Divide the value of Step 3 by that of Step 4.

$$\frac{14,400}{240} = \mathbf{60.00} = SS_{cubic}$$

Step 6. The test of significance for cubic trend is again an F ratio that is equal to the value of Step 5 divided by the mean square within groups of the original analysis. Compute this F, and record the value for future use.

$$F_{cubic} = \frac{60.00}{12.84} = \mathbf{4.67}$$

The df are equal to 1 and the df for ms_{within} (44 in this example).

Step 7. Final check for accuracy: Since the sum of squares between groups was broken into its several trend components, the sums of the linear, quadratic, and cubic components must equal (within rounding error) the sum of squares between groups. (In the present example, $SS_b = 567$.)

$$426.67 + 80.08 + 60.00 = \mathbf{566.75}$$

Note: If the sum of the trend components does not equal the sum of squares between groups, an error in computation has been made.

Step 8. Final tabling of the data: Although there are several ways to do this, the following is most often used:

Source	SS	df	ms	F	p
Total	1132	47	—	—	—
Between groups	567	3	189.00	14.71	<.001
Linear	426.67	1	426.67	33.22	<.001
Quadratic	80.08	1	80.08	6.23	<.025
Cubic	60.00	1	60.00	4.67	<.05
Within groups	565	44	12.84	—	—

The results are interpreted as showing that the data can be best described mathematically by a complex equation. The significant linear component shows that there is some tendency for the data to lie along a straight line. The significant quadratic component shows that there is a tendency for the data to deviate from a straight line in an arcing manner. A quadratic function is represented by a curving line, such as a parabolic arc. The significant cubic component shows that there is a tendency for the data to crisscross a straight line in a regular fashion. A cubic function is similar to two connected parabolic arcs, each peaking in opposite directions.

■ EXAMPLE 2

First, recall the two-factor mixed analysis as presented in Section 4.7. The final table of the results was as follows:

Source	SS	df	ms	F	p
Total	467	98	—	—	—
Between subjects	181	32	—	—	—
Conditions	39	2	19.50	4.12	<.05
Error$_b$	142	30	4.73	—	—
Within subjects	286	66	—	—	—
Trials	170	2	85.00	52.46	<.001
Trials by conditions	19	4	4.75	2.93	<.05
Error$_w$	97	60	1.62	—	—

Question. What level of polynomial functions best describes the form of the data points of the various within-subjects effects?

Step 1. Turn to Appendix N, and obtain the appropriate coefficients for the re-analysis. In the present example, each subject was measured three times (three trials). Therefore, the coefficients for $k = 3$ are:

Linear:	-1	0	$+1$
Quadratic:	$+1$	-2	$+1$

Step 2. The linear component will be analyzed first. Go back to the data recorded in Step 1 of the original analysis (Section 4.7), and multiply each subject's score by the appropriate linear coefficient. In the present example, the retabled data would appear as follows:

	GROUP 1 (LOW-MEANINGFUL MATERIAL)		
Subject	Trial Block 1 Score × −1	Trial Block 2 Score × 0	Trial Block 3 Score × +1
S_1	−3	0	4
S_2	−3	0	4
S_3	−1	0	4
S_4	−1	0	3
S_5	−2	0	5
S_6	−4	0	6
S_7	−4	0	6
S_8	−1	0	5
S_9	−1	0	5
S_{10}	−2	0	3
S_{11}	−2	0	4

GROUP 2 (MEDIUM-MEANINGFUL MATERIAL)		
Trial Block 1	Trial Block 2	Trial Block 3
Subject	Score × −1	Score × 0	Score × +1
S_{12}	−2	0	6
S_{13}	−1	0	5
S_{14}	−3	0	7
S_{15}	−2	0	6
S_{16}	−1	0	3
S_{17}	−4	0	5
S_{18}	−1	0	4
S_{19}	−1	0	4
S_{20}	−2	0	4
S_{21}	−3	0	6
S_{22}	−4	0	7

GROUP 3 (HIGH-MEANINGFUL MATERIAL)		
S_{23}	−2	0	8
S_{24}	−3	0	3
S_{25}	−4	0	7
S_{26}	−1	0	4
S_{27}	−3	0	12
S_{28}	−1	0	2
S_{29}	−1	0	3
S_{30}	−2	0	6
S_{31}	−3	0	6
S_{32}	−1	0	12
S_{33}	−4	0	7

Step 3.   Obtain the algebraic sum of the "weighted scores" for each subject in all groups. (*Note:* All subsequent linear computations will be based on these algebraic sums.)

	Group 1					
Subject	Trial Block 1		Trial Block 2		Trial Block 3	Sum
S_1	−3	+	0	+	4	+1
S_2	−3	+	0	+	4	+1
⋮	⋮		⋮		⋮	⋮
S_{11}	−2	+	0	+	4	+2

Subject	Trial Block 1		Group 2 Trial Block 2		Trial Block 3	Sum
S_{12}	-2	$+$	0	$+$	6	**+4**
S_{13}	-1	$+$	0	$+$	5	**+4**
$\vdots$	$\vdots$		$\vdots$		$\vdots$	$\vdots$
S_{22}	-4	$+$	0	$+$	7	**+3**

			Group 3			
S_{23}	-2	$+$	0	$+$	8	**+6**
S_{24}	-3	$+$	0	$+$	3	**0**
$\vdots$	$\vdots$		$\vdots$		$\vdots$	$\vdots$
S_{33}	-4	$+$	0	$+$	7	**+3**

Step 4.   Add the subject sums obtained in Step 3 to get the algebraic sum for each experimental group. (*Note:* These group sums may be negative.)

$$1 + 1 + \cdots + 2 = \textbf{+25} = \text{sum of Group 1}$$

$$4 + 4 + \cdots + 3 = \textbf{+33} = \text{sum of Group 2}$$

$$6 + 0 + \cdots + 3 = \textbf{+45} = \text{sum of Group 3}$$

Step 5.   Square each of the subject sums obtained in Step 3, and add these squared values to get the overall sum of squares.

$$1^2 + 1^2 + \cdots + 4^2 + 4^2 + \cdots + 6^2 + 0^2 + \cdots + 3^2 = \textbf{473}$$

Step 6.   Add the group sums obtained in Step 4 to get the overall algebraic sum. (*Note:* Again, this may be a negative value.)

$$25 + 33 + 45 = \textbf{+103}$$

Step 7.   Square each of the linear coefficients (Step 1), and add the squared values.

$$(-1)^2 + 0^2 + 1^2 = \textbf{2}$$

Step 8.   Computation of the within-subjects linear component: Divide the sum of the squared values obtained in Step 5 by the value of Step 7.

$$\frac{473}{2} = \textbf{236.5}$$

Step 9. Computation of the repeated-measure effect (trials, in the present example) for the linear component: Square the overall algebraic sum obtained in Step 6, then divide by the value of Step 7 times the total number of subjects in the experiment (33, in the present example).

$$\frac{103^2}{2 \times 33} = \frac{10,609}{66} = \mathbf{160.742}$$

Step 10. Computation of the trials-by-groups effect for the linear component: First, square each of the group sums obtained in Step 4, divide each by the value of Step 7, times the number of subjects in each group (11 in the present example), and add the quotients.

$$\frac{25^2}{2 \times 11} + \frac{33^2}{2 \times 11} + \frac{45^2}{2 \times 11} = \frac{3739}{22} = \mathbf{169.955}$$

Then, from this sum, subtract the value obtained in Step 9.

$$169.955 - 160.742 = \mathbf{9.213}$$

Step 11. Computation of the error term for the linear component: Simply subtract the values obtained in Steps 9 and 10 from the value of Step 8.

$$236.5 - 160.742 - 9.213 = \mathbf{66.545}$$

Step 12. Computation of the df for each of the above components:

df for within subjects (see Step 8) = the total number of subjects used in the experiment.

No. of subjects = **33**

df for trials (see Step 9) = **1** in all instances.

df for the trials-by-groups interaction (see Step 10) = the number of experimental groups minus 1.

$$3 - 1 = \mathbf{2}$$

df for the linear-component error term (see Step 11) = df for within subject minus the df for trials and the df for trials by groups.

$$33 - 1 - 2 = \mathbf{30}$$

Step 13. Computation of the required linear mean squares: Simply divide each sum of squares value as computed in Steps 8, 9, 10 and 11 by its appropriate degrees of freedom (Step 12). The test of significance in each instance is an F ratio of the appropriate linear component divided by the linear error term. Table the mean-square values and the F ratios temporarily as follows:

Source	SS	df	ms	F	p
Within$_{linear}$	236.50	33	(not needed)	—	—
Trials	160.742	1	160.742	72.47	<.001
Trials by groups	9.213	2	4.606	2.08	n.s.
Error$_{linear}$	66.545	30	2.218	—	—

After completing the linear-component computations, the same basic steps must be repeated to analyze the quadratic component.

Step 1.   From Step 1 of the linear analysis (or Appendix N), obtain the coefficients for the quadratic component. In the present example, where $k = 3$, the coefficients are:

Quadratic: +1   −2   +1

Step 2.   The data must again be retabled. The same basic procedure of Step 2 of the linear analysis is followed except that each score is multiplied by its appropriate quadratic coefficient.

	GROUP 1		
Subject	Trial Block 1 Score × +1	Trial Block 2 Score × −2	Trial Block 3 Score × +1
S_1	3	−6	4
S_2	3	−8	4
S_3	1	−6	4
S_4	1	−4	3
S_5	2	−6	5
S_6	4	−10	6
S_7	4	−10	6
S_8	1	−8	5
S_9	1	−8	5
S_{10}	2	−6	3
S_{11}	2	−4	4

	GROUP 2		
S_{12}	2	−6	6
S_{13}	1	−8	5
S_{14}	3	−12	7
S_{15}	2	−8	6
S_{16}	1	−4	3
S_{17}	4	−10	5
S_{18}	1	−6	4
S_{19}	1	−4	4
S_{20}	2	−6	4
S_{21}	3	−10	6
S_{22}	4	−12	7

	GROUP 3		
Subject	Trial Block 1 Score × +1	Trial Block 2 Score × −2	Trial Block 3 Score × +1
S_{23}	2	−8	8
S_{24}	3	−12	3
S_{25}	4	−14	7
S_{26}	1	−14	4
S_{27}	3	−14	12
S_{28}	1	−8	2
S_{29}	1	−10	3
S_{30}	2	−10	6
S_{31}	3	−12	6
S_{32}	1	−10	12
S_{33}	4	−18	7

Step 3. Obtain the algebraic sum of the "weighted scores" for each subject in all groups. (*Note:* All remaining quadratic computations will be based on these sums.)

Subject	Trial Block 1		Trial Block 2		Trial Block 3	Sum
			Group 1			
S_1	3	+	(−6)	+	4	**+1**
S_2	3	+	(−8)	+	4	**−1**
⋮	⋮		⋮		⋮	⋮
S_{11}	2	+	(−4)	+	4	**+2**
			Group 2			
S_{12}	2	+	(−6)	+	6	**+2**
S_{13}	1	+	(−8)	+	5	**−2**
⋮	⋮		⋮		⋮	⋮
S_{22}	4	+	(−12)	+	7	**−1**
			Group 3			
S_{23}	2	+	(−8)	+	8	**+2**
S_{24}	3	+	(−12)	+	3	**−6**
⋮	⋮		⋮		⋮	⋮
S_{33}	4	+	(−18)	+	7	**−7**

Step 4. Add the subject sums obtained in Step 3 to get the algebraic time for each group.

$$1 + (-1) + \cdots + 2 = \quad -3 = \text{sum for Group 1}$$

$$2 + (-2) + \cdots + (-1) = \quad -5 = \text{sum for Group 2}$$

$$2 + (-6) + \cdots + (-7) = -35 = \text{sum for Group 3}$$

Step 5. Square each of the subject sums obtained in Step 3, and add these squared values.

$$1^2 + (-1)^2 + \cdots + 2^2 + (-2)^2 + \cdots 2^2 + (-6)^2 + \cdots + (-7)^2 = \textbf{297}$$

Step 6. Add the group sums obtained in Step 4 to get the overall algebraic sum.

$$(-3) + (-5) + (-35) = \textbf{-43}$$

Step 7. Square each of the quadratic coefficients (Step 1), and add the squared values.

$$1^2 + (-2)^2 + 1^2 = \textbf{6}$$

Step 8. Computation of the within-subjects quadratic component: Divide the value of Step 5 by that of Step 7.

$$\frac{297}{6} = \textbf{49.50}$$

Step 9. Computation of the trials effect for the quadratic component: Square the value of Step 6, and divide it by the value of Step 7 times the total number of subjects used in the experiment (33 in this example).

$$\frac{(-43)^2}{6 \times 33} - \frac{1849}{198} = \textbf{9.34}$$

Step 10. Computation of the trials-by-groups effect for the quadratic component: First, square each sum obtained in Step 4, divide each by the value of Step 7 times the number of subjects in each group (11 in this example), and add the quotients.

$$\frac{(-3)^2}{6 \times 11} + \frac{(-5)^2}{6 \times 11} + \frac{(-35)^2}{6 \times 11} = \frac{1259}{66} = \textbf{19.08}$$

Then, from this sum, subtract the value obtained in Step 9.

$$19.08 - 9.34 = \textbf{9.74}$$

Step 11. Computation of the error term for the quadratic component: Simply subtract the values of Step 9 and 10 from the value of Step 8.

$$49.50 - 9.34 - 9.74 = \textbf{30.42}$$

Step 12.   Computation of the df for each quadratic component:

df for within subjects = total number of subjects
used in the experiment.

No. of subjects = **33**

df for trials = **1** in all instances.

df for trials-by-group interaction = the number of experimental groups minus 1.

$$3 - 1 = 2$$

df for the quadratic component error term = df for within subjects minus the df for trials and the df for trials by groups.

$$33 - 1 - 2 = 30$$

Step 13.   Computation of the quadratic mean squares: Simply divide each of the sums of squares of Steps 9, 10, and 11 by the appropriate df (Step 12). The test of significance in each case is an F ratio of the appropriate quadratic component divided by the quadratic error term. Table the data temporarily as follows:

Source	SS	df	ms	F	p
Within$_{quadratic}$	49.50	33	(not needed)	—	—
Trials	9.34	1	9.34	9.21	<.001
Trials by groups	9.74	2	4.87	4.80	<.05
Error$_{quadratic}$	30.42	30	1.01	—	—

Step 14.   Final check for accuracy: Since each of the within-subjects sums of squares of the original analysis was broken into trend components, the sums of the components must equal (within rounding error) the original values.

Source	Linear		Quadratic		Sum	Original
Within subjects	236.500	+	49.500	=	**286.000**	286.00
Trials	160.742	+	9.340	=	**170.082**	170.00
Trials × groups	9.213	+	9.740	=	**18.953**	19.00
Error$_{within}$	66.545	+	30.420	=	**96.965**	97.00

Step 15.   Final tabling of the analysis: Although there are several techniques, the following is used most often.

Source	SS	df	ms	F	p
Within subjects	286	66	—	—	—
Trials	170	2	85.000	52.46	<.001
Linear	160.742	1	160.742	72.47	<.001
Quadratic	9.340	1	9.340	9.21	<.001
Trials × groups	19	4	4.750	2.93	<.05
Linear	9.213	2	4.606	2.08	n.s.
Quadratic	9.740	2	4.870	4.80	<.05
Error	97	60	1.620	—	—
Linear	66.545	30	2.218	—	—
Quadratic	30.420	30	1.014	—	—

A significant linear component for the trials effect means that there is a tendency for the data to lie along a straight line. The significance of the quadratic component means that there is also a tendency for the data to follow a quadratic (arcing) function.

It is more difficult to interpret the quadratic component of the trials-by-groups interaction, since at least two sets of data must be represented. ■

■ EXAMPLE 3

This example is based on the three-factor mixed design presented in Section 4.8. First, recall the final analysis in that section:

Source	SS	df	ms	F	p
Total	1657	111	—	—	—
Between subjects	576	27	—	—	—
Expectancy (high/low)	4	1	4	<1	—
Feedback (success/failure)	290	1	290	34.27	<.001
Expectancy × feedback	79	1	79	9.34	<.001
Error_b	203	24	8.46	—	—
Within subjects	1081	84	—	—	—
Trials	784	3	261.33	235.43	<.001
Trials × expectancy	1	3	.33	<1	—
Trials × feedback	167	3	55.67	50.15	<.001
Trials × expectancy × feedback	49	3	16.33	14.71	<.001
Error_w	80	72	1.11	—	—

Question.   What level of polynomial functions best describes the form of the data points of the several within-subjects effects in this analysis?

Step 1. Obtain from Appendix N the appropriate coefficients for the re-analysis. In the present example, four measures were recorded for each subject (four trials). Therefore, the coefficients for $k = 4$ are:

Linear: -3 -1 $+1$ $+3$

Quadratic: $+1$ -1 -1 $+1$

Cubic: -1 $+3$ -3 $+1$

Step 2. The linear component will be analyzed first. Multiply each score used in the original analysis by the appropriate linear coefficient, and retable the data as follows.

Subject	Trial 1 Score × −3	Trial 2 Score × −1	Trial 3 Score × +1	Trial 4 Score × +3
\multicolumn{5}{c}{GROUP 1 (HIGH EXPECTANCY/FAILURE)}				
S_1	−12	−6	7	27
S_2	−18	−7	9	33
S_3	−15	−8	10	39
S_4	−9	−4	6	27
S_5	−12	−6	9	30
S_6	−15	−5	6	24
S_7	−21	−8	9	36
\multicolumn{5}{c}{GROUP 2 (HIGH EXPECTANCY/SUCCESS)}				
S_8	−15	−8	9	36
S_9	−9	−5	10	42
S_{10}	−21	−10	12	39
S_{11}	−15	−8	11	45
S_{12}	−12	−9	13	45
S_{13}	−9	−5	9	36
S_{14}	−18	−7	8	33
\multicolumn{5}{c}{GROUP 3 (LOW EXPECTANCY/FAILURE)}				
S_{15}	−9	−4	4	15
S_{16}	−15	−6	8	27
S_{17}	−15	−6	6	24
S_{18}	−15	−6	7	24
S_{19}	−9	−4	4	15
S_{20}	−21	−7	8	21
S_{21}	−18	−8	8	24

	GROUP 4 (LOW EXPECTANCY/SUCCESS)			
S_{22}	-12	-8	10	42
S_{23}	-15	-10	14	54
S_{24}	-9	-7	12	54
S_{25}	-15	-8	11	51
S_{26}	-18	-11	15	57
S_{27}	-18	-8	10	45
S_{28}	-15	-11	17	60

Step 3. Obtain and record the algebraic sum of the "weighted scores" for each subject in all groups. (*Note:* All linear computations will be based on these sums.)

Subject	Trial 1		Trial 2		Trial 3		Trial 4	Sum
					Group 1			
S_1	(-12)	$+$	(-6)	$+$	7	$+$	27	**+16**
S_2	(-18)	$+$	(-7)	$+$	9	$+$	33	**+17**
$\vdots$	$\vdots$		$\vdots$		$\vdots$		$\vdots$	$\vdots$
S_7	(-21)	$+$	(-8)	$+$	9	$+$	36	**+16**
					Group 2			
S_8	(-15)	$+$	(-8)	$+$	9	$+$	36	**+22**
S_9	(-9)	$+$	(-5)	$+$	10	$+$	42	**+38**
$\vdots$	$\vdots$		$\vdots$		$\vdots$		$\vdots$	$\vdots$
S_{14}	(-18)	$+$	(-7)	$+$	8	$+$	33	**+16**
					Group 3			
S_{15}	(-9)	$+$	(-4)	$+$	4	$+$	15	**+6**
S_{16}	(-15)	$+$	(-6)	$+$	8	$+$	27	**+14**
$\vdots$	$\vdots$		$\vdots$		$\vdots$		$\vdots$	$\vdots$
S_{21}	(-18)	$+$	(-8)	$+$	8	$+$	24	**+6**
					Group 4			
S_{22}	(-12)	$+$	(-8)	$+$	10	$+$	42	**+32**
S_{23}	(-15)	$+$	(-10)	$+$	14	$+$	54	**+43**
$\vdots$	$\vdots$		$\vdots$		$\vdots$		$\vdots$	$\vdots$
S_{28}	(-15)	$+$	(-11)	$+$	17	$+$	60	**+51**

Step 4. Add the subject sums obtained in Step 3 to get the algebraic sum for each group. Record these sums and whether they are positive or negative; they will be used later.

$$16 + 17 + \cdots + 16 = + \mathbf{126} = \text{sum of Group 1}$$

$$22 + 38 + \cdots + 16 = + \mathbf{197} = \text{sum of Group 2}$$

$$6 + 14 + \cdots + 6 = + \mathbf{52} = \text{sum of Group 3}$$

$$32 + 43 + \cdots + 51 = + \mathbf{287} = \text{sum of Group 4}$$

Step 5. Square each of the subject sums obtained in Step 3. Add these squared values, and record the sum for later use.

$$16^2 + 17^2 + \cdots + 51^2 = \mathbf{21{,}092}$$

Step 6. Add the group sums obtained in Step 4 to get the overall algebraic sum. Record this sum for later use.

$$126 + 197 + 52 + 287 = \mathbf{+662}$$

Step 7. Square each of the linear coefficients (Step 1), and add the squared values.

$$(-3)^2 + (-1)^2 + 1^2 + 3^2 = \mathbf{20}$$

Step 8. Computation of the within-subjects linear component: Simply divide the overall sum of the squared values obtained in Step 5 by the value of Step 7.

$$\frac{21{,}092}{20} = \mathbf{1054.60}$$

Step 9. Computation of the repeated-measures (trials) effect for the linear component: Square the algebraic sum obtained in Step 6, and divide by the value of Step 7 times the total number of subjects used in the experiment (28 in the present example).

$$\frac{662^2}{20 \times 28} = \frac{438{,}244}{560} = \mathbf{782.58}$$

Step 10. Computation of the trials-by-first-factor (expectancy) linear component: First, obtain the algebraic sums for all subjects who were the same in terms of the first factor (expectancy), disregarding the second factor (feedback). (See Step 4 for group sums to be added.)

$$126 + 197 = \mathbf{323} = \text{sum of all high-expectancy subjects}$$

$$52 + 287 = \mathbf{339} = \text{sum of all low-expectancy subjects}$$

Then, square these sums, divide each by the value of Step 7 times the number of scores on which each sum was based (14 in this example), and add the quotients.

$$\frac{323^2}{20 \times 14} + \frac{339^2}{20 \times 14} = \frac{219,250}{280} = \mathbf{783.03}$$

Then, from this sum, subtract the value obtained in Step 9.

$$783.03 - 782.58 = \mathbf{0.45}$$

Step 11. Computation of the trials-by-second-factor (feedback) linear component: Repeat the computations of Step 10, except use the algebraic sums of subjects who were the same for the second factor, disregarding the first factor (expectancy). (See Step 4 for the group sums to be added). First,

$$126 + 52 = \mathbf{178} = \text{sum of all failure subjects}$$

$$197 + 287 = \mathbf{484} = \text{sum of all success subjects}$$

Then,

$$\frac{178^2}{20 \times 14} + \frac{484^2}{20 \times 14} = \mathbf{949.78}$$

Then,

$$949.78 - 782.58 = \mathbf{167.20}$$

Step 12. Computation of the repeated-measures-by-first-by-second-factor linear component (trials $\times$ expectancy $\times$ feedback, in the present example): Square the algebraic sum of each group (Step 4), divide each square by the value of Step 7 times the number of subjects in each group, and add the quotients.

$$\frac{126^2}{20 \times 7} + \frac{197^2}{20 \times 7} + \frac{52^2}{20 \times 7} + \frac{287^2}{20 \times 7} + \frac{139,758}{140} = \mathbf{998.27}$$

From this sum, subtract the values obtained in Steps 9, 10, and 11.

$$998.27 - 782.58 - .45 - 167.20 = \mathbf{48.04}$$

Step 13. Computation of the linear-component error term: Simply subtract the value obtained in the first computation of Step 12 (998.27, in the present example) from the value of Step 8 (or subtract the values obtained in Steps 9, 10, 11, and 12 from Step 8).

$$1054.60 - 998.27 = \mathbf{56.33}$$

Step 14.   Computation of the df for the linear components:

$$df \text{ for within}_{\text{linear}} = \text{the total number of subjects}$$
$$\text{used in the experiment.}$$

No. of subjects $= \mathbf{28}$

df for repeated measures (trials) $= \mathbf{1}$ (always).

df for trials by first factor (expectancy) $=$ the number of experimental
conditions within the first
factor minus 1.

$$2 - 1 = \mathbf{1}$$

df for trials by second factor (feedback) $=$ the number of experimental
conditions within the second
factor minus 1.

$$2 - 1 = \mathbf{1}$$

df for trials by first by second factor $=$ the df for the first factor times
the df for the second factor.

$$1 \times 1 = \mathbf{1}$$

df for error $=$ df for within subjects minus df
for trials; trials by first factor;
trials by second factor; and
trials by first by second factor.

$$28 - 1 - 1 - 1 - 1 = \mathbf{24}$$

Step 15.   Computation of the mean squares for the linear components: Simply divide each sum-of-squares value as computed in Steps 8, 9, 10, 11, 12, and 13 by its appropriate degrees of freedom. The test of significance in each instance is an F ratio of the appropriate linear component divided by the linear-component error term. The mean squares and F ratios should be tabled as follows for future use:

Source	SS	df	ms	F
Within$_{\text{linear}}$	1054.60	28	(not needed)	—
Trials	782.58	1	782.58	333.01
T × Exp.	.45	1	.45	<1
T × Feed.	167.20	1	167.20	71.15
T × Exp. × Feed.	48.04	1	48.04	20.44
Error$_{\text{linear}}$	56.33	24	2.35	—

The computations for the linear components have been completed. The computations for the quadratic components must now be undertaken.

Step 1.   Obtain the coefficients for the quadratic component from Step 1 of the linear analysis (or Appendix N). In the present example, where $k = 4$:

Quadratic: $+1$ -1 -1 $+1$

Step 2.   The data must again be retabled. The same basic procedure as Step 2 of the linear analysis is followed, except that each score is multiplied by its appropriate quadratic coefficient.

	GROUP 1 (HIGH EXPECTANCY/FAILURE)			
	Trial 1	Trial 2	Trial 3	Trial 4
Subject	Score $\times$ -3	Score $\times$ -1	Score $\times$ $+1$	Score $\times$ $+3$
S_1	4	-6	-7	9
S_2	6	-7	-9	11
S_3	5	-8	-10	13
S_4	3	-4	-6	9
S_5	4	-6	-9	10
S_6	5	-5	-6	8
S_7	7	-8	-9	12

	GROUP 2 (HIGH EXPECTANCY/SUCCESS)			
S_8	5	-8	-9	12
S_9	3	-5	-10	14
S_{10}	7	-10	-12	13
S_{11}	5	-8	-11	15
S_{12}	4	-9	-13	15
S_{13}	3	-5	-9	12
S_{14}	6	-7	-8	11

	GROUP 3 (LOW EXPECTANCY/FAILURE)			
S_{15}	3	-4	-4	5
S_{16}	5	-6	-8	9
S_{17}	5	-6	-6	8
S_{18}	5	-6	-7	8
S_{19}	3	-4	-4	5
S_{20}	7	-7	-8	7
S_{21}	6	-8	-8	8

	GROUP 4 (LOW EXPECTANCY/SUCCESS)			
	Trial 1	Trial 2	Trial 3	Trial 4
Subject	Score $\times$ +1	Score $\times$ -1	Score $\times$ -1	Score $\times$ +1
S_{22}	4	-8	-10	14
S_{23}	5	-10	-14	18
S_{24}	3	-7	-12	18
S_{25}	5	-8	-11	17
S_{26}	6	-11	-15	19
S_{27}	6	-8	-10	15
S_{28}	5	-11	-17	20

Step 3. Using the data of Step 2, obtain and record the algebraic sum of the "weighted scores" of each subject in all groups. (*Note:* All quadratic computations will be based on these scores.)

Group 1								
Subject	Trial 1		Trial 2		Trial 3		Trial 4	Sum
S_1	4	+	(−6)	+	(−7)	+	9	0
S_2	6	+	(−7)	+	(−9)	+	11	+1
⋮	⋮		⋮		⋮		⋮	⋮
S_7	7	+	(−8)	+	(−9)	+	12	+2

Group 2								
S_8	5	+	(−8)	+	(−9)	+	12	0
S_9	3	+	(−5)	+	(−10)	+	14	+2
⋮	⋮		⋮		⋮		⋮	⋮
S_{14}	6	+	(−7)	+	(−8)	+	11	+2

Group 3								
S_{19}	3	+	(−4)	+	(−4)	+	5	0
S_{16}	5	+	(−6)	+	(−8)	+	9	0
⋮	⋮		⋮		⋮		⋮	⋮
S_{21}	6	+	(−8)	+	(−8)	+	8	−2

Group 4								
S_{22}	4	+	(−8)	+	(−10)	+	14	0
S_{23}	5	+	(−10)	+	(−14)	+	18	−1
⋮	⋮		⋮		⋮		⋮	⋮
S_{28}	5	+	(−11)	+	(−17)	+	(20)	−3

Step 4. Add the subject sums of Step 3 to get the algebraic sums for each group. Record these sums and whether they are positive or negative.

$$0 + 1 + \cdots + 2 = +6 = \text{sum of Group 1}$$
$$0 + 2 + \cdots + 2 = +1 = \text{sum of Group 2}$$
$$0 + 0 + \cdots + (-2) = -2 = \text{sum of Group 3}$$
$$0 + (-1) + \cdots + (-3) = +3 = \text{sum of Group 4}$$

Step 5. Square each of the subject sums of Step 3. Add these squared values, and record the sum for later use.

$$0^2 + 1^2 + \cdots + 0^2 + 2^2 + \cdots + 0^2 + 0^2$$
$$+ \cdots + 0^2 + (-1)^2 + \cdots + (-3)^2 = 76$$

Step 6. Add the subject sums of Step 4 to get the overall algebraic sum.

$$6 + 1 + (-2) + 3 = +8$$

Step 7. Square and sum the quadratic coefficients (Step 1).

$$1^2 + (-1)^2 + (-1)^2 + 1^2 = 4$$

Step 8. Computation of the within-subjects quadratic component: Simply divide the value of Step 5 by that of Step 7.

$$\frac{76}{4} = 19.00$$

Step 9. Computation of the trials effect for the quadratic component: Square the value of Step 6, and then divide by the value of Step 7 times the total number of subjects used in the experiment (28 in this example).

$$\frac{8^2}{4 \times 28} = \frac{64}{112} = .57$$

Step 10. Computation of the trials-by-first-factor (expectancy) quadratic component: First, obtain the algebraic sum of the subjects who were the same in terms of the first factor (expectancy in the present example), disregarding the second factor. (See Step 4 for the group sums to be added.)

$$6 + 1 = +7 = \text{sum for all high-expectancy subjects}$$
$$(-2) + 3 = +1 = \text{sum for all low-expectancy subjects}$$

Then square these sums, divide each by the value of Step 7 times the number of scores on which each sum was based (14 in this example), and add the quotients.

$$\frac{7^2}{4 \times 14} + \frac{1^2}{4 \times 14} = \frac{50}{56} = .89$$

Then, from this value, subtract the value of Step 9.

$$.89 - .57 = \textbf{.32}$$

Step 11.   Computation of the trials-by-second-factor (feedback) quadratic component: Repeat the computations of Step 10, except use the algebraic sums of subjects who were the same in terms of the second factor, disregarding the first factor. (See Step 4 for the group sums to be added.) First,

$$6 + (-2) = \textbf{+4} = \text{sum of all failure subjects}$$

$$1 + 3 = \textbf{+4} = \text{sum of all success subjects}$$

Then,

$$\frac{4^2}{4 \times 14} + \frac{4^2}{4 \times 14} = \frac{32}{56} = .57$$

Then,

$$.57 - .57 = \textbf{.00}$$

Step 12.   Computation of the trials-by-first-by-second-factor quadratic component: Square the sums of Step 4, divide each square by the value of Step 7 times the number of subjects in each group, and add the quotients.

$$\frac{6^2}{4 \times 7} + \frac{1^2}{4 \times 7} + \frac{(-2)^2}{4 \times 7} + \frac{3^2}{4 \times 7} = \frac{50}{28} = \textbf{1.79}$$

Then, from this sum, subtract the values obtained in Steps 9, 10, and 11.

$$1.79 - .57 - .32 - .00 = \textbf{.90}$$

Step 13.   Computation of the quadratic component error term: Simply subtract the value obtained in the first computation of Step 12 from the value of Step 8.

$$19.00 - 1.79 = \textbf{17.21}$$

Step 14.   The df computations for the quadratic component are the same as for the linear component.

df for within$_{\text{quadratic}}$ = the total number of subjects used in the experiment.

No. of subjects = **28**

df for trials = 1 (always).

df for trials by first factor = number of first-factor conditions minus 1.

$$2 - 1 = \textbf{1}$$

df for the trials by second factor = number of second-factor conditions minus 1.

$$2 - 1 = 1$$

df for trials by first by second factor = the df for the first factor times the df for the second factor

$$1 \times 1 = 1$$

df for error$_{\text{quadratic}}$ = df for within subjects minus the df for trials, trials by first factor, trials by second factor, and trials by first and second factor.

$$28 - 1 - 1 - 1 - 1 = 24$$

Step 15. Computation of the quadratic mean squares: Again, divide the values of Steps 8, 9, 10, 11, 12, and 13 by the appropriate degrees of freedom. Compute each F ratio by dividing the appropriate quadratic component by the quadratic error term. Table the data temporarily as follows:

Source	SS	df	ms	F
Within$_{\text{quadratic}}$	19.00	28	(not needed)	—
Trials	.57	1	.57	<1
T × Exp.	.32	1	.32	<1
T × Feed.	.00	1	.00	<1
T × Exp. × Feed.	.90	1	.90	1.25
Error$_{\text{quadratic}}$	17.21	24	.72	—

When the computations of the quadratic components have been completed, the computation of the cubic components must be undertaken.

Step 1. Obtain the coefficients for the cubic component from Step 1 of the linear analysis (or Appendix N). In the present example, where $k = 4$:

Cubic: −1   +3   −3   +1

Step 2. Once again, the data must be retabled. This time each score is multiplied by its appropriate cubic coefficient.

	GROUP 1			
	Trial 1	Trial 2	Trial 3	Trial 4
Subject	Score × −1	Score × +3	Score × −3	Score × +1
S_1	−4	18	−21	9
S_2	−6	21	−27	11
S_3	−5	24	−30	13

	GROUP 1			
	Trial 1	Trial 2	Trial 3	Trial 4
Subject	Score $\times$ -1	Score $\times$ $+3$	Score $\times$ -3	Score $\times$ $+1$
S_4	-3	12	-18	9
S_5	-4	18	-27	10
S_6	-5	15	-18	8
S_7	-7	24	-27	12

	GROUP 2			
S_8	-5	24	-27	12
S_9	-3	15	-30	14
S_{10}	-7	30	-36	13
S_{11}	-5	24	-33	15
S_{12}	-4	27	-39	15
S_{13}	-3	15	-27	12
S_{14}	-6	21	-24	11

	GROUP 3			
S_{15}	-3	12	-12	5
S_{16}	-5	18	-24	9
S_{17}	-5	18	-18	8
S_{18}	-5	18	-21	8
S_{19}	-3	12	-12	5
S_{20}	-7	21	-24	7
S_{21}	-6	24	-24	8

	GROUP 4			
S_{22}	-4	24	-30	14
S_{23}	-5	30	-42	18
S_{24}	-3	21	-36	18
S_{25}	-5	24	-33	17
S_{26}	-6	33	-45	19
S_{27}	-6	24	-30	15
S_{28}	-5	33	-51	20

Step 3. Using the data of Step 2, obtain the algebraic sum of each subject's "weighted scores." These sums will be used for all cubic computations.

	GROUP 1								
Subject	Trial 1		Trial 2		Trial 3		Trial 4		Sum
S_1	(-4)	$+$	18	$+$	(-21)	$+$	9		**+2**
S_2	(-6)	$+$	21	$+$	(-27)	$+$	11		**+1**
$\vdots$	$\vdots$		$\vdots$		$\vdots$		$\vdots$		$\vdots$
S_7	(-7)	$+$	24	$+$	(-27)	$+$	12		**+2**

			GROUP 2				
Subject	Trial 1		Trial 2		Trial 3	Trial 4	Sum
S_8	(-5)	+	24	+	(-27) +	12	+4
S_9	(-3)	+	15	+	(-30) +	14	-4
$\vdots$	$\vdots$		$\vdots$		$\vdots$	$\vdots$	$\vdots$
S_{14}	(-6)	+	21	+	(-24) +	11	+2

			GROUP 3				
S_{15}	(-3)	+	12	+	(-12) +	5	+2
S_{16}	(-5)	+	18	+	(-24) +	9	-2
$\vdots$	$\vdots$		$\vdots$		$\vdots$	$\vdots$	$\vdots$
S_{21}	(-6)	+	24	+	(-24) +	8	+2

			GROUP 4				
S_{22}	(-4)	+	24	+	(-30) +	14	+4
S_{23}	(-5)	+	30	+	(-42) +	18	-1
$\vdots$	$\vdots$		$\vdots$		$\vdots$	$\vdots$	$\vdots$
S_{28}	(-5)	+	33	+	(-51) +	20	-3

Step 4. Add the sums of Step 3 to get the algebraic sum for each group.

$2 + (-1) + \cdots + 2 = $ **+2** $=$ sum of Group 1

$4 + (-4) + \cdots + 2 = $ **-1** $=$ sum of Group 2

$2 + (-2) + \cdots + 2 = $ **+4** $=$ sum of Group 3

$4 + 1 + \cdots + (-3) = $ **+9** $=$ sum of Group 4

Step 5. Square the sums of Step 3. Add these squared values, and record them for later use.

$$2^2 + (-1)^2 + \cdots + 4^2 + (-4)^2 + \cdots + 2^2$$
$$+ (-2)^2 + \cdots + 4^2 + 1^2 + \cdots + (-3)^2 = \mathbf{148}$$

Step 6. Add the group sums of Step 4 to obtain the overall algebraic sum.

$2 + (-1) + 4 + 9 = $ **+14**

Step 7. Square and sum the quadratic coefficients (Step 1).

$(-1)^2 + 3^2 + (-3)^2 + 1^2 = \mathbf{20}$

Step 8.   Computation of the within-subjects cubic component: Simply divide Step 5 by Step 7.

$$\frac{148}{20} = \mathbf{7.40}$$

Step 9.   Computation of the cubic-component trials effect: Square the value of Step 6. Then, divide by the value of Step 7 times the total number of subjects used in the experiment.

$$\frac{14^2}{20 \times 28} = \frac{196}{560} = \mathbf{.35}$$

Step 10.   Computation of the trials-by-first-factor (expectancy) cubic component: First, obtain the algebraic sum of the subjects who were the same in terms of the first factor, disregarding the second factor. (See Step 4 for the group sums to be added.)

$$2 + (-1) = \mathbf{+1} = \text{sum of high-expectancy subjects}$$

$$4 + 9 = \mathbf{+13} = \text{sum of low-expectancy subjects}$$

Then, square these sums, divide each by the value of Step 7 times the number of scores on which each sum was based, and add the quotients.

$$\frac{1^2}{20 \times 14} + \frac{13^2}{20 \times 14} = \frac{170}{280} = \mathbf{.61}$$

Then, from this value, subtract the final value of Step 9.

$$.61 - .35 = \mathbf{.26}$$

Step 11.   Computation of the trials-by-second-factor (feedback) cubic component: Repeat the computations of Step 10, except using algebraic sums of the second factor, disregarding the first factor. (See Step 4 for the group sums to be added.) First,

$$2 + 4 = \mathbf{6} = \text{sum of failure subjects}$$

$$(-1) + 9 = \mathbf{8} = \text{sum of success subjects}$$

Then,

$$\frac{6^2}{20 \times 14} + \frac{8^2}{20 \times 14} = \frac{100}{280} = \mathbf{.36}$$

Then,

$$.36 - .35 = \mathbf{.01}$$

Step 12. Computation of the trials-by-first-by-second-factor cubic component: Square the sums of Step 4, divide each by the value of Step 7 times the number of subjects in each group, and add the quotients.

$$\frac{2^2}{20 \times 7} + \frac{(-1)^2}{20 \times 7} + \frac{4^2}{20 \times 7} + \frac{9^2}{20 \times 7} = \frac{102}{140} = .73$$

Then, from this sum, subtract the values of Steps 9, 10, and 11.

$$.73 - .35 - .26 - .01 = .11$$

Step 13. Computation of the cubic-component error term: Simply subtract the value obtained in the initial computation of Step 12 from that of Step 8.

$$7.40 - .73 = 6.67$$

Step 14. The df computations for the cubic components are the same as for the linear and quadratic components. In the present example, these are

df for within$_{cubic}$ = **28**
df for trials = **1**
df for trials by first factor = **1**
df for trials by second factor = **1**
df for trials by first by second factor = **1**
df for error$_{cubic}$ = **24**

Step 15. Computation of the mean squares and F ratios for the cubic component: These are computed in the same manner as for the linear and quadratic components. Again, table the results temporarily as follows.

Source	SS	df	ms	F
Within$_{cubic}$	7.40	28	(not needed)	—
Trials	.35	1	.35	1.25
T × Exp.	.26	1	.26	<1
T × Feed.	.01	1	.01	<1
T × Exp. × Feed.	.11	1	.11	<1
Error$_{cubic}$	6.67	24	.28	—

Step 16. Final check for accuracy: Since each of the within-subjects sums of squares of the original analysis was broken into trend components, the sums of

these components must equal (within rounding error) the original values. In the present example:

Source	Linear		Quadratic		Cubic		Sum	Original
Within subjects	1054.60	+	19.00	+	7.40	=	**1081.00**	1081
Trials	782.58	+	.57	+	.35	=	**783.50**	784
T × Exp.	.45	+	.32	+	.26	=	**1.03**	1
T × Feed.	167.20	+	.00	+	.01	=	**167.21**	167
T × Exp. × Feed.	48.04	+	.90	+	.11	=	**49.05**	49
Error$_{within}$	56.33	+	17.21	+	6.67	=	**80.21**	80

Step 17.   Final tabling of the results: Although several procedures can be used, the following is probably used most often.

Source	SS	df	ms	F	p
Within subjects	1081	84	—	—	—
Trials	784	3	261.33	235.43	<.001
Linear	782.58	1	782.58	333.01	<.001
Quadratic	.57	1	.57	<1	—
Cubic	.35	1	.35	1.25	n.s.
Trials × Exp.	1	3	.33	<1	—
Linear	.45	1	.45	<1	—
Quadratic	.32	1	.32	<1	—
Cubic	.26	1	.26	<1	—
Trials × Feed.	167	3	55.67	50.15	<.001
Linear	167.20	1	167.20	71.15	<.001
Quadratic	.00	1	.00	<1	—
Cubic	.01	1	.01	<1	—
Trials × Exp. × Feed.	49	3	16.33	14.71	<.001
Linear	48.04	1	48.04	20.44	<.001
Quadratic	.90	1	.90	1.25	n.s.
Cubic	.11	1	.11	<1	—
Error$_{within}$	80	72	1.11	—	—
Linear	56.33	24	2.35	—	—
Quadratic	17	24	.72	—	—
Cubic	6.67	24	.28	—	—

The significant linear components mean that the data points tend to lie along a straight line.

If there had been significant quadratic components, it would have meant that there was a tendency for the data to follow quadratic functions (such as a parabola). Significant cubic components would have meant that there was a tendency for the data to follow an even more complex path with two inflections in the functions. The interpretation of linear, quadratic, and cubic components of interactions is very complex because at least two sets of data points are involved in each. Only inspection of the data or additional analyses of each individual set of data points (using the same procedures just outlined) can give an indication as to which of the sets is contributing to the significant findings. ∎

PART 6

Multivariate Analyses

The six sections presented in this part represent an extension of the univariate analyses to the multivariate situation. The univariate analyses presented in Part 4 are conducted to determine whether the sample means differ significantly from the hypothesized population means or from each other. In multivariate analyses, the tests of significance refer to the differences between the coordinates of the means of several variables, or centroids.

In almost all instances, multivariate analyses require the use of a computer. For example, sample size should be fairly large for MANOVA experiments. While appropriate sample size is debatable, a rough rule of thumb is that the total size of the sample should be at least 20 times the number of dependent variables, times the number of experimental groups compared. Thus, if three groups were utilized with two dependent variables recorded, a sample of 120 should be used, i.e., $20 \times 3 \times 2 = 120$. However, for simple problems and for understanding of the concepts, hand calculations of problems are rather easily accomplished with significant enhancement of the understanding of the relationship among univariate, correlational, and multivariate techniques.

The six analyses presented in Part 6 include the following:

Multivariate—One-Sample Tests (Sections 6.1 and 6.2)

The first example, presented in Section 6.1, involves an assumption that the population values of the centroid are known. In fact, this rarely occurs, so the actual utility of this presentation is limited. The second example, presented in Section 6.2, demonstrates the use of difference scores and is the multivariate counterpart of the t-test for matched pairs or related measures described in Section 1.6.

Multivariate—Two-Group Tests (Sections 6.3 and 6.4)

The multivariate tests appropriate for two-sample situations represent the counterpart of the univariate t-test between two independent means presented in Section 1.5. The first example, presented in Section 6.3, represents a direct extension of the univariate t-test. The second example, presented in Section 6.4, also compares two groups but makes use of difference scores [(pre-test)-(post-test)] on each of the variables.

Multivariate—Multiple-Group Tests (Sections 6.5 and 6.6)

The analyses presented in Sections 6.5 and 6.6 represent the multivariate counterparts of the F-test in one-way analysis of variance. Section 6.5 represents the multivariate extension of the completely randomized design presented in Section 4.1, while Section 6.6 represents the multivariate counterpart of the univariate factorial analysis presented in Section 4.2.

In this part, computational formulas will be presented in those instances where a standard set of symbols and terms are used in nearly all textbooks. A minimal understanding of matrix notation is required but this should pose no problem for anyone with even a limited knowledge of algebra since only bivariate cases will be presented.

SECTION 6.1
Multivariate Analysis to Test for a Difference Between a Sample Centroid and the Population Values

This analysis, using Hotelling's T^2 is the logical multivariate extension of the univariate t-test presented in Section 1.4. Use of T^2 assumes that the population values of the centroid are known. If this information is known, the experimenter can then determine whether the sample centroid is significantly different from the population values.

■ EXAMPLE

Assume that an experimenter gives a mathematical aptitude test (Test 1) and an intellectual curiosity test (Test 2) to a group of twelve high school seniors. She knows that the population means (μ) for these tests are 12 and 26, respectively. Use of the following test can determine whether the scores made by her subjects are significantly different from the population centroid.

Step 1. Table the data as follows. Care must be taken to ensure that the scores for each subject are recorded in the proper rows and columns.

Subjects	Test 1 (Mathematics)	Test 2 (Curiosity)
S_1	11	26
S_2	13	29
S_3	18	38
S_4	14	27
S_5	16	30
S_6	15	26
S_7	19	37
S_8	10	22
S_9	10	23
S_{10}	21	39
S_{11}	19	36
S_{12}	20	35

Step 2. Calculate the sum of the scores on Test 1 and Test 2.

Subjects	Test 1	Test 2
S_1	11	26
S_2	13	29
.	.	.
.	.	.
S_{12}	20	35
	186	368

Step 3. Calculate the sum of squared scores for Test 1.

$11 + 13 + 18 + \cdots + 20 = \textbf{3,054}$

Step 4. Calculate the sum of squared scores for Test 2.

$26 + 29 + 38 + \cdots + 35 = \textbf{11,690}$

Step 5. Calculate the sum of the cross products.

$(11 \times 26) + (13 \times 29) + \cdots + (20 \times 35) = \textbf{5,951}$

Step 6. Calculate the sample centroid (from Step 2).

$$\overline{X}_1 = \frac{186}{12} = \textbf{15.5}$$

$$\overline{X}_2 = \frac{368}{12} = \textbf{30.67}$$

Step 7.   Calculate the difference between the population mean (μ) and the sample mean ($\overline{X}$). For this example, it is assumed that the population values for Test 1 and Test 2 are known to be 12 and 26 respectively. Thus,

$$\begin{aligned} \overline{X}_1 - \mu_1 &= 15.5 - 12 = \\ \overline{X}_2 - \mu_2 &= 30.67 - 26 = \end{aligned} \begin{bmatrix} 3.5 \\ 4.67 \end{bmatrix}$$

Step 8.   Calculation of the values required to set up the sample dispersion matrix: For a problem with two variables, the sum of squares for the first variable, the sum of squares for the second variable, and the sum of squares of the cross products must be calculated.

First, calculation for the sum of squares for Test 1: The formula for this computation is

$$\Sigma X^2 - \frac{(\Sigma X)^2}{N}$$

Sum of X^2 (Step 3) = **3054**

Sum of X (Step 2) = **186**

and

$$3054 - \frac{(186)^2}{12} = 3054 - 2883 = \textbf{171}$$

Next, calculation of the sum of squares for Test 2:

Sum of X^2 (Step 3) = **11,690**

Sum of X (Step 2) = **368**

and

$$11,690 - \frac{(368)^2}{12} = 11,690 - 11,285.3 = \textbf{404.7}$$

Finally, calculation of the sum of cross products:

$$\Sigma X_1 X_2 - \frac{(\Sigma X_1)(\Sigma X_2)}{N}$$

Sum of cross products (Step 4) = **5951**

and

$$\Sigma X_1 \times \Sigma X_2 \text{ (Step 2)} = 186 \times 368 = \textbf{68,448}$$

thus,

$$5,951 - \frac{68,448}{12} = 5,951 - 5704 = \textbf{247}$$

Step 9. Calculation of the sample dispersion matrix: The values will be inserted into a symmetric dispersion matrix with the elements arranged like this:

$$\begin{bmatrix} a & b \\ c & d \end{bmatrix}$$

The formula for the dispersion matrix is

$$\mathbf{C}_d = \frac{1}{N-1}\begin{bmatrix} SS_{x_1} & SSCP \\ SSCP & SS_{x_2} \end{bmatrix}$$

using the calculated values

$$\mathbf{C}_d = \frac{1}{11}\begin{bmatrix} 171 & 247 \\ 247 & 404.7 \end{bmatrix}$$

$$\mathbf{C}_d = \begin{bmatrix} (a) & (b) \\ 15.54 & 22.45 \\ (c) & (d) \\ 22.45 & 36.79 \end{bmatrix}$$

Step 10. Calculation of the inverse matrix, $\mathbf{C}_d^{-1}$: The computational formula is

$$\mathbf{C}_d^{-1} = \frac{1}{ad-bc}\begin{bmatrix} d & -b \\ -c & a \end{bmatrix}$$

or, in terms of the current problem (from Step 9),

$$\mathbf{C}_d^{-1} = \frac{1}{(15.54)(36.79)-(-22.45)(-22.45)}\begin{bmatrix} 36.79 & -22.45 \\ -22.45 & 15.54 \end{bmatrix}$$

$$= \frac{1}{67}\begin{bmatrix} 36.79 & -22.45 \\ -22.45 & 15.54 \end{bmatrix}$$

$$= \begin{bmatrix} .55 & -.33 \\ -.33 & .23 \end{bmatrix}$$

Note: For subsequent calculations, the above elements of the inverse matrix will be identified in terms of standard matrix notation, i.e.,

$$\mathbf{C}_d^{-1} = \begin{bmatrix} (a) & (b) \\ .55 & -.33 \\ (c) & (d) \\ -.33 & .23 \end{bmatrix}$$

Step 11. All necessary preparatory calculations have been completed. Hotelling's T^2 statistical test is now applied to determine whether the sample centroid differs significantly from the population value. The formula for calculation of T^2 (values from Steps 7 and 10) is

$$T^2 = N\bar{x}'\mathbf{C}_d^{-1}\bar{x}$$

$$= 12[3.5 \quad 4.67]\begin{bmatrix} .55 & -.33 \\ -.33 & .23 \end{bmatrix}\begin{bmatrix} 3.5 \\ 4.67 \end{bmatrix}$$

In a symmetric matrix such as that presented above, where element $b = c$, the computational formula reduces to

$$T^2 = N[a(\bar{X}_{T1} - \mu_{T1})^2 + 2b(\bar{X}_{T1} - \mu_{T1})(\bar{X}_{T2} - \mu_{T2}) + d(\bar{X}_{T2} - \mu_2)^2]$$
$$T^2 = 12[(.55)(3.5)^2 + (2)(-.33)(3.5)(4.67) + (.23)(4.67)^2]$$
$$= 12[(6.737) + (-10.788) + (5.016)]$$
$$= 12(.965)$$
$$= \mathbf{11.586}$$

Step 12. Calculation of the F ratio: The relationship between T^2 and F is described by the following formula:

$$F = \frac{N - p}{p(N - 1)}T^2$$

where N = the number of subjects
  p = the number of dependent variables measured

Inserting the appropriate values, we have

$$F = \frac{12 - 2}{2(12 - 1)} \times 11.586$$

$$= \frac{10}{22} \times 11.586$$

$$= \mathbf{5.27}$$

Step 13. Computation of the degrees of freedom: The df for this F test are equal to the number of test measures, p, and the number of subjects minus the number of test measures, or $N - p$. Since two tests, mathematics and curiosity, were given, the df for this example would be 2 and $12 - 2$.

Step 14. Test of significance: Looking in the F tables under 2 and 10 degrees of freedom, an F ratio of 3.88 is needed for significance at the .05 level. Since the calculated F ratio exceeds 3.88, it is concluded that the sample centroid differs significantly from the population value.   ∎

SECTION 6.2
Multivariate Analysis for Single-Sample Matched Pairs (Difference Scores)

This analysis also makes use of Hotelling's T^2 as the statistical test and represents the multivariate extension of the univariate t-test for related measures presented in Section 1.6.

Points to Consider When Analyzing Single-Sample Difference Scores

1. Usually, two measures are recorded on each variable (pre and post), and the change or difference between the first and second measurements are the scores actually analyzed.
2. Occasionally, as in the t for related measures, matched pairs of subjects will be employed rather than measuring the same subject's performance twice (see univariate example for the t for related measures in Section 1.6).

■ EXAMPLE

Assume that an experimenter is interested in determining whether subjects change their attitudes toward education for the poor (Test 1) and taxation (Test 2) after watching a short film on the plight of migrant workers. Attitudes are measured by the use of two tests, each administered before the film is shown and again after. The number of statements each subject "agrees" with before and after seeing the film are recorded. The difference scores represent the change in positive responses.

Step 1. After the experiment is completed, table the data as follows:

Subjects	Test 1 (Education)		Test 2 (Taxation)	
	Pre	Post	Pre	Post
S_1	12	19	9	12
S_2	16	19	11	11
S_3	11	10	17	20
S_4	15	14	9	11
S_5	18	25	9	16
S_6	20	22	14	15
S_7	10	11	8	9
S_8	20	23	10	12
S_9	13	21	14	17
S_{10}	7	9	6	11
S_{11}	21	22	14	18
S_{12}	19	20	8	19

Step 2.   Compute the difference between each pair of pre- and post-test scores.

Subjects	Test 1 difference	Test 2 difference
S_1	7	3
S_2	3	0
S_3	-1	3
$\vdots$	$\vdots$	$\vdots$
S_{12}	1	11

Step 3.   Sum the difference scores. Calculate the algebraic sum of the difference scores for Test 1 and Test 2.

For Test 1: $7 + 3 + (-1) + \cdots + 1 =$ **33**
For Test 2: $3 + 0 + 3 + \cdots + 11 =$ **42**

Step 4.   Square the difference scores and sum the squared values.

For Test 1: $7^2 + 3^2 + (-1)^2 + \cdots + 1^2 =$ **193**
For Test 2: $3^2 + 0^2 + 3^2 + \cdots + 11^2 =$ **248**

Step 5.   Calculation of the sum of the cross products: Multiply the Test 1 difference scores times the Test 2 difference scores. Then add these cross products.

$(7 \times 3) + (3 \times 0) + (-1 \times 3) + \cdots + (1 \times 11) =$ **123**

Step 6.   Calculation of the sample centroid (from Step 3):

$$33/12 = \begin{bmatrix} 2.75 \\ 3.50 \end{bmatrix}$$
$$42/12 =$$

Step 7.   All of the necessary preliminary calculations have been completed. Now the sample dispersion matrix must be calculated. The computational formulas are

For the Sum of Squares Test 1: $\Sigma\, d_1^2 - \dfrac{(\Sigma\, d_1)^2}{N}$

For the Sum of Squares Test 2: $\Sigma\, d_2^2 - \dfrac{(\Sigma\, d_2)^2}{N}$

For the Sum of Cross Products: $\Sigma\, d_1 d_2 - \dfrac{(\Sigma\, d_1)(\Sigma\, d_2)}{N(\text{pairs})}$

These values will now be inserted into a symmetric dispersion matrix with the elements arranged as follows:

$$\begin{bmatrix} a & b \\ c & d \end{bmatrix}$$

The formula for the dispersion matrix is

$$\mathbf{C}_d = \frac{1}{N-1}\begin{bmatrix} SS_{x_1} & SSCP \\ SSCP & SS_{x_2} \end{bmatrix}$$

Step 8.   The calculations are as follows (values from Steps 3 and 4):

$$\mathbf{C}_d = \frac{1}{11}\begin{bmatrix} 193 - \dfrac{33^2}{12} & 123 - \dfrac{(33)(42)}{12} \\ 123 - \dfrac{(33)(42)}{12} & 248 - \dfrac{42^2}{12} \end{bmatrix}$$

$$= \frac{1}{11}\begin{bmatrix} 102.25 & 7.50 \\ 7.50 & 101.00 \end{bmatrix}$$

$$= \begin{bmatrix} (a) & (b) \\ 9.30 & .68 \\ (c) & (d) \\ .68 & 9.18 \end{bmatrix}$$

Step 9.   Next the inverse of $\mathbf{C}_d$ must be found. The formula for C_d^{-1} is

$$\mathbf{C}_d^{-1} = \frac{1}{ad-bc}\begin{bmatrix} d & -b \\ -c & a \end{bmatrix}$$

$$= \frac{1}{(9.30 \times 9.18) - (-.68 \times -.68)}\begin{bmatrix} 9.18 & -.68 \\ -.68 & 9.30 \end{bmatrix}$$

$$= \frac{1}{84.91}\begin{bmatrix} 9.18 & -.68 \\ -.68 & 9.38 \end{bmatrix}$$

$$= \begin{bmatrix} .108 & -.008 \\ -.008 & .110 \end{bmatrix}$$

Note: For subsequent calculations, the above elements in the inverse matrix will be referred to in relation to common matrix positioning, i.e.

$$\begin{bmatrix} (a) & (b) \\ .108 & -.008 \\ (c) & (d) \\ -.008 & .110 \end{bmatrix}$$

Step 10.   Computation of T^2. The general formula for T^2 is

$$T^2 = N\bar{x}'C_d^{-1}\bar{x}$$

In this example,

$$T^2 = 12[2.75 \quad 3.50]\begin{bmatrix} .108 & -.008 \\ -.008 & .110 \end{bmatrix}\begin{bmatrix} 2.75 \\ 3.50 \end{bmatrix}$$

Note: The computational formula for a symmetric matrix where the off-diagonal terms (elements b and c) are equal reduces to the following:

$$T^2 = N[a(\bar{X}diff_{T_1})^2 + 2(b)(\bar{X}diff_{T_1})(\bar{X}diff_{T_2}) + d(\bar{X}diff_{T_2})^2]$$

Therefore (values from Steps 6 and 9),

$$T^2 = 12[(.108)(2.75^2) + (2)(-.008)(2.75)(3.50) + (.110)(3.50^2)]$$

$$= 12 \times 2.011$$

$$= \mathbf{24.132}$$

Step 11.   Computation of the F statistic:

$$F = \left(\frac{N - p}{p(N - 1)}\right)T^2$$

where N = the number of subjects

p = the number of dependent variables measured

For the bivariate case in this example, $N = 12$ and $p = 2$, thus,

$$F = \left(\frac{12 - 2}{2(12 - 1)}\right)24.132$$

$$= \frac{241.32}{22}$$

$$= \mathbf{10.97}$$

Step 12.   Computation of the df: The df for the F statistic are

$$F_{p, N-p}$$

In this example, the df would be 2 and 10.

Step 13.   Test of significance: Since the computed F of 10.97 exceeds the tabled value of 4.10 for 2 and 10 df, the conclusion is drawn that the experimental treatment (seeing the movie) did result in a change in attitude toward education of the poor (Test 1) and taxation (Test 2).   ∎

SECTION 6.3
Multivariate Analysis to Test for a Difference Between Two Independent Groups

This analysis represents the multivariate extension of the t-test presented in Section 1.5. As in the case of the two-group univariate experiment, the two groups can be formed by random assignment, or the groups already may be constituted (males versus females). The major difference from the univariate experiment is, of course, that two or more responses (dependent variables) are measured and analyzed in combination.

Points to Consider When Using T^2 to Test for Differences Between Independent Groups

1. For each subject, there will be two or more different measures taken and recorded.
2. It is not necessary to have an equal number of subjects in each group, but it makes comparisons easier if there are equal numbers.

■ EXAMPLE

Assume that fifteen psychology and twelve history majors are randomly selected to participate in an experiment to determine whether choice of major is related to particular intellectual skills. Two tests, Reading Comprehension (Test 1) and Mathematical Concepts (Test 2), are given to each subject. The number of correct answers on each of the tests is recorded for each subject.

Step 1. After the experiment is completed, table the data as follows:

\ Psychology Students			History Students		
Subjects	Test 1	Test 2	Subjects	Test 1	Test 2
S_1	20	21	S_{16}	26	28
S_2	27	27	S_{17}	20	24
S_3	20	23	S_{18}	19	23
S_4	23	22	S_{19}	17	19
S_5	30	31	S_{20}	14	20
S_6	21	21	S_{21}	26	27
S_7	26	28	S_{22}	28	29
S_8	18	18	S_{23}	14	19
S_9	19	23	S_{24}	19	19
S_{10}	27	30	S_{25}	16	21
S_{11}	14	19	S_{26}	14	17
S_{12}	15	14	S_{27}	28	27
S_{13}	17	19			
S_{14}	19	22			
S_{15}	16	21			

Step 2. Obtain the sum of the two test scores for both groups of subjects.

Psychology, Test 1 Sum = **312**
Psychology, Test 2 Sum = **339**
History, Test 1 Sum = **241**
History, Test 2 Sum = **273**

Step 3. Obtain the sum of squared scores of the two test scores for both groups of subjects.

Psychology, Sum of Test 1 scores squared
$20^2 + 27^2 + \cdots + 16^2 =$ **6816**
Psychology, Sum of Test 2 scores squared
$21^2 + 27^2 + \cdots + 21^2 =$ **7965**
History, Sum of Test 1 scores squared
$26^2 + 20^2 + \cdots + 28^2 =$ **5175**
History, Sum of Test 2 scores squared
$28^2 + 24^2 + \cdots + 27^2 =$ **6401**

Step 4. Obtain the sum of the cross products for each group.

Psychology, Sum of cross products for Test 1 and Test 2
$(20 \times 21) + (27 \times 27) + \cdots + (16 \times 21) =$ **7338**
History, Sum of cross products for Test 1 and Test 2
$(26 \times 28) + (20 \times 24) + \cdots + (28 \times 27) =$ **5719**

Step 5. Obtain the centroids for each of the experimental groups.

Centroid for Psychology group (from Step 2)

$$\begin{array}{l} 312/15 = \\ 339/15 = \end{array} \begin{bmatrix} 20.8 \\ 22.6 \end{bmatrix}$$

Centroid for History group (from Step 2)

$$\begin{array}{l} 241/12 = \\ 273/12 = \end{array} \begin{bmatrix} 20.08 \\ 22.75 \end{bmatrix}$$

Step 6. Calculate the sum of squares for Group 1 (Psychology; data from Steps 2 and 3). The general computational formula is

$$\Sigma X^2 - \frac{(\Sigma X)^2}{N}$$

For Test 1: $SS_{G_{p1}T_1} = 6816 - \dfrac{(312)^2}{15} =$ **326.4**

For Test 2: $SS_{G_{p1}T_2} = 7965 - \dfrac{(339)^2}{15} =$ **303.6**

Step 7. Calculate the sum of cross products for Group 1 (Psychology; data from Steps 2 and 4). The general computational formula is

$$\Sigma\, X_1 X_2 - \frac{(\Sigma\, X_1)(\Sigma\, X_2)}{N(\text{pairs})}$$

Sum of cross products: $SSCP_{Gp1} = 7338 - \dfrac{(312)(339)}{15} = \mathbf{286.8}$

Step 8. Calculate the sum of squares for Group 2 (History).

For Test 1: $SS_{Gp_2T_1} = 5175 - \dfrac{(241)^2}{12} = \mathbf{334.92}$

For Test 2: $SS_{Gp_2T_2} = 6401 - \dfrac{(273)^2}{12} = 190.25$

Step 9. Calculate the sum of cross products for Group 2.

Sum of cross products: $SSCP_{Gp2} = 5719 - \dfrac{(241)(273)}{12} = \mathbf{236.25}$

Step 10. All the preliminary calculations have been completed. The next step requires the calculation of the within-groups dispersion matrix, $\mathbf{C}_w$. These values will be inserted into a symmetric matrix with the elements arranged as follows:

$$\begin{bmatrix} a & b \\ c & d \end{bmatrix}$$

The diagonal elements of this matrix (a and d) are the within-groups variance estimates, the off-diagonal elements (b and c) are the within-groups covariance estimates.

The matrix elements to be calculated are as follows:

$$\mathbf{C}_w = \begin{bmatrix} SS_{wT1} & SSCP_w \\ SSCP_w & SS_{wT2} \end{bmatrix}$$

The computational formulas for each of the elements are

Psychology History

Test 1: $SS_{wT1} = \dfrac{SS_{Gp_1T_1} + SS_{Gp_2T_1}}{n_{Gp1} + n_{Gp2} - 2}$

Test 2: $SS_{wT2} = \dfrac{SS_{Gp_1T_2} + SS_{Gp_2T_2}}{n_{Gp_1} + n_{Gp_2} - 2}$

Cross Products: $SSCP_w = \dfrac{SSCP_{Gp1} + SSCP_{Gp2}}{n_1(\text{pairs}) + n_2(\text{pairs}) - 2}$

For Test 1, the SS_{wT_1} is equal to (from Steps 6 and 8):

$$\frac{326.4 + 334.92}{25} = \frac{661.32}{25} = \mathbf{26.45}$$

For Test 2, the SS_{wT_2} is equal to (from Steps 6 and 8):

$$\frac{303.6 + 190.25}{25} = \frac{493.85}{25} = \mathbf{19.75}$$

The $SSCP_w$ elements are equal to (from Steps 7 and 9):

$$\frac{286.8 + 236.25}{25} = \frac{523.05}{25} = \mathbf{20.92}$$

Step 11. Computation of the within-groups dispersion matrix

$$\mathbf{C}_w = \begin{bmatrix} (a) & (b) \\ 26.45 & 20.92 \\ (c) & (d) \\ 20.92 & 19.75 \end{bmatrix}$$

Step 12. The inverse matrix must now be computed. The formula is

$$\mathbf{C}_w^{-1} = \frac{1}{ad - bc} \begin{bmatrix} d & -b \\ -c & a \end{bmatrix}$$

$$= \frac{1}{(26.45)(19.75) - (-20.92)(-20.92)} \begin{bmatrix} 19.75 & -20.92 \\ -20.92 & 26.45 \end{bmatrix}$$

$$= \frac{1}{84.74} \begin{bmatrix} 19.75 & -20.92 \\ -20.92 & 26.45 \end{bmatrix}$$

$$= \begin{bmatrix} .2331 & -.2469 \\ -.2469 & .3121 \end{bmatrix}$$

Note: For subsequent calculations, the above elements of the inverse matrix will be referred to in relation to accepted matrix positioning, i.e.

$$\begin{bmatrix} (a) & (b) \\ .2331 & -.2469 \\ (c) & (d) \\ -.2469 & .3121 \end{bmatrix}$$

Step 13. Computation of the difference between the centroids of the two groups (from Step 5):

$$\begin{bmatrix} \bar{X}_{Gp_1T_1} \\ \bar{X}_{Gp_1T_2} \end{bmatrix} - \begin{bmatrix} \bar{X}_{Gp_2T_1} \\ \bar{X}_{Gp_2T_2} \end{bmatrix} = \begin{bmatrix} 20.8 \\ 22.6 \end{bmatrix} - \begin{bmatrix} 20.08 \\ 22.75 \end{bmatrix} = \begin{bmatrix} .72 \\ -.15 \end{bmatrix}$$

Step 14.   Computation of T^2: The general computational formula for T^2 in matrix form is

$$T^2 = N\bar{\mathbf{x}}'\mathbf{C}_w^{-1}\bar{\mathbf{x}}$$

For the two-group example, the formula is

$$T^2 = \left(\frac{n_1 n_2}{n_1 + n_2}\right)\bar{\mathbf{x}}'\mathbf{C}_w^{-1}\bar{\mathbf{x}}$$

$$= \left(\frac{15 \times 12}{15 + 12}\right)[.72 - .15]\begin{bmatrix} .2331 & -.2469 \\ -.2469 & .3121 \end{bmatrix}\begin{bmatrix} .72 \\ -.15 \end{bmatrix}$$

The computational formula for a symmetric matrix where the off-diagonal terms are equal ($b = c$) reduces to the following:

$$T^2 = \left(\frac{n_1 n_2}{n_1 + n_2}\right)(a)(\bar{X}_{\text{diff}_{T1}})^2 + 2(b)(\bar{X}_{\text{diff}_{T1}})(\bar{X}_{\text{diff}_{T2}}) + (d)(\bar{X}_{\text{diff}_{T2}})^2$$

$$= 6.67(.2331)(.72^2) + (2)(-.2469)(.72)(-.15) + (.3121)(-.15^2)$$

$$= 6.67 \times .1812$$

$$= \mathbf{1.208}$$

Step 15.   Transforming T^2 into F: The formula for transforming T^2 into F when there are two independent groups is

$$F = \left(\frac{N - p - 1}{p(N - 2)}\right)T^2$$

where N = the number of subjects
   p = the number of dependent variables measured

$$= \left(\frac{27 - 2 - 1}{2(27 - 2)}\right)1.208$$

$$= \mathbf{.58}$$

Step 16.   Calculating the *df* for this F ratio:

The *df* for $F = p$ and $N - p - 1$

In this example, *df* = 2 and $27 - 2 - 1$, or **24**.

Step 17.   Test of significance: Looking in the F tables for 2 and 24 degrees of freedom, it is seen that an F ratio of 3.40 is needed for significance at the .05 level. Since the computed F in the present example was only .58, it can be concluded that the Psychology and History subjects did not respond differentially to the tests.   ■

SECTION 6.4
Multivariate Analysis to Test for a Difference in the Change Scores of Two Groups

This analysis is an extension of the multivariate example presented in Section 6.2. In this example, the performance of two groups will be compared to determine whether the changes (pre- to post-experiment) in one group are larger than the other.

Points to Consider When Using T^2 to Test for Differences in Change Scores

1. For each subject, there will be two or more response measures (dependent variables) recorded. In addition, each response measure will be recorded twice) usually before experimental manipulation and again, after).
2. It is not necessary to have an equal number of subjects in each group, but comparisons and understanding of results are easier with equal numbers.

■ EXAMPLE

For this example, assume that a special curriculum enrichment program is initiated in a school system. The school psychologist wishes to determine whether such a program benefits talented and gifted students more than average students. Two tests, one of art appreciation (Test 1) and the other of abstract thinking (Test 2), will be administered to the students. Since it is likely that the talented and gifted students would score higher initially due to superior intellectual ability, the experimenter decides to give the tests prior to the initiation of the program and then administer alternative forms of the tests after the curriculum has been in place for one year. The measures to be analyzed are the change between the pre and post scores of the two groups.

Step 1. Table the data as follows:

	TALENTED AND GIFTED GROUP			
	Test 1 (Art appreciation)		Test 2 (Abstract thinking)	
Subjects	Pre	Post	Pre	Post
S_1	10	10	21	27
S_2	12	13	19	25
S_3	9	9	16	22
S_4	15	17	22	27
S_5	16	18	31	36

	TALENTED AND GIFTED GROUP			
	Test 1 (Art appreciation)		Test 2 (Abstract thinking)	
Subjects	Pre	Post	Pre	Post
S_6	14	19	27	31
S_7	13	16	36	38
S_8	10	11	32	38
S_9	10	12	30	36
S_{10}	13	16	17	19
	AVERAGE GROUP			
S_{11}	11	13	21	21
S_{12}	14	15	25	25
S_{13}	13	18	27	28
S_{14}	19	17	29	29
S_{15}	17	17	31	32
S_{16}	16	17	31	32
S_{17}	14	18	34	35
S_{18}	15	16	27	30
S_{19}	18	17	29	29
S_{20}	16	22	22	23

Step 2. Calculate the difference score between the pre- and post-special curriculum scores for each subject.

	TALENTED AND GIFTED	
	Test 1 Difference	Test 2 Difference
S_1	0	6
S_2	1	6
.	.	.
.	.	.
.	.	.
S_{10}	3	2
	AVERAGE	
S_{11}	2	0
.	.	.
.	.	.
S_{20}	6	1

Step 3. Calculate the sum of the difference scores ($\Sigma\ d$) for each condition.

For Test 1, Talented and Gifted: $0 + 1 + \cdots + 3 = \mathbf{19}$
For Test 2, Talented and Gifted: $6 + 6 + \cdots + 2 = \mathbf{48}$

For Test 1, Average Group: $2 + 1 + \cdots + 6 = 17$
For Test 2, Average Group: $0 + 0 + \cdots + 1 = 8$

Step 4. Calculate the sum of the difference scores squared (d^2)

For Test 1, Talented and Gifted: $0^2 + 1^2 + \cdots 3^2 = 57$
For Test 2, Talented and Gifted: $6^2 + 6^2 + \cdots 2^2 = 254$
For Test 1, Average Group: $2^2 + 1^2 + \cdots + 6^2 = 89$
For Test 2, Average Group: $0^2 + 0^2 + \cdots + 1^2 = 14$

Step 5. Calculate the sum of the cross products of the difference scores on Test 1 and Test 2 for each group. $\Sigma \ (d_{test\ 1} \times d_{test\ 2})$

For Talented and Gifted: $(0 \times 6) + (1 \times 6) + \cdots + (3 \times 2) = 76$
For the Average Group: $(2 \times 0) + (1 \times 0) + \cdots + (6 \times 1) = 19$

Step 6. Calculate the centroid for each group (from Step 3).

Centroid for Talented and Gifted: $\dfrac{19/10 = 1.9}{48/10 = 4.8}$

Centroid for Average Group: $\dfrac{17/10 = 1.7}{8/10 = \ .8}$

Step 7. Calculation of the sum of squares of the difference scores for Group 1 (Talented and Gifted): The necessary values were computed in Steps 3 and 4. The basic computational formula is

$$SS_d = \Sigma \ d^2 - \frac{(\Sigma \ d)^2}{n_{per\ group}}$$

For Test 1: $SS_{Gp_1T_1} = 57 - \dfrac{(19)^2}{10} = \ \mathbf{20.9}$

For Test 2: $SS_{Gp_1T_2} = 254 - \dfrac{(48)^2}{10} = \mathbf{23.6}$

Step 8. Calculation of the sum of cross products of the difference scores for Group 1 (Talented and Gifted). The basic computational formula is

$$SSCP = \Sigma \ d_1d_2 - \frac{(\Sigma \ d_1)(\Sigma \ d_2)}{n(\text{pairs})}$$

The necessary values for the calculations were obtained in Steps 3 and 5.

$$SSCP_{Gp_1} = 76 - \frac{(19)(48)}{10} = \mathbf{-15.2}$$

Step 9. Calculation of the sum of squares for Group 2 (Average): Repeat the calculations of Step 7 using the data from the Average group.

For Test 1: $SS_{Gp_2T_1} = 89 - \dfrac{(17)^2}{10} = \mathbf{60.1}$

For Test 2: $SS_{Gp_2T_2} = 14 - \dfrac{(8)^2}{10} = \mathbf{7.6}$

Step 10. Calculation of the sum of cross products for Group 2: Again, repeat the calculations of Step 8 using the data from the Average group.

$SSCP_{Gp_2} = 19 - \dfrac{(17)(8)}{10} = \mathbf{5.4}$

Step 11. These values will now be arranged into a symmetric dispersion matrix with the elements set up as follows:

$$\begin{bmatrix} a & b \\ c & d \end{bmatrix}$$

The elements of the dispersion matrix ($\mathbf{C}_w$) will now be obtained. The diagonal elements of this matrix are the within-groups variance estimates; the off-diagonal elements are the within-groups covariance estimates.

The elements of the matrix are calculated as follows:

$$\mathbf{C}_w = \begin{bmatrix} SS_{wT1} & SSCP_w \\ SSCP_w & SS_{wT2} \end{bmatrix}$$

The computational formulas for the elements are

Test 1: $\qquad SS_{wT1} = \dfrac{SS_{Gp_1T_1} + SS_{Gp_2T_1}}{n_1 + n_2 - 2}$

Test 2: $\qquad SS_{wT2} = \dfrac{SS_{Gp_1T_2} + SS_{Gp_2T_2}}{n_1 + n_2 - 2}$

Cross products: $SSCP_w = \dfrac{SSCP_{Gp_1} + SSCP_{Gp_2}}{n_1(\text{pairs}) + n_2(\text{pairs}) - 2}$

For Test 1, the SS_{wT1} element is equal to (from Steps 7 and 9):

$SS_{wT1} = \dfrac{20.9 + 60.1}{18} = \mathbf{4.50}$

For Test 2, the SS_{wT2} element is equal to (also from Steps 7 and 9):

$SS_{wT2} = \dfrac{23.6 + 7.6}{18} = \mathbf{1.733}$

And the cross products elements ($SSCP_w$) are equal to (from Steps 8 and 10):

$$SSCP_w = \frac{-15.2 + 5.4}{18} = -.544$$

Thus, the $\mathbf{C}_w$ matrix $= \begin{bmatrix} 4.50 & -.544 \\ -.544 & 1.733 \end{bmatrix}$

Step 12. The inverse matrix must now be computed. The formula for this matrix is

$$\mathbf{C}_w^{-1} = \frac{1}{ad - bc} \begin{bmatrix} d & -b \\ -c & a \end{bmatrix}$$

$$= \frac{1}{(4.50)(1.733) - (-.544)(-.544)} \begin{bmatrix} 1.733 & .544 \\ .544 & 4.50 \end{bmatrix}$$

$$= \frac{1}{7.502} \begin{bmatrix} 1.733 & .544 \\ .544 & 4.50 \end{bmatrix}$$

$$= \begin{bmatrix} .231 & .072 \\ .072 & .600 \end{bmatrix}$$

Note: For subsequent calculations, the above elements of the inverse matrix will be referred to in relation to accepted matrix positioning, i.e.,

$$\mathbf{C}_w^{-1} = \begin{bmatrix} (a) & (b) \\ .231 & .072 \\ (c) & (d) \\ .072 & .600 \end{bmatrix}$$

Step 13. Computation of the difference between the change score centroids:

$$\begin{bmatrix} 1.9 \\ 4.8 \end{bmatrix} - \begin{bmatrix} 1.7 \\ .8 \end{bmatrix} = \begin{bmatrix} .2 \\ 4.0 \end{bmatrix}$$

Step 14. Computation of T^2: The general computational formula for T^2 is

$$T^2 = \left(\frac{n_1 n_2}{n_1 + n_2}\right) \bar{\mathbf{x}}' \mathbf{C}_w^{-1} \bar{\mathbf{x}}$$

$$= \left(\frac{10 \times 10}{10 + 10}\right) [.2 \quad 4.0] \begin{bmatrix} .231 & 0.72 \\ .072 & .600 \end{bmatrix} \begin{bmatrix} .2 \\ 4.0 \end{bmatrix}$$

In the special case where C_w^{-1} is symmetric so that element $b = c$, the above expression simplifies to

$$T^2 = \left(\frac{n_1 n_2}{n_1 + n_2}\right)[(a)(\overline{X}_{\text{diff}Gp_1T_1 - Gp_2T_1})^2 + 2(b)(\overline{X}_{\text{diff}G_1T_1 - G_2T_1})(\overline{X}_{\text{diff}G_1T_2 - G_2T_2})$$
$$+ (d)(\overline{X}_{\text{diff}G_1T_2 - G_2T_2})^2]$$
$$= 5[(.231)(.2)^2 + (2)(.072)(4.0)(.2) + (.6)(4.0)^2]$$
$$= 5 \times 9.724 = \mathbf{48.622}$$

Step 15.   Transforming T^2 to F: The relationship between T^2 and F is as follows:

$$F = \left(\frac{N - p - 1}{p(N - 2)}\right)T^2$$

where N = the number of subjects
  p = the number of dependent variables measured

$$= \left(\frac{20 - 2 - 1}{2(20 - 2)}\right) 48.622$$

$$= \left(\frac{17}{36}\right) 48.622$$

$$= \mathbf{22.96}$$

Step 16.   Calculation of the df for the F ratio: The df are equal to p and $N - p - 1$. In the present example, $p = 2$ and $N = 20$. Thus, the $df = 2$ and 17.

Step 17.   Test of significance: Looking in the F tables for 2 and 17 df, we find that a F ratio larger than 3.59 is needed for significance beyond the .05 level. Since the computed F was 22.96, it is concluded that the change score centroids differ significantly. ∎

SECTION 6.5
Multivariate Analysis of Variance: More Than Two Groups

This multivariate example is the counterpart of the univariate completely randomized design presented in Section 4.1. As pointed out in the preceding sections, more than one response measure will be recorded for each subject. While the F-test is the standard test employed in univariate analyses, several tests are available in the multiple group-multivariate case. The test most widely used is Wilks' *lambda* criterion. This test, which can be related directly to the F-test, will be used in the following example.

Points to Consider When Designing an Experiment for More Than Two Groups

1. For each subject, there will be two or more response measures (dependent variables) recorded.
2. More than two groups of subjects will be employed. The number of groups to be compared is arbitrary, but it is rare that more than four or five groups are compared in one experiment.
3. Although not necessary, it is advantageous to have an equal number of subjects in each of the experimental groups.

■ EXAMPLE

For this example, assume that three groups of subjects are selected and classified on the basis of their self-reported stress levels. Seven subjects are classified as low stress, nine as medium stress, and eight as high stress.

All groups undergo the same fitness and exercise program. After six months in the program, all subjects are measured in terms of self-confidence (T_1) and weight loss (T_2).

Step 1. Following completion of the experiment, table the data as follows:

Low stress			Medium stress			High stress		
Subjects	T_1	T_2	Subjects	T_1	T_2	Subjects	T_1	T_2
S_1	10	14	S_8	11	14	S_{17}	5	6
S_2	14	15	S_9	15	19	S_{18}	7	8
S_3	13	13	S_{10}	16	16	S_{19}	9	9
S_4	17	19	S_{11}	14	19	S_{20}	11	9
S_5	19	22	S_{12}	11	19	S_{21}	9	8
S_6	14	16	S_{13}	9	14	S_{22}	13	13
S_7	9	8	S_{14}	9	13	S_{23}	9	7
			S_{15}	8	15	S_{24}	7	9
			S_{16}	14	19			

Step 2. Obtain the sum for Test 1 and Test 2 for each of the three groups.

Low Group
Test 1: $10 + 14 + \cdots + 9 = \mathbf{96}$
Test 2: $14 + 15 + \cdots + 8 = \mathbf{107}$

Med. Group
Test 1: $11 + 15 + \cdots + 14 = \mathbf{107}$
Test 2: $14 + 19 + \cdots + 19 = \mathbf{148}$

High Group
Test 1: $5 + 7 + \cdots + 7 = \mathbf{70}$
Test 2: $6 + 8 + \cdots + 9 = \mathbf{69}$

Step 3.   Obtain the sum of the scores squared for each test and group.

Low Group
Test 1: $10^2 + 14^2 + \cdots + 9^2 = \mathbf{1392}$
Test 2: $14^2 + 15^2 + \cdots + 8^2 = \mathbf{1755}$

Med. Group
Test 1: $11^2 + 15^2 + \cdots + 14^2 = \mathbf{1341}$
Test 2: $14^2 + 19^2 + \cdots + 19^2 = \mathbf{2486}$

High Group
Test 1: $5^2 + 7^2 + \cdots + 7^2 = \mathbf{656}$
Test 2: $6^2 + 8^2 + \cdots + 9^2 = \mathbf{625}$

Step 4.   Obtain the sum of the cross products for each group.

Low Group: $(10 \times 14) + (14 \times 15) + \cdots + (9 \times 8) = \mathbf{1556}$
Med. Group: $(11 \times 14) + (15 \times 18) + \cdots + (14 \times 19) = \mathbf{1799}$
High Group: $(5 \times 6) + (7 \times 8) + \cdots + (7 \times 9) = \mathbf{633}$

Step 5.   The necessary preliminary calculations have been completed. The test will determine whether the mean vectors represented by the experimental groups are equal. In the univariate ANOVA, the test of significance is the *F* ratio represented by the following general formula:

$$F = \frac{MS_{treatments}}{MS_{error}}$$

In the case of the MANOVA, the test to be employed will be Wilks' criterion, which is defined as:

$$lambda = \Lambda = \frac{|\mathbf{W}|}{|\mathbf{T}|}$$

in which $|\mathbf{W}|$ is the determinant of the within-groups sums of squares and cross products matrix and $|\mathbf{T}|$ is the determinant of the total sums of squares and cross products matrix.

Step 6.   Computation of the elements of the $\mathbf{W}$ matrix: The elements will be arranged in a symmetric matrix as follows:

$$\begin{bmatrix} a & b \\ c & d \end{bmatrix}$$

Note: The determinant of the above matrix is required for later calculations. It is computed as $ad - bc$.

The diagonal elements of the $\mathbf{W}$ matrix (elements a and d) consist of the sum of the SS_w components for Test 1 (self-confidence) and the sum of the SS_w components for Test 2 (weight loss). The basic computational formula for each component is

$$\Sigma X^2 - \frac{(\Sigma X)^2}{N}$$

The components for each group will then be combined to obtain the a and d elements (data from Steps 2 and 3).

$$\text{Low—Test 1} \qquad \text{Med.—Test 1} \qquad \text{Hi—Test 1}$$

$$\text{Element } a = 1392 - \frac{(96)^2}{7} + 1341 - \frac{(107)^2}{7} + 656 - \frac{(70)^2}{8}$$

$$= \quad 75.43 \qquad + \quad 68.89 \qquad + \quad 43.50$$

$$= \mathbf{187.82}$$

$$\text{Low—Test 2} \qquad \text{Med.—Test 2} \qquad \text{Hi—Test 2}$$

$$\text{Element } d = 1755 - \frac{(107)^2}{7} + 2486 - \frac{(148)^2}{9} + 625 - \frac{(69)^2}{8}$$

$$= \mathbf{201.53}$$

Step 7. Computation of the *SSCP* elements (elements b and c): In this case, the *SSCP* consists of the sums of the cross products for each of the three experimental groups. Since two test measures were recorded ($p = 2$), elements b and c will be identical. (Data are from Steps 2 and 4.)

$$\qquad\qquad\qquad\qquad \text{Low} \qquad\qquad\qquad \text{Medium}$$

$$\text{Elements } b \text{ and } c = 1556 - \frac{(96)(107)}{7} + 1799 - \frac{(107)(148)}{9}$$

$$\text{High}$$

$$+ 633 - \frac{(70)(69)}{8} = \mathbf{157.26}$$

Step 8. Collecting the elements

$$\mathbf{W} = \begin{bmatrix} (a) & (b) \\ 187.82 & 157.26 \\ (c) & (d) \\ 157.26 & 201.53 \end{bmatrix}$$

Step 9. Computation of the total sum of squares and total sum of cross products required to set up matrix **T**: The necessary scores must first be totaled so the computations can be completed.

Sum of scores on Test 1 ($\Sigma\, T_1$) (from Step 2): $96 + 107 + 70 = \mathbf{273}$
Sum of scores on Test 2 ($\Sigma\, T_2$) (from Step 2): $107 + 148 + 69 = \mathbf{324}$
Sum of T_1 scores squared ($\Sigma\, T_1^2$) (from Step 3): $1392 + 1341 + 656$
$$= \mathbf{3389}$$
Sum of T_2 scores squared ($\Sigma\, T_2^2$) (from Step 3): $1755 + 2486 + 625$
$$= \mathbf{4866}$$
Sum of cross products ($\Sigma\, T_1 T_2$) (from Step 4): $1556 + 1799 + 633$
$$= \mathbf{3988}$$

Step 10. Computation of the elements of the **T** matrix:

Element a: (self-confidence) $= 3389 - \dfrac{(273)^2}{24} = \mathbf{283.6}$

Element d: (weight loss) $= 4866 - \dfrac{(324)^2}{24} = \mathbf{492}$

Elements b and c: (cross products) $= 3988 - \dfrac{(273)(324)}{24} = \mathbf{302.5}$

Step 11. Collecting the elements

$$\mathbf{T} = \begin{bmatrix} (a) & (b) \\ 283.6 & 302.5 \\ (c) & (d) \\ 302.5 & 492.0 \end{bmatrix}$$

Step 12. The final calculation for the necessary components of the lambda ratio requires computation of the determinants. In both cases, the calculation represents subtraction of elements $b \times c$ from $a \times d$.

$$|\mathbf{W}| = ad - bc = (187.82)(201.53) - (157.26)(157.26) = \mathbf{13{,}120.66}$$
$$|\mathbf{T}| = ad - bc = (283.6)(492) - (302.5)(302.5) = \mathbf{48{,}024.95}$$

Step 13. Calculation of

$$\Lambda = \frac{|\mathbf{W}|}{|\mathbf{T}|} = \frac{13{,}120.66}{48{,}024.95} = \mathbf{.2732}$$

Step 14. The distribution of *lambda* for particular values of G (number of groups) and p (number of dependent variables) in a one-way MANOVA is as follows:

G	P	Distribution as F	Degrees of freedom
Any number of groups	2	$\dfrac{1 - \sqrt{\Lambda}}{\sqrt{\Lambda}}\left(\dfrac{N - G - 1}{G - 1}\right)$	$2(G - 1), 2(N - G - 1)$
2	Any number of measures	$\dfrac{1 - \Lambda}{\Lambda}\left(\dfrac{N - p - 1}{p - 1}\right)$	$p, N - p - 1$
3	Any number of measures	$\dfrac{1 - \sqrt{\Lambda}}{\sqrt{\Lambda}}\left(\dfrac{N - p - 2}{2}\right)$	$2p, 2(N - p - 2)$

Thus, for the special case where the number of variables measured is two ($p = 2$), the relationship between lambda and F is described as follows:

$$F = \frac{1 - \sqrt{\Lambda}}{\sqrt{\Lambda}} \left(\frac{N - G - 1}{G - 1} \right)$$

Step 15. The degrees of freedom are described by the following:

$$df = 2(G - 1) \quad \text{and} \quad 2(N - G - 1)$$

In the present example,

$$df = 2(3 - 1) \quad \text{and} \quad 2(24 - 3 - 1)$$

$$= 2(2) \quad \text{and} \quad 2(20)$$

$$= \mathbf{4} \quad \text{and} \quad \mathbf{40}$$

Step 16. Test of significance:

$$F = \frac{1 - \sqrt{.2732}}{\sqrt{.2732}} \left(\frac{24 - 3 - 1}{3 - 1} \right) = .913(10) = \mathbf{9.13}, \quad \text{with } df = 4, 40$$

Step 17. Looking in the F tables with 4 and 40 df, we see that an F larger than 2.61 is required for significance at the .05 level. Since the computed F is 9.13, it is concluded that the centroids of the three groups are significantly different.

Step 18. Summary table: After the analysis has been completed, all the calculations are usually collected into a single summary table.

	Summary table for one-way MANOVA			
Source	Matrix	Lambda	df of F	F
Groups	not needed			
Within Groups	$\begin{bmatrix} 187.82 & 157.26 \\ 157.26 & 201.53 \end{bmatrix}$	$\dfrac{13{,}120.66}{48{,}024.95}$		
Total	$\begin{bmatrix} 283.6 & 302.5 \\ 302.5 & 492.0 \end{bmatrix}$	$= .2732$	4, 40	9.13

Additional Analyses

In the above example, the three groups of subjects (Low, Medium, and High Stress) clearly responded differently when the criterion measures, self-confidence (T_i) and weight loss (T_2), where considered concurrently. The next likely question would be whether the subjects in the three groups responded differently in terms of the response measures when the measures were considered separately.

To answer this question, the usual practice is to carry out two separate univariate ANOVAs, one on T_1 and the other on T_2. To compute these analyses, the user should turn to Section 4.1 and follow Steps 2 through 13, using the data recorded for T_1 and then repeating that analysis using the data recorded for T_2.

If still further univariate analyses are needed to determine which specific groups differ from each other, the experimenter should turn to Part 5 and undertake one of the appropriate supplemental computations presented in Sections 5.4 through 5.9. ■

SECTION 6.6
Multivariate Analysis: Two-Factor Comparisons

The following example represents the multivariate counterpart of the factorial analysis of variance presented in Section 4.2. As in the preceding section, more than one response measure (dependent variable) is recorded for each subject. Wilks' *lambda* criterion will be the test of significance employed. As in the case of the univariate factorial design, the multivariate two-factor design permits investigation of factors in combination with each other.

Points to Consider When Using the Two-Factor Multivariate Design

1. For each subject there will be two or more response measures (dependent variables) recorded. (*Note:* If more than two response measures are recorded, the analysis almost certainly will require use of a computer.)
2. It is usually best to have an equal number of subjects in each of the experimental groups and conditions. If equality cannot be achieved, the groups must be proportional in size.
3. The number of treatment groups within each factor is determined by the nature of the problem. However, it is rare that more than four or five groups are included in either of the two factors.

■ EXAMPLE
For this example, assume that an experimenter wishes to determine whether there are differences between kindergarten students, first graders, and second graders in their intellectual curiosity. He also wishes to determine whether boys and girls show the same changes. To investigate these questions, the experimenter sets up a factorial design involving three grade levels (kindergarten, first, and second) and two sexes (boys and girls). Two response measures (dependent

variables) are recorded. The first (T_1) is a standardized test of creativity, the second (T_2) is based on teachers' judgments of each child's behavior in a variety of standardized problem situations.

Step 1. After the experiment is completed, table the data as follows:

	GIRLS							
	Kindergarten			First Grade			Second Grade	
S_s	T_1	T_2	S_s	T_1	T_2	S_s	T_1	T_2
S_1	10	14	S_{11}	15	30	S_{21}	17	30
S_2	11	18	S_{12}	17	26	S_{22}	19	35
S_3	19	19	S_{13}	18	25	S_{23}	22	36
S_4	16	7	S_{14}	15	17	S_{24}	22	35
S_5	18	16	S_{15}	15	26	S_{25}	19	31
S_6	17	14	S_{16}	12	25	S_{26}	23	29
S_7	9	13	S_{17}	14	21	S_{27}	26	31
S_8	12	15	S_{18}	17	21	S_{28}	23	29
S_9	12	15	S_{19}	19	23	S_{29}	21	30
S_{10}	16	15	S_{20}	21	26	S_{30}	21	25
	BOYS							
S_{31}	31	31	S_{41}	15	30	S_{51}	10	12
S_{32}	30	40	S_{42}	19	26	S_{52}	12	13
S_{33}	26	43	S_{43}	17	22	S_{53}	14	15
S_{34}	26	36	S_{44}	16	21	S_{54}	19	18
S_{35}	25	32	S_{45}	18	25	S_{55}	14	14
S_{36}	28	31	S_{46}	16	21	S_{56}	18	15
S_{37}	21	36	S_{47}	14	21	S_{57}	16	17
S_{38}	21	36	S_{48}	12	19	S_{58}	12	14
S_{39}	32	32	S_{49}	14	28	S_{59}	10	14
S_{40}	27	34	S_{50}	16	25	S_{60}	19	14

Step 2. Calculate the sum of each group.

	GIRLS							
S_1	10	14	S_{11}	15	30	S_{21}	17	30
S_2	11	18	S_{12}	17	26	S_{22}	19	35
	+	+		+	+		+	+
	.	.		.	.		.	.
	.	.		.	.		.	.
S_{10}	16	15	S_{20}	21	26	S_{30}	21	25
Sum =	**140**	**146**		**163**	**240**		**213**	**311**

	Kindergarten			First Grade			Second Grade	
BOYS								
S_s	T_1	T_2	S_s	T_1	T_2	S_s	T_1	T_2
S_{31}	31	31	S_{41}	15	30	S_{51}	10	12
S_{32}	30	40	S_{42}	19	26	S_{52}	12	13
	+	+		+	+		+	+
	.	.		.	.		.	.
	.	.		.	.		.	.
S_{40}	27	34	S_{50}	16	25	S_{60}	19	14
Sum =	**267**	**351**		**157**	**238**		**144**	**146**

Step 3. Calculate the sum of the squared scores for each group.

	GIRLS							
S_1	10^2	14^2	S_{11}	15^2	30^2	S_{21}	17^2	30^2
	+	+		+	+		+	+
	.	.		.	.		.	.
	.	.		.	.		.	.
S_{10}	16^2	15^2	S_{20}	21^2	26^2	S_{30}	21^2	25^2
Sum =	**2076**	**2226**		**2719**	**5878**		**4595**	**9775**

	BOYS							
S_{31}	31^2	31^2	S_{41}	15^2	30^2	S_{51}	10^2	12^2
	+	+		+	+		+	+
	.	.		.	.		.	.
	.	.		.	.		.	.
S_{40}	27^2	34^2	S_{50}	16^2	25^2	S_{60}	9^2	14^2
Sum =	**7257**	**12,463**		**2503**	**5778**		**2182**	**2160**

Step 4. Calculate the sum of the cross products.

	GIRLS			
S_1	$10 \times 14 = 140$	S_{11}	$15 \times 30 = 450$	S_{21}	$17 \times 30 = 510$
	+		+		+
	.		.		.
	.		.		.
S_{10}	$6 \times 15 = 90$	S_{20}	$21 \times 26 = 546$	S_{30}	$21 \times 25 = 525$
Sum =	**2054**		**3921**		**6621**

		BOYS			
S_{31}	$31 \times 31 = 961$	S_{41}	$15 \times 30 = 450$	S_{51}	$10 \times 12 = 120$
	$+$		$+$		$+$
	$\vdots$		$\vdots$		$\vdots$
S_{40}	$27 \times 34 = 918$	S_{50}	$16 \times 25 = 400$	S_{60}	$9 \times 14 = 126$
Sum $=$	**9337**		**3754**		**2140**

Step 5. Calculate the correction term for T_1 (creativity in this example). First, add the sums of all of the T_1 subtotals (Step 2) to obtain the grand sum of the T_1 scores for the entire table.

$$140 + 163 + \cdots + 144 = \textbf{1084}$$

Then square this value and divide by the total number of T_1 measures recorded. (See Step 1.) This yields the T_1 correction term.

$$\frac{1084^2}{60} = \frac{1,175,056}{60} = \textbf{19,584.267}$$

Step 6. Calculation of the correction term for T_2 (teacher's judgment in this example). Repeat the above steps for T_2

$$146 + 240 + \cdots + 146 = \textbf{1432}$$

and

$$\frac{1432^2}{60} = \frac{2,050,624}{60} = \textbf{34,177.067}$$

Step 7. Calculate the cross products correction term. First, multiply the sum of the T_1 scores (Step 5) times the sum of the T_2 scores (Step 6).

$$1084 \times 1432 = \textbf{1,552,288}$$

Then divide by the number of measures on which each sum was based.

$$\frac{1,552,288}{60} = \textbf{25,871.467}$$

Step 8. Calculate the total sum of squares for T_1. First, obtain the sum of the T_1 scores squared (from Step 3).

$$2076 + 2719 + 4595 + 7257 + 2503 + 2182 = \textbf{21,332}$$

Then, subtract the correction term obtained in Step 5.

$$21,332 - 19,584.267 = \textbf{1747.733}$$

Step 9.   Calculate the total sum of squares for T_2. First, obtain the sum of the T_2 scores squared (from Step 3).

$$2226 + 5878 + 9775 + 12,463 + 5778 + 2160 = \mathbf{38{,}280}$$

Then, subtract the correction term obtained in Step 6.

$$38{,}280 - 34{,}177.067 = \mathbf{4102.933}$$

Step 10.   Calculate the total sum of squares for cross products. First, obtain the total sum of cross products (from Step 4).

$$2054 + 3921 + 6621 + 9337 + 3754 + 2140 = \mathbf{27{,}827}$$

Then, subtract the correction term obtained in Step 7.

$$27{,}827 - 25{,}871.467 = \mathbf{1955.533}$$

Step 11.   Calculate the sum of squares for rows on T_1 (the overall effects of girls versus boys on the creativity test).

Sum of girls' scores on the creativity test: $140 + 163 + 213 = \mathbf{516}$
Sum of boys' scores on the creativity test: $267 + 157 + 144 = \mathbf{568}$

Then, square the above sums, divide by the number of measures on which each was based, and add the quotients.

$$\frac{516^2}{30} + \frac{568^2}{30} = \frac{588{,}880}{30} = \mathbf{19{,}629.333}$$

Finally, subtract the correction term for T_1 (Step 5) from this value.

$$19{,}629.333 - 19{,}584.267 = \mathbf{45.066}$$

Step 12.   Calculation of the sum of squares for rows on T_2 (the overall difference between girls and boys based on teachers' judgments): These calculations repeat Step 11, using the scores recorded as T_2.

Sum of girls' scores (judgment): $146 + 240 + 311 = \mathbf{697}$
Sum of boys' scores (judgment): $351 + 238 + 146 = \mathbf{735}$

Then, square and divide the scores:

$$\frac{697^2}{30} + \frac{735^2}{30} = \frac{1{,}026{,}034}{30} = \mathbf{34{,}201.133}$$

Then, subtract the correction term (Step 6).

$$34{,}201.133 - 34{,}177.067 = \mathbf{24.066}$$

Step 13.   Calculation of the sum of squares of cross products for rows (boys versus girls.)

First, obtain the overall sum of the T_1 and T_2 scores for the first (girls) condition (from Step 2).

$$140 + 163 + 213 = \textbf{516}$$

and

$$146 + 240 + 311 = \textbf{697}$$

Then, multiply the overall sum of the T_1 scores times the overall sum of the T_2 scores.

$$697 \times 516 = \textbf{359,652}$$

Then, divide by the number of scores on which each sum was based.

$$\frac{359,652}{30} = \textbf{11,988.4}$$

Now, repeat the above steps for the second (boys) condition.

Sum of the T_1 scores: $267 + 157 + 144 = \textbf{568}$
Sum of the T_2 scores: $351 + 238 + 146 = \textbf{735}$

and

$$\frac{568 \times 735}{30} = \frac{417,480}{30} = \textbf{13,916}$$

Finally, add the sums of cross products for girls and boys computed above.

$$11,988.4 + 13,916 = \textbf{25,904.4}$$

From that value, subtract the sum of the cross products correction term (Step 7).

$$25,904.4 - 25,871.467 = \textbf{32.933}$$

Step 14. Calculation of the sum of squares for columns on T_1 (the overall effects of grade level on creativity):

First, add the sums of the kindergarten, first, and second grade level on the creativity test (T_1) (from Step 2).

K on T_1: $140 + 267 = \textbf{407}$
First on T_1: $163 + 157 = \textbf{320}$
Second on T_1: $213 + 144 = \textbf{357}$

Square the above sums, divide by the number of measures on which each of the sums was based, and add the quotients.

$$\frac{407^2}{20} + \frac{320^2}{20} + \frac{357^2}{20} + \frac{684,342}{20} = \textbf{19,774.9}$$

Then, subtract the correction term for T_1 (Step 5).

$$19,774.9 - 19,584.267 = \textbf{190.633}$$

Step 15. Computation of the sum of squares for columns on T_2 (the overall effects of grade level on judgments).

Again, add the sums of the teacher judgment scores recorded for the kindergarten, first, and second graders.

K on T_2: 146 + 351 = **497**
First on T_2: 240 + 238 = **478**
Second on T_2: 311 + 146 = **457**

Square the sums, divide by the number of measures on which each was based, and add the quotients.

$$\frac{497^2}{20} + \frac{478^2}{20} + \frac{457^2}{20} + \frac{684,342}{20} = \textbf{34,217.1}$$

Then, subtract the correction term for T_2 (Step 6).

34,217.1 − 34,177.067 = **40.033**

Step 16. Calculation of the sum of squares for cross products for columns (grade levels): First, obtain the overall sum of T_1 scores and the overall sum of T_2 scores for kindergarten group (from Step 2).

Creativity/kindergarten: 140 + 267 = **407**
Judgments/kindergarten: 146 + 351 = **497**

Then multiply these sums times each other and divide by the number of scores on which each sum was based.

$$\frac{407 \times 497}{20} = \frac{202,279}{20} = \textbf{10,113.95}$$

Then, repeat the same set of computations for first and second graders.

Creativity/first graders: 163 + 157 = **320**
Judgments/first graders: 240 + 238 = **478**

and

$$\frac{320 \times 478}{20} = \frac{152,900}{20} = \textbf{7,648}$$

Creativity/second graders: 213 + 144 = **357**
Judgments/second graders: 311 + 146 = **457**

and

$$\frac{357 \times 457}{20} = \frac{163,149}{20} = \textbf{8,157.45}$$

Then, add the sums of cross products for the three groups (kindergarten, first, and second graders) computed above.

10,113.95 + 7,520 + 8,157.45 = **25,919.4**

Finally, from that value, subtract the sum of squares for the cross products correction term (Step 7).

$$25{,}919.4 - 25{,}871.467 = \mathbf{47.933}$$

Note: The sum of squares for cross products can be a negative value; the sum of squares value is always positive.

Step 17.   Calculation of the sum of squares of rows by columns ($SS_{r\times c}$) for T_1 (the interactive effects of boys and girls by grade level for the creativity test): First, square the sum of each of the group's scores on T_1, divide each by the number of scores added to obtain that sum, then sum these quotients (data from Step 2).

$$\frac{140^2}{10} + \frac{163^2}{10} + \frac{213^2}{10} + \frac{267^2}{10} + \frac{157^2}{10} + \frac{144^2}{10} = \frac{208{,}212}{10} = \mathbf{20{,}821.2}$$

Then, subtract the correction term for T_1 (Step 5), the SS for rows$_{T_1}$ (Step 11), and the SS for columns$_{T_1}$ (Step 14).

$$20{,}821.2 - 19{,}584.267 - 45.066 - 190.633 = \mathbf{1001.234}$$

Step 18.   Calculation of the $SS_{r\times c}$ for T_2: Repeat the above calculations for the performance of boys and girls at each grade level for the comprehension test (data from Step 2). Square the group scores on T_2, and divide by the number of scores added to obtain the sum.

$$\frac{146^2}{10} + \frac{240^2}{10} + \frac{311^2}{10} + \frac{351^2}{10} + \frac{238^2}{10} + \frac{146^2}{10} = \mathbf{37{,}679.8}$$

Then, subtract the correction term for T_2 (Step 6), the SS for rows (Step 12), and the SS for columns (Step 15).

$$37{,}679.8 - 34{,}177.067 - 24.066 - 40.033 = \mathbf{3438.634}$$

Step 19.   Calculation of the sum of squares of cross products for the rows by columns ($SSCP_{r\times c}$):
First, multiply the sum of T_1 scores for each condition times the sum of the T_2 scores for each condition (from Step 2). Then divide by the number of pairs of scores.

$$\frac{140 \times 146}{10} + \frac{163 \times 240}{10} + \frac{213 \times 311}{10} + \frac{267 \times 351}{10} + \frac{157 \times 238}{10}$$

$$+ \frac{144 \times 146}{10} + \frac{277{,}910}{10} = \mathbf{27{,}791}$$

Then subtract the SSCP correction term (Step 7), the $SSCP_{T_1}$ for rows (Step 13), and the $SSCP_{T_2}$ for columns (Step 16).

$$27{,}791 - 25{,}871.467 - 32.933 - 47.933 = \mathbf{1838.667}$$

Step 20.   Computation of the $SS_{\text{within groups}}$ for each of the components. These values are computed as residuals according to the following formula:

Total − Rows − Columns − Rows × Columns = Within Variability

For $SS_{W_{T1}}$: 1747.733 (Step 8) − 45.066(Step 11)

− 190.633 (Step 14) − 1001.234 (Step 17) = **510.8**

For $SS_{W_{T2}}$: 4102.933 (Step 9) − 24.066 (Step 12)

− 40.033 (Step 15) − 3438.634 (Step 18) = **600.2**

For $SSCP_{W_{T1T2}}$: 1955.533 (Step 10) − 974.633 (Step 13)

− 47.933 (Step 16) − 896.967 (Step 19) = **36**

Note: As a double check of the computations, each of the above terms can be computed directly. For example, for the cross products values ($SSCP_{T_1T_2}$):

$$2054 - \frac{140 \times 146}{10} + 3921 - \frac{163 \times 240}{10}$$

$$+ \cdots + 2140 - \frac{144 \times 146}{10} = 36$$

Step 21.   The above computed values will now be inserted into a series of symmetric matricies with the elements identified as follows:

$$\begin{bmatrix} a & b \\ c & d \end{bmatrix}$$

The above symmetric matricies will serve as the bases for all of the calculations needed to set up the necessary tests of significance. The general formula for Wilks' *lambda* is

$$lambda = \Lambda = \frac{|\mathbf{W}|}{|\mathbf{T}|}$$

where $|\mathbf{W}|$ = the *error* sums of squares and cross products determinant
and $|\mathbf{T}|$ = the determinant of the *error* sums of squares and cross products added to the determinant of the sums of squares and cross products of the effects being measured.

The ratio calculation will involve the determinants for each of several matrices. Each determinant will be calculated as:

$$(a \times d) - (b \times c)$$

Step 22.   Summary of computational steps as they relate to the several matrix elements: The several tests of significance will be based on the following matrices. In each, SS_{T_1} forms element a, SS_{T_2} forms element d, and $SSCP_{T_1T_2}$ forms elements b and c.

$$\text{Total} = \begin{bmatrix} 1747.733 & 1955.533 \\ 1955.533 & 4102.933 \end{bmatrix} \quad \text{(computed in Steps 8, 9, and 10)}$$

$$\text{Rows} = \begin{bmatrix} 45.066 & 32.933 \\ 32.933 & 24.066 \end{bmatrix} \quad \text{(computed in Steps 11, 12, and 13)}$$

$$\text{Columns} = \begin{bmatrix} 190.633 & 47.933 \\ 47.933 & 40.033 \end{bmatrix} \quad \text{(computed in Steps 14, 15, and 16)}$$

$$\text{Rows} \times \text{Cols} = \begin{bmatrix} 1001.234 & 1838.667 \\ 1838.667 & 3438.634 \end{bmatrix} \quad \text{(computed in Steps 17, 18, and 19)}$$

$$\text{Within} = \begin{bmatrix} 510.8 & 36.0 \\ 36.0 & 600.2 \end{bmatrix} \quad \text{(computed in Step 20)}$$

Step 23. Computation of the necessary ratios: As stated above, the general relationship is

$$\Lambda = \frac{|\mathbf{W}|}{|\mathbf{T}|}$$

and the actual ratios are equal to:

$$\frac{|\mathbf{W}|}{|\mathbf{T}|} = \frac{\text{Determinant}_{\text{within}}}{\text{Determinant}_{\text{effects}} + \text{Determinant}_{\text{within}}}$$

Thus, the above ratios are calculated on the appropriate matrix addition followed by calculation of $ad - bc$.

Since the test ratios always involve the determinant of the within component, that value must be calculated first.

$$\overset{a}{} \quad \overset{d}{} \quad - \quad \overset{b}{} \quad \overset{c}{}$$

$$\text{Determinant}_{\text{within}} = \mathbf{D}_w = (510.8)(600.2) - (36.0)(36.0) = \mathbf{305{,}286.16}$$

$$\text{Determinant}_{\text{total}} = \mathbf{D}_t = \text{Not needed for significance test}$$

$$\text{Rows} = \mathbf{D}_r + \mathbf{D}_w = \begin{bmatrix} 45.066 & 32.933 \\ 32.933 & 24.066 \end{bmatrix} + \begin{bmatrix} 510.8 & 36.0 \\ 36.0 & 600.2 \end{bmatrix}$$

$$= \begin{bmatrix} 555.866 & 68.933 \\ 68.933 & 624.266 \end{bmatrix}$$

And, multiplication of $ad - bc = (555.866)(624.266)$

$$- (68.933)(68.933)$$

$$= 347{,}008.244 - 4751.7578$$

$$= \mathbf{342{,}256.486}$$

$$\text{Columns} = \mathbf{D}_c + \mathbf{D}_w = \begin{bmatrix} 190.633 & 47.933 \\ 47.933 & 40.033 \end{bmatrix} + \begin{bmatrix} 510.8 & 36.0 \\ 36.0 & 600.2 \end{bmatrix}$$

$$= \begin{bmatrix} 701.433 & 83.933 \\ 83.933 & 640.233 \end{bmatrix}$$

$$= (701.433)(640.233) - (83.933)(83.933)$$

$$= 449,080.544 - 7,044.748 = \mathbf{442,035.806}$$

$$\text{Rows} \times \text{Cols} = \mathbf{D}_{r \times c} + \mathbf{D}_w = \begin{bmatrix} 1001.234 & 1838.667 \\ 1838.667 & 3438.634 \end{bmatrix}$$

$$+ \begin{bmatrix} 510.8 & 36.0 \\ 36.0 & 600.2 \end{bmatrix}$$

$$= \begin{bmatrix} 1512.034 & 1874.667 \\ 1874.667 & 4038.834 \end{bmatrix}$$

$$= (1512.034)(4038.834)$$

$$- (1874.667)(1874.667)$$

$$= 6,106,854.328 - 3,514,372.444$$

$$= \mathbf{2,592,481.884}$$

Step 24. The relationship between *lambda* and *F*: The distribution of *lambda* for certain numbers of dependent variables (p), the *df* associated with the within-groups error (w), and the *df* for the particular effects (e) being analyzed are as follows:

Value of e	Value of p	Distribution of F	Degrees of freedom of F
Any number	2	$\dfrac{1 - \sqrt{\Lambda_e}}{\sqrt{\Lambda_e}}\left(\dfrac{w - 1}{e}\right)$	$2e, 2(w - 1)$
1	Any number	$\dfrac{1 - \Lambda_e}{\Lambda_e}\left(\dfrac{w + e - p}{p}\right)$	$p, w + e - p$
2	Any number	$\dfrac{1 - \sqrt{\Lambda_e}}{\sqrt{\Lambda_e}}\left(\dfrac{w + e - p - 1}{p}\right)$	$2p, 2(w + e - p - 1)$

For the example just completed, there are two dependent variables ($p = 2$). Thus, the following formula is appropriate to describe the exact functional relationship between *lambda* and *F*.

$$F = \frac{1 - \sqrt{\Lambda_e}}{\sqrt{\Lambda_e}}\left(\frac{w - 1}{e}\right)$$

where $w =$ rows $\times$ columns $\times (n_{\text{per gp.}} - 1)$

and

$e = (\text{rows} - 1)$, or $(\text{columns} - 1)$, or $(\text{rows} - 1) \times (\text{columns} - 1)$

Step 25.   Computation of the *lambda* ratios:

$$\Lambda_{\text{rows}} = \frac{305{,}286.160}{342{,}256.486} = .8920$$

$$\Lambda_{\text{cols}} = \frac{305{,}286.160}{442{,}035.806} = .6906$$

$$\Lambda_{\text{rows} \times \text{cols}} = \frac{305{,}286.160}{2{,}592{,}481.884} = .1178$$

Step 26.   The degrees of freedom, *df*, for the *F* ratio are equal to:

$$\text{Rows} = 2(r - 1) \quad \text{and} \quad 2[(r \times c)(n_{\text{per gp.}} - 1) - 1]$$
$$= 2(1) \quad \text{and} \quad 2[(2 \times 3)(10 - 1) - 1]$$
$$= 2 \quad \text{and} \quad 2[(6)(9) - 1]$$
$$= \mathbf{2} \quad \text{and} \quad \mathbf{106}$$

$$\text{Columns} = 2(c - 1) \quad \text{and} \quad 2[(r \times c)(n_{\text{per gp.}} - 1) - 1]$$
$$= 2(2) \quad \text{and} \quad 2[(6)(9) - 1]$$
$$= \mathbf{4} \quad \text{and} \quad \mathbf{106}$$

$$\text{Rows} \times \text{Columns} = 2(r - 1)(c - 1) \quad \text{and}$$
$$2[(r \times c)(n_{\text{per gp.}} - 1) - 1]$$
$$= \mathbf{4} \quad \text{and} \quad \mathbf{106}$$

Step 27.   The tests of significance:

For Rows (boys versus girls): $F_{2,\,106} = 1 - \dfrac{\sqrt{.8920}}{\sqrt{.8920}}\left(\dfrac{53}{1}\right) = \mathbf{3.1203}$

For Columns (grade level): $F_{4,\,106} = 1 - \dfrac{\sqrt{.6906}}{\sqrt{.6906}}\left(\dfrac{53}{2}\right) = \mathbf{5.3893}$

For Rows by Columns: $F_{4,\,106} = 1 - \dfrac{\sqrt{.1178}}{\sqrt{.1178}}\left(\dfrac{53}{2}\right) = \mathbf{50.7145}$

Step 28.   First, looking in the *F* tables under the *df* for rows (2,106) we find that an *F* ratio of 3.10 is needed for significance.

Since the computed *F* is 3.1203, we conclude that the centroid of T_1 and T_2 is significantly different for boys and girls.

Looking now in the F tables under the df for rows and rows $\times$ columns (4, 106), we find that an F ratio of 2.48 is needed for significance. Since the computed F of 5.3893 for columns exceeds that value, we conclude that the centroid of T_1 and T_2 is significantly different for the three grade levels. Similarly, the interaction ($F_{4,106} = 50.7145$) of boy/girls by grade level is also significant beyond the .05 level.

Step 29. Summary table: Following completion of all the computations, the final results of the analysis are summarized as follows:

Source	df	Matrix		lambda$_e$	df of F	F
Rows (Boys/ Girls)	$R - 1$	$\begin{bmatrix} 555.866 & 68.933 \\ 68.933 & 624.266 \end{bmatrix}$		$\dfrac{305,286.160}{342,256.486}$ = .8920	2, 106	3.1203
Columns (Grade level)	$C - 1$	$\begin{bmatrix} 701.433 & 83.933 \\ 83.933 & 640.233 \end{bmatrix}$		$\dfrac{305,286.160}{442,035.806}$ = .6906	4, 106	5.3895
Rows $\times$ Cols (Interaction)	$(R - 1) \times (C - 1)$	$\begin{bmatrix} 1512.034 & 1874.667 \\ 1874.667 & 4038.834 \end{bmatrix}$		$\dfrac{305,286.160}{2,592,481.884}$ = .1178	4, 106	50.7145
Within Gps. (Error)	$RC(n - 1)$	$\begin{bmatrix} 510.800 & 36.000 \\ 36.000 & 600.200 \end{bmatrix}$				
Total	$nRC - 1$					

Further Analyses

In the above example, the boys and girls responded differently in terms of the standardized test scores of creativity and their teachers' judgments. Also there were clear differences among the kindergarten, first, and second graders. Finally, there was a strong interaction between the sex of the subjects and grade level in terms of the response measures recorded.

The usual first step to further analyze these differences is to perform two separate univariate, two-way ANOVAs. The first would be carried out using the T_1 scores, and the second using the T_2 scores. To compute these analyses, the experimenter should turn to Section 4.2 and follow Steps 2 through 13. If still further univariate analyses are felt necessary to determine which specific groups differ on each measure, the experimenter should turn to Part 5 and compute one or more of the appropriate supplemental computations presented in Sections 5.4 through 5.10. ∎

PART 7

Nonparametric Tests, Miscellaneous Tests of Significance, and Indexes of Relationship

In many cases where it is desirable to make comparisons of two proportions, or two medians, or within a table of frequency counts, there are some very simple tests that can be used. Some of these are listed in the following nine sections. Various names—such as *nonparametric tests* or *distribution-free tests*—have been applied to many such tests of significance. We will not attempt to argue the merits and deficiencies of these tests, but will merely point out that they are relatively easy to use and that they are often applicable when the various tests presented elsewhere are not.

The nine sections in this part are discussed below in four sets. These discussions should help you choose the correct analysis for your particular problem.

1. Significance tests for proportions
2. Significance tests for differences between two or more groups
3. Nonparametric parallels of analysis of variance tests
4. Tests for (1) significance of differences or (2) relationships, when data are gathered into contingency tables
5. Tests for trends

Tests for Proportions (Sections 7.1 and 7.2)

If you have a proportion that has been computed from experimental data (such as the proportion of all American men over forty who have been married at least twice) and you wish to find whether it differs from some specific value (such as a guess that one third, or .33, of all American men over forty have been married at least twice), the material presented in Section 7.1 will help you solve the problem. If you wish to find whether two independently computed proportions are different, use the analysis presented in Section 7.2.

Tests for Differences Between Two or More Groups (Sections 7.3, 7.4, 7.5, and 7.6)

Section 1.5 (*t*-test for independent means) shows how to find whether two *mean* values are different. If you wish to find whether two independent *median* values are different, use the procedure in Section 7.3.

Section 1.6 (*t*-test for related measures) presents the method for finding whether two *means* are different when the samples are paired, matched, or otherwise related. If you wish to test whether two related groups differ on the basis of a simple sign test, use the analysis in Section 7.4. The tests presented in Sections 7.5 and 7.6 represent the nonparametric parallels to the analyses of variance demonstrated in Sections 4.1 and 4.5.

Tests for Data in Contingency Tables (Sections 7.7 and 7.8)

When you have frequency data (counts of the people exhibiting the characteristic of interest to you) that can be put into the form of a contingency table, you probably wish to ask one side or the other of a two-sided question: (1) Do these variables (treatments) produce different results? or (2) Are these variables related, and if so, how highly related? Both questions can be answered by the tests presented in Sections 7.7 and 7.8. The first question is a chi-square question, and the first part of either Section 7.7 (if you have a 2×2 table of data) or Section 7.8 (if you have a large number of cells in the table) will help you answer it. The second question is a *phi*-coefficient question or a contingency-coefficient question, depending on the number of cells in your table, and the last part of either Section 7.7 and 7.8 will help you answer it.

Tests for Trends, Runs, and Randomness (Section 7.9)

When recorded scores represent an event occurring over time, questions often arise as to whether the scores are patterned in some fashion or are random. The tests in this section represent a few of the ways scores recorded to describe a recurring event can be tested to determine their degree of patterning.

In the following sections, computational formulas are again presented when they contribute to the understanding of the analysis. In those instances where the computation involves only a count or a ranking, the formula is omitted.

SECTION 7.1

Test for Significance of a Proportion

In a situation where a logically dichotomous variable, such as passing or failing a course, is considered, the use of proportions can sometimes facilitate the statistical analysis of significance. Before the test of significance can be executed, it is necessary to know the proportion to be expected. If you toss a coin, for example, you expect to get heads one half of the time (in the long run); thus, the expected proportion is .50. If you toss a die, you expect to get a one-spot one time in six; thus, the expected proportion is 1/6. When the dichotomy is on a variable such as passing or failing a course, you must either (1) know the expected proportion from some previous experience, (2) insist on some a priori proportion, such as "10 percent will fail," or (3) in some other way determine or state the expected proportion. Then, when the actual proportion has been determined and the expected proportion has been decided upon, the test for significance can be carried out.

■ **EXAMPLE**

Assume that a teacher wishes to determine whether a particular class of fifteen students is under par in its performance on an arithmetic achievement test. This can be done simply by determining if the proportions who passed and failed correspond to those proportions in classes taught in previous years.

Step 1.   In order to determine the actual or observed proportion, the first step is to record and table the data on which the proportion will be based (in this case, the arithmetic scores).

Student	Score
A	64
B	35
C	81
D	77
E	65
F	48
G	56
H	31
I	64
J	72
K	43
L	44
M	63
N	59
O	38

Step 2. In order to compute the proportion of students who passed, the teacher must set a pass-fail cutoff point. Suppose it is decided that a score of 50 or more is passing and a score of 49 or less is failing. We can quickly see that Students B, F, H, K, L, and O failed. Six out of fifteen failed; thus, nine out of fifteen passed. The proportion (p) of students who passed is the number who passed divided by the total number of students.

$$p = \frac{9}{15} = .60$$

Step 3. Suppose the teacher's information from previous classes indicates that, on the average, 80 percent (or .80) of the students got a passing grade on this examination. The .80 expected to pass is the P value. The significance test (z-test) for the obtained proportion is computed by use of the following formula.

$$z = \frac{p - P}{\sqrt{\dfrac{P(1 - P)}{N}}}$$

Thus, for this case,

$$z = \frac{.60 - .80}{\sqrt{\dfrac{.80(1 - .80)}{15}}} = \frac{-.20}{\sqrt{\dfrac{.80(.20)}{15}}} = \frac{-.20}{\sqrt{\dfrac{.16}{15}}}$$

$$= \frac{-.20}{\sqrt{.0107}} = \frac{-.20}{.1034} = -1.93$$

In order to have a significant difference, at the .05 level using a two-tailed test, the z would need to be at least ± 1.96 (see Appendix A). A significant z would mean that the p value is significantly different from the P value. In this case, it is concluded that the scores of the fifteen students are not under par for the arithmetic achievement test. ∎

SECTION 7.2
Test for Significance of a Difference Between Two Proportions

Often, data are collected that are dichotomous in nature and there is a wish to determine whether the responses from two groups are different from each other. For example, men and women may be asked whether they "will" or "will not" vote for a candidate; students in rural and urban schools take a test where the score assigned is either "pass" or "fail"; or older and younger consumers are asked whether they will "buy" or "not buy" a particular product. When dealing with two groups and data that are logically dichotomous, it is easy to test whether there is a significant difference between the groups.

■ **EXAMPLE**

In an experiment on short-term memory for a single item, the following conditions were used. The item was presented to all subjects for two seconds. One
group of twenty subjects was tested to determine if they did or did not recall the
item after five seconds; the other group of twenty subjects was tested after
ten seconds. If the item was correctly recalled, a "+" was recorded for that
subject; if an incorrect response was made, a "0" was recorded.

The formula for the significance of the difference between two proportions is:

$$z = \frac{P_1 - P_2}{\sqrt{\dfrac{p(1-p)}{N_1} + \dfrac{p(1-p)}{N_2}}}$$

Step 1. To compute the two proportions P_1 and P_2, from Groups 1 and 2
respectively, first table the data as follows:

Group 1		Group 2	
Subject	Recall (5 sec.)	Subject	Recall (10 sec.)
S_1	+	S_{21}	0
S_2	+	S_{22}	0
S_3	+	S_{23}	+
S_4	+	S_{24}	0
S_5	+	S_{25}	+
S_6	+	S_{26}	+
S_7	+	S_{27}	0
S_8	+	S_{28}	+
S_9	+	S_{29}	0
S_{10}	0	S_{30}	0
S_{11}	+	S_{31}	+
S_{12}	0	S_{32}	0
S_{13}	0	S_{33}	0
S_{14}	+	S_{34}	0
S_{15}	+	S_{35}	0
S_{16}	0	S_{36}	+
S_{17}	+	S_{37}	0
S_{18}	+	S_{38}	0
S_{19}	+	S_{39}	+
S_{20}	+	S_{40}	+

Step 2. Subjects 10, 12, 13, and 16 in Group 1 missed the item; thus, a total
of sixteen subjects recalled correctly. The number correctly recalling, divided

by the number of subjects in the group, gives the proportion who correctly recalled the item.

$$P_1 = \frac{16}{20} = .80$$

Step 3. Subjects 21, 22, 24, 27, 29, 30, 32, 33, 34, 35, 37, and 38 in Group 2 missed the item. Thus, 12 subjects missed and only 8 correctly recalled the item. Again, the number who correctly recalled, divided by the number of subjects in the group, gives the proportion who correctly recalled the item.

$$P_2 = \frac{8}{20} = .40$$

Step 4. The p value needed for the calculations is computed as follows. First, add the numerators used in the computations of Steps 2 and 3 (the numbers of individuals in each group who got the item correct).

$$16 + 8 = 24$$

Then, divide that answer by the total number of scores (subjects) in the experiment ($N_1 + N_2 = 40$)

$$p = 24/40 = .60$$

Step 5. Subtract the final result of Step 4 from the number 1.

$$1 - p = 1 - .60 = .40$$

Then, multiply that number by the final result of Step 4.

$$p(1 - p) = .60 \times .40 = .24$$

Step 6. Divide the result of Step 5 by N_1 (the size of the first sample).

$$p(1 - p)/N_1 = .24/20 = .012$$

Step 7. Divide the result of Step 5 by N_2 (the size of the second sample).

$$p(1 - p)/N_2 = .24/20 = .012$$

Step 8. Add the result of Step 6 to the result of Step 7.

$$p(1 - p)/N_1 + p(1 - p)/N_2 = .012 + .012 = .024$$

Then, take the square root of that sum. This gives the denominator of the formula for testing the difference between two proportions.

$$\sqrt{.024} = .155$$

Step 9. Subtract the result of Step 3 from that of Step 2. This gives the numerator of the formula for testing the difference between two proportions

$$P_1 - P_2 = .80 - .40 = .40$$

Step 10. Divide the result of Step 9 by the result of Step 8.

$$z = .40/.155 = 2.48$$

A z having a value equal to or greater than ± 1.96 is considered significant at the .05 level (two-tailed test; see Appendix A). Thus, a z of 2.48 tells us that the two proportions are significantly different. ∎

SECTION 7.3

The Mann-Whitney U-Test for Differences Between Independent Samples

Occasionally the data collected by an experimenter are badly skewed. For this reason, the Mann-Whitney U-test might be chosen rather than the t-test for independent groups.

The basic formula for the Mann-Whitney U-test is

$$U = n_1 n_2 + \frac{n_1(n_1 + 1)}{2} - R_1$$

or

$$U' = n_1 n_2 + \frac{n_2(n_2 + 1)}{2} - R_2$$

where n_1 = size of the smaller sample
n_2 = size of the larger sample
R_1 = sum of the ranks of the smaller sample
R_2 = sum of the ranks of the larger sample

When either U or U' has been computed, the other can be quickly found by

$$U = n_1 n_2 - U'$$

or

$$U' = n_1 n_2 - U$$

Therefore, it is necessary to compute only one; the other is then obtained by subtraction.

∎ EXAMPLE

Suppose that the following data have been collected representing weekly incomes for office managers who are members of two different ethnic groups. The experimenter wishes to determine whether there is a significant difference between these incomes.

	Group 1		Group 2	
Subject	Weekly Income (dollars)	Subject	Weekly Income (dollars)
S_1	387	S_{10}	431
S_2	372	S_{11}	394
S_3	365	S_{12}	377
S_4	354	S_{13}	388
S_5	367	S_{14}	416
S_6	376	S_{15}	390
S_7	373	S_{16}	387
S_8	382	S_{17}	376
S_9	404	S_{18}	395
		S_{19}	464
		S_{20}	427
		S_{21}	377

Step 1. Rank *all* the numbers in *both* groups taken together according to the size of the number, beginning with the smallest. (*Note:* When there are equal measures, the same rank is assigned to each. But notice that the rank assigned is the mean value of the tied ranks. For example, there are two incomes of 376 dollars, which are tied for sixth and seventh positions. Therefore, they are both assigned the rank of 6.5.)

Group 1		Group 2	
Income	Rank	Income	Rank
387	11.5	431	20
372	4	394	15
365	2	377	8.5
354	1	388	13
367	3	416	18
376	6.5	390	14
373	5	387	11.5
382	10	376	6.5
404	17	395	16
		464	21
		427	19
		377	8.5

Step 2. Count the number of measures in each group, and then multiply these numbers. (Here, there are 9 measures in Group 1 and 12 in Group 2.)

$$n_1 n_2 = 9 \times 12 = \mathbf{108}$$

Step 3. Add 1 to the number of measures in Group 1; then multiply that sum by the original number (9 in this example), and divide the product by 2.

$$\frac{n_1(n_1 + 1)}{2} = \frac{9(9 + 1)}{2} = \frac{90}{2} = 45$$

Step 4. Add the ranks for Group 1.

$R_1 = 11.5 + 4 + \cdots + 15 = 60$

Step 5. Add the result of Step 2 to the result of Step 3, and subtract the sum of Step 4. This yields the value of U.

$U = 108 + 45 - 60 = 93$

Step 6. Subtract the result of Step 5 from the result of Step 2. This yields the value of U'.

$U' = 108 - 93 = 15$

If the number of measures in the larger group is greater than 8, and the number of measures in either group is less than 21, take whichever answer from Steps 5 or 6 is *smaller,* and look in the tables of U values to check for significance (see Appendix H). In the present example, $n_1 = 9$ and $n_2 = 12$ so both requirements are satisfied. Thus, go to Appendix H and look in the table for the appropriate alpha level. Using a two-tailed test and alpha $= .05$, if the value of either U or U' is 26 or less, the difference is significant. Since U' in the present example is equal to 15, we conclude that the two groups differ significantly.

If the number of measures in *either* group is greater than 20, carry out the following steps.

Step 7. Divide the result of Step 2 by 2.

$$\frac{108}{2} = 54$$

Then, subtract that quotient from the result of Step 5.

$93 - 54 = 39$

Step 8. Add together the number of measures in each group; then add the number 1.

$9 + 12 + 1 = 22$

Step 9. Multiply the result of Step 2 by the sum of Step 8.

$108 \times 22 = 2376$

Step 10. Divide the result of Step 9 by the number 12. (*Note:* The number 12 is always used.)

$$\frac{2376}{12} = 198$$

Then, take the square root of that quotient.

$$\sqrt{198} = 14.071$$

Step 11. Divide the result of Step 7 by the result of Step 10.

$$\frac{39}{14.071} = 2.77$$

This is a z, or critical-ratio, test. A value greater than ± 1.96 is significant at the .05 level using a two-tailed test (see Appendix A). The hypothesis tested by the Mann-Whitney analysis is that the *medians* of the two groups are equal. A z value that is large enough so that the hypothesis is rejected tells us that the chance of the medians being the same is very small. It is concluded, then, that there is a significant difference between the median incomes of office managers in the two ethnic groups. ∎

SECTION 7.4
A Sign Test (Wilcoxon) for Differences Between Related Samples

The Mann-Whitney U-test presented in Section 7.3 is a nonparametric test for *independent* samples. The Wilcoxon signed-ranks test is applicable where the samples are related (i.e., not independent).

■ EXAMPLE
Suppose we have collected the reading-rate scores for a group of ten people before and after they enrolled in a course in speed reading. We wish to determine if the course made any significant difference in reading rate.

Step 1. Table the data as follows. Since these are related measures, they must be tabled in appropriate pairs.

Subject	Rate Before	Rate After
A	150	145
B	135	138
C	102	121
D	96	115

Subject	Rate Before	Rate After
E	127	134
F	118	132
G	132	138
H	124	145
I	115	126
J	103	94

Step 2. Subtract each number in the first column from its paired number in the second column, and record the differences.

Subject	After	Before	Difference
A	145	150	−5
B	138	135	3
C	121	102	19
D	115	96	19
E	134	127	7
F	132	118	14
G	138	132	6
H	145	124	21
I	126	115	11
J	94	103	−9

Step 3. Rank the difference values (Step 2) according to the size of the number, beginning with the smallest. Ignore the sign (i.e., use absolute values).

Difference	Rank
−5	2
3	1
19	8.5
19	8.5
7	4
14	7
6	3
21	10
11	6
−9	5

Step 4. Add the ranks for all the difference values that are negative (see Step 3). (In this example, the two negative differences, -5 and -9, are ranked 2 and 5, respectively.)

$2 + 5 = 7$ ■

Note: Zero differences are not used in the computation. The N which is used in consulting the table (Appendix M) must be reduced by the number of zero difference cases.

Step 5. Add the ranks for all the difference values that are positive (see Step 3).

$1 + 8.5 + 8.5 + 4 + 7 + 3 + 10 + 6 = \textbf{48}$

Step 6. The results of Steps 4 and 5 are the signed-rank values. Take the result that is smaller (7 in this example) and look in a table of Wilcoxon's signed-rank probabilities (see Appendix M) to check for significance. When the number of pairs is 10, as it is in this example, a value of 8 or less is significant at the .05 level using a two-tailed test. Since the result of Step 4 (i.e., 7) is smaller than 8, we have a significant difference. We conclude that the reading rate *after* training was significantly faster than *before* training.

SECTION 7.5
The Kruskal-Wallis *H* Test: Differences Among Three or More Groups

The Kruskal-Wallis H test is the nonparametric parallel to the completely randomized design presented in Section 4.1. The test also can be viewed as the generalized version of the Mann-Whitney U-test presented in Section 7.3.

Assume an example similar to that presented in Section 4.1, where an experimenter is interested in determining the effects of four levels of electric shock on learning. Subjects in Group 1 receive no shock, Group 2 receives periodic low level of shock, Group 3 receives a medium level, and Group 4 receives a high level. The total time required to solve the problems is recorded.

Step 1. Table the data as follows:

Group 1 (No Shock)		Group 2 (Low Shock)		Group 3 (Med. Shock)		Group 4 (High Shock)	
Subj.	Time	Subj.	Time	Subj.	Time	Subj.	Time
S_1	10	S_6	12	S_{11}	6	S_{16}	14
S_2	7	S_7	3	S_{12}	12	S_{17}	13
S_3	6	S_8	5	S_{13}	16	s_{18}	17
S_4	8	S_9	4	S_{14}	31	S_{19}	39
S_5	9	S_{10}	6	S_{15}	42	S_{20}	50

Step 2. Since the data are badly skewed, the Kruskal-Wallis *H* test will be used to analyze the data instead of the completely randomized design. The second step, then, is to rank-order *all* of the scores.

Group 1		Group 2		Group 3		Group 4	
S_1	10	S_6	11.5	S_{11}	5	S_{16}	14
S_2	7	S_7	1	S_{12}	11.5	S_{17}	13
S_3	5	S_8	3	S_{13}	15	S_{18}	16
S_4	8	S_9	2	S_{14}	17	S_{19}	18
S_5	9	S_{10}	5	S_{15}	19	S_{20}	20

Step 3. Obtain the sum of the ranks of each group.

Sum of ranks of Group 1 = **39**
Sum of ranks of Group 2 = **22.5**
Sum of ranks of Group 3 = **67.5**
Sum of ranks of Group 4 = **81**

Step 4. Compute the test statistic. The formula for the test statistic is:

$$H = \frac{12}{N(N + 1)} \Sigma \frac{(\Sigma T_j)^2}{n_j} - 3(N + 1)$$

First, sum the ranks for each group, square those values and divide each squared value by the *n* of each group. Then obtain the grand sum.

$$\frac{(\Sigma T_1)^2}{n_1} = 1521/5 = 304.20$$

$$\frac{(\Sigma T_2)^2}{n_2} = 506.25/5 = 101.25$$

$$\frac{(\Sigma T_3)^2}{n_3} = 4556.25 = 911.25$$

$$\frac{(\Sigma T_4)^2}{n_4} = 6561/5 = 1312.20$$

The total $= \Sigma \frac{(\Sigma T_j)^2}{n_j} = $ **2628.9**

Next, using the formula, we have:

$$H = 12/(20 + 21) \times 2628.9 - 3(20 + 1) = 75.11 - 63 = \mathbf{12.11}$$

The above value of *H* can be referred to the chi-square distribution of Appendix D where the *df* to enter the table will be the number of groups minus 1, or 4 − 1 = 3. From Appendix D with $\alpha = .05$ and $df = 3$, we find that a chi-square value of 7.8 or larger is needed for significance. Since the computed value is 12.11, it is concluded that the distributions differ significantly. ■

SECTION 7.6

The Friedman Test for Repeated Measures or Matched Groups

In much the same way that the Kruskal-Wallis test represents an extension of the Mann-Whitney U test and is the nonparametric parallel of the completely randomized design, the Friedman test is an extension of the Wilcoxon test presented in Section 7.4 and the treatment by subjects, or repeated measures, design presented in Section 4.5.

Assume that as in Section 4.5, an experimenter is interested in collecting I.Q. test data over a four-year period. The data in this case, however, represent individuals who have suffered a significant brain injury. $Test_0$ represents a baseline and is the most recent test score recorded before the injury occurred. $Test_1$ represents the first testing that occurred after the injury; $Test_2$ represents a testing six months after the injury, and T_3, a test score eighteen months after the injury. The data are as follows.

	T_0	T_1	T_2	T_3
S_1	138	118	110	124
S_2	142	96	91	92
S_3	136	95	88	96
S_4	94	77	89	88
S_5	87	75	86	85

Since the data are badly skewed, the Friedman test will be used instead of the repeated measures design of Section 4.5.

Step 1.   Rank order the scores for *each* subject. In the present example, each subject's scores will be ranked from 1 through 4.

	T_0	T_1	T_2	T_3
S_1	4	2	1	3
S_2	4	3	1	2
S_3	4	2	1	3
S_4	4	1	3	2
S_5	4	1	3	2

Step 2.   Sum the ranks for each testing period.

Sum $T_0 = 20$
Sum $T_1 = 9$
Sum $T_2 = 9$
Sum $T_3 = 12$

Step 3. Computation of the test statistic: The test statistic is distributed approximately as a chi-square with df = treatments per subject minus 1. The formula for its computation is

$$\chi^2 = \frac{12}{KJ(J + 1)} \Sigma T_j^2 - 3K(J + 1)$$

where T_j = the sum of the ranks for each treatment
J = the number of treatments
K = the number of subjects

and the values "12" and "3" are constants and always used for the present example:

$$\chi^2 = \frac{12}{5 \times 4(4 + 1)}(20^2 + 9^2 + 9^2 + 12^2) - 3 \times 5(4 + 1)$$

$$= 12/100 \times 706 - 15 \times 5$$

$$= 84.72 - 75$$

$$= \mathbf{9.72}$$

The above value can be referred to the chi-square distribution of Appendix D where the df to enter the table will be the number of treatments minus 1, or, $4 - 1 = 3$. From Appendix D with $\alpha = .05$ and $df = 3$, we find that a chi-square value of 7.8 or larger is needed for significance. Since the computed value was 9.72, it is concluded that there was a significant change in I.Q. scores. ■

SECTION 7.7
Simple Chi-Square and the *Phi* Coefficient

When you have frequency data comparing the effects of two variables and there are two groups on both variables, the *phi* coefficient can be quickly computed to show the degree of the relationship between the two variables. Then, the simple chi-square can be easily computed from the *phi* coefficient. The chi-square test will establish whether the variables are related. A significant chi-square is interpreted as showing a relationship between the two variables. The *phi* coefficient gives a numerical value, ranging from 0 to +1, for that relationship.

■ **EXAMPLE**
Consider data collected on the two variables (1) gum-chewing activity and (2) educational background. The experimenter simply sampled two groups with differing educational backgrounds. Within each group, the subjects were classified according to their gum-chewing behavior.

The basic computational formula for chi-square is

$$\chi^2 = \frac{N(AD - BC)^2}{(A + B)(C + D)(A + C)(B + D)}$$

where the numbers represented by the letters A, B, C, and D come from the contingency table.

A	B
C	D

and the formula for *phi*(ϕ) is

$$\phi = \sqrt{\frac{\chi^2}{N}}$$

where N = the total frequency in the entire contingency table.

Step 1.   Organize the data into a contingency table as follows. The values in the table represent the number of persons in each category.

		Gum Behavior	
		Chews	Eschews
Educational History	High-School Dropout	90	50
	College Graduate	20	30

Step 2.   Add all the numbers in the table.

90 + 50 + 20 + 30 = **190**

Step 3.   Add the numbers in each row to get the row sums.

90 + 50 = **140** = sum for Row 1
20 + 30 = **50** = sum for Row 2

Then, add the numbers in each column to get the column sums.

	Column 1	Column 2
	90	50
	+20	+30
Sums:	**110**	**80**

Step 4.   Multiply together the four sums from Step 3.

140 × 50 × 110 × 80 = **61,600,000**

Step 5.   Multiply the number from the upper-left square by the number from the lower-right square (Step 1).

90 × 30 = **2700**

Step 6. Multiply the number from the upper-right square by the number from the lower-left square (Step 1).

$50 \times 20 = \mathbf{1000}$

Step 7. Get the results of Steps 5 and 6, and subtract the smaller from the larger:

$2700 - 1000 = \mathbf{1700}$

Step 8. Square the results of Step 7, and then multiply by the total number of scores in the contingency table. In this example $N = 190$.

$1700^2 = 2{,}890{,}000$

and

$2{,}890{,}000 \times 190 = \mathbf{549{,}100{,}000}$

Step 9. Divide the result of Step 8 by the result of Step 4. The answer is the chi-square.

$$\chi^2 = \frac{549{,}100{,}000}{61{,}600{,}000} = \mathbf{8.91}$$

The number of degrees of freedom for this simple 2×2 chi-square will always be 1. A chi-square value larger than 3.8, with one *df* is significant at the .05 level (see Appendix D). It is concluded, therefore, that educational background and gum-chewing behavior are significantly related.

Step 10. Computation of *phi*. Divide the chi-square value obtained in Step 9 by N, then take the square root of the quotient.

$$\frac{8.91}{190} = \mathbf{.0468}$$

and

$$\phi = \sqrt{.0468} = \mathbf{.217}$$

The value of *phi* is an indicator of the degree of relationship between the two variables in this example; it is similar in meaning to a correlation coefficient.

■

Supplement

In a 2×2 contingency table, if the frequency of any cell is less than 10, it is often recommended that Yates' correction for continuity be applied to account for the fact that an χ^2 computed with very small ns will overestimate the true χ^2 value. Yates' correction is applied to the basic χ^2 formula as follows (note the absolute value signs):

$$\chi^2 = \frac{N[|AD - BC| - N/2]^2}{(A + B)(C + D)(A + C)(B + D)}$$

In the data presented (even though it is not needed since the N in every cell is greater than 10), the computations would be

$$\chi^2 = \frac{190[|2700 - 1000| - 190/2]^2}{140 \times 50 \times 110 \times 80}$$

$$= \frac{190(1700 - 95)^2}{140 \times 50 \times 110 \times 80}$$

$$= \frac{489,444,750}{61,600,000}$$

$$= 7.94$$

SECTION 7.8
Complex Chi-Square and the Contingency Coefficient (C)

When you have frequency data comparing the effects of two variables, and there are more than two groups on either of the two variables, the complex chi-square can be used to test the hypothesis of no relationship between the variables. If the chi-square test shows that there is most likely a relationship between the variables, then the contingency coefficient can be computed to give an indication of the degree of the relationship.

■ **EXAMPLE**

Suppose we gather income information for three groups of people: (1) those under 26 years of age, (2) those between 26 and 60 years of age, and (3) those 61 years of age and older. The incomes are categorized according to $3,000 ranges, and a frequency count is made for each category.

The basic formula for chi-square to be used here is

$$\chi^2 = \Sigma \frac{(O - E)^2}{E}$$

where O = the *observed* frequency for a particular cell of the contingency table (see Step 1)

E = the *expected* frequency for a cell, based upon marginal totals (see Steps 2 through 6 for a complete definition)

The relationship between the contingency coefficient (C) and chi-square is

$$C = \sqrt{\frac{\chi^2}{\chi^2 + N}}$$

where X^2 = the chi-square value

N = the total of all the values in the contingency table

Step 1.   Organize the data into a contingency table as follows. As indicated above, the values in the table represent the number of persons falling into each category.

	Income Groups (dollars)			
	Under 3,000	3,000— 6,000	6,000— 9,000	Over 9,000
Under 26	40	30	10	20
26 through 60	50	60	20	70
Over 60	10	20	20	10

Age Group is labeled to the left spanning the three age rows.

Step 2.   Add all the numbers in the table to obtain a grand total.

$$40 + 30 + \cdots + 20 + 50 + \cdots + 70 + 10 + \cdots + 10 = \mathbf{360}$$

Step 3.   Add the numbers in each row to obtain the row sums.

$$40 + 30 + 10 + 20 = \mathbf{100} = \text{sum for Row 1}$$
$$50 + 60 + 20 + 70 = \mathbf{200} = \text{sum for Row 2}$$
$$10 + 20 + 20 + 10 = \mathbf{60} = \text{sum for Row 3}$$

Step 4.   Add the numbers in each column to obtain the column sums.

	Column 1	Column 2	Column 3	Column 4
	40	30	10	20
	50	60	20	70
	⼁10	⼁20	+20	+10
Sums:	**100**	**110**	**50**	**100**

Step 5.   Make a new table similar to the one in Step 1, but get the new numbers as follows.

Compute the new number for each square in the table by using the row sum from Step 3 and the column sum from Step 4 of the row and column that intersect at the square in which you are interested. For example, to compute the new number that goes into the upper-left square, get the sum for Row 1 from Step 3 and the sum for Column 1 from Step 4; multiply these numbers together, and divide by the result of Step 2.

$$\frac{100 \times 100}{360} = \frac{10,000}{360} = \mathbf{27.778}$$

Continue this operation for each square in the new table.

$$\text{Row 1} \times \text{Column 2: } \frac{100 \times 110}{360} = 30.556$$

$$\text{Row 1} \times \text{Column 3: } \frac{100 \times 50}{360} = 13.889$$

$$\text{Row 1} \times \text{Column 4: } \frac{100 \times 100}{360} = 27.778$$

$$\text{Row 2} \times \text{Column 1: } \frac{200 \times 100}{360} = 55.556$$

$$\text{Row 2} \times \text{Column 2: } \frac{200 \times 110}{360} = 61.111$$

$$\text{Row 2} \times \text{Column 3: } \frac{200 \times 50}{360} = 27.778$$

$$\text{Row 2} \times \text{Column 4: } \frac{200 \times 100}{360} = 55.556$$

$$\text{Row 3} \times \text{Column 1: } \frac{60 \times 100}{360} = 16.667$$

$$\text{Row 3} \times \text{Column 2: } \frac{60 \times 110}{360} = 18.833$$

$$\text{Row 3} \times \text{Column 3: } \frac{60 \times 50}{360} = 8.333$$

$$\text{Row 3} \times \text{Column 4: } \frac{60 \times 100}{360} = 16.667$$

Step 6. Put the numbers from Step 5 into the same tabular form as that of Step 1.

		Income Groups (dollars)			
		Under 3,000	3,000—6,000	6,000—9,000	Over 9,000
	Under 26	27.778	30.556	13.889	27.778
Age Group	26 through 60	55.556	61.111	27.778	55.556
	Over 60	16.667	18.333	18.333	16.667

Step 7. The chi-square values can now be computed using the two tables of Step 1 and Step 6. To get these values, take the numbers from the same squares

of the two tables, subtract the smaller from the larger, and square that value; then divide by the number that came from the table of Step 6. For example, the number in the upper-left square of the table of Step 1 is 40; the number from the same square in the table of Step 6 is 27.778. To get the first number for the chi-square, subtract 27.778 from 40, square that difference, and then divide the square by 27.778.

$$\frac{(40 - 27.778)^2}{27.778} = \frac{12.222^2}{27.778} = \frac{149.337}{27.778} = \textbf{5.378}$$

Continue for each of the other values.

Row 1:

$$\frac{(30.556 - 30)^2}{30.556} = \frac{.556^2}{30.556} = \frac{.309}{30.556} = \textbf{.01}$$

$$\frac{(13.889 - 10)^2}{13.889} = \frac{3.889^2}{13.889} = \frac{15.124}{13.889} = \textbf{1.089}$$

$$\frac{(27.778 - 20)^2}{27.778} = \frac{7.778^2}{27.778} = \frac{60.497}{27.778} = \textbf{2.178}$$

Row 2:

$$\frac{(55.556 - 50)^2}{55.556} = \frac{5.556^2}{55.556} = \frac{30.869}{55.556} = \textbf{.556}$$

$$\frac{(61.111 - 60)^2}{61.111} = \frac{1.111^2}{61.111} = \frac{1.234}{61.111} = \textbf{.02}$$

$$\frac{(27.778 - 20)^2}{27.778} = \frac{7.778^2}{27.778} = \frac{60.497}{27.778} = \textbf{2.178}$$

$$\frac{(70 - 55.556)^2}{55.556} = \frac{14.444^2}{55.556} = \frac{208.629}{55.556} = \textbf{3.755}$$

Row 3:

$$\frac{(16.667 - 10)^2}{16.667} = \frac{6.667^2}{16.667} = \frac{44.449}{16.667} = \textbf{2.667}$$

$$\frac{(20 - 18.333)^2}{18.333} = \frac{1.667^2}{18.333} = \frac{2.779}{18.333} = \textbf{.152}$$

$$\frac{(20 - 8.333)^2}{8.333} = \frac{11.667^2}{8.333} = \frac{136.119}{8.333} = \textbf{16.335}$$

$$\frac{(16.667 - 10)^2}{16.667} = \frac{6.667^2}{16.667} = \frac{44.449}{16.667} = \textbf{2.667}$$

Step 8.   Chi-square is computed by adding all the values that were computed in Step 7.

$$\chi^2 = 5.378 + .01 + \cdots + 2.667 = \mathbf{36.985}$$

Step 9.   The degrees of freedom for this chi-square will always be the number of rows minus 1, multiplied by the number of columns minus 1. (In the present example, there are 3 rows and 4 columns.)

$$df = (3 - 1)(4 - 1) = 2 \times 3 = \mathbf{6}$$

A chi-square value larger than 12.6, with 6 degrees of freedom, is significant at the .05 level (see Appendix D).

Step 10.   The extent of the relationship between the two variables can be found by first adding the result of Step 8 to the result of Step 2.

$$36.985 + 360 = \mathbf{396.985}$$

Step 11.   Divide the result of Step 8 by the answer of Step 10.

$$\frac{36.985}{396.985} = \mathbf{.093}$$

Then, take the square root of that quotient. This yields the contingency coefficient.

$$C = \sqrt{.093} = \mathbf{.305}$$

This contingency coefficient, which is similar in meaning to the correlation coefficient, has already been shown to be significantly different from zero by the test concluded in Step 9. Thus, it is concluded that age and income are significantly related.   ■

SECTION 7.9
Tests for Trends, Runs, and Randomness

Scores representing an event occurring over time are often recorded. The questions that arise usually relate to the randomness or the extent to which the scores are patterned in some fashion. For example, the temperature recorded at noon daily during the months of February, March, and April would show day-to-day fluctuation, but clearly the trend would be upward as summer approached. Similar nonrandom patterns might be observed in situations as different as the bar-pressing behavior of a rat during successive five-minute periods and the number of letters in the alphabet a child is able to recite on successive days.

   The tests described below represent only a small fraction of the tests that can be employed. These were chosen because of their simplicity or their familiarity. The reader who is interested in learning more about the many types and uses of tests of randomness, runs, etc., is referred to the texts listed below.* In addition to those listed, many statistics books in the areas of economics and finance deal at great length with runs and various forms of trend analyses required for making financial projections.

■ EXAMPLE

Assume that a researcher has recorded the number of times an autistic child speaks a complete sentence during successive half-hour therapy sessions. The number of complete sentences is recorded each day for a 20-day period. The data are recorded as follows:

Day	1	2	3	4	5	6	7	8	9	10	11	12	13	14	15	16	17	18	19	20
Complete Sentences	6	5	4	5	6	8	9	10	7	6	8	10	11	13	15	12	9	10	13	15

Several questions (hypotheses) will be formulated and answers obtained by use of one or more of the following tests. Each of the computations demonstrated below represents one way of answering a particular question or testing a particular hypothesis.

When dealing with repeated measures of a single event, it is advisable first to graph the data. This is especially true if the number of scores recorded is large.

The graph below will prove useful for several of the computations that follow.

Figure 7.5

---

*Many textbooks concerned with nonparametric or distribution-free statistics include a section on tests for trends, runs, and randomness. There are also many texts available that deal with analysis of time series. Two texts for consideration by the reader are James V. Bradley, *Distribution-Free Statistical Tests;* Prentice-Hall, 1968, and M. G. Kendall, *Time-Series;* Griffin, London, 1973.

Question 1. If the number of sentences spoken each day shows a consistent tendency to increase or decrease, runs (successive increasing or decreasing scores) would tend to be longer and fewer in number. The specific question to be answered by the following analysis is "Are there fewer runs than would be expected by chance?"

Step 1. The actual number of runs (both up and down) in the data must be counted. The direction of change will be represented by a + when there is an increase from one day to the next and by a − when there is a decrease.

Days	1 2 3 4 5 6 7 8	9 10 11 12 13 14 15 16 17 18 19 20
Complete Sentences	6 5 4 5 6 8 9 10	7 6 8 10 11 13 15 12 9 10 13 15
Change	− − + + + + +	− − + + + + + − − + + +

During the twenty-day period used in the example, there were a total of six runs. These occurred between days 1 and 3, 3 and 8, 8 and 10, 10 and 15, 15 and 17, and 17 and 20.

Step 2. Turn to Appendix O, which gives the probability of the total number of runs (both up and down) occurring for up to 25 observations. In the present example, six or fewer runs would occur in 20 observations by chance alone less than once in 10,000 times. Therefore, it is concluded that there are fewer runs than would be expected by chance.

When the number of observations exceeds 25, the following formula approximates a z score and can be referred to the normal tables.

$$z = \frac{r - \left(\frac{2n - 1}{3}\right)}{\sqrt{\frac{16n - 29}{90}}}$$

where r = the total number of runs
n = the number of observations

Question 2. While the above analysis indicates that the total number of runs is significantly fewer than would be expected by chance, a second question relates to the length of the longest run. Specifically, "Is the length of the longest run greater than would be expected by chance alone?"

Step 1.   Using the data as reformulated above, it can be noted that the longest run is five (there actually are two runs of length five). To determine the probability of a run of length five, the following formula is employed:

$$P = \frac{2 + 2(n - S)(S + 1)}{(S + 2)!}$$

where n = the number of observations
      S = the length of the longest run

$$= \frac{2 + 2(20 - 5)(5 + 1)}{7 \times 6 \times 5 \times 4 \times 3 \times 2 \times 1}$$

$$= \frac{182}{5,040}$$

$$= .036$$

Thus, the probability of a run of five or more signs of the same type is approximately .036. It is thus concluded that a run of five would not be expected by chance. (If the expected direction of the run, + or −, had been hypothesized prior to the conduct of the experiment, the probability of a positive run of five would have been .036/2.)

Question 3.   Further inspection of the data indicates that performance seems to increase more frequently than it decreases. A simple analysis of this observation can be undertaken by use of the test for significance of a proportion, as presented in Section 7.1.

Referring again to the reformulated data of Question 1, it is noted that of the 19 possible changes up or down, 13 are positive. In terms of proportion, 13/19 or .684 are positive. If there were no pattern or trend shown in the data, the expected proportion of increases would be .50.

Step 1.   Turn to Section 7.1 and begin the analysis with Step 2. In the above example, the observed proportion will be equal to .684, and the expected equal to .50.

Results of the calculations for the above example show the z for proportion to be equal to 1.60. Thus, it is concluded that the number of positive changes in relation to the total number of changes is not greater than could be expected by chance.

Question 4. Inspection of the data reveals a tendency for the number of complete sentences to increase as days progress. If this is the case, the scores of days 11 through 20 would be expected to be higher than those of days 1 through 10. Adaptation of the Mann-Whitney U-test described in Section 7.3 permits examination of this hypothesis.

Step 1. Arrange the scores recorded over the 20-day period into two "groups," one representing the first half of the series, the other representing the second half.

Days	Sentences Spoken	Days	Sentences Spoken
1	6	11	8
2	5	12	10
3	4	13	11
4	5	14	13
5	6	15	15
6	8	16	12
7	9	17	9
8	10	18	10
9	7	19	13
10	6	20	15

Step 2. Turn to Section 7.3 and begin the calculation with Step 1.

Analysis of the above data, using the Mann-Whitney U-test, indicates that the distributions of the scores in the two groups are different beyond the .001 probability level. Thus, it is concluded that significantly more sentences were spoken during the last ten days than during the first ten days.

Question 5. Use of the Mann-Whitney U-test indicates whether the distribution of scores on the last half of the series is different from the first half. Another question might be whether the pattern of increase or decrease is similar during the first and second half of the data series. Use of Spearman's *rho* will permit analysis of this question.

Step 1. Arrange the scores in the first and second half of data sequence in the same fashion as for the Mann-Whitney U-test.

Days	Sentences Spoken	Days	Sentences Spoken
1	6	11	8
2	5	12	10
3	4	13	11
4	5	14	13
5	6	15	15
6	8	16	12
7	9	17	9
8	10	18	10
9	7	19	13
10	6	20	15

Then turn to Section 3.2 and begin the analysis with Step 1. For the data used in this example, the calculated *rho* is equal to $-.05$. Thus, it is concluded that while the number of sentences spoken during the second half of the observation period is larger than the number spoken during the first half (results of the Mann-Whitney U-test), the pattern of increase or decrease during the first and second half is not similar.

The above tests represent a few of the tools available to assist in the decision-making process when data on a single event or subject have been collected. As mentioned initially, the particular test chosen depends in large measure on the hypotheses or questions under study.   ■

APPENDIX A

Normal-Curve Areas

To read this table, first find the z value in which you are interested by looking down the first column for the units and tenths values and across the first row for the hundredths value. Whether the sign of z is positive or negative is not important for reading the table since it merely indicates whether the z lies to the left or right of the mean. After locating the z value of interest, find the number in the body of the table representing the proportional part of the area from the mean ($z = 0.00$) to your particular z value. For example, if the z of interest were -1.24, the proportion would be .3925. To compute the proportional part of the area in one half of the distribution that lies beyond the z value of interest, subtract the number found above from .5000. Thus, the area below a z of -1.24 would be .5000 − .3925 = .1075.

					APPENDIX A. NORMAL CURVE					
z	.00	.01	.02	.03	.04	.05	.06	.07	.08	.09
0.0	.0000	.0040	.0080	.0120	.0160	.0199	.0239	.0279	.0319	.0359
0.1	.0398	.0438	.0478	.0517	.0557	.0596	.0636	.0675	.0714	.0753
0.2	.0793	.0832	.0871	.0910	.0948	.0987	.1026	.1064	.1103	.1141
0.3	.1179	.1217	.1255	.1293	.1331	.1368	.1406	.1443	.1480	.1517
0.4	.1554	.1591	.1628	.1664	.1700	.1736	.1772	.1808	.1844	.1879
0.5	.1915	.1950	.1985	.2019	.2054	.2088	.2123	.2157	.2190	.2224
0.6	.2257	.2291	.2324	.2357	.2389	.2422	.2454	.2486	.2517	.2549
0.7	.2580	.2611	.2642	.2673	.2704	.2734	.2764	.2794	.2823	.2852
0.8	.2881	.2910	.2939	.2967	.2995	.3023	.3051	.3078	.3106	.3133
0.9	.3159	.3186	.3212	.3238	.3264	.3289	.3315	.3340	.3365	.3389
1.0	.3413	.3438	.3461	.3485	.3508	.3531	.3554	.3577	.3599	.3621
1.1	.3643	.3665	.3686	.3708	.3729	.3749	.3770	.3790	.3810	.3830
1.2	.3849	.3869	.3888	.3907	.3925	.3944	.3962	.3980	.3997	.4015
1.3	.4032	.4049	.4066	.4082	.4099	.4115	.4131	.4147	.4162	.4177
1.4	.4192	.4207	.4222	.4236	.4251	.4265	.4279	.4292	.4306	.4319
1.5	.4332	.4345	.4357	.4370	.4382	.4394	.4406	.4418	.4429	.4441
1.6	.4452	.4463	.4474	.4484	.4495	.4505	.4515	.4525	.4535	.4545
1.7	.4554	.4564	.4573	.4582	.4591	.4599	.4608	.4616	.4625	.4633
1.8	.4641	.4649	.4656	.4664	.4671	.4678	.4686	.4693	.4699	.4706
1.9	.4713	.4719	.4726	.4732	.4738	.4744	.4750	.4756	.4761	.4767
2.0	.4772	.4778	.4783	.4788	.4793	.4798	.4803	.4808	.4812	.4817
2.1	.4821	.4826	.4830	.4834	.4838	.4842	.4846	.4850	.4854	.4857
2.2	.4861	.4864	.4868	.4871	.4875	.4878	.4881	.4884	.4887	.4890
2.3	.4893	.4896	.4898	.4901	.4904	.4906	.4909	.4911	.4913	.4916
2.4	.4918	.4920	.4922	.4925	.4927	.4929	.4931	.4932	.4934	.4936
2.5	.4938	.4940	.4941	.4943	.4945	.4946	.4948	.4949	.4951	.4952
2.6	.4953	.4955	.4956	.4957	.4959	.4960	.4961	.4962	.4963	.4964
2.7	.4965	.4966	.4967	.4968	.4969	.4970	.4971	.4972	.4973	.4974
2.8	.4974	.4975	.4976	.4977	.4977	.4978	.4979	.4979	.4980	.4981
2.9	.4981	.4982	.4982	.4983	.4984	.4984	.4985	.4985	.4986	.4986
3.0	.4987	.4987	.4987	.4988	.4988	.4989	.4989	.4989	.4990	.4990
3.1	.49903									
3.2	.49931									
3.3	.49952									
3.4	.49966									
3.5	.49977									
3.6	.49984									
3.7	.49989									
3.8	.49993									
3.9	.49995									
4.0	.50000									

APPENDIX B

Critical Values of "Student's" *t* Statistic

To read this table, first find the degrees of freedom (*df*) in the column at the left. The minimum *t* values for the several alpha levels of significance are given in the columns to the right of the *df* column. Note that the alpha levels are given for both directional (one-tailed) and nondirectional (two-tailed) tests of significance. Nearly all tests of significance are, however, nondirectional.

To demonstrate the use of this table, assume that a computed *t* value of 3.25 was obtained with *df* equal to 15. Entering the table at the row headed by 15 *df*, read to the right. Note that the *t* of 3.25 is larger than the .01 value (2.947) for a two-tailed test but less than the .001 value (4.073). Therefore, it is concluded that this *t* value is significant beyond the .01 level.

	APPENDIX B. t STATISTIC					
	Alpha level of significance for directional (one-tailed) tests					
	.25	.05	.025	.01	.005	.0005
df						
	Alpha level of significance for nondirectional (two-tailed) tests					
	.50	.10	.05	.02	.01	.001
1	1.000	6.314	12.706	31.821	63.657	636.619
2	.816	2.920	4.303	6.965	9.925	31.598
3	.765	2.353	3.182	4.541	5.841	12.941
4	.741	2.132	2.776	3.747	4.604	8.610
5	.727	2.015	2.571	3.365	4.032	6.859
6	.718	1.943	2.447	3.143	3.707	5.959
7	.711	1.895	2.365	2.998	3.499	5.405
8	.706	1.860	2.306	2.896	3.355	5.041
9	.703	1.833	2.262	2.821	3.250	4.781
10	.700	1.812	2.228	2.764	3.169	4.587
11	.697	1.796	2.201	2.718	3.106	4.437
12	.695	1.782	2.179	2.681	3.055	4.318
13	.694	1.771	2.160	2.650	3.012	4.221
14	.692	1.761	2.145	2.624	2.977	4.140
15	.691	1.753	2.131	2.602	2.947	4.073
16	.690	1.746	2.120	2.583	2.921	4.015
17	.689	1.740	2.110	2.567	2.898	3.965
18	.688	1.734	2.101	2.552	2.878	3.992
19	.688	1.729	2.093	2.539	2.861	3.883
20	.687	1.725	2.086	2.528	2.845	3.850
21	.686	1.721	2.080	2.518	2.831	3.819
22	.686	1.717	2.074	2.508	2.819	3.792
23	.685	1.714	2.069	2.500	2.807	3.767
24	.685	1.711	2.064	2.492	2.797	3.745
25	.684	1.708	2.060	2.485	2.787	3.725
26	.684	1.706	2.056	2.479	2.779	3.707
27	.684	1.703	2.052	2.473	2.771	3.690
28	.683	1.701	2.048	2.467	2.763	3.674
29	.683	1.699	2.045	2.462	2.756	3.659
30	.683	1.697	2.042	2.457	2.750	3.646
40	.681	1.684	2.021	2.423	2.704	3.551
60	.679	1.671	2.000	2.390	2.660	3.460
120	.677	1.658	1.980	2.358	2.617	3.373
∞	.674	1.645	1.960	2.326	2.576	3.291

SOURCE: Appendix B is taken from Table III of Fisher & Yates: *Statistical Tables for Biological, Agricultural and Medical Research,* 6/e published by Addison Wesley Longman Ltd., (1974). Reprinted by permission of the authors and publishers.

APPENDIX C

Critical Values for Sandler's A Statistic

To read this table, first find the degrees of freedom (pairs of scores minus one) in the column at the left. The *maximum A* values for the several alpha levels of significance are given in the columns to the right of the *df* column. Note that values for both one-tailed and two-tailed tests are given.

To demonstrate the use of this table, assume that a computed *A* value of .261 was obtained with *df* equal to 18. Entering the table at the row for 18 *df*, read to the right. The computed *A* of .261 is *smaller* than the .05 value (.267) but larger than the .02 value for a two-tailed test. Therefore, it is concluded that the difference is significant beyond the .05 level.

APPENDIX C. CRITICAL VALUES OF A

For any given value of $n - 1$, the table shows the values of A corresponding to various levels of probability. A is significant at a given level if it is equal to or *less than* the value shown in the table.

| | Level of significance for one-tailed test | | | | |
	.05	.025	.01	.005	.0005
	Level of significance for two-tailed test				
$n - 1$*	.10	.05	.02	.01	.001
1	0.5125	0.5031	0.50049	0.50012	0.5000012
2	0.412	0.369	0.347	0.340	0.334
3	0.385	0.324	0.286	0.272	0.254
4	0.376	0.304	0.257	0.238	0.211
5	0.372	0.293	0.240	0.218	0.184
6	0.370	0.286	0.230	0.205	0.167
7	0.369	0.281	0.222	0.196	0.155
8	0.368	0.278	0.217	0.190	0.146
9	0.368	0.276	0.213	0.185	0.139
10	0.368	0.274	0.210	0.181	0.134
11	0.368	0.273	0.207	0.178	0.130
12	0.368	0.271	0.205	0.176	0.126
13	0.368	0.270	0.204	0.174	0.124
14	0.368	0.270	0.202	0.172	0.121
15	0.368	0.269	0.201	0.170	0.119
16	0.368	0.268	0.200	0.169	0.117
17	0.368	0.268	0.199	0.168	0.116
18	0.368	0.267	0.198	0.167	0.114
19	0.368	0.267	0.197	0.166	0.113
20	0.368	0.266	0.197	0.165	0.112
21	0.368	0.266	0.196	0.165	0.111
22	0.368	0.266	0.196	0.164	0.110
23	0.368	0.266	0.195	0.163	0.109
24	0.368	0.265	0.195	0.163	0.108
25	0.368	0.265	0.194	0.162	0.108
26	0.368	0.265	0.194	0.162	0.107
27	0.368	0.265	0.193	0.161	0.107
28	0.368	0.265	0.193	0.161	0.106
29	0.368	0.264	0.193	0.161	0.106
30	0.368	0.264	0.193	0.160	0.105
40	0.368	0.263	0.191	0.158	0.102
60	0.369	0.262	0.189	0.155	0.099
120	0.369	0.261	0.187	0.153	0.095
∞	0.370	0.260	0.185	0.151	0.092

*Number of pairs.

SOURCE: Critical values of A by J. Sandler from *British Journal of Psychology*, 1955, **46**, 225–226. Reprinted by permission of Cambridge University Press.

APPENDIX D

Values of the Chi-Square Statistic

To read this table, first find the degrees of freedom (*df*) in the column at the left. The minimum chi-square values for the several alpha levels are given in the columns to the right of the *df* column. The subscript values for each chi-square column indicate the probability of a real difference existing.

To demonstrate the use of this table, assume that a computed chi-square of 25 was obtained with 15 *df*. Entering the table at the row headed by 15 *df*, read to the right. The value of 25 is listed in the .05 column. Thus it is concluded that the probability is .05 that the difference is due to chance alone.

APPENDIX D. CHI-SQUARE STATISTIC

df	$x^2.995$	$x^2.99$	$x^2.975$	$x^2.95$	$x^2.90$	$x^2.75$	$x^2.50$	$x^2.25$	$x^2.10$	$x^2.05$	$x^2.025$	$x^2.01$	$x^2.005$	$x^2.001$
1	—	—	—	—	.02	.10	.45	1.3	2.7	3.8	5.0	6.6	7.9	10.8
2	.01	.02	.05	.10	.21	.58	1.4	2.8	4.6	6.0	7.4	9.2	10.6	13.8
3	.07	.11	.22	.35	.58	1.21	2.4	4.1	6.3	7.8	9.4	11.3	12.8	16.3
4	.21	.30	.48	.71	1.1	1.92	3.4	5.4	7.8	9.5	11.1	13.3	14.9	18.5
5	.41	.55	.83	1.1	1.6	2.7	4.4	6.6	9.2	11.1	12.8	15.1	16.7	20.5
6	.68	.87	1.2	1.6	2.2	3.5	5.4	7.8	10.6	12.6	14.4	16.8	18.5	22.5
7	.99	1.24	1.7	2.2	2.8	4.3	6.4	9.0	12.0	14.1	16.0	18.5	20.3	24.3
8	1.3	1.65	2.2	2.7	3.5	5.1	7.3	10.2	13.4	15.5	17.5	20.1	22.0	26.1
9	1.7	2.09	2.7	3.3	4.2	5.9	8.3	11.4	14.7	16.9	19.0	21.7	23.6	27.9
10	2.2	2.56	3.2	3.9	4.9	6.7	9.3	12.5	16.0	18.3	20.5	23.2	25.2	29.6
11	2.6	3.05	3.8	4.6	5.6	7.6	10.3	13.7	17.3	19.7	21.9	24.7	26.8	31.3
12	3.1	3.57	4.4	5.2	6.3	8.4	11.3	14.8	18.5	21.0	23.3	26.2	28.3	32.9
13	3.6	4.11	5.0	5.9	7.0	9.3	12.3	16.0	19.8	22.4	24.7	27.7	29.8	34.5
14	4.1	4.66	5.6	6.6	7.8	10.2	13.3	17.1	21.1	23.7	26.1	29.1	31.3	36.1
15	4.6	5.23	6.3	7.3	8.5	11.0	14.3	18.2	22.3	25.0	27.5	30.6	32.8	37.7
16	5.1	5.81	6.9	8.0	9.3	11.9	15.3	19.4	23.5	26.3	28.8	32.0	34.3	39.3
17	5.7	6.41	7.6	8.7	10.1	12.8	16.3	20.5	24.8	27.6	30.2	33.4	35.7	40.8
18	6.3	7.01	8.2	9.4	10.9	13.7	17.3	21.6	26.0	28.9	31.5	34.8	37.2	42.3
19	6.8	7.63	8.9	10.1	11.7	14.6	18.3	22.7	27.2	30.1	32.9	36.2	38.6	43.8
20	7.4	8.26	9.6	10.9	12.4	15.5	19.3	23.8	28.4	31.4	34.2	37.6	40.0	45.3
21	8.0	8.9	10.3	11.6	13.2	16.3	20.3	24.9	29.6	32.7	35.5	38.9	41.4	46.8
22	8.6	9.5	11.0	12.3	14.0	17.2	21.3	26.0	30.8	33.9	36.8	40.3	42.8	48.3
23	9.3	10.2	11.7	13.1	14.8	18.1	22.3	27.1	32.0	35.2	38.1	41.6	44.2	49.7
24	9.9	10.9	12.4	13.8	15.7	19.0	23.3	28.2	33.2	36.4	39.4	43.0	45.6	51.2
25	10.5	11.5	13.1	14.6	16.5	19.9	24.3	29.3	34.4	37.7	40.6	44.3	46.9	52.6
26	11.2	12.2	13.8	15.4	17.3	20.8	25.3	30.4	35.6	38.9	41.9	45.6	48.3	54.0
27	11.8	12.9	14.6	16.2	18.1	21.7	26.3	31.5	36.7	40.1	43.2	47.0	49.6	55.5
28	12.5	13.6	15.3	16.9	18.9	22.7	27.3	32.6	37.9	41.3	44.5	48.3	51.0	56.9
29	13.1	14.3	16.0	17.7	19.8	23.6	28.3	33.7	39.1	42.6	45.7	49.6	52.3	58.3
30	13.8	15.0	16.8	18.5	20.6	24.5	29.3	34.8	40.3	43.8	47.0	50.9	53.3	59.7

APPENDIX E

Probabilities of the F Distribution

To read this table, the degrees of freedom (df) for both mean-square values of the F ratio must be located. The df for the numerator is located in the top row (df_1). The df for the denominator of the F ratio is located in the column to the far left of the table (df_2). The values in the block where the row and column intersect represent the F values at the different alpha levels of significance.

To demonstrate the use of this table, assume that a computed F ratio of 3.54 was obtained with df equal to 5 and 15. Entering the table by the column headed by df_1 equal to 5 and the row headed by df_2 equal to 15, we find that the values range from 1.68 for the .20 level to 7.57 for the .001 level. The F ratio of 3.54 falls just short of the value required for the .025 level. It is concluded, then, that the F of 3.54 with df equal to 5 and 15 is significant at the .05 level.

APPENDIX E. F DISTRIBUTION

df_2 \ df_1		1	2	3	4	5	6	8	12	24	∞
1	.001	405284	500000	540379	562500	576405	585937	598144	610667	623497	636619
	.005	16211	20000	21615	22500	23056	23437	23925	24426	24940	25465
	.01	4052	4999	5403	5625	5764	5859	5981	6106	6234	6366
	.025	647.79	799.50	864.16	899.58	921.85	937.11	956.66	976.71	997.25	1018.30
	.05	161.45	199.50	215.71	224.58	230.16	233.99	238.88	243.91	249.05	254.32
	.10	39.86	49.50	53.59	55.83	57.24	58.20	59.44	60.70	62.00	63.33
	.20	9.47	12.00	13.06	13.73	14.01	14.26	14.59	14.90	15.24	15.58
2	.001	998.5	999.0	999.2	999.2	999.3	999.3	999.4	999.4	999.5	999.5
	.005	198.50	199.00	199.17	199.25	199.30	199.33	199.37	199.42	199.46	199.51
	.01	98.49	99.00	99.17	99.25	99.30	99.33	99.36	99.42	99.46	99.50
	.025	38.51	39.00	39.17	39.25	39.30	39.33	39.37	39.42	39.46	39.50
	.05	18.51	19.00	19.16	19.25	19.30	19.33	19.37	19.41	19.45	19.50
	.10	8.53	9.00	9.16	9.24	9.29	9.33	9.37	9.41	9.45	9.49
	.20	3.56	4.00	4.16	4.24	4.28	4.32	4.36	4.40	4.44	4.48
3	.001	167.5	148.5	141.1	137.1	134.6	132.8	130.6	128.3	125.9	123.5
	.005	55.55	49.80	47.47	46.20	45.39	44.84	44.13	43.39	42.62	41.83
	.01	34.12	30.81	29.46	28.71	28.24	27.91	27.49	27.05	26.60	26.12
	.025	17.44	16.04	15.44	15.10	14.89	14.74	14.54	14.34	14.12	13.90
	.05	10.13	9.55	9.28	9.12	9.01	8.94	8.84	8.74	8.64	8.53
	.10	5.54	5.46	5.39	5.34	5.31	5.28	5.25	5.22	5.18	5.13
	.20	2.68	2.89	2.94	2.96	2.97	2.97	2.98	2.98	2.98	2.98
4	.001	74.14	61.25	56.18	53.44	51.71	50.53	49.00	47.41	45.77	44.05
	.005	31.33	26.28	24.26	23.16	22.46	21.98	21.35	20.71	20.03	19.33
	.01	21.20	18.00	16.69	15.98	15.52	15.21	14.80	14.37	13.93	13.46
	.025	12.22	10.65	9.98	9.60	9.36	9.20	8.98	8.75	8.51	8.26
	.05	7.71	6.94	6.59	6.39	6.26	6.16	6.04	5.91	5.77	5.63
	.10	4.54	4.32	4.19	4.11	4.05	4.01	3.95	3.90	3.83	3.76
	.20	2.35	2.47	2.48	2.48	2.48	2.47	2.47	2.46	2.44	2.43
5	.001	47.04	36.61	33.20	31.09	29.75	28.84	27.64	26.42	25.14	23.78
	.005	22.79	18.31	16.53	15.56	14.94	14.51	13.96	13.38	12.78	12.14
	.01	16.26	13.27	12.06	11.39	10.97	10.67	10.29	9.89	9.47	9.02
	.025	10.01	8.43	7.76	7.39	7.15	6.98	6.76	6.52	6.28	6.02
	.05	6.61	5.79	5.41	5.19	5.05	4.95	4.82	4.68	4.53	4.36
	.10	4.06	3.78	3.62	3.52	3.45	3.40	3.34	3.27	3.19	3.10
	.20	2.18	2.26	2.25	2.24	2.23	2.22	2.20	2.18	2.16	2.13
6	.001	35.51	27.00	23.70	21.90	20.81	20.03	19.03	17.99	16.89	15.75
	.005	18.64	14.54	12.92	12.03	11.46	11.07	10.57	10.03	9.47	8.88
	.01	13.74	10.92	9.78	9.15	8.75	8.47	8.10	7.72	7.31	6.88
	.025	8.81	7.26	6.60	6.23	5.99	5.82	5.60	5.37	5.12	4.85
	.05	5.99	5.14	4.76	4.53	4.39	4.28	4.15	4.00	3.84	3.67
	.10	3.78	3.46	3.29	3.18	3.11	3.05	2.98	2.90	2.82	2.72
	.20	2.07	2.13	2.11	2.09	2.08	2.06	2.04	2.02	1.99	1.95

SOURCE: Appendix E is taken from Table V of Fisher & Yates: *Statistical Tables for Biological, Agricultural and Medical Research*, 6/e published by Addison Wesley Longman Ltd., (1974). Reprinted by permission of the authors and publishers.

APPENDIX E. *F* DISTRIBUTION *(cont.)*

df_2		df_1 1	2	3	4	5	6	8	12	24	∞
7	.001	29.22	21.69	18.77	17.19	16.21	15.52	14.63	13.71	12.73	11.69
	.005	16.24	12.40	10.88	10.05	9.52	9.16	8.68	8.18	7.65	7.08
	.01	12.25	9.55	8.45	7.85	7.46	7.19	6.84	6.47	6.07	5.65
	.025	8.07	6.54	5.89	5.52	5.29	5.12	4.90	4.67	4.42	4.14
	.05	5.59	4.74	4.35	4.12	3.97	3.87	3.73	3.57	3.41	3.23
	.10	3.59	3.26	3.07	2.96	2.88	2.83	2.75	2.67	2.58	2.47
	.20	2.00	2.04	2.02	1.99	1.97	1.96	1.93	1.91	1.87	1.83
8	.001	25.42	18.49	15.83	14.39	13.49	12.86	12.04	11.19	10.30	9.34
	.005	14.69	11.04	9.60	8.81	8.30	7.95	7.50	7.01	6.50	5.95
	.01	11.26	8.65	7.59	7.01	6.63	6.37	6.03	5.67	5.28	4.86
	.025	7.57	6.06	5.42	5.05	4.82	4.65	4.43	4.20	3.95	3.67
	.05	5.32	4.46	4.07	3.84	3.69	3.58	3.44	3.28	3.12	2.93
	.10	3.46	3.11	2.92	2.81	2.73	2.67	2.59	2.50	2.40	2.29
	.20	1.95	1.98	1.95	1.92	1.90	1.88	1.86	1.83	1.79	1.74
9	.001	22.86	16.39	13.90	12.56	11.71	11.13	10.37	9.57	8.72	7.81
	.005	13.61	10.11	8.72	7.96	7.47	7.13	6.69	6.23	5.73	5.19
	.01	10.56	8.02	6.99	6.42	6.06	5.80	5.47	5.11	4.73	4.31
	.025	7.21	5.71	5.08	4.72	4.48	4.32	4.10	3.87	3.61	3.33
	.05	5.12	4.26	3.86	3.63	3.48	3.37	3.23	3.07	2.90	2.71
	.10	3.36	3.01	2.81	2.69	2.61	2.55	2.47	2.38	2.28	2.16
	.20	1.91	1.94	1.90	1.87	1.85	1.83	1.80	1.76	1.72	1.67
10	.001	21.04	14.91	12.55	11.28	10.48	9.92	9.20	8.45	7.64	6.76
	.005	12.83	9.43	8.08	7.34	6.87	6.54	6.12	5.66	5.17	4.64
	.01	10.04	7.56	6.55	5.99	5.64	5.39	5.06	4.71	4.33	3.91
	.025	6.94	5.46	4.83	4.47	4.24	4.07	3.85	3.62	3.37	3.08
	.05	4.96	4.10	3.71	3.48	3.33	3.22	3.07	2.91	2.74	2.54
	.10	3.28	2.92	2.73	2.61	2.52	2.46	2.38	2.28	2.18	2.06
	.20	1.88	1.90	1.86	1.83	1.80	1.78	1.75	1.72	1.67	1.62
11	.001	19.69	13.81	11.56	10.35	9.58	9.05	8.35	7.63	6.85	6.00
	.005	12.23	8.91	7.60	6.88	6.42	6.10	5.68	5.24	4.76	4.23
	.01	9.65	7.20	6.22	5.67	5.32	5.07	4.74	4.40	4.02	3.60
	.025	6.72	5.26	4.63	4.28	4.04	3.88	3.66	3.43	3.17	2.88
	.05	4.84	3.98	3.59	3.36	3.20	3.09	2.95	2.79	2.61	2.40
	.10	3.23	2.86	2.66	2.54	2.45	2.39	2.30	2.21	2.10	1.97
	.20	1.86	1.87	1.83	1.80	1.77	1.75	1.72	1.68	1.63	1.57
12	.001	18.64	12.97	10.80	9.63	8.89	8.38	7.71	7.00	6.25	5.42
	.005	11.75	8.51	7.23	6.52	6.07	5.76	5.35	4.91	4.43	3.90
	.01	9.33	6.93	5.95	5.41	5.06	4.82	4.50	4.16	3.78	3.36
	.025	6.55	5.10	4.47	4.12	3.89	3.73	3.51	3.28	3.02	2.72
	.05	4.75	3.88	3.49	3.26	3.11	3.00	2.85	2.69	2.50	2.30
	.10	3.18	2.81	2.61	2.48	2.39	2.33	2.24	2.15	2.04	1.90
	.20	1.84	1.85	1.80	1.77	1.74	1.72	1.69	1.65	1.60	1.54
13	.001	17.81	12.31	10.21	9.07	8.35	7.86	7.21	6.52	5.78	4.97
	.005	11.37	8.19	6.93	6.23	5.79	5.48	5.08	4.64	4.17	3.65
	.01	9.07	6.70	5.74	5.20	4.86	4.62	4.30	3.96	3.59	3.16
	.025	6.41	4.97	4.35	4.00	3.77	3.60	3.39	3.15	2.89	2.60
	.05	4.67	3.80	3.41	3.18	3.02	2.92	2.77	2.60	2.42	2.21
	.10	3.14	2.76	2.56	2.43	2.35	2.28	2.20	2.10	1.98	1.85
	.20	1.82	1.83	1.78	1.75	1.72	1.69	1.66	1.62	1.57	1.51

APPENDIX E. F DISTRIBUTION (cont.)

df_2	df_1	1	2	3	4	5	6	8	12	24	∞
14	.001	17.14	11.78	9.73	8.62	7.92	7.43	6.80	6.13	5.41	4.60
	.005	11.06	7.92	6.68	6.00	5.56	5.26	4.86	4.43	3.96	3.44
	.01	8.86	6.51	5.56	5.03	4.69	4.46	4.14	3.80	3.43	3.00
	.025	6.30	4.86	4.24	3.89	3.66	3.50	3.29	3.05	2.79	2.49
	.05	4.60	3.74	3.34	3.11	2.96	2.85	2.70	2.53	2.35	2.13
	.10	3.10	2.73	2.52	2.39	2.31	2.24	2.15	2.05	1.94	1.80
	.20	1.81	1.81	1.76	1.73	1.70	1.67	1.64	1.60	1.55	1.48
15	.001	16.59	11.34	9.34	8.25	7.57	7.09	6.47	5.81	5.10	4.31
	.005	10.80	7.70	6.48	5.80	5.37	5.07	4.67	4.25	3.79	3.26
	.01	8.68	6.36	5.42	4.89	4.56	4.32	4.00	3.67	3.29	2.87
	.025	6.20	4.77	4.15	3.80	3.58	3.41	3.20	2.96	2.70	2.40
	.05	4.54	3.68	3.29	3.06	2.90	2.79	2.64	2.48	2.29	2.07
	.10	3.07	2.70	2.49	2.36	2.27	2.21	2.12	2.02	1.90	1.76
	.20	1.80	1.79	1.75	1.71	1.68	1.66	1.62	1.58	1.53	1.46
16	.001	16.12	10.97	9.00	7.94	7.27	6.81	6.19	5.55	4.85	4.06
	.005	10.58	7.51	6.30	5.64	5.21	4.91	4.52	4.10	3.64	3.11
	.01	8.53	6.23	5.29	4.77	4.44	4.20	3.89	3.55	3.18	2.75
	.025	6.12	4.69	4.08	3.73	3.50	3.34	3.12	2.89	2.63	2.32
	.05	4.49	3.63	3.24	3.01	2.85	2.74	2.59	2.42	2.24	2.01
	.10	3.05	2.67	2.46	2.33	2.24	2.18	2.09	1.99	1.87	1.72
	.20	1.79	1.78	1.74	1.70	1.67	1.64	1.61	1.56	1.51	1.43
17	.001	15.72	10.66	8.73	7.68	7.02	6.56	5.96	5.32	4.63	3.85
	.005	10.38	7.35	6.16	5.50	5.07	4.78	4.39	3.97	3.51	2.98
	.01	8.40	6.11	5.18	4.67	4.34	4.10	3.79	3.45	3.08	2.65
	.025	6.04	4.62	4.01	3.66	3.44	3.28	3.06	2.82	2.56	2.25
	.05	4.45	3.59	3.20	2.96	2.81	2.70	2.55	2.38	2.19	1.96
	.10	3.03	2.64	2.44	2.31	2.22	2.15	2.06	1.96	1.84	1.69
	.20	1.78	1.77	1.72	1.68	1.65	1.63	1.59	1.55	1.49	1.42
18	.001	15.38	10.39	8.49	7.46	6.81	6.35	5.76	5.13	4.45	3.67
	.005	10.22	7.21	6.03	5.37	4.96	4.66	4.28	3.86	3.40	2.87
	.01	8.28	6.01	5.09	4.58	4.25	4.01	3.71	3.37	3.00	2.57
	.025	5.98	4.56	3.95	3.61	3.38	3.22	3.01	2.77	2.50	2.19
	.05	4.41	3.55	3.16	2.93	2.77	2.66	2.51	2.34	2.15	1.92
	.10	3.01	2.62	2.42	2.29	2.20	2.13	2.04	1.93	1.81	1.66
	.20	1.77	1.76	1.71	1.67	1.64	1.62	1.58	1.53	1.48	1.40
19	.001	15.08	10.16	8.28	7.26	6.61	6.18	5.59	4.97	4.29	3.52
	.005	10.07	7.09	5.92	5.27	4.85	4.56	4.18	3.76	3.31	2.78
	.01	8.18	5.93	5.01	4.50	4.17	3.94	3.63	3.30	2.92	2.49
	.025	5.92	4.51	3.90	3.56	3.33	3.17	2.96	2.72	2.45	2.13
	.05	4.38	3.52	3.13	2.90	2.74	2.63	2.48	2.31	2.11	1.88
	.10	2.99	2.61	2.40	2.27	2.18	2.11	2.02	1.91	1.79	1.63
	.20	1.76	1.75	1.70	1.66	1.63	1.61	1.57	1.52	1.46	1.39
20	.001	14.82	9.95	8.10	7.10	6.46	6.02	5.44	4.82	4.15	3.38
	.005	9.94	6.99	5.82	5.17	4.76	4.47	4.09	3.68	3.22	2.69
	.01	8.10	5.85	4.94	4.43	4.10	3.87	3.56	3.23	2.86	2.42
	.025	5.87	4.46	3.86	3.51	3.29	3.13	2.91	2.68	2.41	2.09
	.05	4.35	3.49	3.10	2.87	2.71	2.60	2.45	2.28	2.08	1.84
	.10	2.97	2.59	2.38	2.25	2.16	2.09	2.00	1.89	1.77	1.61
	.20	1.76	1.75	1.70	1.65	1.62	1.60	1.56	1.51	1.45	1.37

APPENDIX E. F DISTRIBUTION *(cont.)*

df_2	df_1	1	2	3	4	5	6	8	12	24	∞
21	.001	14.59	9.77	7.94	6.95	6.32	5.88	5.31	4.70	4.03	3.26
	.005	9.83	6.89	5.73	5.09	4.68	4.39	4.01	3.60	3.15	2.61
	.01	8.02	5.78	4.87	4.37	4.04	3.81	3.51	3.17	2.80	2.36
	.025	5.83	4.42	3.82	3.48	3.25	3.09	2.87	2.64	2.37	2.04
	.05	4.32	3.47	3.07	2.84	2.68	2.57	2.42	2.25	2.05	1.81
	.10	2.96	2.57	2.36	2.23	2.14	2.08	1.98	1.89	1.75	1.59
	.20	1.75	1.74	1.69	1.65	1.61	1.59	1.55	1.50	1.44	1.36
22	.001	14.38	9.61	7.80	6.81	6.19	5.79	5.19	4.58	3.92	3.15
	.005	9.73	6.81	5.65	5.02	4.61	4.32	3.94	3.54	3.08	2.55
	.01	7.94	5.72	4.82	4.31	3.99	3.76	3.45	3.12	2.75	2.31
	.025	5.79	4.38	3.78	3.44	3.22	3.05	2.84	2.60	2.33	2.00
	.05	4.30	3.44	3.05	2.82	2.66	2.55	2.40	2.23	2.03	1.78
	.10	2.95	2.56	2.35	2.22	2.13	2.06	1.97	1.86	1.73	1.57
	.20	1.75	1.73	1.68	1.64	1.61	1.58	1.54	1.49	1.43	1.35
23	.001	14.19	9.47	7.67	6.69	6.08	5.65	5.09	4.48	3.82	3.05
	.005	9.63	6.73	5.58	4.95	4.54	4.26	3.88	3.47	3.02	2.48
	.01	7.88	5.66	4.76	4.26	3.94	3.71	3.41	3.07	2.70	2.26
	.025	5.75	4.35	3.75	3.41	3.18	3.02	2.81	2.57	2.30	1.97
	.05	4.28	3.42	3.03	2.80	2.64	2.53	2.38	2.20	2.00	1.76
	.10	2.94	2.55	2.34	2.21	2.11	2.05	1.95	1.84	1.72	1.55
	.20	1.74	1.73	1.68	1.63	1.60	1.57	1.53	1.49	1.42	1.34
24	.001	14.03	9.34	7.55	6.59	5.98	5.55	4.99	4.39	3.74	2.97
	.005	9.55	6.66	5.52	4.89	4.49	4.20	3.83	3.42	2.97	2.43
	.01	7.82	5.61	4.72	4.22	3.90	3.67	3.36	3.03	2.66	2.21
	.025	5.72	4.32	3.72	3.38	3.15	2.99	2.78	2.54	2.27	1.94
	.05	4.26	3.40	3.01	2.78	2.62	2.51	2.36	2.18	1.98	1.73
	.10	2.93	2.54	2.33	2.19	2.10	2.04	1.94	1.83	1.70	1.53
	.20	1.74	1.72	1.67	1.63	1.59	1.57	1.53	1.48	1.42	1.33
25	.001	13.88	9.22	7.45	6.49	5.88	5.46	4.91	4.31	3.66	2.89
	.005	9.48	6.60	5.46	4.84	4.43	4.15	3.78	3.37	2.92	2.38
	.01	7.77	5.57	4.68	4.18	3.86	3.63	3.32	2.99	2.62	2.17
	.025	5.69	4.29	3.69	3.35	3.13	2.97	2.75	2.51	2.24	1.91
	.05	4.24	3.38	2.99	2.76	2.60	2.49	2.34	2.16	1.96	1.71
	.10	2.92	2.53	2.32	2.18	2.09	2.02	1.93	1.82	1.69	1.52
	.20	1.73	1.72	1.66	1.62	1.59	1.56	1.52	1.47	1.41	1.32
26	.001	13.74	9.12	7.36	6.41	5.80	5.38	4.83	4.24	3.59	2.82
	.005	9.41	6.54	5.41	4.79	4.38	4.10	3.73	3.33	2.87	2.33
	.01	7.72	5.53	4.64	4.14	3.82	3.59	3.29	2.96	2.58	2.13
	.025	5.66	4.27	3.67	3.33	3.10	2.94	2.73	2.49	2.22	1.88
	.05	4.22	3.37	2.98	2.74	2.59	2.47	2.32	2.15	1.95	1.69
	.10	2.91	2.52	2.31	2.17	2.08	2.01	1.92	1.81	1.68	1.50
	.20	1.73	1.71	1.66	1.62	1.58	1.56	1.52	1.47	1.40	1.31
27	.001	13.61	9.02	7.27	6.33	5.73	5.31	4.76	4.17	3.52	2.75
	.005	9.34	6.49	5.36	4.74	4.34	4.06	3.69	3.28	2.83	2.29
	.01	7.68	5.49	4.60	4.11	3.78	3.56	3.26	2.93	2.55	2.10
	.025	5.63	4.24	3.65	3.31	3.08	2.92	2.71	2.47	2.19	1.85
	.05	4.21	3.35	2.96	2.73	2.57	2.46	2.30	2.13	1.93	1.67
	.10	2.90	2.51	2.30	2.17	2.07	2.00	1.91	1.80	1.67	1.49
	.20	1.73	1.71	1.66	1.61	1.58	1.55	1.51	1.46	1.40	1.30

APPENDIX E. *F* DISTRIBUTION *(cont.)*

df_2 \ df_1		1	2	3	4	5	6	8	12	24	∞
28	.001	13.50	8.93	7.19	6.25	5.66	5.24	4.69	4.11	3.46	2.70
	.005	9.28	6.44	5.32	4.70	4.30	4.02	3.65	3.25	2.79	2.25
	.01	7.64	5.45	4.57	4.07	3.75	3.53	3.23	2.90	2.52	2.06
	.025	5.61	4.22	3.63	3.29	3.06	2.90	2.69	2.45	2.17	1.83
	.05	4.20	3.34	2.95	2.71	2.56	2.44	2.29	2.12	1.91	1.65
	.10	2.89	2.50	2.29	2.16	2.06	2.00	1.90	1.79	1.66	1.48
	.20	1.72	1.71	1.65	1.61	1.57	1.55	1.51	1.46	1.39	1.30
29	.001	13.39	8.85	7.12	6.19	5.59	5.18	4.64	4.05	3.41	2.64
	.005	9.23	6.40	5.28	4.66	4.26	3.98	3.61	3.21	2.76	2.21
	.01	7.60	5.42	4.54	4.04	3.73	3.50	3.20	2.87	2.49	2.03
	.025	5.59	4.20	3.61	3.27	3.04	2.88	2.67	2.43	2.15	1.81
	.05	4.18	3.33	2.93	2.70	2.54	2.43	2.28	2.10	1.90	1.64
	.10	2.89	2.50	2.28	2.15	2.06	1.99	1.89	1.78	1.65	1.47
	.20	1.72	1.70	1.65	1.60	1.57	1.54	1.50	1.45	1.39	1.29
30	.001	13.29	8.77	7.05	6.12	5.53	5.12	4.58	4.00	3.36	2.59
	.005	9.18	6.35	5.24	4.62	4.23	3.95	3.58	3.18	2.73	2.18
	.01	7.56	5.39	4.51	4.02	3.70	3.47	3.17	2.84	2.47	2.01
	.025	5.57	4.18	3.59	3.25	3.03	2.87	2.65	2.41	2.14	1.79
	.05	4.17	3.32	2.92	2.69	2.53	2.42	2.27	2.09	1.89	1.62
	.10	2.88	2.49	2.28	2.14	2.05	1.98	1.88	1.77	1.64	1.46
	.20	1.72	1.70	1.64	1.60	1.57	1.54	1.50	1.45	1.38	1.28
40	.001	12.61	8.25	6.60	5.70	5.13	4.73	4.21	3.64	3.01	2.23
	.005	8.83	6.07	4.98	4.37	3.99	3.71	3.35	2.95	2.50	1.93
	.01	7.31	5.18	4.31	3.83	3.51	3.29	2.99	2.66	2.29	1.80
	.025	5.42	4.05	3.46	3.13	2.90	2.74	2.53	2.29	2.01	1.64
	.05	4.08	3.23	2.84	2.61	2.45	2.34	2.18	2.00	1.79	1.51
	.10	2.84	2.44	2.23	2.09	2.00	1.93	1.83	1.71	1.57	1.38
	.20	1.70	1.68	1.62	1.57	1.54	1.51	1.47	1.41	1.34	1.24
60	.001	11.97	7.76	6.17	5.31	4.76	4.37	3.87	3.31	2.69	1.90
	.005	8.49	5.80	4.73	4.14	3.76	3.49	3.13	2.74	2.29	1.69
	.01	7.08	4.98	4.13	3.65	3.34	3.12	2.82	2.50	2.12	1.60
	.025	5.29	3.93	3.34	3.01	2.79	2.63	2.41	2.17	1.88	1.48
	.05	4.00	3.15	2.76	2.52	2.37	2.25	2.10	1.92	1.70	1.39
	.10	2.79	2.39	2.18	2.04	1.95	1.87	1.77	1.66	1.51	1.29
	.20	1.68	1.65	1.59	1.55	1.51	1.48	1.44	1.38	1.31	1.18
120	.001	11.38	7.31	5.79	4.95	4.42	4.04	3.55	3.02	2.40	1.56
	.005	8.18	5.54	4.50	3.92	3.55	3.28	2.93	2.54	2.09	1.43
	.01	6.85	4.79	3.95	3.48	3.17	2.96	2.66	2.34	1.95	1.38
	.025	5.15	3.80	3.23	2.89	2.67	2.52	2.30	2.05	1.76	1.31
	.05	3.92	3.07	2.68	2.45	2.29	2.17	2.02	1.83	1.61	1.25
	.10	2.75	2.35	2.13	1.99	1.90	1.82	1.72	1.60	1.45	1.19
	.20	1.66	1.63	1.57	1.52	1.48	1.45	1.41	1.35	1.27	1.12
∞	.001	10.83	6.91	5.42	4.62	4.10	3.74	3.27	2.74	2.13	1.00
	.005	7.88	5.30	4.28	3.72	3.35	3.09	2.74	2.36	1.90	1.00
	.01	6.64	4.60	3.78	3.32	3.02	2.80	2.51	2.18	1.79	1.00
	.025	5.02	3.69	3.12	2.79	2.57	2.41	2.19	1.94	1.64	1.00
	.05	3.84	2.99	2.60	2.37	2.21	2.09	1.94	1.75	1.52	1.00
	.10	2.71	2.30	2.08	1.94	1.85	1.77	1.67	1.55	1.38	1.00
	.20	1.64	1.61	1.55	1.50	1.46	1.43	1.38	1.32	1.23	1.00

APPENDIX F

Fisher's z-Transformation Function for Pearson's r Correlation Coefficient:
$$z = 1/2 \, [\log_e(1 + r) - \log_e(1 - r)]$$

To read this table, simply find the correlation coefficient value in the r column, and then read the corresponding z value from the adjacent column. For example, if the r value were .46, the z would be .497.

APPENDIX F. FISHER'S z TRANSFORMATION									
r	z	r	z	r	z	r	z	r	z
.000	.000	.200	.203	.400	.424	.600	.693	.800	1.099
.005	.005	.205	.208	.405	.430	.605	.701	.805	1.113
.010	.010	.210	.213	.410	.436	.610	.709	.810	1.127
.015	.015	.215	.218	.415	.442	.615	.717	.815	1.142
.020	.020	.220	.224	.420	.448	.620	.725	.820	1.157
.025	.025	.225	.229	.425	.454	.625	.733	.825	1.172
.030	.030	.230	.234	.430	.460	.630	.741	.830	1.188
.035	.035	.235	.239	.435	.466	.635	.750	.835	1.204
.040	.040	.240	.245	.440	.472	.640	.758	.840	1.221
.045	.045	.245	.250	.445	.478	.645	.767	.845	1.238
.050	.050	.250	.255	.450	.485	.650	.775	.850	1.256
.055	.055	.255	.261	.455	.491	.655	.784	.855	1.274
.060	.060	.260	.266	.460	.497	.660	.793	.860	1.293
.065	.065	.265	.271	.465	.504	.665	.802	.865	1.313
.070	.070	.270	.277	.470	.510	.670	.811	.870	1.333
.075	.075	.275	.282	.475	.517	.675	.820	.875	1.354
.080	.080	.280	.288	.480	.523	.680	.829	.880	1.376
.085	.085	.285	.293	.485	.530	.685	.838	.885	1.398
.090	.090	.290	.299	.490	.536	.690	.848	.890	1.422
.095	.095	.295	.304	.495	.543	.695	.858	.895	1.447
.100	.100	.300	.310	.500	.549	.700	.867	.900	1.472
.105	.105	.305	.315	.505	.556	.705	.877	.905	1.499
.110	.110	.310	.321	.510	.563	.710	.887	.910	1.528
.115	.116	.315	.326	.515	.570	.715	.897	.915	1.557
.120	.121	.320	.332	.520	.576	.720	.908	.920	1.589
.125	.126	.325	.337	.525	.583	.725	.918	.925	1.623
.130	.131	.330	.343	.530	.590	.730	.929	.930	1.658
.135	.136	.335	.348	.535	.597	.735	.940	.935	1.697
.140	.141	.340	.354	.540	.604	.740	.950	.940	1.738
.145	.146	.345	.360	.545	.611	.745	.962	.945	1.783
.150	.151	.350	.365	.550	.618	.750	.973	.950	1.832
.155	.156	.355	.371	.555	.626	.755	.984	.955	1.886
.160	.161	.360	.377	.560	.633	.760	.996	.960	1.946
.165	.167	.365	.383	.565	.640	.765	1.008	.965	2.014
.170	.172	.370	.388	.570	.648	.770	1.020	.970	2.092
.175	.177	.375	.394	.575	.655	.775	1.033	.975	2.185
.180	.182	.380	.400	.580	.662	.780	1.045	.980	2.298
.185	.187	.385	.406	.585	.670	.785	1.058	.985	2.443
.190	.192	.390	.412	.590	.678	.790	1.071	.990	2.647
.195	.198	.395	.418	.595	.685	.795	1.085	.995	2.994

SOURCE: From *Statistical Methods* by Allen L. Edwards, Copyright 1954. © 1967 by Allen L. Edwards. Reprinted by permission of Holt, Rinehart & Winston, Inc.

APPENDIX G

Critical Values of Pearson's r Correlation Coefficient for Five Alpha Significance Levels

To read this table, find the appropriate degrees of freedom for the correlation coefficient in the column headed by $n' - 2$. When this value has been located, read to the right to find the values that represent the minimum r values for significance at the .10, .05, .02, .01, and .001 alpha levels of significance. For example, if the degrees of freedom were 25, an r of at least .3233 would be needed for significance at the .10 level, .3809 at the .05 level, etc.

	APPENDIX G. PEARSON'S r				
$n' - 2$	.10	.05	.02	.01	.001
1	.98769	.99692	.999507	.999877	.9999988
2	.90000	.95000	.98000	.990000	.99900
3	.8054	.8783	.93433	.95873	.99116
4	.7293	.8114	.8822	.91720	.97406
5	.6694	.7545	.8329	.8745	.95074
6	.6215	.7067	.7887	.8343	.92493
7	.5822	.6664	.7498	.7977	.8982
8	.5494	.6319	.7155	.7646	.8721
9	.5214	.6021	.6851	.7348	.8471
10	.4973	.5760	.6581	.7079	.8233
11	.4762	.5529	.6339	.6835	.8010
12	.4575	.5324	.6120	.6614	.7800
13	.4409	.5139	.5923	.6411	.7603
14	.4259	.4973	.5742	.6226	.7420
15	.4124	.4821	.5577	.6055	.7246
16	.4000	.4683	.5425	.5897	.7084
17	.3887	.4555	.5285	.5751	.6932
18	.3783	.4438	.5155	.5614	.6787
19	.3687	.4329	.5034	.5487	.6652
20	.3598	.4227	.4921	.5368	.6524
25	.3233	.3809	.4451	.4869	.5974
30	.2960	.3494	.4093	.4487	.5541
35	.2746	.3246	.3810	.4182	.5189
40	.2573	.3044	.3578	.3932	.4896
45	.2428	.2875	.3384	.3721	.4648
50	.2306	.2732	.3218	.3541	.4433
60	.2108	.2500	.2948	.3248	.4078
70	.1954	.2319	.2737	.3017	.3799
80	.1829	.2172	.2565	.2830	.3568
90	.1726	.2050	.2422	.2673	.3375
100	.1638	.1946	.2301	.2540	.3211

SOURCE: Appendix G is taken from Table VI of Fisher & Yates: *Statistical Tables for Biological, Agricultural and Medical Research,* 6/e published by Addison Wesley Longman Ltd., (1974). Reprinted by permission of the authors and publishers.

APPENDIX H

Critical Values of the *U* Statistic of the Mann-Whitney Test

To read this table, you must locate the number of cases in both groups in the particular subtable that lists the level of significance desired with either a one-tailed or a two-tailed test. Assume that you wish to find the critical value using a two-tailed test at the .05 level of significance. To do this, the first step is to locate n_1 and n_2 in subtable "c." The point at which the n_1 row and the n_2 column intersect represents the maximum critical value for significance at the .05 level. If, for example, n_1 equals 10, n_2 equals 15, and the computed value equals 23, it is concluded that the difference between the groups is significant—i.e., the tabled critical value for $n_1 = 10$ and $n_2 = 15$ is 39, and 23 is obviously smaller than 39.

APPENDIX H. U STATISTIC

(a) Critical Values of U for a One-Tailed Test at .001 or for a Two-Tailed Test at .002

n_1 \ n_2	9	10	11	12	13	14	15	16	17	18	19	20
1												
2												
3									0	0	0	0
4		0	0	0	1	1	1	2	2	3	3	3
5	1	1	2	2	3	3	4	5	5	6	7	7
6	2	3	4	4	5	6	7	8	9	10	11	12
7	3	5	6	7	8	9	10	11	13	14	15	16
8	5	6	8	9	11	12	14	15	17	18	20	21
9	7	8	10	12	14	15	17	19	21	23	25	26
10	8	10	12	14	17	19	21	23	25	27	29	32
11	10	12	15	17	20	22	24	27	29	32	34	37
12	12	14	17	20	23	25	28	31	34	37	40	42
13	14	17	20	23	26	29	32	35	38	42	45	48
14	15	19	22	25	29	32	36	39	43	46	50	54
15	17	21	24	28	32	36	40	43	47	51	55	59
16	19	23	27	31	35	39	43	48	52	56	60	65
17	21	25	29	34	38	43	47	52	57	61	66	70
18	23	27	32	37	42	46	51	56	61	66	71	76
19	25	29	34	40	45	50	55	60	66	71	77	82
20	26	32	37	42	48	54	59	65	70	76	82	88

(b) Critical Values of U for a One-Tailed Test at .01 or for a Two-Tailed Test at .02

n_1 \ n_2	9	10	11	12	13	14	15	16	17	18	19	20
1												
2					0	0	0	0	0	0	1	1
3	1	1	1	2	2	2	3	3	4	4	4	5
4	3	3	4	5	5	6	7	7	8	9	9	10
5	5	6	7	8	9	10	11	12	13	14	15	16
6	7	8	9	11	12	13	15	16	18	19	20	22
7	9	11	12	14	16	17	19	21	23	24	26	28
8	11	13	15	17	20	22	24	26	28	30	32	34
9	14	16	18	21	23	26	28	31	33	36	38	40
10	16	19	22	24	27	30	33	36	38	41	44	47
11	18	22	25	28	31	34	37	41	44	47	50	53
12	21	24	28	31	35	38	42	46	49	53	56	60
13	23	27	31	35	39	43	47	51	55	59	63	67
14	26	30	34	38	43	47	51	56	60	65	69	73
15	28	33	37	42	47	51	56	61	66	70	75	80
16	31	36	41	46	51	56	61	66	71	76	82	87
17	33	38	44	49	55	60	66	71	77	82	88	93
18	36	41	47	53	59	65	70	76	82	88	94	100
19	38	44	50	56	63	69	75	82	88	94	101	107
20	40	47	53	60	67	73	80	87	93	100	107	114

SOURCE: Adapted and abridged from Tables 1, 3, 5 and 7 of D. Aube, "Extended Tables for the Mann-Whitney Statistic," *Bulletin of the Institute of Educational Research of Indiana University,* 1953, **1**, No. 2. Reproduced from S. Siegel, *Nonparametric Statistics for the Behavioral Sciences.* New York: McGraw-Hill Book Company, 1956. Reprinted by permission of the Institute of Educational Research and McGraw-Hill Book Company.

n_1 \ n_2	(c) Critical Values of *U* for a One-Tailed Test at .025 or for a Two-Tailed Test at .05											
	9	10	11	12	13	14	15	16	17	18	19	20
1												
2	0	0	1	1	1	1	1	1	2	2	2	2
3	2	3	3	4	4	5	5	6	6	7	7	8
4	4	5	6	7	8	9	10	11	11	12	13	13
5	7	8	9	11	12	13	14	15	17	18	19	20
6	10	11	13	14	16	17	19	21	22	24	25	27
7	12	14	16	18	20	22	24	26	28	30	32	34
8	15	17	19	22	24	26	29	31	34	36	38	41
9	17	20	23	26	28	31	34	37	39	42	45	48
10	20	23	26	29	33	36	39	42	45	48	52	55
11	23	26	30	33	37	40	44	47	51	55	58	62
12	26	29	33	37	41	45	49	53	57	61	65	69
13	28	33	37	41	45	50	54	59	63	67	72	76
14	31	36	40	45	50	55	59	64	67	74	78	83
15	34	39	44	49	54	59	64	70	75	80	85	90
16	37	42	47	53	59	64	70	75	81	86	92	98
17	39	45	51	57	63	67	75	81	87	93	99	105
18	42	48	55	61	67	74	80	86	93	99	106	112
19	45	52	58	65	72	78	85	92	99	106	113	119
20	48	55	62	69	76	83	90	98	105	112	119	127

n_1 \ n_2	(d) Critical Values of *U* for a One-Tailed Test at .05 or for a Two-Tailed Test at .10											
	9	10	11	12	13	14	15	16	17	18	19	20
1											0	0
2	1	1	1	2	2	2	3	3	3	4	4	4
3	3	4	5	5	6	7	7	8	9	9	10	11
4	6	7	8	9	10	11	12	14	15	16	17	18
5	9	11	12	13	15	16	18	19	20	22	23	25
6	12	14	16	17	19	21	23	25	26	28	30	32
7	15	17	19	21	24	26	28	30	33	35	37	39
8	18	20	23	26	28	31	33	36	39	41	44	47
9	21	24	27	30	33	36	39	42	45	48	51	54
10	24	27	31	34	37	41	44	48	51	55	58	62
11	27	31	34	38	42	46	50	54	57	61	65	69
12	30	34	38	42	47	51	55	60	64	68	72	77
13	33	37	42	47	51	56	61	65	70	75	80	84
14	36	41	46	51	56	61	66	71	77	82	87	92
15	39	44	50	55	61	66	72	77	83	88	94	100
16	42	48	54	60	65	71	77	83	89	95	101	107
17	45	51	57	64	70	77	83	89	96	102	109	115
18	48	55	61	68	75	82	88	95	102	109	116	123
19	51	58	65	72	80	87	94	101	109	116	123	130
20	54	62	69	77	84	92	100	107	115	123	130	138

APPENDIX

Critical Values for Hartley's Maximum *F*-Ratio Significance Test for Homogeneity of Variances

Since the sample size in all groups is the same, the *df* column represents the value for each group. To use this table, simply locate the appropriate *df* row heading and the column headed by the number of variances that are being compared; then read the value from the point at which the row and column intersect. For example, assume that the *df* of each sample is 20, that six variances were compared, and that the F_{max} ratio is 4.2. Entering the table at the row headed by 20 *df* and reading across to the $k = 6$ column, it is noted that .05 value is 3.76 and the .01 value is 4.9. Therefore, the $F_{max} = 4.2$ is considered significant at the .05 level.

APPENDIX I. F_{max} STATISTIC
Alpha = .05 and .01 (in italics)

df \ k	2	3	4	5	6	7	8	9	10	11	12
2	39.0	87.5	142.	202.	266.	333.	403.	475.	550.	626.	704.
	199.	*448.*	*729.*	*1036.*	*1362.*	*1705.*	*2063.*	*2432.*	*2813.*	*3204.*	*3605.*
3	15.4	27.8	39.2	50.7	62.0	72.9	83.5	93.9	104.	114.	124.
	47.5	*85.*	*120.*	*151.*	*184.*	*216.**	*249.**	*281.**	*310.**	*337.**	*361.**
4	9.60	15.5	20.6	25.2	29.5	33.6	37.5	41.1	44.6	48.0	51.4
	23.2	*37.*	*49.*	*59.*	*69.*	*79.*	*89.*	*97.*	*106.*	*113.*	*120.*
5	7.15	10.8	13.7	16.3	18.7	20.8	22.9	24.7	26.5	28.2	29.9
	14.9	*22.*	*28.*	*33.*	*38.*	*42.*	*46.*	*50.*	*54.*	*57.*	*60.*
6	5.82	8.38	10.4	12.1	13.7	15.0	16.3	17.5	18.6	19.7	20.7
	11.1	*15.5*	*19.1*	*22.*	*25.*	*27.*	*30.*	*32.*	*34.*	*36.*	*37.*
7	4.99	6.94	8.44	9.70	10.8	11.8	12.7	13.5	14.3	15.1	15.8
	8.89	*12.1*	*14.5*	*16.5*	*18.4*	*20.*	*22.*	*23.*	*24.*	*26.*	*27.*
8	4.43	6.00	7.18	8.12	9.03	9.78	10.5	11.1	11.7	12.2	12.7
	7.50	*9.9*	*11.7*	*13.2*	*14.5*	*15.8*	*16.9*	*17.9*	*18.9*	*19.8*	*21.*
9	4.03	5.34	6.31	7.11	7.80	8.41	8.95	9.45	9.91	10.3	10.7
	6.54	*8.5*	*9.9*	*11.1*	*12.1*	*13.1*	*13.9*	*14.7*	*15.3*	*16.0*	*16.6*
10	3.72	4.85	5.67	6.34	6.92	7.42	7.87	8.28	8.66	9.01	9.34
	5.85	*7.4*	*8.6*	*9.6*	*10.4*	*11.1*	*11.8*	*12.4*	*12.9*	*13.4*	*13.9*
12	3.28	4.16	4.79	5.30	5.72	6.09	6.42	6.72	7.00	7.25	7.48
	4.91	*6.1*	*6.9*	*7.6*	*8.2*	*8.7*	*9.1*	*9.5*	*9.9*	*10.2*	*10.6*
15	2.86	3.54	4.01	4.37	4.68	4.95	5.19	5.40	5.59	5.77	5.93
	4.07	*4.9*	*5.5*	*6.0*	*6.4*	*6.7*	*7.1*	*7.3*	*7.5*	*7.8*	*8.0*
20	2.46	2.95	3.29	3.54	3.76	3.94	4.10	4.24	4.37	4.49	4.59
	3.32	*3.8*	*4.3*	*4.6*	*4.9*	*5.1*	*5.3*	*5.5*	*5.6*	*5.8*	*5.9*
30	2.07	2.40	2.61	2.78	2.91	3.02	3.12	3.21	3.29	3.36	3.39
	2.63	*3.0*	*3.3*	*3.4*	*3.6*	*3.7*	*3.8*	*3.9*	*4.0*	*4.1*	*4.2*
60	1.67	1.85	1.96	2.04	2.11	2.17	2.22	2.26	2.30	2.33	2.36
	1.96	*2.2*	*2.3*	*2.4*	*2.5*	*2.5*	*2.5*	*2.6*	*2.6*	*2.7*	*2.7*
∞	1.00	1.00	1.00	1.00	1.00	1.00	1.00	1.00	1.00	1.00	1.00
	1.00	*1.00*	*1.00*	*1.00*	*1.00*	*1.00*	*1.00*	*1.00*	*1.00*	*1.00*	*1.00*

*Values in the column $k = 2$ and in the rows $df = 2$ and ∞ are exact. Elsewhere the third digit may be in error by a few units for F_{95} and several units for F_{99}. The third digit figures of values marked be an asterisk are the most uncertain.

SOURCE: Reproduced from Table 31 of E. S. Pearson and H. O. Hartley, *Biometrika Tables for Statisticians,* Vol. 1, Third Edition, 1966. Used by permission of the Biometrika Trustees.

APPENDIX J

Significant Studentized Ranges for Duncan's New Multiple-Range Test

To use these tables, the df and the range of the pairs of groups being compared must be located in the particular subtable that lists the level of significance desired. Assume that you wish to find the critical value using a two-tailed test at the .05 level of significance. To do this, first locate the df and r values in the subtable for alpha equal to .05. The point at which the df row and the r column intersect represents the minimum significant value (k) at the .05 level. This is then multiplied by the standard error of the means to obtain the minimum critical differences for each of the several ranges. If, for example, the df are equal to 15, the range of the pair being compared is equal to 6, and the standard error of the means is equal to 1.50, then the critical difference would be equal to 3.36×1.50, or 5.04. For the next pair, with a range of 5, the critical differences would be 3.31×1.50, or 4.96. The same procedure would be followed for the remainder of the range comparisons.

APPENDIX J. DUNCAN'S NEW MULTIPLE-RANGE TEST

Error df	Protection Level	r = number of means for range being tested					
		2	3	4	5	6	7
1	.05	18.0	18.0	18.0	18.0	18.0	18.0
	.01	90.0	90.0	90.0	90.0	90.0	90.0
2	.05	6.09	6.09	6.09	6.09	6.09	6.09
	.01	14.0	14.0	14.0	14.0	14.0	14.0
3	.05	4.50	4.50	4.50	4.50	4.50	4.50
	.01	8.26	8.5	8.6	8.7	8.8	8.9
4	.05	3.93	4.01	4.02	4.02	4.02	4.02
	.01	6.51	6.8	6.9	7.0	7.1	7.1
5	.05	3.64	3.74	3.79	3.83	3.83	3.83
	.01	5.70	5.96	6.11	6.18	6.26	6.33
6	.05	3.46	3.58	3.64	3.68	3.68	3.68
	.01	5.24	5.51	5.65	5.73	5.81	5.88
7	.05	3.35	3.47	3.54	3.58	3.60	3.61
	.01	4.95	5.22	5.37	5.45	5.53	5.61
8	.05	3.26	3.39	3.47	3.52	3.55	3.56
	.01	4.74	5.00	5.14	5.23	5.32	5.40
9	.05	3.20	3.34	3.41	3.47	3.50	3.52
	.01	4.60	4.86	4.99	5.08	5.17	5.25
10	.05	3.15	3.30	3.37	3.43	3.46	3.47
	.01	4.48	4.73	4.88	4.96	5.06	5.13
11	.05	3.11	3.27	3.35	3.39	3.43	3.44
	.01	4.39	4.63	4.77	4.86	4.94	5.01
12	.05	3.08	3.23	3.33	3.36	3.40	3.42
	.01	4.32	4.55	4.68	4.76	4.84	4.92
13	.05	3.06	3.21	3.30	3.35	3.38	3.41
	.01	4.26	4.48	4.62	4.69	4.74	4.84
14	.05	3.03	3.18	3.27	3.33	3.37	3.39
	.01	4.21	4.42	4.55	4.63	4.70	4.78
15	.05	3.01	3.16	3.25	3.31	3.36	3.38
	.01	4.17	4.37	4.50	4.58	4.64	4.72

SOURCE: Abridged from D. B. Duncan, Multiple range and multiple F tests, *Biometrics*, 1955, **11**, 1–41. Reprinted by permission of the Biometric Society.

8	9	10	12	14	16	18	20
18.0	18.0	18.0	18.0	18.0	18.0	18.0	18.0
90.0	90.0	90.0	90.0	90.0	90.0	90.0	90.0
6.09	6.09	6.09	6.09	6.09	6.09	6.09	6.09
14.0	14.0	14.0	14.0	14.0	14.0	14.0	14.0
4.50	4.50	4.50	4.50	4.50	4.50	4.50	4.50
8.9	9.0	9.0	9.0	9.1	9.2	9.3	9.3
4.02	4.02	4.02	4.02	4.02	4.02	4.02	4.02
7.2	7.2	7.3	7.3	7.4	7.4	7.5	7.5
3.83	3.83	3.83	3.83	3.83	3.83	3.83	3.83
6.40	6.44	6.5	6.6	6.6	6.7	6.7	6.8
3.68	3.68	3.68	3.68	3.68	3.68	3.68	3.68
5.95	6.00	6.0	6.1	6.2	6.2	6.3	6.3
3.61	3.61	3.61	3.61	3.61	3.61	3.61	3.61
5.69	5.73	5.8	5.8	5.9	5.9	6.0	6.0
3.56	3.56	3.56	3.56	3.56	3.56	3.56	3.56
5.47	5.51	5.5	5.6	5.7	5.7	5.8	5.8
3.52	3.52	3.52	3.52	3.52	3.52	3.52	3.52
5.32	5.36	5.4	5.5	5.5	5.6	5.7	5.7
3.47	3.47	3.47	3.47	3.47	3.47	3.47	3.48
5.20	5.24	5.28	5.36	5.42	5.48	5.54	5.55
3.45	3.46	3.46	3.46	3.46	3.46	3.47	3.48
5.06	5.12	5.15	5.24	5.28	5.34	5.38	5.39
3.44	3.44	3.46	3.46	3.46	3.46	3.47	3.48
4.96	5.02	5.07	5.13	5.17	5.22	5.24	5.26
3.42	3.44	3.45	3.45	3.46	3.46	3.47	3.47
4.88	4.94	4.98	5.04	5.08	5.13	5.14	5.15
3.41	3.42	3.44	3.45	3.46	3.46	3.47	3.47
4.83	4.87	4.91	4.96	5.00	5.04	5.06	5.07
3.40	3.42	3.43	3.44	3.45	3.46	3.47	3.47
4.77	4.81	4.84	4.90	4.94	4.97	4.99	5.00

APPENDIX J. DUNCAN'S NEW MULTIPLE-RANGE TEST (*cont.*)

Error df	Protection Level	r = number of means for range being tested						
		2	3	4	5	6	7	8
16	.05	3.00	3.15	3.23	3.30	3.34	3.37	3.39
	.01	4.13	4.34	4.45	4.54	4.60	4.67	4.72
17	.05	2.98	3.13	3.22	3.28	3.33	3.36	3.38
	.01	4.10	4.30	4.41	4.50	4.56	4.63	4.68
18	.05	2.97	3.12	3.21	3.27	3.32	3.35	3.37
	.01	4.07	4.27	4.38	4.46	4.53	4.59	4.64
19	.05	2.96	3.11	3.19	3.26	3.31	3.35	3.37
	.01	4.05	4.24	4.35	4.43	4.50	4.56	4.61
20	.05	2.95	3.10	3.18	3.25	3.30	3.34	3.36
	.01	4.02	4.22	4.33	4.40	4.47	4.53	4.58
22	.05	2.93	3.08	3.17	3.24	3.29	3.32	3.35
	.01	3.99	4.17	4.28	4.36	4.42	4.48	4.53
24	.05	2.92	3.07	3.15	3.22	3.28	3.31	3.34
	.01	3.96	4.14	4.24	4.33	4.39	4.44	4.49
26	.05	2.91	3.06	3.14	3.21	3.27	3.30	3.34
	.01	3.93	4.11	4.21	4.30	4.36	4.41	4.46
28	.05	2.90	3.04	3.13	3.20	3.26	3.30	3.33
	.01	3.91	4.08	4.18	4.28	4.34	4.39	4.43
30	.05	2.89	3.04	3.12	3.20	3.25	3.29	3.32
	.01	3.89	4.06	4.16	4.22	4.32	4.36	4.41
40	.05	2.86	3.01	3.10	3.17	3.22	3.27	3.30
	.01	3.82	3.99	4.10	4.17	4.24	4.30	4.34
60	.05	2.83	2.98	3.08	3.14	3.20	3.24	3.28
	.01	3.76	3.92	4.03	4.12	4.17	4.23	4.27
100	.05	2.80	2.95	3.05	3.12	3.18	3.22	3.26
	.01	3.71	3.86	3.93	4.06	4.11	4.17	4.21
∞	.05	2.77	2.92	3.02	3.09	3.15	3.19	3.23
	.01	3.64	3.80	3.80	3.98	4.04	4.09	4.14

9	10	12	14	16	18	20
3.41	3.43	3.44	3.45	3.46	3.47	3.47
4.76	4.79	4.84	4.88	4.91	4.93	4.94
3.40	3.42	3.44	3.45	3.46	3.47	3.47
4.72	4.75	4.80	4.83	4.86	4.88	4.89
3.39	3.41	3.43	3.45	3.46	3.47	3.47
4.68	4.71	4.76	4.79	4.82	4.84	4.85
3.39	3.41	3.43	3.44	3.46	3.47	3.47
4.64	4.67	4.72	4.76	4.79	4.81	4.82
3.38	3.40	3.43	3.44	3.46	3.46	3.47
4.61	4.65	4.69	4.73	4.76	4.78	4.79
3.37	3.39	3.42	3.44	3.45	3.46	3.47
4.57	4.60	4.65	4.68	4.71	4.74	4.75
3.37	3.38	3.41	3.44	3.45	3.46	3.47
4.53	4.57	4.62	4.64	4.67	4.70	4.72
3.36	3.38	3.41	3.43	3.45	3.46	3.47
4.50	4.53	4.58	4.62	4.65	4.67	4.69
3.35	3.37	3.40	3.43	3.45	3.46	3.47
4.47	4.51	4.56	4.60	4.62	4.65	4.67
3.35	3.37	3.40	3.43	3.44	3.46	3.47
4.45	4.48	4.54	4.58	4.61	4.63	4.65
3.33	3.35	3.39	3.42	3.44	3.46	3.47
4.37	4.41	4.46	4.51	4.54	4.57	4.59
3.31	3.33	3.37	3.40	3.43	3.45	3.47
4.31	4.34	4.39	4.44	4.47	4.50	4.58
3.29	3.32	3.36	3.40	3.42	3.45	3.47
4.25	4.29	4.35	4.38	4.42	4.45	4.48
3.26	3.29	3.34	3.38	3.41	3.44	3.47
4.17	4.20	4.26	4.31	4.34	4.38	4.44

APPENDIX K

Significant Studentized Ranges for the Newman-Keuls' and Tukey Multiple-Comparison Tests

To use these tables, the *df* and the range (*r*) of the pairs of groups being compared must be located in the table where the desired level of significance is listed. Assume that you wish to find a significant value at the .05 level. To do this, first locate the *df* and the *r* values in the table for alpha equal to .05. The point at which the *df* row and the *r* column intersect (*q*) represents the minimum significant value at the .05 level. This value is then multiplied by the standard error of the means to obtain the minimum critical value.

If, for example, the tables are being used for the Newman-Keuls' test, where the *df* are equal to 15, alpha $= .05$, the range of the first pair to be compared is 6, and the standard error of the means is equal to 1.50, then a minimum critical value of 6.88 would be needed for significance (4.59 $\times$ 1.50). For the next comparison, with a range of 5, the critical value would have to be equal to or larger than 6.56 (4.37 $\times$ 1.50). For a range of 4, the critical value would have to be at least 6.12, etc.

Using the tables for the Tukey test, only the value for the largest range is needed. Thus, where the *df* are equal to 15, alpha $= .05$, the largest range is equal to 6, and the standard error of the means is equal to 1.50, a critical value larger than 6.88 would be needed for all comparisons.

APPENDIX K. SIGNIFICANT STUDENTIZED RANGES (TWO-TAILED)

Error df	α	r = number of means or number of steps between ordered means									
		2	3	4	5	6	7	8	9	10	11
5	.05	3.64	4.60	5.22	5.67	6.03	6.33	6.58	6.80	6.99	7.17
	.01	5.70	6.98	7.80	8.42	8.91	9.32	9.67	9.97	10.24	10.48
6	.05	3.46	4.34	4.90	5.30	5.63	5.90	6.12	6.32	6.49	6.65
	.01	5.24	6.33	7.03	7.56	7.97	8.32	8.61	8.87	9.10	9.30
7	.05	3.34	4.16	4.68	5.06	5.36	5.61	5.82	6.00	6.16	6.30
	.01	4.95	5.92	6.54	7.01	7.37	7.68	7.94	8.17	8.37	8.55
8	.05	3.26	4.04	4.53	4.89	5.17	5.40	5.60	5.77	5.92	6.05
	.01	4.75	5.64	6.20	6.62	6.96	7.24	7.47	7.68	7.86	8.03
9	.05	3.20	3.95	4.41	4.76	5.02	5.24	5.43	5.59	5.74	5.87
	.01	4.60	5.43	5.96	6.35	6.66	6.91	7.13	7.33	7.49	7.65
10	.05	3.15	3.88	4.33	4.65	4.91	5.12	5.30	5.46	5.60	5.72
	.01	4.48	5.27	5.77	6.14	6.43	6.67	6.87	7.05	7.21	7.36
11	.05	3.11	3.82	4.26	4.57	4.82	5.03	5.20	5.35	5.49	5.61
	.01	4.39	5.15	5.62	5.97	6.25	6.48	6.67	6.84	6.99	7.13
12	.05	3.08	3.77	4.20	4.51	4.75	4.95	5.12	5.27	5.39	5.51
	.01	4.32	5.05	5.50	5.84	6.10	6.32	6.51	6.67	6.81	6.94
13	.05	3.06	3.73	4.15	4.45	4.69	4.88	5.05	5.19	5.32	5.43
	.01	4.26	4.96	5.40	5.73	5.98	6.19	6.37	6.53	6.67	6.79
14	.05	3.03	3.70	4.11	4.41	4.64	4.83	4.99	5.13	5.25	5.36
	.01	4.21	4.89	5.32	5.63	5.88	6.08	6.26	6.41	6.54	6.66
15	.05	3.01	3.67	4.08	4.37	4.59	4.78	4.94	5.08	5.20	5.31
	.01	4.17	4.84	5.25	5.56	5.80	5.99	6.16	6.31	6.44	6.55

SOURCE: Reproduced from Table 29 of E. S. Pearson and H. O. Hartley, *Biometrika Tables for Statisticans,* Vol. 1, Third Edition, 1966. Used by permission of the Biometrika Trustees.

Error df	α	r = number of means or number of steps between ordered means									
		2	3	4	5	6	7	8	9	10	11
16	.05	3.00	3.65	4.05	4.33	4.56	4.74	4.90	5.03	5.15	5.26
	.01	4.13	4.79	5.19	5.49	5.72	5.92	6.08	6.22	6.35	6.46
17	.05	2.98	3.63	4.02	4.30	4.52	4.70	4.86	4.99	5.11	5.21
	.01	4.10	4.74	5.14	5.43	5.66	5.85	6.01	6.15	6.27	6.38
18	.05	2.97	3.61	4.00	4.28	4.49	4.67	4.82	4.96	5.07	5.17
	.01	4.07	4.70	5.09	5.38	5.60	5.79	5.94	6.08	6.20	6.31
19	.05	2.96	3.59	3.98	4.25	4.47	4.65	4.70	4.92	5.04	5.14
	.01	4.05	4.67	5.05	5.33	5.55	5.73	6.89	6.02	6.14	6.25
20	.05	2.95	3.58	3.96	4.23	4.45	4.62	4.77	4.90	5.01	5.11
	.01	4.02	4.64	5.02	5.29	5.51	5.69	5.84	5.97	6.09	6.19
24	.05	2.92	3.53	3.90	4.17	4.37	4.54	4.68	4.81	4.92	5.01
	.01	3.96	4.55	4.91	5.17	5.37	5.54	5.69	5.81	5.92	6.02
30	.05	2.89	3.49	3.85	4.10	4.30	4.46	4.60	4.72	4.82	4.92
	.01	3.89	4.45	4.80	5.05	5.24	5.40	5.54	5.65	5.76	5.85
40	.05	2.86	3.44	3.79	4.04	4.23	4.39	4.52	4.63	4.73	4.82
	.01	3.82	4.37	4.70	4.93	5.11	5.26	5.39	5.50	5.60	5.69
60	.05	2.83	3.40	3.74	3.98	4.16	4.31	4.44	4.55	4.65	4.73
	.01	3.76	4.28	4.59	4.82	4.99	5.13	5.25	5.36	5.45	5.53
120	.05	2.80	3.36	3.68	3.92	4.10	4.24	4.36	4.47	4.56	4.64
	.01	3.70	4.20	4.50	4.71	4.87	5.01	5.12	5.21	5.30	5.37
∞	.05	2.77	3.31	3.63	3.86	4.03	4.17	4.29	4.39	4.47	4.55
	.01	3.64	4.12	4.40	4.60	4.76	4.88	4.99	5.08	5.16	5.23

APPENDIX K. SIGNIFICANT STUDENTIZED RANGES (*cont.*)

| Error df | α | \(r\) = number of means or number of steps between ordered means |||||||||
		12	13	14	15	16	17	18	19	20
5	.05	7.32	7.47	7.60	7.72	7.83	7.93	8.03	8.12	8.21
	.01	10.70	10.89	11.08	11.24	11.40	11.55	11.68	11.81	11.93
6	.05	6.79	6.92	7.03	7.14	7.24	7.34	7.43	7.51	7.59
	.01	9.48	9.65	9.81	9.95	10.08	10.21	10.32	10.43	10.54
7	.05	6.43	6.55	6.66	6.76	6.85	6.94	7.02	7.10	7.17
	.01	8.71	8.86	9.00	9.12	9.24	9.35	9.46	9.55	9.65
8	.05	6.18	6.29	6.39	6.48	6.57	6.65	6.73	6.80	6.87
	.01	8.18	8.31	8.44	8.55	8.66	8.76	8.85	8.94	9.03
9	.05	5.98	6.09	6.19	6.28	6.36	6.44	6.51	6.58	6.64
	.01	7.78	7.91	8.03	8.13	8.23	8.33	8.41	8.49	8.57
10	.05	5.83	5.93	6.03	6.11	6.19	6.27	6.34	6.40	6.47
	.01	7.49	7.60	7.71	7.81	7.91	7.99	8.08	8.15	8.23
11	.05	5.71	5.81	5.90	5.98	6.06	6.13	6.20	6.27	6.33
	.01	7.25	7.36	7.46	7.56	7.65	7.73	7.81	7.88	7.95
12	.05	5.61	5.71	5.80	5.88	5.95	6.02	6.09	6.15	6.21
	.01	7.06	7.17	7.26	7.36	7.44	7.52	7.59	7.66	7.73
13	.05	5.53	5.63	5.71	5.79	5.86	5.93	5.99	6.05	6.11
	.01	6.90	7.01	7.10	7.19	7.27	7.35	7.42	7.48	7.55
14	.05	5.46	5.55	5.64	5.71	5.79	5.85	5.91	5.97	6.03
	.01	6.77	6.87	6.96	7.05	7.13	7.20	7.27	7.33	7.39
15	.05	5.40	5.49	5.57	5.65	5.72	5.78	5.85	5.90	5.96
	.01	6.66	6.76	6.84	6.93	7.00	7.07	7.14	7.20	7.26

Error df	α	r = number of means or number of steps between ordered means								
		12	13	14	15	16	17	18	19	20
16	.05	5.35	5.44	5.52	5.59	5.66	5.73	5.79	5.84	5.90
	.01	6.56	6.66	6.74	6.82	6.90	6.97	7.03	7.09	7.15
17	.05	5.31	5.39	5.47	5.54	5.61	5.67	5.73	5.79	5.84
	.01	6.48	6.57	6.66	6.73	6.81	6.87	6.94	7.00	7.05
18	.05	5.27	5.35	5.43	5.50	5.57	5.63	5.69	5.74	5.79
	.01	6.41	6.50	6.58	6.65	6.73	6.79	6.85	6.91	6.97
19	.05	5.23	5.31	5.39	5.46	5.53	5.59	5.65	5.70	5.75
	.01	6.34	6.43	6.51	6.58	6.65	6.72	6.78	6.84	6.89
20	.05	5.20	5.28	5.36	5.43	5.49	5.55	5.61	5.66	5.71
	.01	6.28	6.32	6.45	6.52	6.59	6.65	6.71	6.77	6.82
24	.05	5.10	5.18	5.25	5.32	5.38	5.44	5.49	5.55	5.59
	.01	6.11	6.19	6.26	6.33	6.39	6.45	6.51	6.56	6.61
30	.05	5.00	5.08	5.15	5.21	5.27	5.33	5.38	5.43	5.47
	.01	5.93	6.01	6.08	6.14	6.20	6.26	6.31	6.36	6.41
40	.05	4.90	4.98	5.04	5.11	5.16	5.22	5.27	5.31	5.36
	.01	5.76	5.83	5.90	5.96	6.02	6.07	6.12	6.16	6.21
60	.05	4.81	4.88	4.94	5.00	5.06	5.11	5.15	5.20	5.24
	.01	5.60	5.67	5.73	5.78	5.84	5.89	5.93	5.97	6.01
120	.05	4.71	4.78	4.84	4.90	4.95	5.00	5.04	5.09	5.13
	.01	5.44	5.50	5.56	5.61	5.66	5.71	5.75	5.79	5.83
∞	.05	4.62	4.68	4.74	4.80	4.85	4.89	4.93	4.97	5.01
	.01	5.29	5.35	5.40	5.45	5.49	5.54	5.57	5.61	5.65

APPENDIX L

Dunnett's Test: Comparison of Treatment Means with a Control

To use this table, the *df* and the range (*r*) of the pairs of groups being compared must be located in the table where the desired level of significance is listed. Assume that you wish to compare four means with the control group. To do this, first locate the *df* and the *r* in the table for alpha equal to .05. The point at which the *df* and *r* intersect (*d*) represents the minimum significant value. This value is then multiplied by the standard error of the means to obtain the minimum critical value. If, for example, the *df* are equal to 15, the maximum range of the means being compared is equal to 4, and the standard error of the means is equal to 1.70, then the critical difference for all comparisons would be equal to 2.61 × 1.70, or 4.44.

APPENDIX L. COMPARISON OF TREATMENT MEANS WITH A CONTROL
(TWO-TAILED)

Error df	α	r = number of treatment means, including control								
		2	3	4	5	6	7	8	9	10
5	.05	2.57	3.03	3.29	3.48	3.62	3.73	3.82	3.90	3.97
	.01	4.03	4.63	4.98	5.22	5.41	5.56	5.69	5.80	5.89
6	.05	2.45	2.86	3.10	3.26	3.39	3.49	3.57	3.64	3.71
	.01	3.71	4.21	4.51	5.71	4.87	5.00	5.10	5.20	5.28
7	.05	2.36	2.75	2.97	3.12	3.24	3.33	3.41	3.47	3.53
	.01	3.50	3.95	4.21	4.39	4.53	4.64	4.74	4.82	4.89
8	.05	2.31	2.67	2.88	3.02	3.13	3.22	3.29	3.35	3.41
	.01	3.36	3.77	4.00	4.17	4.29	4.40	4.48	4.56	4.62
9	.05	2.26	2.61	2.81	2.95	3.05	3.14	3.20	3.26	3.32
	.01	3.25	3.63	3.85	4.01	4.12	4.22	4.30	4.37	4.43
10	.05	2.23	2.57	2.76	2.89	2.99	3.07	3.14	3.19	3.24
	.01	3.17	3.53	3.74	3.88	3.99	4.08	4.16	4.22	4.28
11	.05	2.20	2.53	2.72	2.84	2.94	3.02	3.08	3.14	3.19
	.01	3.11	3.45	3.65	3.79	3.89	3.98	4.05	4.11	4.16
12	.05	2.18	2.50	2.68	2.81	2.90	2.98	3.04	3.09	3.14
	.01	3.05	3.39	3.58	3.71	3.81	3.89	3.96	4.02	4.07
13	.05	2.16	2.48	2.65	2.78	2.87	2.94	3.00	3.06	3.10
	.01	3.01	3.33	3.52	3.65	3.74	3.82	3.89	3.94	3.99
14	.05	2.14	2.46	2.63	2.75	2.84	2.91	2.97	3.02	3.07
	.01	2.98	3.29	3.47	3.59	3.69	3.76	3.83	3.88	3.93
15	.05	2.13	2.44	2.61	2.73	2.82	2.89	2.95	3.00	3.04
	.01	2.95	3.25	3.43	3.55	3.64	3.71	3.78	3.83	3.88

SOURCE: Table reproduced from C.W. Dunnett, New tables for multiple comparisons with a control, *Biometrics,* 1964, **20,** 482–491. Reprinted by permission of the Biometric Society.

Error df	α	r = number of treatment means, including control								
		2	3	4	5	6	7	8	9	10
16	.05	2.12	2.42	2.59	2.71	2.80	2.87	2.92	2.97	3.02
	.01	2.92	3.22	3.39	3.51	3.60	3.67	3.73	3.78	3.83
17	.05	2.11	2.41	2.58	2.69	2.78	2.85	2.90	2.95	3.00
	.01	2.90	3.19	3.36	3.47	3.56	3.63	3.69	3.74	3.79
18	.05	2.10	2.40	2.56	2.68	2.76	2.83	2.89	2.94	2.98
	.01	2.88	3.17	3.33	3.44	3.53	3.60	3.66	3.71	3.75
19	.05	2.09	2.39	2.55	2.66	2.75	2.81	2.87	2.92	2.96
	.01	2.86	3.15	3.31	3.42	3.50	3.57	3.63	3.68	3.72
20	.05	2.09	2.38	2.54	2.65	2.73	2.80	2.86	2.90	2.95
	.01	2.85	3.13	3.29	3.40	3.48	3.55	3.60	3.65	3.69
24	.05	2.06	2.35	2.51	2.61	2.70	2.76	2.81	2.86	2.90
	.01	2.80	3.07	3.22	3.32	3.40	3.47	3.52	3.57	3.61
30	.05	2.04	2.32	2.47	2.58	2.66	2.72	2.77	2.82	2.86
	.01	2.75	3.01	3.15	3.25	3.33	3.39	3.44	3.49	3.52
40	.05	2.02	2.29	2.44	2.54	2.62	2.68	2.73	2.77	2.81
	.01	2.70	2.95	3.09	3.19	3.26	3.32	3.37	3.41	3.44
60	.05	2.00	2.27	2.41	2.51	2.58	2.64	2.69	2.73	2.77
	.01	2.66	2.90	3.03	3.12	3.19	3.25	3.29	3.33	3.37
120	.05	1.98	2.24	2.38	2.47	2.55	2.60	2.65	2.69	2.73
	.01	2.62	2.85	2.97	3.06	3.12	3.18	3.22	3.26	3.29
∞	.05	1.96	2.21	2.35	2.44	2.51	2.57	2.61	2.65	2.69
	.01	2.58	2.79	2.92	3.00	3.06	3.11	3.15	3.19	3.22

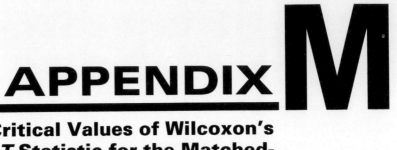

APPENDIX M

Critical Values of Wilcoxon's T Statistic for the Matched-Pairs Signed-Ranks Test

To use this table, first locate the number of *pairs* of scores in the n' column. The critical values for the several levels of significance are listed in the columns to the right. For example, if n' were 20 and the computed value 25, it would be concluded that since 25 is less than 38, this value is significant beyond the .01 level of significance for a two-tailed test.

	Level of significance for one-tailed test		
	.025	.01	.005
	Level of significance for two-tailed test		
n'	.05	.02	.01
6	1	—	—
7	2	0	—
8	4	2	0
9	6	3	2
10	8	5	3
11	11	7	5
12	14	10	7
13	17	13	10
14	21	16	13
15	25	20	16
16	30	24	19
17	35	28	23
18	40	33	28
19	46	38	32
20	52	43	37
21	59	49	43
22	66	56	49
23	73	62	55
24	81	69	61
25	90	77	68

Note that n' is the number of matched pairs.

SOURCE: Adapted from Table 2 of F. Wilcoxon and R. A. Wilcox, *Some Rapid Approximate Statistical Procedures,* rev. ed. Pearl River, New York: American Cyanamid Company, 1964. Reproduced from S. Siegel, *Nonparametric Statistics for the Behavioral Sciences.* New York: McGraw-Hill Book Company, 1956. Reprinted by permission of the Institute of Educational Research and McGraw-Hill Book Company.

APPENDIX N

Coefficients for Orthogonal Polynomials

In this table, the column headed by k indicates the number of components being compared. The columns headed by the ten X values indicate the actual coefficients to be used. Thus, if $k = 3$ groups were being analyzed, the coefficients for analysis of the linear component would be -1 for Group 1, 0 for Group 2, and 1 for Group 3. The quadratic coefficients would be 1, -2, and 1 for the three respective groups.

k	Polynomial	X = 1	2	3	4	5	6	7	8	9	10
3	Linear	−1	0	1							
	Quadratic	1	−2	1							
4	Linear	−3	−1	1	3						
	Quadratic	1	−1	−1	1						
	Cubic	−1	3	−3	1						
5	Linear	−2	−1	0	1	2					
	Quadratic	2	−1	−2	−1	2					
	Cubic	−1	2	0	−2	1					
	Quartic	1	−4	6	−4	1					
6	Linear	−5	−3	−1	1	3	5				
	Quadratic	5	−1	−4	−4	−1	5				
	Cubic	−5	7	4	−4	−7	5				
	Quartic	1	−3	2	2	−3	1				
7	Linear	−3	−2	−1	0	1	2	3			
	Quadratic	5	0	−3	−4	−3	0	5			
	Cubic	−1	1	1	0	−1	−1	1			
	Quartic	3	−7	1	6	1	−7	3			
8	Linear	−7	−5	−3	−1	1	3	5	7		
	Quadratic	7	1	−3	−5	−5	−3	1	7		
	Cubic	−7	5	7	3	−3	−7	−5	7		
	Quartic	7	−13	−3	9	9	−3	−13	7		
	Quintic	−7	23	−17	−15	15	17	−23	7		
9	Linear	−4	−3	−2	−1	0	1	2	3	4	
	Quadratic	28	7	−8	−17	−20	−17	−8	7	28	
	Cubic	−14	7	13	9	0	−9	−13	−7	14	
	Quartic	14	−21	−11	9	18	9	−11	−21	14	
	Quintic	−4	11	−4	−9	0	9	4	−11	4	
10	Linear	−9	−7	−5	−3	−1	1	3	5	7	9
	Quadratic	6	2	−1	−3	−4	−4	−3	−1	2	6
	Cubic	−42	14	35	31	12	−12	−31	−35	−14	42
	Quartic	18	−22	−17	3	18	18	3	−17	−22	18
	Quintic	−6	14	−1	−11	−6	6	11	1	−14	6

SOURCE: Abridged from Table B.10 of *Statistical Principles in Experimental Design* by B. J. Winer, Copyright 1962 by McGraw-Hill Book Company. Used by permission of McGraw-Hill Book Company.

APPENDIX O

Cumulative Probability Distribution for r', the Total Number of Runs Up or Down

To use this table, the number of observations (n) and the number of runs (r') must be known. Enter the table according to the number of observations (n) and runs (r'). For example, if there are twenty observations and six runs, the probability of six or fewer runs occurring by chance alone is less than one in ten thousand.

APPENDIX O. CUMULATIVE PROBABILITY DISTRIBUTION FOR r', THE TOTAL NUMBER OF RUNS UP AND DOWN

$P(r \leq r')$

Number of runs r'	\multicolumn{12}{c}{Number of observations, n}
	1	2	3	4	5	6	7	8	9	10	11	12
1	...	1.0000	.3333	.0833	.0167	.0028	.0004	.0000	.0000	.0000	.0000	.0000
2	...		1.0000	.5833	.2500	.0861	.0250	.0063	.0014	.0003	.0001	.0000
3	...			1.0000	.7333	.4139	.1909	.0749	.0257	.0079	.0022	.0005
4	...				1.0000	.8306	.5583	.3124	.1500	.0633	.0239	.0082
5	...					1.0000	.8921	.6750	.4347	.2427	.1196	.0529
6	...						1.0000	.9313	.7653	.5476	.3438	.1918
7	...							1.0000	.9563	.8329	.6460	.4453
8	...								1.0000	.9722	.8823	.7280
9	...									1.0000	.9823	.9179
10	...										1.0000	.9887
11	...											1.0000
12	...											
13	...											
14	...											
15	...											
16	...											
17	...											
18	...											
19	...											
20	...											
21	...											
22	...											
23	...											
24	...											

SOURCE: From "Probability Table for Number of Runs of Signs of First Differences in Ordered Series" by Eugene S. Edgington, *Journal of the American Statistical Association*, **56**(1961), 156–159. Copyright © 1961 by the American Statistical Association. Reprinted by permission.

APPENDIX O. CUMULATIVE PROBABILITY DISTRIBUTION FOR r (cont.)

$P(r \leq r')$

Number of runs r'

Number of observations, n

13	14	15	16	17	18	19	20	21	22	23	24	25
.0000	.0000	.0000	.0000	.0000	.0000	.0000	.0000	.0000	.0000	.0000	.0000	.0000
.0000	.0000	.0000	.0000	.0000	.0000	.0000	.0000	.0000	.0000	.0000	.0000	.0000
.0001	.0000	.0000	.0000	.0000	.0000	.0000	.0000	.0000	.0000	.0000	.0000	.0000
.0026	.0007	.0002	.0001	.0000	.0000	.0000	.0000	.0000	.0000	.0000	.0000	.0000
.0213	.0079	.0027	.0009	.0003	.0001	.0000	.0000	.0000	.0000	.0000	.0000	.0000
.0964	.0441	.0186	.0072	.0026	.0009	.0003	.0001	.0000	.0000	.0000	.0000	.0000
.2749	.1534	.0782	.0367	.0160	.0065	.0025	.0009	.0003	.0001	.0000	.0000	.0000
.5413	.3633	.2216	.1238	.0638	.0306	.0137	.0058	.0023	.0009	.0003	.0001	.0000
.7942	.6278	.4520	.2975	.1799	.1006	.0523	.0255	.0117	.0050	.0021	.0008	.0003
.9432	.8464	.7030	.5369	.3770	.2443	.1467	.0821	.0431	.0213	.0099	.0044	.0018
.9928	.9609	.8866	.7665	.6150	.4568	.3144	.2012	.1202	.0674	.0356	.0177	.0084
1.0000	.9954	.9733	.9172	.8188	.6848	.5337	.3873	.2622	.1661	.0988	.0554	.0294
	1.0000	.9971	.9818	.9400	.8611	.7454	.6055	.4603	.3276	.2188	.1374	.0815
		1.0000	.9981	.9877	.9569	.8945	.7969	.6707	.5312	.3953	.2768	.1827
			1.0000	.9988	.9917	.9692	.9207	.8398	.7286	.5980	.4631	.3384
				1.0000	.9992	.9944	.9782	.9409	.8749	.7789	.6595	.5292
					1.0000	.9995	.9962	.9846	.9563	.9032	.8217	.7148
						1.0000	.9997	.9975	.9892	.9679	.9258	.8577
							1.0000	.9998	.9983	.9924	.9765	.9436
								1.0000	.9999	.9989	.9947	.9830
									1.0000	.9999	.9993	.9963
										1.0000	1.0000	.9995
											1.0000	1.0000
												1.0000

APPENDIX P

Sample Size and Power

To read this table, first identify the power level desired and the α level to be employed. After locating the appropriate section of the table, read down the column at the left to find the number of treatment levels (groups) planned for your experiment. Then, read across until the column headed by the value closest to the estimated *effect size* is located. The number at the intercept is the *N per group* needed to achieve the desired level of power.

To demonstrate the use of this table, assume that an experiment with three groups is planned. An α of .05 will be used and the desired level of power is .90. The estimated effect size based on data from similar studies is 1.30σ. Entering the .90 power table for $\alpha = .05$, $k = 3$, and an effect size of 1.25σ, the *N per group* should be set at 17, or a total of 51 subjects in the experiment.

APPENDIX P. SAMPLE SIZES FOR TREATMENT LEVELS AND EFFECT SIZES

Power = .75

$\alpha = .05$

Number of treatment levels (k)	Sample size per treatment level with effect sizes				
	$.5\sigma$	$.75\sigma$	1.0σ	1.25σ	1.5σ
2	55	26	15	10	7
3	69	31	18	12	9
4	79	35	21	14	10
5	88	39	23	15	10
6	95	42	24	16	11
7	101	45	26	17	11
8	107	48	27	18	12

$\alpha = .01$

2	85	39	23	15	11
3	103	46	27	18	13
4	117	53	30	20	14
5	130	58	33	21	15
6	137	61	35	22	16
7	143	64	37	23	17
8	148	66	38	24	18

Power = .80

$\alpha = .05$

2	62	29	17	12	8
3	78	35	20	14	10
4	88	40	23	16	11
5	96	43	25	17	12
6	103	47	27	18	13
7	110	50	29	19	13
8	117	52	30	20	14

$\alpha = .01$

2	93	43	25	17	12
3	112	52	29	20	14
4	124	56	32	22	16
5	134	60	34	23	17
6	144	64	36	25	18
7	150	68	38	26	19
8	156	71	40	27	19

SOURCE: Appendix P is from Hinkle, D. E., and Oliver, J. D. How large should the sample be? A question with no simple answer? Or . . . , *Educational and Psychological Measurement*, 1983, **43**, 1051–1060. Reprinted by permission of Sage Periodicals Press.

Power = .85

Number of treatment levels (k)	Sample size per treatment level with effect sizes				
	$.5\sigma$	$.75\sigma$	1.0σ	1.25σ	1.5σ

$\alpha = .05$

2	72	32	19	13	9
3	87	39	22	15	11
4	98	44	25	17	12
5	108	48	28	18	13
6	116	52	30	19	14
7	123	55	31	20	14
8	129	57	32	21	15

$\alpha = .01$

2	103	48	28	18	13
3	124	56	32	21	15
4	138	62	35	23	17
5	150	67	38	25	18
6	162	72	41	27	19
7	169	76	44	29	19
8	176	79	46	30	20

Power = .90

$\alpha = .05$

2	85	39	22	14	11
3	101	45	26	17	12
4	114	51	29	19	13
5	124	56	31	20	14
6	133	59	33	22	15
7	140	62	35	23	16
8	146	65	37	24	17

$\alpha = .01$

2	120	55	32	21	15
3	142	64	37	24	17
4	158	72	41	26	19
5	170	77	44	28	20
6	180	81	46	30	21
7	187	84	48	32	22
8	192	87	50	33	23

Power = .95

$\alpha = .05$

2	104	47	27	18	13
3	124	56	32	21	15
4	139	63	36	23	16
5	149	67	39	25	17
6	158	71	41	27	18
7	167	75	43	28	19
8	176	79	45	29	20

APPENDIX P. SAMPLE SIZES FOR TREATMENT LEVELS AND EFFECT SIZES (*cont.*)

Power = .95

$\alpha = .01$

Number of treatment levels (k)	Sample size per treatment level with effect sizes				
	$.5\sigma$	$.75\sigma$	1.0σ	1.25σ	1.5σ
2	144	64	37	24	18
3	167	76	43	28	20
4	183	82	47	31	22
5	197	88	50	33	24
6	207	93	53	35	25
7	217	98	56	36	26
8	226	102	59	37	27

Power = .99

$\alpha = .05$

2	148	67	38	25	17
3	173	77	44	28	20
4	192	85	48	31	22
5	208	93	52	34	24
6	218	98	55	36	25
7	227	102	58	38	26
8	235	105	60	39	27

$\alpha = .01$

2	194	87	49	32	23
3	222	100	57	37	26
4	240	109	62	40	29
5	258	117	67	43	31
6	274	122	70	45	32
7	284	127	72	47	33
8	294	133	74	49	34

Index